Office for Disarmament Affairs
New York, 2020

The United Nations
DISARMAMENT YEARBOOK

Volume 44 (Part II): 2019

Guide to the user

The *United Nations Disarmament Yearbook*, in print and electronic format, is designed to be a concise reference tool for diplomats, researchers, students and the general public on disarmament, non-proliferation and arms control issues under consideration by the international community.

Part I of the 2019 *Yearbook* was published in April this year. It contains all the resolutions and decisions of the seventy-fourth session of the General Assembly.

Part II is divided among the main multilateral issues under consideration throughout the year. It includes developments and trends on the issues and a convenient issue-oriented timeline, as well as short summaries found in appendix II, of First Committee and General Assembly actions taken on resolutions and decisions.

Because much of the background information is condensed, it is helpful to consult previous editions for expanded historical knowledge. Factual information is provided in the appendices. Websites of United Nations departments and specialized agencies, intergovernmental organizations, research institutes and non-governmental organizations are referenced as hyperlinks in the online version of the *Yearbook*.

Symbols of United Nations documents are composed of capital letters combined with figures. Hyperlinks to these documents are included in the online version of the *Yearbook*. Alternatively, they can be accessed, in the official languages of the United Nations, from https://documents.un.org/. Specific disarmament-related documents are also available from the disarmament reference collection at https://www.un.org/disarmament/publications/library/.

Electronically available in PDF format at
www.un.org/disarmament

UNITED NATIONS PUBLICATION
E.20.IX.7

ISBN 978-92-1-139192-3
eISBN 978-92-1-005235-1
Print ISSN 0252-5607
Online ISSN 2412-1193

Contents

Page

Foreword   xi

Acknowledgements.   xiii

Multilateral disarmament timeline
Highlights, 2019   xiv

Chapter I. Nuclear disarmament and non-proliferation

Developments and trends, 2019   3

Issues related to the Treaty on the Non-Proliferation of Nuclear Weapons   5

*Third session of the Preparatory Committee for the 2020 Review
Conference of the Parties to the Treaty on the Non-Proliferation of
Nuclear Weapons*   6

Issues related to the Comprehensive Nuclear-Test-Ban Treaty   14

Entry into force and universality   14

Eleventh Article XIV Conference   15

*Comprehensive Nuclear-Test-Ban Treaty Science and Technology
Conference*.   15

International Day against Nuclear Tests   16

Youth Group.   17

Group of Eminent Persons   17

*Preparatory Commission for the Comprehensive Nuclear-Test-Ban
Treaty Organization*.   18

Integrated capacity-building, education and training   18

Treaty on the Prohibition of Nuclear Weapons   19

Bilateral agreements and other issues   20

*Implementation of the Treaty on Measures for the Further Reduction
and Limitation of Strategic Offensive Arms*   20

*Implementation of the Treaty on the Elimination of Intermediate-
Range and Shorter-Range Missiles*   22

*Joint Comprehensive Plan of Action and Security Council
resolution 2231 (2015)*   23

Democratic People's Republic of Korea.   26

Group of Governmental Experts to consider the role of verification
in advancing nuclear disarmament   30

International Atomic Energy Agency verification   31

   Nuclear verification   32

   Safeguards conclusions   32

   Safeguards agreements, additional protocols and small quantities protocols   33

   Verification activities   34

   Application of safeguards in the Middle East   36

   Assurances of nuclear fuel supply   36

   Nuclear security   37

Export controls   40

   Missile Technology Control Regime   40

   Hague Code of Conduct against Ballistic Missile Proliferation   41

   Nuclear Suppliers Group   42

Fissile materials   43

Chapter II. Biological and chemical weapons

Developments and trends, 2019   49

Chemical weapons   50

   Twenty-fourth session of the Conference of the States Parties   50

   Organisation for the Prohibition of Chemical Weapons   51

   National implementation, assistance and protection against chemical weapons, and international cooperation on promoting peaceful uses of chemistry   52

   Science and technology-related activities   55

   United Nations project on lessons learned from the Organisation for the Prohibition of Chemical Weapons–United Nations Joint Investigative Mechanism   55

Biological weapons   56

   Meetings of Experts to the Biological Weapons Convention   56

   Meeting of States Parties to the Biological Weapons Convention   61

   Work of the Implementation Support Unit   63

Secretary-General's Mechanism for Investigation of Alleged Use of Chemical and Biological Weapons   68

Export controls   69

   Australia Group   69

Chapter III. Conventional weapons

Developments and trends, 2019 73

Arms Trade Treaty 75

    Fifth Conference of States Parties 76

Small arms and light weapons 81

    Programme of Action on Small Arms and Light Weapons 81

    Security Council 85

    Modular Small-arms-control Implementation Compendium 88

    Coordinating Action on Small Arms mechanism 89

    Protocol against the Illicit Manufacturing of and Trafficking
    in Firearms, Their Parts and Components and Ammunition 90

Ammunition 90

    General Assembly 92

    International Ammunition Technical Guidelines and United Nations
    SaferGuard activities 93

Improvised explosive devices 95

    Amended Protocol II of the Convention on Certain Conventional
    Weapons 97

    United Nations Mine Action Service activities 97

Explosive weapons in populated areas 98

    Vienna Conference and development of a political declaration 101

    Relevant discussions under the Convention on Certain Conventional
    Weapons 102

    Data collection and civilian casualty recording. 103

Transparency in conventional arms transfers and military expenditures . . 103

    United Nations Register of Conventional Arms 103

    Objective information on military matters, including transparency
    of military expenditures 106

Export controls 107

    Wassenaar Arrangement 107

United Nations Trust Facility Supporting Cooperation on Arms
Regulation 108

Confidence-building measures in the field of conventional arms 109

Convention on Certain Conventional Weapons 110

> Group of Governmental Experts on Emerging Technologies in the
> Area of Lethal Autonomous Weapons Systems 110

> Protocol V: Meeting of Experts and thirteenth Conference of the
> High Contracting Parties 112

> Amended Protocol II: Group of Experts and twenty-first Annual
> Conference of the High Contracting Parties 113

> Meeting of the High Contracting Parties to the Convention on
> Certain Conventional Weapons 116

> Work of the Implementation Support Unit of the Convention on
> Certain Conventional Weapons 118

Cluster munitions 119

> Ninth Meeting of States Parties to the Convention on Cluster
> Munitions 119

Anti-personnel mines 121

> Intersessional activities and the fourth Review Conference of the
> States Parties to the Anti-Personnel Mine Ban Convention 121

Chapter IV. Regional disarmament

Developments and trends, 2019 131

Nuclear-weapon-free zones 134

> Treaty for the Prohibition of Nuclear Weapons in Latin America
> and the Caribbean (Treaty of Tlatelolco) 136

> South Pacific Nuclear Free Zone (Rarotonga Treaty) 138

> Treaty on the Southeast Asia Nuclear Weapon-Free Zone
> (Bangkok Treaty) 139

> African Nuclear-Weapon-Free Zone Treaty (Pelindaba Treaty) 140

> Treaty on a Nuclear-Weapon-Free Zone in Central Asia 141

Establishment of a Middle East zone free of nuclear weapons and other
weapons of mass destruction 142

> First session of the Conference on the Establishment of a
> Middle East Zone Free of Nuclear Weapons and Other Weapons
> of Mass Destruction 142

United Nations Office for Disarmament Affairs regional centres 144

> United Nations Regional Centre for Peace and Disarmament
> in Africa 144

*United Nations Regional Centre for Peace, Disarmament and
Development in Latin America and the Caribbean* 148

*United Nations Regional Centre for Peace and Disarmament in Asia
and the Pacific* 150

Disarmament and arms regulation at the regional level 153

Africa 153

Americas 157

Asia 159

Europe 163

Middle East 175

United Nations Development Programme 176

United Nations Office on Drugs and Crime 178

Chapter V. Emerging, cross-cutting and other issues

Developments and trends, 2019 183

Emerging issues 185

Outer space 185

*Developments in the field of information and telecommunications
in the context of international security.* 188

Missiles 190

Armed uncrewed aerial vehicles 191

Emerging technologies relevant to small arms and light weapons 192

Cross-cutting issues 194

Relationship between disarmament and development 194

Terrorism and disarmament. 195

*Promotion of multilateralism in the area of disarmament and
non-proliferation* 200

*Developments in science and technology and their potential impact
on international security and disarmament efforts.* 200

*Observance of environmental norms in the drafting and
implementation of agreements on disarmament and arms control* 201

Implementation of Security Council resolution 1540 (2004) 201

Status of implementation 201

Monitoring and national implementation 202

Assistance 203

Cooperation with international, regional and subregional organizations 203

Transparency and outreach 204

Chapter VI. Gender and disarmament

Developments and trends, 2019 207

Integrating gender perspectives 208

Equal participation 211

Conventional weapons 215

Nuclear weapons. 219

Other weapons of mass destruction. 220

New weapons technologies. 221

Regional disarmament and arms control 223

Peace operations 225

Disarmament, demobilization and reintegration 227

Security sector reform 228

United Nations police 231

Mine action. 231

Chapter VII. Disarmament machinery

Developments and trends, 2019 235

First Committee of the General Assembly 237

Organization of work. 237

Overview of key substantive discussions in the Committee 239

United Nations Disarmament Commission 262

Conference on Disarmament. 265

2019 session of the Conference on Disarmament 267

Advisory Board on Disarmament Matters. 270

Chapter VIII. Information and outreach

Developments and trends, 2019 277

Disarmament Information Programme 279

Print and e-publications 279

Websites. 281

Databases 282

International days 283

Media. 286

Exhibits 287

Disarmament and non-proliferation education 289

Youth and disarmament 289

Disarmament fellowships 293

Vienna Office of the United Nations Office for Disarmament Affairs 295

United Nations Institute for Disarmament Research. 296

Weapons of mass destruction and other strategic weapons 297

Conventional arms 298

Security and technology. 299

Gender and disarmament 300

Appendix I. Status of multilateral arms regulation and disarmament agreements. 309

Appendix II. Disarmament resolutions and decisions listed by chapter. 323

Foreword

Welcome to Part II of the 2019 *United Nations Disarmament Yearbook*. Prepared each year at the request of the General Assembly, the *Yearbook* offers a comprehensive and authoritative guide to recent developments and trends in the field of multilateral disarmament, non-proliferation and arms control.

The Office for Disarmament Affairs makes every effort to maintain the *Yearbook* as a consistent source of objective information for the diplomatic community, academia and the general public. I am pleased to note that this latest volume incorporates a number of innovations meant to expand on what then-Secretary-General Kurt Waldheim, in his introduction to the very first edition, set out as the publication's aim: contributing to "a better and broader understanding of disarmament issues". This forty-fourth edition features, for the first time, a collection of graphics and charts that provide key historical context while highlighting opportunities for further progress.

Additionally, in recognition that gender issues are crucial to address in creating the conditions for lasting peace and security, the present volume of the *Yearbook* is the first to devote a full chapter to the topic of "gender and disarmament". It is hoped that this information will assist policymakers and practitioners in considering how gender-responsive approaches can improve their disarmament-related work, including through the pursuit of equal participation by women and men in relevant multilateral forums and decision-making.

Although women continued to be significantly underrepresented in these processes throughout 2019, the General Assembly prioritized women's full, equal and meaningful participation in forums tackling issues such as ammunition management, nuclear disarmament verification and the global ban on biological weapons. The First Committee of the General Assembly voiced direct support for pursuing gender parity or addressing gender considerations in 17 of the resolutions it adopted during its seventy-fourth session, and implementing gender-responsive approaches and training was a growing focus of entities working on disarmament issues both in and beyond the United Nations system. Also, as a personal contribution to raising awareness, I authored an op-ed in which I made the case for gender to be placed "at the heart of arms policy".

In the following pages, you will find a detailed accounting of 2019's progress and setbacks across the disarmament field, where policymakers and practitioners acted on priorities that included limiting risks from strategic competition between States; preserving the international norm against chemical-weapon use; effectively managing conventional weapons and ammunition and countering their illicit manufacturing and trade; developing meaningful responses to emerging weapon technologies; and improving the functioning of the intergovernmental disarmament machinery. Meanwhile, Member States partnered with the Secretary-General to achieve notable movement towards fulfilling commitments that he made in 2018 as part of his Agenda for Disarmament, *Securing Our Common Future*.

Still, the many challenges in these areas underscore the need for disarmament processes to become more inclusive in order to facilitate fresh ideas and approaches. This makes 2019 particularly notable as a landmark year for youth participation in disarmament, with the United Nations and its Member States taking significant new steps aimed at supporting the entry of young people into the field. The General Assembly passed, for the first time, a resolution on "Youth, disarmament and non-proliferation", reaffirming the important and positive contribution that young people can make in sustaining peace and security. Meanwhile, under a new outreach initiative called "Youth4Disarmament", the Office for Disarmament Affairs undertook a variety of programming to connect geographically diverse young people with experts to learn about current international security challenges, the work of the United Nations and how they can be active participants.

I encourage you to consider the following pages from the perspective of these young people, for each edition of the *Yearbook* is written not just as a convenient reference for our time, but also as a chronicle for succeeding generations. Let us do our utmost to preserve and build further upon the legacy recalled in these volumes in the hope that future readers might find in our efforts a narrative of humanity's shared journey towards peace.

Izumi Nakamitsu
Under-Secretary-General
High Representative for Disarmament Affairs
August 2020

Acknowledgements

Volume 44 (Part II) of the *United Nations Disarmament Yearbook*, like editions before it, was a collaborative endeavour to which the staff of the United Nations Office for Disarmament Affairs devoted considerable time and effort. It was prepared under the overall direction of the High Representative for Disarmament Affairs, Izumi Nakamitsu, and the Director of the Office, Thomas Markram.

I would like to extend my gratitude to the following writers and contributors: Nora Allgaier, Ismail Balla, Katja Boettcher, Aaron Buckley, Tam Chung, Amanda Cowl, Courtney Cresap, Radha Day, Amy Dowler, Adedeji Ebo, John Ennis, Estela Evangelista, Daniel Feakes, Ivor Fung, Claudia Garcia Guiza, Melanie Gerber, Gillian Goh, Takuma Haga, Jan Havlicek, René Holbach, Ana Izar, Rebecca Jovin, Heegyun Jung, Erika Kawahara, Soo Hyun Kim, Christopher King, Peter Kolarov, Tsutomu Kono, Yuriy Kryvonos, Iina Kuuttila, Qi Lai, Hermann Lampalzer, Gabiden Laumulin, Su-Yin Lew, Valère Mantels, Tak Mashiko, Hideki Matsuno, Silvia Mercogliano, Jiaming Miao, Aleksander Micic, Laurie Mincieli, Charles Ovink, Daniël Prins, Katherine Prizeman, Cecile Salcedo, Fiona Simpson, Ingmar Snabile, Mary Soliman, Michael Spies, Frida Thomassen, Ngoc Phuong van der Blij, Xiaoyu Wang, Anselme Yabouri and Yue Yao.

I also would like to thank the many others who contributed to this publication on behalf of other agencies and organizations.

Diane Barnes
Editor-in-Chief
August 2020

Multilateral disarmament timeline
Highlights, 2019

January	February	March	April	May	June

21 Jan.–29 Mar.
Conference on Disarmament, 1st session

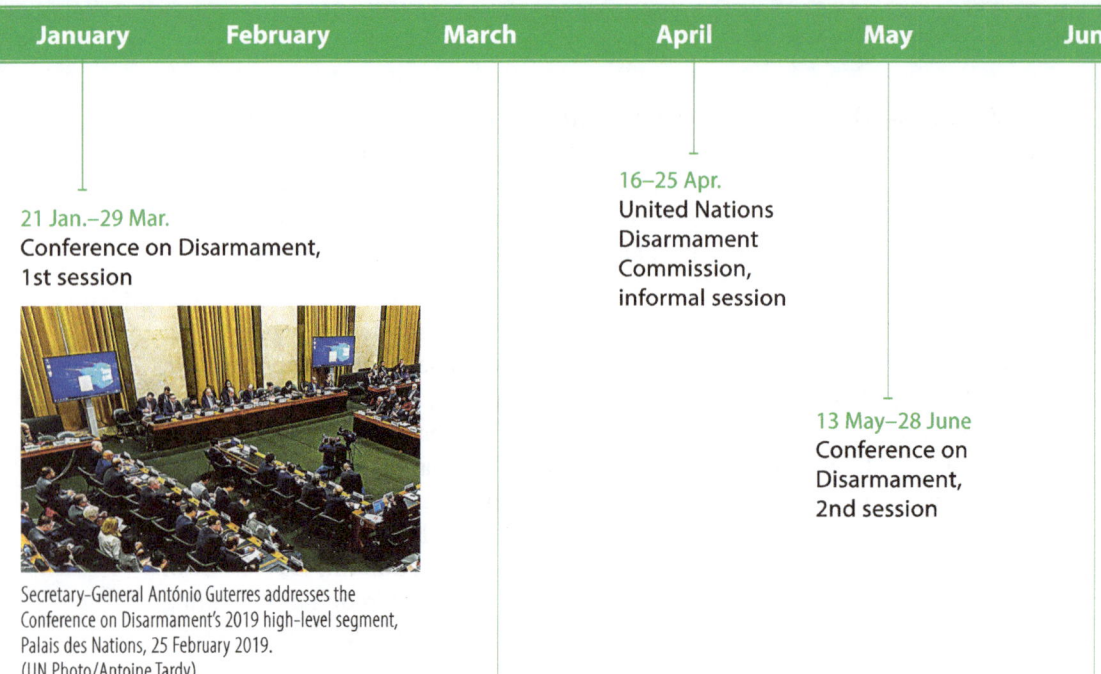

Secretary-General António Guterres addresses the
Conference on Disarmament's 2019 high-level segment,
Palais des Nations, 25 February 2019.
(UN Photo/Antoine Tardy)

16–25 Apr.
United Nations Disarmament Commission, informal session

13 May–28 June
Conference on Disarmament, 2nd session

1 Mar.
20th anniversary: entry into force of the Anti-Personnel Mine Ban Convention

The first female clearance team in Viet Nam.
Photo: Nguyen Thi Kim Thanh, Norwegian Embassy in Hanoi, 8 May 2019

7 June
20th anniversary: opening for signature of the Inter-American Convention on Transparency in Conventional Weapons Acquisitions

Security forces participate in a workshop on physical
security and stockpile management, weapons marking
and data record-keeping, held from 6 to 18 May 2019
in Vontovorona, Madagascar.

July	August	September	October	November	December

3 Oct.–8 Nov.
Seventy-fourth session of the First Committee of the General Assembly

11 July
35th anniversary: entry into force of the Agreement Governing the Activities of States on the Moon and Other Celestial Bodies

1 Dec.
60th anniversary: signing of the Antarctic Treaty

18–22 Nov.
Conference on the Establishment of a Middle East Zone Free of Nuclear Weapons and All Other Weapons of Mass Destruction, 1st session

15 July
10th anniversary: entry into force of the Pelindaba Treaty

29 July–13 Sep.
Conference on Disarmament, 3rd session

26–29 Nov.
Fourth Review Conference of the Anti-Personnel Mine Ban Convention

24 Dec.
5th anniversary: entry into force of the Arms Trade Treaty

Thirty-two youth delegates from 18 countries delivered a powerful statement during the closing ceremony of the Oslo Review Conference.
(Photo: Stine Østby/Medvind/Ministry of Foreign Affairs, Oslo)

The United Nations Regional Centre for Peace and Disarmament in Africa assists Togo with the destruction of seized and obsolete weapons and ammunition, 21 September 2019.

chapter

Nuclear disarmament and non-proliferation

Opening ceremony of the "Comprehensive Nuclear-Test-Ban Treaty: Science and Technology 2019 Conference", Hofburg Palace, Vienna, Austria, 24 June 2019.

CHAPTER I

Nuclear disarmament and non-proliferation

There are many pathways to a world free of nuclear weapons. ... Our focus must be on taking steps in eliminating nuclear weapons and doing so in good faith.

ANTÓNIO GUTERRES, SECRETARY-GENERAL OF THE UNITED NATIONS[1]

Developments and trends, 2019

THE YEAR 2019 witnessed a continuation—and, in some cases, a worsening—of negative trends that had plagued nuclear disarmament efforts in previous years: deteriorating geostrategic conditions, growing distrust and acrimony among nuclear-armed States, and widening fissures between Member States over how to achieve the common goal of eliminating all nuclear weapons. Together, those developments placed growing pressure on the web of agreements and instruments that make up the disarmament and non-proliferation regime, undermining existing efforts and imposing new obstacles to progress. As the Secretary-General stated at the Conference on Disarmament in February, "Key components of the international arms control architecture are collapsing."

The third session of the Preparatory Committee for the 2020 Review Conference of the Parties to the Treaty on the Non-Proliferation of Nuclear Weapons (Nuclear Non-Proliferation Treaty)—considered by most States to be the cornerstone of the disarmament and non-proliferation regime—saw heated debates and the exposure of significant divisions between States parties over commitments made under the Treaty, particularly with regard to their enduring relevance and issues of compliance. Divisions were noted among nuclear-weapon States, between nuclear-weapon and non-nuclear-weapon States, and between groups of non-nuclear-weapon States. Although States parties reiterated their commitment to the Treaty and its goals, their discussions reflected the challenge they faced in seeking a successful outcome at the 2020 Review Conference.

Relations between States possessing nuclear weapons worsened significantly during 2019, with dire consequences for the disarmament and non-proliferation regime. In August, the United States of America announced its withdrawal from the Treaty between the United States of America and the Union of Soviet Socialist Republics on the Elimination of Their Intermediate-Range and Shorter-Range Missiles (Intermediate-Range Nuclear Forces Treaty) of 1987 due to continued

---

[1] Remarks on the occasion of the International Day for the Total Elimination of Nuclear Weapons, New York, 26 September 2019.

violations by the Russian Federation.[2] As the first agreement on eliminating an entire category of nuclear-capable weapons, the Treaty was widely seen as a pillar of the international arms-control regime, and its demise represented a significant blow to that architecture. Its collapse also placed in doubt the future of the Treaty between the United States of America and the Russian Federation on Measures for the Further Reduction and Limitation of Strategic Offensive Arms (New START Treaty) of 2011, which, despite repeated calls from the international community—including the Secretary-General—would expire in 2021 if not extended,.

In parallel, all States possessing nuclear weapons continued to modernize their nuclear arsenals, including through the testing and deployment of new weapon systems. In December, the Ministry of Defence of the Russian Federation announced it had fit intercontinental ballistic missiles with a new hypersonic glide vehicle, consistent with a 2018 announcement by the President of the Russian Federation, Vladimir Putin. Similarly, the Russian Federation continued testing a new silo-based intercontinental ballistic missile. Meanwhile, following its withdrawal from the Intermediate-Range Nuclear Forces Treaty, the United States conducted two series of tests with missiles that would have been prohibited under the Treaty.

Regional crises with nuclear dimensions also worsened in 2019. In May, responding to the United States' withdrawal from the Joint Comprehensive Plan of Action and reimposition of related unilateral sanctions, the Islamic Republic of Iran said that it would scale back its nuclear commitments under the agreement in 60-day increments in the absence of meaningful sanctions relief.

Separately, the Democratic People's Republic of Korea and the United States achieved no substantial progress towards the complete and verifiable denuclearization of the Korean Peninsula, including through implementing the Joint Statement[3] from their 2018 summit in Singapore. Inter-Korean relations also continued to deteriorate following the signing of the Panmunjom Declaration[4] of April 2018, with the Democratic People's Republic of Korea refusing to engage in dialogue with the Republic of Korea. Throughout the year, the Democratic People's Republic of Korea appeared to continue the development of its nuclear and missile capabilities, including by launching over 20 short-range ballistic missiles and large-calibre artillery rockets on 13 separate occasions. With the expiration of a year-end deadline set by the Democratic People's Republic of Korea for the United States to propose "new calculations" to advance the stalled talks, 2019 ended with uncertain prospects for future dialogue.

---

[2] United States of America, Department of State, "U.S. Withdrawal from the INF Treaty on August 2, 2019", 2 August 2019.

[3] United States of America, The White House, "Joint Statement of President Donald J. Trump of the United States of America and Chairman Kim Jong Un of the Democratic People's Republic of Korea at the Singapore Summit", 12 June 2018.

[4] Republic of Korea, Ministry of Foreign Affairs, "Panmunjom Declaration for the Peace, Prosperity and Unification of the Korean Peninsula", 11 September 2018.

Against that background, however, there were several positive developments. "Disarmament to Save Humanity"—the pillar of the Secretary-General's Agenda for Disarmament[5] dedicated to eliminating all nuclear weapons and other weapons of mass destruction—gained new State "champions" and "supporters" in 2019, with totals of 15 and 14, respectively, as at the end of the year. Furthermore, several cross-regional initiatives were launched in 2019 to support a successful Nuclear Non-Proliferation Treaty Review Conference in 2020.

Many Member States also signalled their commitment to the complete elimination of nuclear weapons through support to the Treaty on the Prohibition of Nuclear Weapons, which at the end of 2019 had 80 signatories and 34 ratifications or accessions. Nevertheless, the Treaty remained divisive, with States possessing nuclear weapons asserting that it undermined existing efforts.

Also in 2019, a Group of Governmental Experts established to consider the role of verification in advancing nuclear disarmament delivered its final report[6] to the General Assembly, identifying possible points of convergence and suggesting a list of principles on verification in advancing nuclear disarmament.

In August, representatives from the five nuclear-weapon-free zones and Mongolia met in Nur-Sultan, Kazakhstan, for a seminar on fostering cooperation and enhancing consultation mechanisms among the existing nuclear-weapon-free zones. Participants discussed ways to improve coordination and achieve more robust cooperation among the zones, strengthen disarmament initiatives and the nuclear non-proliferation regime, and provide impetus to the development of new zones.

The first session of the Conference on the Establishment of a Middle East Zone Free of Nuclear Weapons and Other Weapons of Mass Destruction was held in November, pursuant to General Assembly decision 73/546 of 22 December 2018. The strong commitment of the participating States and their constructive approach resulted in a successful session. By adopting a political declaration,[7] the participating States conveyed a clear message to the wider international community about their renewed commitment to working towards achieving the establishment of the Middle East zone, while keeping the door of the process open to participation by all States from the region.

Issues related to the Treaty on the Non-Proliferation of Nuclear Weapons

The Nuclear Non-Proliferation Treaty is a landmark international treaty whose objective is to prevent the spread of nuclear weapons and weapons

---

[5] António Guterres, *Securing Our Common Future: An Agenda for Disarmament* (United Nations publication, Sales No. E.18.IX.6).

[6] A/74/90.

[7] A/CONF.236/6, annex.

technology, to promote cooperation in the peaceful uses of nuclear energy and to further the goal of achieving nuclear disarmament and general and complete disarmament.

Third session of the Preparatory Committee for the 2020 Review Conference of the Parties to the Treaty on the Non-Proliferation of Nuclear Weapons

The Preparatory Committee for the 2020 Review Conference of the Parties to the Treaty on the Non-Proliferation of Nuclear Weapons[8] held its third session in New York from 29 April to 10 May, with Syed Md Hasrin Syed Hussin (Malaysia) serving as Chair. Representatives from 143 States parties,[9] 6 international organizations (NGOs)[10] and 95 non-governmental organizations[11] participated in the session. The Committee adopted its final report[12] for the 2020 Review Conference and achieved several procedural outcomes to facilitate the Conference, notably the adoption of its provisional agenda and rules of procedure, as well as the endorsement of its President-designate. The Committee could not obtain consensus on recommendations to the Review Conference; the Chair consequently submitted recommendations as a working paper[13] under his own authority.

---

[8] The text and adherence status of the Treaty are available at the Disarmament Treaty Database of the Office for Disarmament Affairs.

[9] Afghanistan, Algeria, Andorra, Argentina, Armenia, Australia, Austria, Azerbaijan, Bahamas, Bahrain, Bangladesh, Barbados, Belarus, Belgium, Belize, Bolivia (Plurinational State of), Bosnia and Herzegovina, Botswana, Brazil, Brunei Darussalam, Bulgaria, Burkina Faso, Burundi, Cabo Verde, Cambodia, Canada, Chile, China, Colombia, Congo, Costa Rica, Côte d'Ivoire, Croatia, Cuba, Cyprus, Czechia, Democratic Republic of the Congo, Denmark, Djibouti, Dominican Republic, Ecuador, Egypt, Estonia, Fiji, Finland, France, Germany, Ghana, Greece, Grenada, Guatemala, Guyana, Holy See, Honduras, Hungary, Iceland, Indonesia, Iran (Islamic Republic of), Iraq, Ireland, Italy, Jamaica, Japan, Jordan, Kazakhstan, Kenya, Kuwait, Kyrgyzstan, Lao People's Democratic Republic, Latvia, Lebanon, Libya, Liechtenstein, Lithuania, Luxembourg, Madagascar, Malawi, Malaysia, Maldives, Mali, Malta, Mauritius, Mexico, Micronesia (Federated States of), Monaco, Mongolia, Morocco, Myanmar, Nepal, Netherlands, New Zealand, Nicaragua, Niger, Nigeria, North Macedonia, Norway, Oman, Panama, Paraguay, Peru, Philippines, Poland, Portugal, Qatar, Republic of Korea, Republic of Moldova, Romania, Russian Federation, Saint Lucia, Saint Vincent and the Grenadines, Samoa, San Marino, Saudi Arabia, Serbia, Singapore, Slovakia, South Africa, Spain, Sri Lanka, State of Palestine, Sudan, Suriname, Sweden, Switzerland, Syrian Arab Republic, Thailand, Togo, Trinidad and Tobago, Tunisia, Turkey, Uganda, Ukraine, United Arab Emirates, United Kingdom of Great Britain and Northern Ireland, United Republic of Tanzania, United States, Uruguay, Uzbekistan, Venezuela (Bolivarian Republic of), Viet Nam, Yemen, Zambia and Zimbabwe.

[10] Brazilian-Argentine Agency for Accounting and Control of Nuclear Materials; the European Union; the International Committee of the Red Cross; the League of Arab States; the North Atlantic Treaty Organization; the Preparatory Commission for the Comprehensive Nuclear-Test-Ban Treaty Organization.

[11] For the list of NGOs, see NPT/CONF.2020/PC.III/INF/6.

[12] NPT/CONF.2020/1.

[13] NPT/CONF.2020/PC.III/WP.49.

In her statement[14] to the Preparatory Committee, the High Representative for Disarmament Affairs, Izumi Nakamitsu, expressed hope that States parties would reaffirm their commitment to the Treaty, to its complete and balanced implementation, and to the fulfilment of the obligations assumed under it. She highlighted the deteriorating geopolitical environment and real concerns about the erosion of the global arms control regime, and underscored the need to secure the collective benefits provided by the Treaty to all States parties.

The Preparatory Committee set aside five meetings for a general debate on issues related to all aspects of its work. It heard 93 statements[15] by States parties and 10 by groups of States parties, as well as several by NGOs. In a joint statement[16] delivered by China, the nuclear-weapon States referenced their eighth formal conference held in January in Beijing, which focused on the theme "Strengthening the P5 Coordination and Safeguarding the Nuclear Non-Proliferation Treaty Regime". The five States highlighted their agreement to enhance dialogue on nuclear policies and doctrines, promote strategic trust and common security, and make utmost efforts to prevent nuclear risks. They also recalled the importance of maintaining the existing arms-control architecture, undertook to jointly safeguard the Nuclear Non-Proliferation Treaty regime, and agreed to work on making the international security environment more conducive to further progress on nuclear disarmament and on achieving a world without nuclear weapons with undiminished security for all, through a gradual approach.

As in 2018, the Preparatory Committee was marked by occasionally heated rhetoric between States parties that highlighted enduring obstacles to securing a successful conclusion to the 2020 Review Conference. External sources of division that were predominantly of a geostrategic nature—in particular, the increasingly strained relationship between the Russian Federation and the United States, as well as various crises in the Middle East—clearly impacted the session. States engaged in heated debate and rights of reply over developments in the previous 12 months, such as the withdrawal by the United States from the Joint Comprehensive Plan of Action on the nuclear programme of the Islamic Republic of Iran, the announced withdrawal of the United States from the Intermediate-Range Nuclear Forces Treaty and the ongoing allegations of use of chemical weapons in the Syrian Arab Republic.

Treaty-based dynamics also contributed to the fissures between States parties. Those included ongoing frustration over the implementation of past commitments—especially those related to disarmament—as well as diverging

---

[14] Izumi Nakamitsu, High Representative for Disarmament Affairs, statement at the third session of the Preparatory Committee for the 2020 Review Conference of the Nuclear Non-Proliferation Treaty, New York, 29 April 2019.

[15] United Nations PaperSmart, "Preparatory Committee for the 2020 Review Conference of the Parties to the Treaty on the Non-Proliferation of Nuclear Weapons Third Session".

[16] Fu Cong (China), statement on behalf of the P5 States at the general debate of the third session of the Preparatory Committee for the 2020 Review Conference of the Nuclear Non-Proliferation Treaty, New York, 1 May 2019.

views on how to achieve and maintain a world free of nuclear weapons, as reflected by disagreement between supporters and opponents of the Treaty on the Prohibition of Nuclear Weapons.

Nevertheless, States parties reaffirmed both their commitment to the Nuclear Non-Proliferation Treaty and its status as the cornerstone of the nuclear non-proliferation and disarmament regime. They emphasized the integral contribution of the Treaty to international peace, security and stability, and they stressed the importance of: (a) full and effective implementation of and compliance with the Treaty's obligations; and (b) the pursuit of policies fully compatible with the Treaty. They also emphasized the importance of ensuring the balanced implementation of the three pillars of the Treaty—nuclear disarmament, nuclear non-proliferation and peaceful uses of nuclear energy—and noted their mutually reinforcing nature.

States parties recalled the need for the full and effective implementation of decisions 1 and 2 of the 1995 Review and Extension Conference, as well as of the resolution on the Middle East adopted at that meeting. Likewise, most States parties argued in favour of the Final Document adopted at the 2000 Review Conference, as well as the conclusions and recommendations for follow-on actions adopted at the 2010 Review Conference. States parties further committed to making every effort to achieve a successful outcome at the Review Conference in 2020, the fiftieth year since the Treaty entered into force.

Following the general exchange of views, the Committee organized its meetings into three clusters, according equal time to each of the Treaty's three pillars: (a) non-proliferation of nuclear weapons, disarmament and international peace and security; (b) non-proliferation of nuclear weapons, safeguards and nuclear-weapon-free zones; and (c) the inalienable right of all States parties to the Treaty to the development, research, production and use of nuclear energy for peaceful purposes, without discrimination and in conformity with articles I and II of the Treaty. Under those clusters, the following blocs of issues were addressed: (a) nuclear disarmament and security assurances; (b) regional issues, such as the Middle East and the implementation of the 1995 resolution on the Middle East; and (c) peaceful uses of nuclear energy and other provisions of the Treaty. Discussion also took place on the issue of improving the effectiveness of the strengthened review process.

Cluster 1

States parties reaffirmed their commitment to the full and effective implementation of article VI of the Treaty. In that regard, they recalled the unequivocal undertaking by the nuclear-weapon States in 2000 to accomplish the total elimination of their nuclear arsenals leading to nuclear disarmament, as well as the responsibility of all States parties to pursue negotiations in good faith on effective measures relating to cessation of the nuclear arms race and to nuclear disarmament.

Disagreement persisted among States parties over the pace and scale of nuclear disarmament, with many expressing concern that the slow progress to date was inconsistent with obligations made under the Treaty and in various review conference outcomes. Similarly, it was asserted that modernization programmes in nuclear-weapon States were not consistent with commitments to diminish the role of nuclear weapons in military and security concepts, doctrines and policies. In response, nuclear-weapon States argued that modernization programmes were intended to increase the safety and security of nuclear arsenals.

Some participants highlighted the catastrophic humanitarian consequences of any use of nuclear weapons, as well as the need for all States to comply at all times with applicable international law, including international humanitarian law. In that context, many States parties expressed the view that the Treaty on the Prohibition of Nuclear Weapons was an "effective measure" as defined under article VI, as it created a legally binding prohibition on nuclear weapons and strengthened the existing disarmament and nuclear non-proliferation regime. That argument was rejected by some States parties on the grounds that the Treaty on the Prohibition of Nuclear Weapons contradicted and risked undermining the Nuclear Non-Proliferation Treaty.

In addition, some participants noted that all States had a responsibility to work together to improve the geopolitical environment to facilitate an environment conducive to further nuclear disarmament. In that regard, States parties encouraged steps that promoted international stability, peace and security and that also were based on the principle of equal and undiminished security for all.

Participants also noted that increasing transparency was important to building confidence and trust at regional and international levels. In that connection, many States parties commented that regular reporting could enhance transparency, benefiting the Treaty review cycle.

With regard to doctrine and posture, it was recalled that nuclear-weapon States had committed to reduce the operational status of nuclear-weapon systems in ways that promoted international stability and security. The Committee urged further progress in that regard. States parties discussed the relevance of security assurances by nuclear-weapon States, as well as the legitimate interest of non-nuclear-weapon States in receiving unequivocal security assurances, including through legally binding instruments.

The Committee highlighted the need for a robust and credible verification mechanism for nuclear disarmament as an essential element for achieving and maintaining a world without nuclear weapons. States parties welcomed efforts to develop capabilities for nuclear disarmament verification, including through the Group of Governmental Experts established by the General Assembly.

Many States parties articulated their alarm at the erosion of the bilateral arms-control regime between the Russian Federation and the United States, in particular the Intermediate-Range Nuclear Forces Treaty. The Committee called for the urgent extension of the Treaty on Measures for the Further Reduction and Limitation of Strategic Offensive Arms (New START Treaty) and the negotiation of a successor agreement leading to further reductions.

Furthermore, States parties reaffirmed the status of the Comprehensive Nuclear-Test-Ban Treaty as a core element of the nuclear-disarmament and non-proliferation regime, as well as the urgent need for the Treaty to enter into force. Emphasizing its link with the Nuclear Non-Proliferation Treaty, they urged States that had not yet signed and ratified the Comprehensive Nuclear-Test-Ban Treaty—especially the remaining eight Annex 2 States—to do so without delay. The Conference also encouraged all States to refrain from any action that would defeat the object and purpose of the Comprehensive Nuclear-Test-Ban Treaty, pending its entry into force.

The Committee also expressed deep regret at the continued stalemate in the Conference on Disarmament, despite further attempts to achieve consensus. However, States parties welcomed the Conference's decision of 19 February 2018 on the creation of subsidiary bodies to reach understanding on areas of commonalities; deepen technical discussions and broaden areas of agreement; and consider effective measures, including legal instruments for negotiation.

Cluster 2

States parties emphasized that International Atomic Energy Agency (IAEA) safeguards were a fundamental component of the nuclear non-proliferation regime and played an indispensable role in the implementation of the Nuclear Non-Proliferation Treaty and helped to create an environment conducive to nuclear cooperation.

They reaffirmed that IAEA was the competent authority responsible for verifying and assuring compliance with safeguards agreements, which States parties undertake to fulfil Treaty obligations with a view to preventing diversion of nuclear energy from peaceful uses to nuclear weapons or other nuclear explosive devices. They also stressed that nothing should be done to undermine the authority of the Agency in that regard.

States parties welcomed the fact that 175 non-nuclear-weapon States had brought into force comprehensive safeguards agreements with IAEA, and the Committee encouraged those States without such agreements to bring them into force as soon as possible. Many States parties noted that although comprehensive safeguards agreements were successful in providing assurance regarding declared nuclear material, an additional protocol could increase confidence about the absence of undeclared material and, together with the comprehensive safeguards agreement, constituted the current verification standard. They welcomed the growing number of States parties, which had reached 136, that had brought additional protocols into force. However, the Committee also emphasized that it was the sovereign decision of any State to conclude an additional protocol. The

Committee stressed the importance of continuing to strengthen the safeguards system and, in that context, some States parties welcomed the work by IAEA to conceptualize and further implement State-level approaches to safeguards in order to increase the system's efficiency and effectiveness.

In response to concerns about non-compliance with non-proliferation obligations, participants stressed that complying with all such obligations and addressing all non-compliance matters were important practices, both for the Treaty's integrity and for the authority of IAEA safeguards system. States parties also highlighted the importance of resolving all cases of non-compliance with safeguards obligations in full conformity with the statute of the Agency and the respective legal obligations of States parties. In addition, they underlined the primary responsibility of the Security Council in cases of non-compliance.

Participants recalled the need to ensure that all nuclear-related exports were undertaken in full conformity with the objectives and purposes of the Nuclear Non-Proliferation Treaty. While concern was expressed regarding restrictions on exports, a number of States parties expressed the view that export controls were a legitimate, necessary and desirable means of implementing the obligations of States parties under article III of the Treaty.

In addition, States parties highlighted the need to provide effective physical protection for all nuclear material and nuclear facilities. All States, within their responsibility, were called upon to achieve and maintain highly effective nuclear security, including by protecting sensitive information and by providing physical protection both for nuclear and other radioactive material during use, storage and transport, and for the associated facilities at all stages in the life cycle. Reaffirming the central role of IAEA in strengthening the global nuclear-security framework and coordinating international activities in the field of nuclear security, the Committee encouraged the Agency to continue to assist States upon request in strengthening their national regulatory controls on nuclear material, including through the establishment and maintenance of State systems to account for and control nuclear material.

The Committee expressed concerns regarding the threat of terrorism and the risk that non-State actors might acquire nuclear weapons and their means of delivery. In that connection, it recalled the obligation of all States to fully implement Security Council resolution 1540 (2004). The Committee also encouraged all States that had not yet done so to become parties to the International Convention for the Suppression of Acts of Nuclear Terrorism, as soon as possible.

Separately, the Committee recognized the contributions to the objectives of nuclear disarmament and nuclear non-proliferation made by: (a) internationally recognized nuclear-weapon-free zones established on the basis of arrangements freely arrived at among the States of the region concerned and in accordance with the guidelines adopted in 1999 by the United Nations Disarmament Commission; and (b) the parallel declarations concerning the nuclear-weapon-free status of Mongolia. States parties also encouraged increased cooperation among the members of those zones. Furthermore, participants highlighted the importance of the expeditious signing and ratification by nuclear-weapon States of the relevant protocols to the treaties establishing nuclear-weapon-free zones.

The Committee reaffirmed universal support for the resolution on the Middle East adopted by the 1995 Review and Extension Conference, describing it as an essential element both of the Conference outcome and of the basis on which the Treaty was extended indefinitely without a vote. States parties recalled the affirmation of the resolution's goals and objectives by the 2000 and 2010 Review Conferences. However, the Committee was divided in its response to General Assembly decision 73/546 of 22 December 2018 on the convening of a conference on the establishment of a Middle East zone free of nuclear and other weapons of mass destruction. A majority of States parties supported the decision, but some expressed concern that it would set back prospects for inclusive regional dialogue on the issue and potentially for a successful Review Conference in 2020.

Participants strongly supported the Joint Comprehensive Plan of Action as an important contribution to the non-proliferation regime and a successful, multilateral endeavour endorsed by the Security Council, and they regretted the decision by the United States to withdraw from the agreement. The Committee underscored the vital role played by IAEA in verifying and monitoring the implementation of the Plan of Action. It also emphasized the importance of strict adherence by the Islamic Republic of Iran to all of its nuclear-related commitments under the Plan and its full cooperation with the Agency to achieve international confidence in the exclusively peaceful nature of the Iranian nuclear programme. All parties concerned were encouraged to maintain constructive positions so as to ensure continued progress towards the full implementation of the Plan.

While States parties expressed grave concern about the nuclear weapon and ballistic missile programmes of the Democratic People's Republic of Korea, they welcomed the two summits held between the United States and the Democratic People's Republic of Korea, as well as the three inter-Korean summits held in 2018, which helped to reduce tensions and restore dialogue. The Committee strongly urged the Democratic People's Republic of Korea to: abandon all nuclear weapons and existing nuclear programmes, as well as all other existing weapons of mass destruction and ballistic missile programmes; return, as early as possible, to the Treaty and IAEA safeguards; come into full compliance with the Treaty and cooperate promptly with the Agency in the full and effective implementation of comprehensive safeguards; and sign and ratify the Comprehensive Nuclear-Test-Ban Treaty. The Conference reiterated that the Democratic People's Republic of Korea could not have the status of a nuclear-weapon State in accordance with the Treaty. The Committee called upon all States to comply fully with relevant

Security Council resolutions. Meanwhile, 70 States parties released a joint statement entitled "Addressing the North Korean Nuclear Challenge".[17]

Fifty-two States parties released a joint statement[18] regretting that the Syrian Arab Republic did not cooperate with IAEA regarding the Board of Governors' finding in 2011 that failure by that country to declare the Dair Alzour reactor constituted non-compliance with its obligations under its IAEA safeguards agreement. Those States parties also stressed that the Syrian Arab Republic's safeguards non-compliance remained a serious concern.

Cluster 3

As in previous years, States parties agreed that nothing in the Treaty should be interpreted as affecting the inalienable right of all parties to the Treaty to develop research, production and use of nuclear energy for peaceful purposes without discrimination and in conformity with articles I, II and III of the Treaty. That right, they agreed, constituted one of the fundamental objectives of the Treaty. They also stressed that the use of nuclear energy must be safeguarded at all stages and accompanied by high levels of safety and security, consistent with States parties' national legislation and respective international obligations.

The Committee recognized the indispensable role of nuclear science and technology in achieving social and economic development for all States parties, as well as the need for enhanced international cooperation to expand the utilization of nuclear sciences and applications to improve the quality of life and the well-being of the peoples of the world. Such enhanced cooperation, States parties agreed, could support the achievement of the goals of the 2030 Agenda for Sustainable Development and the Paris Agreement on climate change.

States parties acknowledged the centrality of the IAEA Technical Cooperation Programme in enhancing the application of nuclear science and technology, especially in developing countries. Recognizing the Technical Cooperation Fund

---

[17] The joint statement (NPT/CONF.2020/PC.III/13) was endorsed by Albania, Andorra, Australia, Austria, Bahrain, Belgium, Bosnia and Herzegovina, Brazil, Bulgaria, Canada, Colombia, Croatia, Cyprus, Czechia, Denmark, El Salvador, Estonia, Finland, France, Georgia, Germany, Greece, Honduras, Hungary, Iceland, Iraq, Ireland, Italy, Japan, Jordan, Kuwait, Latvia, Liechtenstein, Lithuania, Luxembourg, Malaysia, Malta, Mexico, Monaco, Montenegro, Morocco, Netherlands, New Zealand, the Niger, Nigeria, North Macedonia, Norway, Papua New Guinea, Paraguay, Peru, Poland, Portugal, Qatar, Republic of Korea, Republic of Moldova, Romania, San Marino, Saudi Arabia, Serbia, Singapore, Slovakia, Slovenia, Spain, Sweden, Switzerland, Turkey, Ukraine, United Arab Emirates, United Kingdom and United States.

[18] The joint statement (NPT/CONF.2020/PC.III/12/Rev.1) was endorsed by Albania, Andorra, Australia, Austria, Belgium, Bulgaria, Brazil, Canada, Colombia, Croatia, Cyprus, Czechia, Denmark, Estonia, Finland, France, Georgia, Germany, Greece, Hungary, Iceland, Ireland, Italy, Japan, Latvia, Liechtenstein, Lithuania, Luxembourg, Malawi, Malta, Monaco, Montenegro, Netherlands, New Zealand, North Macedonia, Norway, Panama, Peru, Poland, Portugal, Republic of Korea, Romania, San Marino, Slovakia, Slovenia, Spain, Sweden, Switzerland, Turkey, Ukraine, United Kingdom and United States.

as the most important mechanism for the implementation of the Programme, they stressed the need to ensure that the Agency's resources for technical cooperation activities were sufficient, assured and predictable. States parties noted the ongoing collaborative efforts by IAEA and its member States to enhance the effectiveness and efficiency of the Programme. They also welcomed progress made in the construction of new IAEA laboratory buildings and infrastructure, judging the additions to be central to the Agency's efforts to provide opportunities for training in and research and development of nuclear applications.

States parties recognized that, although the primary responsibility for nuclear safety rested with individual States, IAEA played a central role in promoting international cooperation on matters relating to nuclear safety, including through the establishment of nuclear safety standards. States that had not yet done so were called upon to become parties to the relevant nuclear-safety instruments, including the Convention on Nuclear Safety. The Committee welcomed the Agency's provision of international peer review services, support to regulatory bodies and other relevant areas of Member States' infrastructures, noting with appreciation the continuous work of IAEA to strengthen nuclear, radiation, transport and waste safety, as well as emergency preparedness and response.

On the issue of article X and withdrawal, States parties recalled that each State party, in exercising its national sovereignty, had the right to withdraw from the Treaty, in accordance with its provisions. However, it was also underscored that, under international law, a withdrawing party would remain responsible for violations of the Treaty committed prior to its withdrawal.

Pursuant to the decisions taken at the 1995 Review and Extension Conference of the Treaty and the consensus final outcome document of the 2000 Review Conference, which required the third Preparatory Committee session to make every effort to produce a consensus report containing recommendations to the Review Conference, the Chair duly submitted draft recommendations for consideration by States parties. However, as agreement could not be reached, the Chair decided to issue the recommendations as a working paper under his own authority.[19]

Issues related to the Comprehensive Nuclear-Test-Ban Treaty

Entry into force and universality

Political support for the Comprehensive Nuclear-Test-Ban Treaty and its entry into force and universalization continued to increase in 2019. With Zimbabwe's ratification on 13 February, the Treaty had 168 ratifying States and 184 signatory States as at 31 December.

---

[19] NPT/CONF.2020/PC.III/WP.49.

Importantly, during the 2019 session of the Preparatory Committee for the 2020 Review Conference of the Parties to the Treaty on the Non-Proliferation of Nuclear Weapons, in New York, a majority of States parties expressed strong support for the Comprehensive Nuclear-Test-Ban Treaty and its verification regime, highlighting the Treaty's vital role in nuclear disarmament and non-proliferation.

Eleventh Article XIV Conference

Ministers and high-ranking officials from 85 States gathered at the United Nations Headquarters on 25 September for the biennial Conference on Facilitating the Entry into Force of the Comprehensive Nuclear-Test-Ban Treaty, commonly known as the "Article XIV Conference". During the Conference, which was held on the sidelines of the general debate of the General Assembly's seventy-fourth session, participants aimed to intensify efforts to bring the Treaty into force as a core element of the global nuclear arms control and non-proliferation architecture.

In a declaration adopted by the Conference, States that had already ratified the Treaty were joined by other signatory States in vowing to "spare no effort and use all avenues open to us to encourage further signature and ratification of the Treaty".

"We reaffirm the vital importance and urgency of the entry into force of the [Treaty] and urge all States to remain seized of the issue at the highest political level", the declaration read.

Comprehensive Nuclear-Test-Ban Treaty Science and Technology Conference

From 24 to 28 June, more than 1,100 scientists, technologists, policymakers, diplomats, academics, students, journalists and others from around the world gathered in Vienna for the "Comprehensive Nuclear-Test-Ban Treaty: Science and Technology 2019 Conference", where they exchanged views and expertise on Treaty verification issues in pursuit of a world free of nuclear explosions.

The seventh in a flagship series of biennial, multidisciplinary meetings, the 2019 Conference was the largest to date. The aim of the Conference was to help ensure that the Treaty's global verification regime would remain at the forefront of scientific and technical innovation, further reinforce the strong relationship between the scientific and technological community and the Preparatory Commission for the Comprehensive Nuclear-Test-Ban-Treaty Organization, and strengthen the alignment of science and technology matters with policy issues.

Building on its core technical agenda of presentations and discussions, as well as a scientific poster competition, the Conference took notable steps to engage with young people. The activities included a Youth Forum, held jointly with the Ban Ki-moon Centre for Global Citizens, an Innovation Challenge, during which members of the Preparatory Commission's Youth Group presented original ideas linking the Treaty with efforts to achieve the 2030 Agenda for Sustainable Development, and an awards ceremony for an international children's art competition—organized in collaboration with Paz y Cooperación, a Spanish NGO, which welcomed children from as far away as Azerbaijan, Bosnia and Herzegovina, China and Namibia.

The Conference featured a number of new elements. Underscoring the Preparatory Commission's commitment to multilingualism, two round-table discussions were held in Spanish and French, respectively. In addition, a special evening panel session explored the theme "Women in Science and Technology".

Other highlights included discussions on the challenges of communicating about science with wider audiences, artificial intelligence, and potential avenues for Treaty data to contribute to civilian aims, such as studying climate change and mitigating disaster risks.

International Day against Nuclear Tests

The International Day against Nuclear Tests was commemorated on 29 August with events in Nur-Sultan and at the United Nations in Vienna. To mark the occasion, the Executive Secretary of the Provisional Technical Secretariat of the Preparatory Commission, Lassina Zerbo, and the Minister of Foreign Affairs of Kazakhstan, Beibut Atamkulov, issued a joint statement[20] calling for a world free from nuclear testing and urging those States that had not yet signed or ratified the Comprehensive Nuclear-Test-Ban Treaty to do so without delay. The President of the General Assembly's seventy-third session also gave a statement.[21]

The commemorative ceremony in Vienna was held at the Preparatory Commission's headquarters with the support of Kazakhstan and the United Nations Information Service.

In addition to a reading of the above-mentioned joint statement, the ceremony included a message[22] from the Secretary-General, in which he reiterated his call for all States that had not yet done so, especially those whose ratification was needed for its entry into force, to sign and ratify the Treaty.

The event in Vienna also included an exhibition of winning artwork from a children's art campaign launched in 2018 by the Preparatory Commission and Paz y Cooperación.

On 9 September, the General Assembly held a high-level plenary meeting to commemorate and promote the day at the United Nations Headquarters in New York.

---

[20] Joint statement on the occasion of the International Day against Nuclear Tests, Nur-Sultan, 29 August 2019.

[21] María Fernanda Espinosa Garcés, President of the General Assembly, statement on the occasion of the International Day against Nuclear Tests, New York, 29 August 2019.

[22] Message on the occasion of the International Day against Nuclear Tests, New York, 29 August 2019.

Youth Group

Launched in 2016, the Preparatory Commission's Youth Group[23] grew to include, as at the end of 2019, more than 800 members from 100 States, including a considerable number from non-ratifying Annex 2 States. Throughout the year, members of the Group actively engaged in national, regional and international events and activities to promote the entry into force and universalization of the Treaty.

In 2019, members of the Youth Group participated in a number of events, including: the Paris Talks forum on 15 March; a Youth for Peace and Disarmament event co-hosted with the Ban Ki-Moon Centre for Global Citizens on 31 May in Seoul; the Comprehensive Nuclear-Test-Ban Treaty Science and Technology Conference from 22 to 28 June; a workshop entitled "New Tools for Verifying Disarmament and Nonproliferation", hosted by the James Martin Center for Nonproliferation Studies from 8 to 10 July in Monterey, United States; a Science Diplomacy Workshop, held on 12 and 13 September in Quito; the eleventh Article XIV Conference; the 2019 Annual Meeting of the Mexican Geophysical Union, held from 27 October to 1 November in Puerto Vallarta, Mexico; the 2019 Moscow Nuclear Nonproliferation Conference held from 7 to 9 November; and a young professionals' seminar to discuss the Treaty's impact on the international non-proliferation regime and an assessment of the current state of affairs, held in Saint Petersburg, Russian Federation, from 10 to 12 November.

Group of Eminent Persons

At its annual coordination meeting held on 24 and 25 June in Vienna, the Preparatory Commission's Group of Eminent Persons[24] reaffirmed its "unwavering commitment" to promoting the Comprehensive Nuclear-Test-Ban Treaty as a pillar of the global non-proliferation and disarmament architecture.

After convening on the sidelines of the Treaty's biennial Science and Technology Conference, the Group issued a declaration,[25] in which it recognized that the Treaty "constitutes the most effective and practical non-proliferation and disarmament measure within grasp of the international community", and called on all States to "continue their support in advancing the entry into force of the

---

[23] The Youth Group was launched in January 2016 during a symposium on "Science and Diplomacy for Peace and Security". It is open to students and young professionals dedicated to achieving the entry into force and universalization of the Treaty, the continued build-up of the verification regime, and the promotion of the Treaty and its verification technologies for international peace and security.

[24] The Group of Eminent Persons is made up of eminent personalities and internationally recognized experts who examine political and technical developments related to the Treaty and identify concrete actions and new initiatives that could be explored to accelerate its entry into force. It was launched on 26 September 2013 at the United Nations Headquarters in New York.

[25] Preparatory Commission for the Comprehensive Nuclear-Test-Ban Treaty Organization, "[Group of Eminent Persons] Declaration June 2019".

Treaty as the most practical step towards nuclear disarmament, notably during the upcoming 2020 [Nuclear Non-Proliferation Treaty] Review Conference".

Preparatory Commission for the Comprehensive Nuclear-Test-Ban Treaty Organization

The Preparatory Commission for the Comprehensive Nuclear-Test-Ban Treaty Organization held its fifty-second and fifty-third sessions on 17 and 18 June and from 25 to 27 November, respectively.[26] The fifty-second session was chaired by Shin Dong-ik (Republic of Korea), while the fifty-third session was chaired by Ganeson Sivagurunathan (Malaysia).

During each of the sessions, the Executive Secretary of the Preparatory Commission reported on various high-level meetings focused on the Treaty, as well as his bilateral meetings with signatory States. In addition, he welcomed recent bilateral and multilateral efforts for the denuclearization of the Korean Peninsula and called addressed technical issues, such as the inauguration of the Preparatory Commission's Technology Support and Training Centre, its new Operations Centre, and the re-engineering of application software for the International Data Centre.

Integrated capacity-building, education and training

The Preparatory Commission continued organizing integrated capacity-building, education and training activities for signatory States and other key stakeholders throughout 2019. Those activities and events were aimed at enhancing understanding of the Treaty and its verification regime, while promoting its entry into force and universalization. By strengthening capacities, the activities helped enable signatory States and other stakeholders to more actively support efforts to reinforce the Treaty and the international norm against nuclear testing, as well as the build-up and sustainment of the verification regime.

The Preparatory Commission offered signatory States training courses and workshops on technologies associated with the three pillars of the verification regime—the International Monitoring System, the International Data Centre and on-site inspections—as well as the Treaty's political, diplomatic and legal aspects. Those courses helped to strengthen national scientific capabilities in relevant areas and develop capacities in signatory States to effectively confront the political, legal, technical and scientific challenges facing the Treaty and its verification regime.

The activities included 9 station operator courses, 11 National Data Centre training events, the 2019 regional infrasound workshop and integrated training for Latin America and the Caribbean, a National Data Centre workshop on the Progressive Commissioning Plan for the International Data Centre, a technical

---

[26] See the reports of the fifty-second (CTBT/PC-52/2 and Add.1) and fifty-third (CTBT/PC-53/2/Rev.1) sessions.

meeting on the International Data Centre validation and acceptance test plan, a regional National Data Centre workshop and training event held in Thailand, a regional National Data Centre workshop and training event in Costa Rica, four technical and two expert meetings on advances in waveform processing and special studies, and special studies and expert technical analysis with radionuclide and atmospheric transport modelling methods. Additionally, the Preparatory Commission's Provisional Technical Secretariat organized three technical workshops: the International Hydroacoustic Workshop 2019, the Infrasound Technology Workshop 2019 and the International Noble Gas Experiment Workshop 2019.

Over the course of the year, 103 participants subscribed to the National Data Centre e-learning course on accessing and applying International Monitoring System data and International Data Centre products. Separately, the Provisional Technical Secretariat released version 5.0 of its seismic, hydroacoustic and infrasound "National Data Centre-in-a-box" software in June.

Meanwhile, an on-site inspection build-up exercise took place from 11 to 15 November with a focus on an inspection launch phase. Drawing 70 participants from the Provisional Technical Secretariat and 19 trained experts from 15 signatory States, the exercise was intended to test the Preparatory Commission's new Operations Centre, equipment handling at the Technology Support and Training Centre, and use of the newly developed Geospatial Information Management system for on-site inspections.[27]

On 15 November, the Provisional Technical Secretariat welcomed representatives from Permanent Missions and technical experts on an observer visit to the Technology Support and Training Centre in Seibersdorf, Austria, where the Preparatory Commission stores the bulk of its equipment for on-site inspections. The visitors viewed material handling and rapid deployment capabilities, as well as observed inspection team out briefings, and the handover of an inspection mandate.

Treaty on the Prohibition of Nuclear Weapons

The Treaty on the Prohibition of Nuclear Weapons, adopted in 2017, includes a comprehensive set of prohibitions on participating in any nuclear-weapon activity.

---

[27] The exercise was the first of three planned within the framework of the 2016–2020 on-site inspection exercise plan. This multi-year exercise plan was designed to validate key deliverables from the action plan for on-site inspections and to test progress in the further build-up of operational capability for on-site inspections.

In 2019, 11 States[28] signed the Treaty and 15 States[29] ratified it. As at 31 December, the number of signatory States stood at 80 and the number of ratifying or acceding States at 34. According to article 15, paragraph 1, the Treaty shall enter into force 90 days after the deposit of the fiftieth instrument of ratification, acceptance, approval or accession.

At the signature and ratification ceremony held on 26 September, on the margins of the general debate of the General Assembly, nine States signed the Treaty and five States deposited their instruments of ratification.[30] In her remarks at the event,[31] the High Representative for Disarmament Affairs noted that, in the face of a deteriorating international security environment, the goals of the Treaty remained as necessary as ever. She congratulated the States that had signed or ratified the Treaty for their commitment to multilateral disarmament.

Bilateral agreements and other issues

Implementation of the Treaty on Measures for the Further Reduction and Limitation of Strategic Offensive Arms

On 5 February 2018, the United States and the Russian Federation met the central limits of the Treaty on Measures for the Further Reduction and Limitation of Strategic Offensive Arms (New START Treaty). Under the Treaty, the parties shall possess no more than 700 deployed intercontinental ballistic missiles, submarine-launched ballistic missiles and heavy bombers and no more than 1,550 warheads associated with those deployed launchers.

According to data published by the United States and the Russian Federation pursuant to the biannual exchange of data required by the Treaty, as at 1 September 2019, the parties possessed aggregate total numbers of strategic offensive arms as shown in the table below.

---

[28] Botswana, Cambodia, Dominica, Grenada, Lesotho, Maldives, Nauru, Saint Kitts and Nevis, Trinidad and Tobago, United Republic of Tanzania and Zambia.

[29] Antigua and Barbuda, Bangladesh, Bolivia (Plurinational State of), Dominica, Ecuador, El Salvador, Kazakhstan, Kiribati, Lao People's Democratic Republic, Maldives, Panama, Saint Lucia, Saint Vincent and the Grenadines, South Africa, and Trinidad and Tobago.

[30] States that signed the Treaty were Botswana, Dominica, Grenada, Lesotho, Maldives, Saint Kitts and Nevis, Trinidad and Tobago, United Republic of Tanzania and Zambia. States that ratified the Treaty were Bangladesh, Kiribati, Lao People's Democratic Republic, Maldives, and Trinidad and Tobago.

[31] Izumi Nakamitsu, High Representative for Disarmament Affairs, remarks at the signature and ratification ceremony for the Treaty on the Prohibition of Nuclear Weapons, New York, 26 September 2018.

New START Treaty aggregate numbers of strategic offensive arms

Category of data	United States	Russian Federation
Deployed intercontinental ballistic missiles, deployed submarine-launched ballistic missiles and deployed heavy bombers	668	513
Warheads on deployed intercontinental ballistic missiles, and on deployed submarine-launched ballistic missiles, and nuclear warheads counted for deployed heavy bombers	1,376	1,426
Deployed and non-deployed launchers of intercontinental ballistic missiles, deployed and non-deployed launchers of submarine-launched ballistic missiles, and deployed and non-deployed heavy bombers	800	757

Source: United States Department of State, Bureau of Arms Control, Verification and Compliance, Fact Sheet, October 2, 2018.

The Treaty remains in force until 2021, although it can be extended for a period of up to five years without legislative approval.

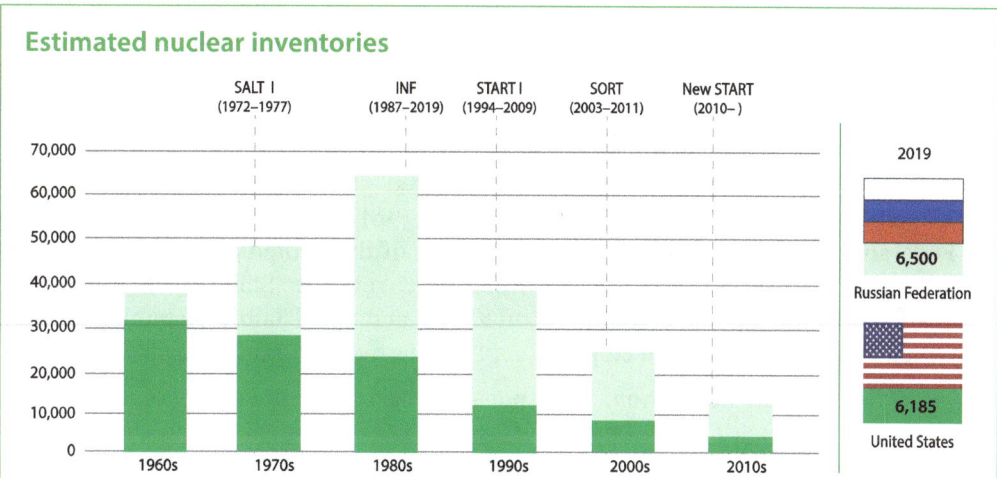

Estimated nuclear inventories

For over 50 years, but especially since the end of the cold war, the United States and the Russian Federation (formerly the Soviet Union) have engaged in a series of bilateral arms control measures that have drastically reduced their strategic nuclear arsenals from a peak of around 60,000. The most recent of those measures, the New START Treaty, limits the number of deployed strategic nuclear weapons to 1,550 per State. New START is scheduled to expire on 5 February 2021; should it expire without a successor or not be extended, it will be the first time that the strategic arsenals of the United States and the Russian Federation have not been constrained since the 1970s.*

* The New START Treaty entered into effect on 5 February 2011 for a period of 10 years. It can be extended for up to five years, unless it is replaced earlier by another agreement.

Source: Federation of American Scientists

Acronyms: SALT I=Strategic Arms Limitation Treaty; INF=Intermediate-Range Nuclear Forces Treaty; START=Strategic Arms Reduction Treaty; SORT=Strategic Offensive Reductions Treaty; New START=Treaty on Measures for the Further Reduction and Limitation of Strategic Offensive Arms.

Implementation of the Treaty on the Elimination of Intermediate-Range and Shorter-Range Missiles

On 2 February, the United States provided its six-month notice of withdrawal from the Treaty on the Elimination of Intermediate-Range and Shorter-Range Missiles (Intermediate-Range Nuclear Forces Treaty) of 1987, citing the Russian Federation's "continuing violation of the treaty".[32] On 4 March, Mr. Putin formally suspended Russian participation in the Treaty. The agreement prohibits parties from possessing, producing or conducting flight tests of ground-launched missiles with a range capability of 500 to 5,500 km or to possess or produce launchers of such missiles.

Since 2014, the United States had alleged that the Russian Federation had been in violation of the Treaty through the development, testing and deployment of a ground-launched cruise missile with a prohibited range. In November 2017, the United States revealed the specific missile of concern to be the SSC-8, designated by the Russian Federation as 9M729. The SSC-8 was alleged to have entered into service in February 2017 and to have an approximate range of 1,500 to 2,000 km.

On 2 August 2019, the United States' withdrawal took effect. A statement by the United States Secretary of State declared that the Russian Federation was "solely responsible" for the Treaty's demise. He stated that "dating back to at least the mid-2000s, Russia developed, produced, flight tested, and has now fielded multiple battalions of its noncompliant missile".[33]

The United States had previously cited the following reasons for its withdrawal: (a) the testing of the SSC-8 (9M729) missile by the Russian Federation "gravely" undermined the security of the United States and that of its allies and partners; and (b) the Treaty did not cover other States, including China, the Democratic People's Republic of Korea and the Islamic Republic of Iran, which were thus free to develop and deploy intermediate-range missiles.

The Russian Federation, in response, reiterated its own concerns regarding alleged violations of the Treaty, focusing on the deployment by the United States of the ground-based MK-41 vertical launch system, which could launch, inter alia, missile-defence interceptors and cruise missiles.[34] The United States had stated that the launchers deployed in Eastern Europe were only capable of launching missile interceptors.[35]

The Secretary-General expressed his deep regret at the withdrawal of the United States from the Intermediate-Range Nuclear Forces Treaty and his disappointment at the parties' inability to resolve their differences through the

---

[32] United States Department of State, "U.S. Withdrawal from the INF Treaty on August 2, 2019".
[33] Ibid.
[34] Russian Federation, Ministry of Foreign Affairs, "Deputy Foreign Minister Sergey Ryabkov's briefing on developments involving the INF Treaty, Moscow, November 26, 2018".
[35] United States Department of State, "Refuting Russian Allegations of U.S. Noncompliance with the INF Treaty", 8 December 2017.

consultation mechanisms provided for in the Treaty. He further emphasized the need to avoid destabilizing developments and to urgently seek agreement on a new common path for international arms control. The Secretary-General called on the Russian Federation and the United States to extend the New START Treaty and to undertake urgent negotiations on further arms control measures.[36]

Joint Comprehensive Plan of Action and Security Council resolution 2231 (2015)

On 8 May, the first anniversary of the announcement by the President of the United States of America, Donald Trump, that the United States would cease its participation in the Joint Comprehensive Plan of Action, the President of the Islamic Republic of Iran, Hassan Rouhani, stated in a letter addressed to the remaining parties[37] to the agreement that, in line with paragraphs 26 and 36 of the Plan of Action,[38] his country would not commit itself to respecting the limits set by the Plan regarding low-enriched uranium and heavy-water reserves.[39] In addition, if European parties to the Plan "failed to fulfil their obligations", especially with regard to banking and oil, the Islamic Republic of Iran would, after 60 days, suspend compliance with the Plan's limits on its uranium-enrichment level and on measures to modernize the Arak Heavy Water Research Reactor.[40] On 1 July, IAEA reported[41] that the Islamic Republic of Iran had amassed 205 kilograms of uranium enriched up to 3.67 per cent, thereby surpassing the Plan's limit on the material.[42]

---

[36] Statement attributable to the Spokesperson for the Secretary-General on the ending of the Intermediate-range Nuclear Forces Treaty, New York, 2 August 2019.

[37] China, France, Germany, Russian Federation and United Kingdom.

[38] Paragraph 26 states: "The United States will refrain from re-introducing or re-imposing the sanctions specified in Annex II that it has ceased applying under this JCPOA" and "will refrain from imposing new nuclear-related sanctions. The Islamic Republic of Iran has stated that it will treat such a re-introduction or re-imposition of the sanctions specified in Annex II, or such an imposition of new nuclear-related sanctions, as grounds to cease performing its commitments under this JCPOA in whole or in part." Paragraph 36 sets out procedures for a dispute resolution mechanism.

[39] Paragraph 7 states that the Islamic Republic of Iran "will keep its uranium stockpile under 300 kilograms of up to 3.67% enriched uranium hexafluoride (UF6) or the equivalent in other chemical forms". Three hundred kilograms of uranium hexafluoride corresponds to 202.8 kilograms of uranium enriched up to 3.67 per cent, considering the standard atomic weight of uranium and fluorine. Annex I, paragraph 14 states: "Iran's needs, consistent with the parameters above, are estimated to be 130 metric tonnes of nuclear grade heavy water or its equivalent in different enrichments prior to commissioning of the modernised Arak research reactor."

[40] Paragraph 8 states: "Iran will redesign and rebuild a modernised heavy water research reactor in Arak, based on an agreed conceptual design ... The reactor will support peaceful nuclear research and radioisotope production for medical and industrial purposes. The redesigned and rebuilt Arak reactor will not produce weapons grade plutonium."

[41] IAEA document GOV/INF/2019/8.

[42] The quantity of 300 kilograms of uranium hexafluoride corresponds to 202.8 kilograms of uranium.

On 7 July, to mark the second step of the phased scale-back of its commitments under the Plan of Action, the Islamic Republic of Iran announced that it had started to enrich uranium above the limit of 3.67 per cent set by the Plan. On 8 July, IAEA confirmed that the country had enriched a quantity of uranium up to 4.5 per cent.[43]

On 4 September, Mr. Rouhani announced that, as of 6 September, his country's "commitments for research and development under the [Joint Comprehensive Plan of Action][44] will be completely removed". On 8 September, IAEA confirmed that various types of centrifuges had either been installed or were being installed at the Pilot Fuel Enrichment Plant in Natanz.[45] In addition, the Atomic Energy Organization of Iran stated on 4 November that it had begun operating 60 IR-6 advanced centrifuges.[46] The Islamic Republic of Iran also announced that it was working on a prototype IR-9 centrifuge.

On 5 November, Mr. Rouhani said that his country would begin injecting uranium gas into centrifuges at the Fordow Fuel Enrichment Plant.[47] On 7 November, IAEA reported that a cylinder of natural uranium hexafluoride had been connected at the Fordow Fuel Enrichment Plant in preparation for feeding uranium hexafluoride into centrifuges.[48]

The Islamic Republic of Iran stated that the withdrawal from its nuclear-related commitments under the Plan of Action—in four phases, each starting approximately 60 days apart—was undertaken with a view to creating balance in the commitments by the participants, and the phased withdrawal would continue in the same intervals unless its demands were met. The Islamic Republic of Iran also stated that those measures were fully reversible upon implementation of commitments by the European participants in the Plan of Action.

The Joint Commission of the Joint Comprehensive Plan of Action discussed the action of the Islamic Republic of Iran at a quarterly meeting in Vienna on 28 June, at an extraordinary meeting in Vienna on 28 July, at an extraordinary ministerial meeting in New York on 25 September and at an additional meeting in Vienna on 6 December. Following the meeting of 6 December, Helga Schmid, the Chair of the meeting, and the Secretary-General of the European External

---

[43] See IAEA document GOV/INF/2019/8.

[44] The Islamic Republic of Iran is only permitted to build or test, with or without uranium, only those gas centrifuges specified in the Joint Comprehensive Plan of Action (para. G.32). On Implementation Day, the Islamic Republic of Iran was also required to remove and store its 164-machine IR-2m and 164-machine IR-4 cascades at the Pilot Fuel Enrichment Plant (paras. G.33, G.34).

[45] See IAEA document GOV/INF/2019/8.

[46] Under the Joint Comprehensive Plan of Action, the Islamic Republic of Iran is only allowed to test IR-6 centrifuges in 2023 (eight and a half years after the Implementation Day of the Plan of Action).

[47] Under the Joint Comprehensive Plan of Action, the Fordow plant was converted to a nuclear, physics and technology centre; up to 1,044 IR-1 centrifuges stored there are to be used for non-enrichment purposes, such as producing stable medical radioisotopes.

[48] See IAEA document GOV/INF/2019/16.

Action Service issued a statement[49] voicing deep concern over the reduction of the commitments of the Islamic Republic of Iran under the Plan and stressed the importance of full and effective enforcement by all parties. She also expressed the participants' determination to follow up on efforts to preserve the agreement.

With the aim of bringing tangible economic benefits to the Islamic Republic of Iran, on 31 January, France, Germany and the United Kingdom announced the establishment of the Instrument in Support of Trade Exchanges, a special-purpose vehicle to facilitate transactions for non-sanctioned trade with the Islamic Republic of Iran. On 19 March, the Islamic Republic of Iran announced that it had registered the Special Trade and Finance Institute, which was its counterpart to the Instrument. On 28 June, at the meeting of the Joint Commission, France, Germany and the United Kingdom announced that the Instrument had been made operational and that the first transactions were being processed. On 29 November, the Ministry for Foreign Affairs of Finland announced that six European countries—Belgium, Denmark, Finland, Netherlands, Norway and Sweden—would join the Instrument. However, the Governor of the Central Bank of the Islamic Republic of Iran reportedly said that the Instrument would be of no use, unless Iranian oil revenues were also included.

Implementation of the Joint Comprehensive Plan of Action

In 2019, IAEA continued to report quarterly to its Board of Governors and to the Security Council on the implementation of the nuclear-related commitments of the Islamic Republic of Iran under the Plan of Action, as well as on matters related to verification and monitoring in the country in light of Security Council resolution 2231 (2015).[50] In the reports, IAEA stated that it continued to: (a) verify the non-diversion of declared nuclear material in the Islamic Republic of Iran, pursuant to the Iranian safeguards agreement; and (b) carry out its evaluation regarding the absence of undeclared nuclear materials and activities in the country.

In its report of 11 November,[51] IAEA stated that it had detected, on 7 November, natural uranium particles of anthropogenic origin at an undeclared location in the Islamic Republic of Iran. The Agency called on the Islamic Republic of Iran to continue to engage with it in order to resolve the matter as soon as possible. In the report, IAEA also noted that the Islamic Republic of Iran had been engaging in several activities that were inconsistent with the Plan of Action,[52] effectively confirming the four announcements made by the Islamic Republic of Iran since May.

---

[49] Statement following the meeting of the Joint Commission of the Joint Comprehensive Plan of Action, Vienna, 6 December 2019.

[50] IAEA documents GOV/2019/10, GOV/2019/21, GOV/2019/32 and GOV/2019/55.

[51] IAEA document GOV/2019/55.

[52] The Agency had previously reported many of these activities in ad hoc reports. See IAEA documents GOV/INF/2019/8, GOV/INF/2019/9, GOV/INF/2019/10, GOV/INF/2019/12, GOV/INF/2019/16 and GOV/INF/2019/17.

Implementation of Security Council resolution 2231 (2015)

By its resolution 2231 (2015) endorsing the Plan of Action, the Security Council requested the Secretary-General to report every six months on the resolution's implementation. In his seventh and eighth reports[53] issued on 13 June and 10 December, respectively, the Secretary-General continued to focus on the provisions set forth in annex B of the resolution, which included: (a) restrictions applicable to nuclear-related transfers, ballistic missile–related and arms-related transfers to or from the Islamic Republic of Iran; and (b) provisions for asset freezes and travel bans.

In the two reports, the Secretary-General addressed the examination of debris from cruise missiles and uncrewed aerial vehicles used in attacks against oil facilities and an airport in Saudi Arabia, as well as arms and related materials recovered in the United Arab Emirates and Yemen. The Secretary-General also reported on other allegations concerning activities related to ballistic missiles, as well as transfers of related items, technologies and other arms by the Islamic Republic of Iran.

Democratic People's Republic of Korea

The year 2019 ended with little progress towards sustainable peace on the Korean Peninsula despite signs of improved relations between key parties in 2018, including the Joint Statement[54] of the United States and the Democratic People's Republic of Korea from their summit in Singapore. Although the Democratic People's Republic of Korea complied in 2019 with its self-established moratorium on nuclear and intercontinental ballistic missiles, it conducted over twenty launches of short-range ballistic missiles and long-range artillery rockets, as well as two engine tests. Diplomatic efforts failed to produce tangible steps in support of the country's complete and verifiable denuclearization.

In his annual New Year address in January 2019, Kim Jong Un—Chairman of the Workers' Party of Korea, Chairman of the State Affairs Commission of the Democratic People's Republic of Korea and Supreme Commander of the Korean People's Army—expressed dissatisfaction at the lack of advancement towards sanctions relief with the United States. While calling for the United States to take reciprocal measures and to ease sanctions, and expressing his willingness to freeze the nuclear programme of the Democratic People's Republic of Korea, Mr. Kim

---

[53] S/2019/492 and S/2019/934.

[54] The Joint Statement from the summit in Singapore committed the United States to provide unspecified "security guarantees" in exchange for the "complete denuclearization of the Korean Peninsula". It also covered a number of other issues, including new peaceful relations, denuclearization of the Korean Peninsula, recovery of soldiers' remains and follow-up negotiations between high-level officials. However, it did not include specific measures leading to the dismantlement of the nuclear weapons of the Democratic People's Republic of Korea, instead leaving the matter for future negotiations.

warned that his country may seek a "new path" forward if talks remained at an impasse. However, he spoke favourably about the Panmunjom Declaration, which is meant to enhance relations with the Republic of Korea. He also expressed the desire to reopen the Kumgang Mountain resort, an inter-Korean economic cooperation project, setting a hopeful tone for inter-Korean relations in 2019.

The struggle to make meaningful progress in negotiations between the United States and the Democratic People's Republic of Korea was apparent at the second summit between Mr. Trump and Mr. Kim, held in Hanoi on 27 and 28 February. The meeting concluded early when the sides determined that they could not reach an agreement. In a press conference afterwards, Mr. Trump said that he could not agree to the full lifting of sanctions for the dismantlement of Yongbyon, one of the major nuclear facilities of the Democratic People's Republic of Korea. While both parties portrayed the meeting as a positive development and worthwhile endeavour, its stunted conclusion marked another setback in efforts to achieve denuclearization and ease tensions on the Korean Peninsula.

The Democratic People's Republic of Korea then adopted a harder line, announcing that it was considering a suspension of talks and would reconsider its freeze on long-range ballistic missile and nuclear tests unless the United States made additional concessions. In April, Chairman Kim gave the United States until the end of the year to present a more flexible negotiating proposal. On 4 May, he supervised the test firing of a new short-range missile and other short-range projectiles from Wonsan. That launch—the first of its kind in 2019—was quickly followed by test launches of two short-range missiles on 9 May.

In June, Mr. Kim undertook a series of bilateral meetings, including with the President of China, Xi Jinping, in Pyongyang, to discuss deepening cooperation and expanding bilateral ties. Mr. Kim also met with Mr. Trump on 30 June at Panmunjom. Following that meeting, Mr. Trump announced that the two sides had agreed to designate negotiators to resume working-level talks within the next few weeks.

In parallel to those diplomatic efforts, the Democratic People's Republic of Korea conducted additional missile launches, including tests of two "tactical guided weapons" on 25 July that were intended to send a "solemn warning" to the Republic of Korea.[55] Furthermore, on 31 July, the Democratic People's Republic of Korea fired two missiles that it described as a "newly developed multiple launch-guided rocket system".[56] On 2 August, the Democratic People's Republic of Korea fired another two projectiles, the first launches from Yonghung on its east coast. On 5 August, it conducted two more short-range missile launches from

---

[55] Democratic People's Republic of Korea, Korean Central News Agency, "Supreme Leader Kim Jong Un Guides Power Demonstration Fire of New Type Tactical Guided Weapon", 25 July 2019.

[56] Democratic People's Republic of Korea, Korean Central News Agency, "Supreme Leader Kim Jong Un Guides Test-Fire of New-type Large-caliber Multiple Launch Guided Rocket System", 1 August 2019.

another location, followed by additional test flights on 10, 16 and 24 August and 10 September.

On 2 October, the Democratic People's Republic of Korea flight tested the Pukguksong-3 submarine-launched ballistic missile for the first time from an underwater platform in waters off of Wonsan, prompting a Security Council meeting on 8 October. The Democratic People's Republic of Korea described the test in its State media as ushering in a "new phase" in containing the threat from "outside forces".[57] As the country's first test since November 2017 of a system unambiguously designed specifically as a nuclear-weapon delivery vehicle, the launch represented another step forward in its sea-based nuclear capability. Notably, the launch took place one day after the Democratic People's Republic of Korea confirmed that it would participate in new working-level talks with the United States.

The working-level negotiations restarted on 5 October, since the breakdown in January, with the goal of finding a diplomatic solution to the impasse. However, the talks in Stockholm ended quickly with no outcome. Following the collapse, the chief negotiator of the Democratic People's Republic of Korea, Kim Myong Gil, said that the United States had not been able to provide the new proposal needed. Reiterating the year-end deadline his country had announced previously, the chief negotiator warned that a "terrible" event may take place if the United States failed to offer a better deal.[58] In contrast, the United States expressed satisfaction with the dialogue and indicated its willingness to meet again quickly; however, the Democratic People's Republic of Korea rejected that idea.

On 22 October, inter-Korean diplomatic efforts were diminished when the Democratic People's Republic of Korea demanded the destruction of facilities that the Republic of Korea had built at Mount Kumgang, one of two major inter-Korean economic projects providing a token of cooperation between the two States on the Korean Peninsula. On 28 October, the Republic of Korea proposed working-level talks to discuss the issue, but that suggestion was rebuffed by the Democratic People's Republic of Korea, which thereafter refused to engage in further inter-Korean dialogue.

With the impasse in diplomatic relations and the approaching year-end deadline, tensions between the United States and the Democratic People's Republic of Korea increased in late 2019. On 31 October and 28 November, the Democratic People's Republic of Korea launched a total of four short-range missiles, similar in type to those launched on 24 August and 10 September. The November tests were the country's thirteenth and final set of firings in 2019,

---

[57] Democratic People's Republic of Korea, Korean Central News Agency, "DPRK Academy of Defence Science Succeeds in Test-firing New-type SLBM", 3 October 2019.

[58] NK News "N. Korean Diplomat Warns of "Terrible" Results if the US Fails to Offer Better Deal", 7 October 2019.

resulting in a total of over twenty ballistic missiles and long-range artillery rockets fired throughout the year.

In addition to the missile launches, the Democratic People's Republic of Korea tested two rocket engines on 7 and 13 December, describing the tests as "significant" and "crucial" to its defensive capabilities. The tests occurred at a test stand at the Sohae Satellite Launching Ground, which the Democratic People's Republic of Korea had previously pledged to dismantle during negotiations with the United States. The Democratic People's Republic of Korea described the second test as part of a "reliable strategic nuclear deterrent".

On 11 December, the Security Council convened to discuss the current situation of the Democratic People's Republic of Korea; Japan and the Republic of Korea attended that meeting.[59] Member States stressed the need for the Council's continued unity, while expressing support for dialogue efforts by the United States and the Democratic People's Republic of Korea. Many Council members condemned the missile launches by the Democratic People's Republic of Korea in 2019 as a violation of the Security Council's decisions.

From 28 to 31 December, Kim Jong Un led the fifth plenary meeting of the seventh Central Committee of the Workers' Party of Korea where he gave a statement in lieu of a traditional New Year address. Speaking to the body during its second plenary of the year, Mr. Kim focused on strengthening the country's economy and military simultaneously. He also expressed belief that the United States and the Democratic People's Republic of Korea would remain in a prolonged stalemate and warned that "the world will witness a new strategic weapon … in the near future".[60] Mr. Kim further stated that, should the United States fail to change its "hostile policy", hopes for a denuclearized Korean Peninsula would be finished. However, Mr. Kim did not explicitly suspend negotiations with the United States nor rescind the self-imposed moratorium on nuclear and long-range ballistic missile testing, leaving open a possibility for resumed diplomacy in 2020.

Despite the Democratic People's Republic of Korea's threat of a "Christmas gift" for the United States, 2019 ended without any further missile launches or other incidents.[61] Key States, including China and the Republic of Korea, and the Secretary-General called on the United States and the Democratic People's Republic of Korea to resume denuclearization talks in order to make tangible progress in bringing peace to the Korean Peninsula in 2020.

---

[59] S/PV.8682.

[60] Democratic People's Republic of Korea, Korean Central News Agency, "Report on the 5th Plenary Meeting of the 7th C.C., WPK", 1 January 2020

[61] Democratic People's Republic of Korea, Korean Central News Agency, "Deputy Foreign Minister Issues Statement", 4 December 2019.

Group of Governmental Experts to consider the role of verification in advancing nuclear disarmament

By its resolution 71/67 of 5 December 2016, the General Assembly requested the Secretary-General to establish a group of governmental experts with up to 25 participants[62] on the basis of equitable geographical distribution to consider the role of verification in advancing nuclear disarmament. The Group met in Geneva for three five-day sessions, in 2018 and 2019, with Knut Langeland (Norway) serving as Chair.[63]

The Group held its third and final session in Geneva from 8 to 12 April 2019.[64] The session was preceded by an informal meeting organized by the Ministry of Foreign Affairs of Norway, the Federal Department of Foreign Affairs of Switzerland and the Federal Foreign Office of Germany, held from 30 January to 1 February at Wilton Park in West Sussex, United Kingdom, where the participants discussed nuclear disarmament verification.

At the April 2019 session, the Group agreed on a final report[65] to submit to the General Assembly, summarizing the discussions during their three sessions. The Group concluded, inter alia, that advancing nuclear disarmament was an ongoing undertaking in need of continued international examination of all its aspects, including verification and agreed on seven principles[66] on verification in advancing nuclear disarmament.

Throughout the sessions, the Group of Governmental Experts considered the role of verification in advancing nuclear disarmament with a view to achieving and maintaining a world without nuclear weapons. Noting that a nuclear disarmament verification regime must be linked to specific treaty obligations, the Group emphasized that it was not within its mandate to create a specific verification regime. A number of experts, however, stressed the importance of discussing general verification aspects applicable to any treaty.

The Group listened to presentations on national experiences with nuclear disarmament in South Africa and Kazakhstan, and on verification in the context of three bilateral and multilateral agreements—the Treaty between the United States of America and the Russian Federation on Measures for the Further Reduction

---

[62] The Secretary-General invited nominations of members from 25 States: Algeria, Argentina, Brazil, Chile, China, Finland, France, Germany, Hungary, India, Indonesia, Japan, Kazakhstan, Mexico, Morocco, Netherlands, Nigeria, Norway, Pakistan, Poland, Russian Federation, South Africa, Switzerland, United Kingdom and United States.

[63] The group was asked to take into account the views of Member States expressed in a report of the Secretary-General, issued in 2017 as A/72/304, on the development and strengthening of practical and effective nuclear disarmament verification measures and on the importance of such measures in achieving and maintaining a world without nuclear weapons.

[64] The Group of Governmental Experts held its first and second sessions from 14 to 18 May 2018 and from 12 to 16 November 2018 in Geneva.

[65] A/74/90.

[66] Ibid., para. 38.

and Limitation of Strategic Offensive Arms (New START Treaty); the Brazilian-Argentine Agency for Accounting and Control of Nuclear Materials; and the Chemical Weapons Convention. The Group also received briefings on the technical elements of the Comprehensive Nuclear-Test-Ban Treaty and IAEA safeguards and heard presentations on three recent and ongoing initiatives and exercises relating to nuclear disarmament verification—the United Kingdom-Norway Initiative on nuclear dismantlement verification, the Quad Nuclear Verification Partnership and the International Partnership for Nuclear Disarmament Verification. In considering each presentation, the Group focused on extracting lessons that may be applicable for nuclear disarmament verification, and identifying possible common denominators. A Chair's summary of the presentations, made on his own responsibility, is contained in an annex to the report.

The Group discussed the capacities that might be needed in developing technologies and methodologies for nuclear disarmament verification and exchanged views on the issue of capacity-building, including through voluntary cooperation among States. Two working papers on the issue[67] were circulated.

Experts put forward a number of proposals[68] on possible next steps for consideration, but none received consensus agreement. The submissions included one working paper[69] suggesting the creation of a group of scientific and technical experts on nuclear disarmament verification within the Conference on Disarmament and another working paper[70] proposing the establishment of a voluntary funding mechanism for capacity-building.

The Group of Governmental Experts recommended that Member States, as well as relevant components of the international disarmament machinery, consider the final report in accordance with their respective mandates. It also recommended further consideration of the work related to the role of verification in advancing nuclear disarmament, taking into account its final report.

International Atomic Energy Agency verification

Since its founding in 1957, the International Atomic Energy Agency (IAEA) has served as the focal point for worldwide cooperation in the peaceful uses of nuclear technology for promoting global nuclear security and safety and, through its verification activities, for providing assurances that States' international undertakings to use nuclear material and facilities for peaceful purposes are being honoured. The following is a brief survey of the work of IAEA in 2019 in the areas of nuclear verification, nuclear security, peaceful uses of nuclear energy and nuclear fuel assurances.

---

[67] GE-NDV/2018/12 and GE-NDV/2018/16.
[68] A/74/90, para. 14.
[69] GE-NDV/2019/1.
[70] GE-NDV/2019/3.

Nuclear verification

A major pillar of the IAEA programme involves activities that enable the Agency to provide assurances to the international community regarding the peaceful use of nuclear material and facilities. The IAEA verification programme thus remains at the core of multilateral efforts to prevent the proliferation of nuclear weapons by verifying that States are complying with their safeguards obligations.[71]

Safeguards conclusions

At the end of each year, IAEA draws safeguards conclusions for each State with a safeguards agreement in force for which safeguards are applied, based on an evaluation of all safeguards-related information available for that year.[72] For a "broader conclusion" to be drawn that "all nuclear material remained in peaceful activities", a State must have both a comprehensive safeguards agreement[73] and an additional protocol[74] in force, IAEA must have been able to conduct all necessary verification and evaluation activities for the State and have found no indication that, in its judgment, would give rise to a proliferation concern. For States that have a comprehensive safeguards agreement but no additional protocol in force, and IAEA draws a safeguards conclusion regarding only the non-diversion of declared nuclear material, as IAEA does not have sufficient tools to provide credible assurances regarding the absence of undeclared nuclear material and activities.

For States for which broader conclusions have been drawn, IAEA has implemented integrated safeguards—an optimized combination of measures available under comprehensive safeguards agreements and additional protocols—to maximize effectiveness and efficiency in fulfilling its safeguards obligations.

In 2019, safeguards were applied for 183 States[75,76] with safeguards agreements in force. Of the 131 States that had both a comprehensive safeguards agreement and an additional protocol in force,[77] IAEA concluded that all nuclear material remained in peaceful activities in 69 States.[78] Since the necessary evaluation regarding the absence of undeclared nuclear material and activities

---

[71] The designations employed and the presentation of material in this section, including the members cited, do not imply the expression of any opinion whatsoever on the part of the Agency or its Member States concerning the legal status of any country or territory or of its authorities, or concerning the delimitation of its frontiers.

[72] For more information, see IAEA, "Safeguards and verification". See also article III (1) of the Treaty on the Non-Proliferation of Nuclear Weapons.

[73] Comprehensive safeguards agreements are based on INFCIRC/153 (Corrected).

[74] Additional protocols are based on INFCIRC/540 (Corrected).

[75] Those States do not include the Democratic People's Republic of Korea, for which IAEA did not implement safeguards and, therefore, could not draw any conclusions.

[76] Safeguards were also applied for Taiwan Province of China.

[77] Or an additional protocol being provisionally applied, pending its entry into force.

[78] IAEA drew the same conclusion for Taiwan Province of China.

remained ongoing in the other 62 States, IAEA was unable to draw the same conclusion. For those 62 States and for the 44 States with a comprehensive safeguards agreement but no additional protocol in force, IAEA concluded only that declared nuclear material remained in peaceful activities.

Integrated safeguards were implemented for the whole or a part of 2019 for 67 States.[79,80]

For the three States for which IAEA implemented safeguards pursuant to item-specific safeguards agreements based on INFCIRC/66/Rev.2, IAEA concluded that nuclear material, facilities or other items to which safeguards had been applied remained in peaceful activities. Safeguards were also implemented with regard to nuclear material in selected facilities in the five nuclear-weapon States party to the Nuclear Non-Proliferation Treaty under their respective voluntary offer agreements. For these five States, IAEA concluded that the nuclear material in selected facilities to which safeguards had been applied remained in peaceful activities or had been withdrawn from safeguards as provided for in the agreements.

As at 31 December, 11 States parties[81] to the Treaty had yet to bring comprehensive safeguards agreements into force pursuant to article III of the Treaty. For those States parties, IAEA could not draw any safeguards conclusions.

Safeguards agreements, additional protocols and small quantities protocols

Safeguards agreements and additional protocols are legal instruments that provide the basis for IAEA verification activities. The entry into force of such instruments therefore continues to be crucial to effective and efficient IAEA safeguards.

IAEA continued to implement the Plan of Action to Promote the Conclusion of Safeguards Agreements and Additional Protocols,[82] which was updated in September. IAEA organized an outreach workshop in Vienna in April for diplomats at permanent missions and embassies located in Berlin, Brussels and Geneva; a national workshop for Oman in Muscat in June; and a country visit to

---

[79] Albania, Andorra, Armenia, Australia, Austria, Bangladesh, Belgium, Botswana, Bulgaria, Burkina Faso, Canada, Chile, Croatia, Cuba, Czechia, Denmark, Ecuador, Estonia, Finland, Germany, Ghana, Greece, Holy See, Hungary, Iceland, Indonesia, Ireland, Italy, Jamaica, Japan, Kazakhstan, Kuwait, Latvia, Liechtenstein, Lithuania, Luxembourg, Madagascar, Mali, Malta, Mauritius, Monaco, Montenegro, Netherlands, New Zealand, North Macedonia, Norway, Palau, Peru, Philippines, Poland, Portugal, Republic of Korea, Romania, Seychelles, Singapore, Slovakia, Slovenia, South Africa, Spain, Sweden, Switzerland, Tajikistan, Ukraine, United Republic of Tanzania, Uruguay, Uzbekistan and Viet Nam.

[80] Integrated safeguards were also implemented for Taiwan Province of China.

[81] The number of States parties is based on the number of instruments of ratification, accession or succession that had been deposited in respect of the Nuclear Non-Proliferation Treaty.

[82] IAEA, "Plan of Action to Promote the Conclusion of Safeguards Agreements and Additional Protocols", September 2019.

Eritrea in January. During those outreach activities, IAEA encouraged States to conclude comprehensive safeguards agreements and additional protocols, as well as to amend their small quantities protocols. IAEA also held consultations with representatives from a number of member and non-member States in Addis Ababa, Bangkok, Geneva, New York and Vienna at various times throughout the year.

During the year, a comprehensive safeguards agreement with a small quantities protocol and an additional protocol entered into force for Benin and a comprehensive safeguards agreement with a small quantities protocol was signed for the State of Palestine.[83] In addition, IAEA Board of Governors approved a comprehensive safeguards agreement with a small quantities protocol and an additional protocol for Sao Tome and Principe, while an additional protocol entered into force for Ethiopia and an additional protocol was signed for the Plurinational State of Bolivia.

IAEA also continued to communicate with States to implement the decisions taken in 2005 by its Board of Governors regarding small quantities protocols, with a view to amending or rescinding such protocols. Also during the year, small quantities protocols were amended for Cameroon, Ethiopia, France[84] and Papua New Guinea. As at the end of 2019, 68 States had accepted the revised text of the small quantities protocol, which was in force for 62 of those States, and 8 States had rescinded their small quantities protocols.

Verification activities

Throughout 2019, the Agency continued to verify and monitor the nuclear-related commitments of the Islamic Republic of Iran under the Joint Comprehensive Plan of Action. Four quarterly reports, as well as six reports, providing updates on developments in between the issuance of the quarterly reports, were submitted to the Board of Governors and to the Security Council. The ten reports were entitled "Verification and monitoring in the Islamic Republic of Iran in light of United Nations Security Council resolution 2231 (2015)".[85]

In August, IAEA Director General submitted to the Board of Governors a report entitled "Implementation of the NPT Safeguards Agreement in the Syrian Arab Republic",[86] covering relevant developments since the previous report in August 2018.[87] The Director General informed the Board of Governors that no new

---

[83] The designation employed does not imply the expression of any opinion whatsoever concerning the legal status of any country or territory or of its authorities, or concerning the delimitation of its frontiers.

[84] France has amended its small quantities protocol to the safeguards agreement reproduced in INFCIRC/718 between France, the European Atomic Energy Community and IAEA pursuant to Additional Protocol I of the Treaty of Tlatelolco, covering France's Protocol I territories.

[85] IAEA documents GOV/2019/10, GOV/2019/21, GOV/INF/2019/8, GOV/INF/2019/9, GOV/INF/2019/10, GOV/2019/32, GOV/INF/2019/12, GOV/INF/2019/16, GOV/INF/2019/17 and GOV/2019/55.

[86] IAEA document GOV/2019/34.

[87] IAEA document GOV/2018/35.

information had come to the knowledge of IAEA that would have had an impact on its assessment that a building destroyed at the Dair Alzour site was very likely a nuclear reactor that should have been declared by the Syrian Arab Republic.[88] In 2019, the Director General renewed his call on that State to cooperate fully with IAEA in connection with unresolved issues related to the Dair Alzour site and other locations. The Syrian Arab Republic had yet to respond to those calls.

On the basis of the evaluation of information provided by the Syrian Arab Republic and all other safeguards-relevant information available to it, IAEA found no indication of diversion of declared nuclear material from peaceful activities. For 2019, IAEA concluded for the country that declared nuclear material remained in peaceful activities.

In August, IAEA Acting Director General submitted to the Board of Governors and the General Conference a report entitled "Application of Safeguards in the Democratic People's Republic of Korea",[89] which provided an update of developments since the Director General's report of August 2018.[90]

Since 1994, IAEA had not been able to conduct all necessary safeguards activities provided for in the Nuclear Non-Proliferation Treaty Safeguards Agreement of the Democratic People's Republic of Korea. From the end of 2002 until July 2007—and again since April 2009—IAEA has not been able to implement any verification measures in the Democratic People's Republic of Korea; therefore, it could not draw any safeguards conclusion for that country.

In 2019, no verification activities were implemented in the field, but IAEA continued to monitor developments in the nuclear programme of the Democratic People's Republic of Korea and to evaluate all safeguards-relevant information available to it, including open-source information and satellite imagery.

In 2019, IAEA secretariat intensified efforts to enhance its readiness to play its essential role in verifying the nuclear programme of the Democratic People's Republic of Korea. The country team increased the frequency of collection of satellite imagery, procured equipment and supplies, updated verification approaches and procedures, conducted specialized training, commenced new knowledge management activities, and ensured the availability of appropriate verification technologies and equipment. Once a political agreement has been reached among the countries concerned, IAEA is ready to return to the Democratic People's Republic of Korea in a timely manner, if requested by the Government and subject to approval of the Board of Governors.

---

[88] The Board of Governors, in its resolution GOV/2011/41 of June 2011 (adopted by a vote), had, inter alia, called on the Syrian Arab Republic to urgently remedy its non-compliance with its Nuclear Non-Proliferation Treaty safeguards agreement and, in particular, to provide the Agency with updated reporting under its safeguards agreement and access to all information, sites, material and persons necessary for it to verify such reporting and resolve all outstanding questions, and provide the necessary assurance as to the exclusively peaceful nature of the Syrian nuclear programme.

[89] IAEA document GOV/2019/33-GC(63)/20.

[90] IAEA document GOV/2018/34-GC(62)/12.

Application of safeguards in the Middle East

As requested in operative paragraph 13 of resolution GC(62)/RES/12 on the application of IAEA safeguards in the Middle East, adopted at the sixty-second regular session of the General Conference of IAEA in 2018, the Director General submitted to the Board of Governors and to the General Conference at its sixty-third regular session a report[91] on the implementation of that resolution. In the report on the application of IAEA safeguards in the Middle East, the Director General described, inter alia, the steps he had undertaken in his efforts to further the implementation of the mandates conferred by the General Conference in resolution GC(62)/RES/12 and in decision GC(44)/DEC/12.

In relation to that, in September 2013, following the discussions of the Board of Governors, the Director General provided IAEA member States with the "background documentation prepared for the 2012 Conference on the establishment of a Middle East zone free of nuclear weapons and all other weapons of mass destruction", which contained descriptions of the work that IAEA had undertaken and the experience it had gained with regard to modalities for a zone free of nuclear weapons in the Middle East region.[92]

Assurances of nuclear fuel supply

In December 2010, IAEA Board of Governors approved the establishment of IAEA Low-Enriched Uranium Bank,[93] a physical stock of up to 60 Type-30B cylinders containing standard commercial low-enriched uranium hexafluoride with enrichment levels of up to 4.95 per cent. The Low-Enriched Uranium Bank would serve as a supply mechanism of last resort in the event that an eligible member State's supply of low-enriched uranium is disrupted and cannot be restored by commercial means.

The Low-Enriched Uranium Bank was established and became operational in 2019; it was a major milestone for the project. The achievement came after IAEA Low-Enriched Uranium Storage Facility—located at Ulba Metallurgical Plant in Ust-Kamenogorsk, Kazakhstan—had received 32 full 30B cylinders on 17 October under IAEA low-enriched uranium supply contract with Orano Cycle. The material was successfully transported from France through the Russian Federation and Kazakhstan under IAEA contracts with Orano Cycle, TENEX and KTZ Express. In addition, the transfer successfully tested one of the

---

[91] IAEA document GOV/2019/35-GC(63)/14(Corrected).

[92] The 2010 Review Conference endorsed requesting IAEA and other relevant international organizations to prepare background documentation for the 2012 Conference on the establishment of a Middle East zone free of nuclear weapons and all other weapons of mass destruction, taking into account work previously undertaken and experience gained (NPT/CONF.2010/50 (Vol. I), p. 30, para. 7 (d)). For the background documentation, see IAEA document GOV/2013/33/Add.1-GC(57)/10/Add.1.

[93] Other assurances of nuclear fuel supply mechanisms are described in previous editions of the *United Nations Disarmament Yearbook*.

transport routes for supply out of the Low-Enriched Uranium Bank. The transport contracts with TENEX and KTZ Express remained available for future use in both directions.

On 10 December, the Low-Enriched Uranium Storage Facility received an additional 28 full 30B cylinders under a supply contract with Kazatomprom, completing the stock of the Low-Enriched Uranium Bank.

Nuclear security

Nuclear Security Plan 2018-2021

IAEA continued to assist States, at their request, in making their national nuclear security regimes more robust, sustainable and effective, while also playing a central role in enhancing international cooperation in nuclear security. In 2019, IAEA continued to implement the Nuclear Security Plan 2018-2021,[94] thereby contributing to global efforts to achieve effective nuclear security. Under the Plan, IAEA established comprehensive nuclear security guidance and promoted its use through peer reviews, advisory services and capacity-building, including education and training. IAEA also worked to assist with: (a) adherence to, and implementation of, relevant international legal instruments; and (b) strengthening international cooperation and coordination of assistance.

International nuclear security framework

In 2019, progress continued towards the universalization of the principal binding international instruments relating to nuclear security, which had been adopted under the auspices of IAEA: the Convention on the Physical Protection of Nuclear Material and the 2005 Amendment thereto. During the year, the number of States parties to the original Convention increased to 160, while the total number of States parties to the Amendment rose to 123. The Amendment entered into force in May 2016, establishing a legal basis for a strengthened framework to protect nuclear facilities and nuclear material in domestic use, storage and transport.

IAEA continued to promote universal adherence to the Amendment through technical meetings, regional workshops and promotional efforts. In two informal meetings from 22 to 26 July and from 12 to 15 November, over 100 experts from more than 70 States parties initiated informal preparations for the 2021 Conference of the Parties to the amended Convention. IAEA also organized the fifth Technical Meeting of the Representatives of the Parties to the Convention and its Amendment, drawing more than 60 States parties to Vienna on 11 November to discuss various aspects of implementing the Convention and its Amendment, as well as efforts to universalize the amended Convention. IAEA also held one international seminar on 13 and 14 May for States parties to the amended

---

[94] IAEA document GC(61)/24.

Convention and non-IAEA member States without permanent representation in Vienna. At the regional level, it conducted a July event in Kenya for English-speaking African countries, followed by an event in Costa Rica in October for Latin American countries.

Nuclear security guidance for member States

IAEA continued to establish and maintain its Nuclear Security Series as part of its central role in providing nuclear security-related international support and coordination. In 2019, IAEA continued to publish a broad range of technical nuclear security guidance, releasing five new publications and one revision of an existing publication in the Series, bringing the total number of published volumes to 37. It also held two meetings of the Nuclear Security Guidance Committee, to which 59 member States nominated representatives. IAEA approved four draft publications for the Series, while overseeing the development of 11 others. IAEA also issued translations of nine publications that had been initially released in English in other official United Nations languages.

Incident and Trafficking Database

IAEA Incident and Trafficking Database continued to be an important source of information for assisting the secretariat, participating States and selected international organizations in strengthening nuclear security. In 2019, Comoros joined the Database, bringing the total number of participating States to 139. IAEA held two subregional information-exchange meetings to share information among current and potential participating States and organized one training course for new and prospective Database points of contact. In 2019, States reported 189 incidents of nuclear and other radioactive material out of regulatory control—six of which were either confirmed or likely acts of trafficking[95]—increasing the number in the Database to 3,686. The Database is a component of the information management systems supporting the implementation of the IAEA Nuclear Security Plan.

Nuclear-security human-resource development

IAEA continued to provide comprehensive assistance to States on human resource development relating to nuclear security, including through programme development, needs analysis, training events, instructor training, educational programmes and further development of nuclear security support centres. In 2019, IAEA conducted 104 security-related training activities—42 at the national level and 62 at the international or regional level—providing training to more than 2,560 participants from 143 States. Participation in the 17 e-learning courses on

---

[95] In order to accurately categorize all reported trafficking incidents and distinguish them from other unauthorized activities, a definition of "trafficking" was agreed for communication purposes among the points of contact or the Incident and Trafficking Database. According to that definition, incidents are categorized based on whether the intent to commit an act of trafficking or malicious use is confirmed, is not known or is absent.

nuclear security offered by IAEA continued to grow, generating more than 4,600 completion certificates by almost 2,000 users in 2019.

In March, the Abdus Salam International Centre for Theoretical Physics (ICTP) hosted the annual event "Joint IAEA-ICTP International School on Nuclear Security" in Trieste, Italy, providing a comprehensive introduction to the field of nuclear security. In September, the "Regional School on Nuclear Security for French-speaking Countries" took place in Kenitra, Morocco, followed in November by the "Regional School on Nuclear Security for English-speaking Countries in Africa" in Cape Town, South Africa. In October, the Faculty Professional Development Course on Nuclear Security Education for Countries in the Asia-Pacific took place in Singapore. IAEA also convened the annual meeting of the International Network for Nuclear Security Training and Support Centres in Tokai, Japan, from 5 to 9 March, as well as the annual meeting of the International Nuclear Security Education Network in Vienna from 8 to 12 July.

IAEA fellowships enabled five students from four developing States to attend a Master's programme in nuclear security at the University of National and World Economy in Sofia. IAEA fellowships also provided support to nine students from seven developing States to attend a Master's programme in nuclear security at Brandenburg University of Applied Sciences in Germany.

Nuclear-security peer reviews and advisory services

IAEA continued to implement peer reviews and advisory services to help States evaluate their nuclear security. It conducted missions with a focus on national nuclear security regimes, including practical security measures for nuclear and other radioactive material and associated facilities and activities.

In 2019, IAEA conducted several expert missions and workshops to provide guidance to States on drafting regulatory principles, reviewing regulatory frameworks and finalizing nuclear-security regulations and associated administrative measures.

IAEA International Physical Protection Advisory Service conducted five missions in Belgium, Lebanon, Madagascar, Paraguay and Uruguay, bringing the total number of such missions since 1996 to 90. In addition, IAEA completed revisions of guidelines aimed at improving assistance to States through the Advisory Service.

Coordinated Research Projects

The Agency continued to coordinate with educational, operational, and research and development institutions to implement Coordinated Research Projects focused on various scientific and technical areas of nuclear security to address evolving threats and technologies, including the establishment and sustainability of national nuclear security regimes. In 2019, IAEA launched three new projects on applying nuclear forensic science to respond to a nuclear security event; on improving preventive and protective measures against insider threats; and on advancing maintenance, repair and calibration of radiation detection equipment. As part of other Coordinated Research Project activities, IAEA circulated to member States the report and findings of a separate project focused on the development of enhancement solutions for national security cultures.

Risk reduction

IAEA continued to advise States on formal threat characterization and assessment; the development, use and maintenance of design-basis threats; the conduct and evaluation of exercises; methodologies for nuclear-material accounting and control for security purposes; and the evaluation and inspection of physical protection systems. IAEA also continued its assistance throughout 2019 with securing vulnerable radioactive sources and upgrading facilities.

Export controls

Missile Technology Control Regime

The Missile Technology Control Regime held its thirty-second plenary meeting in Auckland, New Zealand, from 7 to 10 October.[96] Dell Higgie (New Zealand) served as Chair—the first woman to chair a meeting of the Regime. More than 230 experts from the 35 partner States attended.

The partner States discussed developments related to missile proliferation and expressed concern about global missile proliferation activities, in particular ongoing missile programmes in Asia and the Middle East, which might fuel missile proliferation activities elsewhere. Addressing specific situations, the partner States reiterated the need for full compliance by the Democratic People's Republic of Korea with relevant resolutions of the Security Council—including resolutions 2371 (2017), 2357 (2017) and 2397 (2017)—as well as States' commitment to exercising the necessary vigilance when controlling transfers that could contribute to the ballistic missile programme of the Democratic People's Republic of Korea. With respect to the Islamic Republic of Iran, the partner States took note of the international community's continued obligations under resolution 2231 (2015) and expressed concern regarding the implementation of the resolution.

The partner States also appealed to all States to support the non-proliferation aims of the Missile Technology Control Regime by observing its Guidelines and establishing appropriate national legislation and law enforcement mechanisms. They discussed issues related to future membership, as well as individual applications for membership.

---

[96] See the public statement from the plenary meeting of the Missile Technology Control Regime, Auckland, New Zealand, 11 October 2019.

In addition, the partner States expressed appreciation for the continuous work in 2019 on the Equipment, Software and Technology Annex, including through discussions on ballistic missile developments and tests, proliferation trends and procurement activities, evolving strategies in support of programmes for weapons of mass destruction delivery means, serious risks and challenges posed by intangible technology transfers, catch-all controls for non-listed items, transit and trans-shipment issues, approaches to outreach to industry, and national experiences to strengthen export control enforcement. The States also reflected on the evolution of procurement strategies, exchanging views on how to most effectively address related challenges through effective implementation of export controls.

Hague Code of Conduct against Ballistic Missile Proliferation

The subscribing States of the Hague Code of Conduct against Ballistic Missile Proliferation held their eighteenth annual regular meeting in Vienna on 3 and 4 June.[97] Delegations from 74 States attended, and participants reaffirmed the importance of the Code as a unique confidence-building and transparency instrument against ballistic missile proliferation.

Norway, the incoming Chair for 2019–2020, introduced main objectives for the year that included universalizing and fully implementing the Code in order to enhance its multinational confidence-building ability. The subscribing States decided that Switzerland would chair the nineteenth regular meeting in 2020.

The subscribing States stressed the ongoing need to prevent and curb the proliferation of weapons of mass destruction and their means of delivery and to encourage new subscriptions to the Hague Code of Conduct, particularly by countries with space launch vehicle and ballistic missile capabilities.

They reaffirmed the threat to international peace and security posed by the proliferation of weapons of mass destruction and their means of delivery. They discussed developments in the missile programme of the Democratic People's Republic of Korea in the context of relevant Security Council resolutions.

The subscribing States separately stressed the importance of achieving full implementation of the Code, in particular with regard to the timely submission of pre-launch notifications and annual declarations.

They also reaffirmed the right to exploration and use of outer space for peaceful purposes, as provided for in the Outer Space Treaty. Participants emphasized the need to exercise necessary vigilance in considering possible assistance to space launch vehicle programmes so as to not contribute to, support or assist any ballistic missile programme in contravention of international norms and obligations, as provided for in the Code.

---

[97] See Hague Code of Conduct subscribing States, press release on the seventeenth regular meeting of the subscribing States to the Hague Code of Conduct against Ballistic Missile Proliferation, Vienna, 4 June 2019.

The subscribing States agreed to continue efforts to universalize the Code.

Nuclear Suppliers Group

The Nuclear Suppliers Group[98] held its twenty-ninth plenary in Nur-Sultan on 20 and 21 June, with Kairat Sarybay (Kazakhstan) serving as Chair. The President of Kazakhstan, Kassym-Jomart Tokayev, delivered the welcoming remarks.

In a public statement[99] to the plenary meeting, the Group reiterated its firm support for the full, complete and effective implementation of the Treaty on the Non-Proliferation of Nuclear Weapons as the cornerstone of the international non-proliferation regime.

During the plenary, the Group noted developments in the Democratic People's Republic of Korea since its 2018 plenary and reconfirmed its commitment to Security Council resolutions 2371 (2017), 2375 (2017) and 2397 (2017), as well as previous relevant resolutions of the Council. The Group also noted that the supply of all controlled items to the Democratic People's Republic of Korea was prohibited.

The Group took note of the international community's obligations under Security Council resolution 2231 (2015) and urged compliance. Since its previous plenary meeting, the Group had continued to receive briefings from the coordinator of the Procurement Working Group, established under the Joint Comprehensive Plan of Action, regarding the work of the Procurement Channel for Member States and international organizations to participate in the supply, sale or transfer of nuclear, ballistic missile or arms-related dual-use equipment and material to or activities with the Islamic Republic of Iran. The Group expressed interest in receiving further such briefings.

Also at the plenary meeting, members of the Group exchanged views and agreed on several proposals to clarify and update its control list and guidelines. The Group further emphasized the importance of updating its guidelines to keep pace with technical developments in nuclear-related industries.

In addition, the Group exchanged views on national practices for raising awareness, interacting with industry and engaging with academic and research institutions.

---

[98] As at the end of 2019, the participating Governments of the Group were the following: Argentina, Australia, Austria, Belarus, Belgium, Brazil, Bulgaria, Canada, China, Croatia, Cyprus, Czechia, Denmark, Estonia, Finland, France, Germany, Greece, Hungary, Iceland, Ireland, Italy, Japan, Kazakhstan, Latvia, Lithuania, Luxembourg, Malta, Mexico, Netherlands, New Zealand, Norway, Poland, Portugal, Republic of Korea, Romania, Russian Federation, Serbia, Slovakia, Slovenia, South Africa, Spain, Sweden, Switzerland, Turkey, Ukraine, United Kingdom and United States. The European Commission and the Chair of the Zangger Committee participated as permanent observers.

[99] Nuclear Suppliers Group, public statement of the 2019 plenary, Nur-Sultan, 21 June 2019.

Furthermore, members of the Group continued to consider all aspects of the Statement on Civil Nuclear Cooperation with India of 2008 and discussed their relationship with that State.

Fissile materials

The Office for Disarmament Affairs organized a series of activities in 2019 as part of a three-year project that was launched the previous year, pursuant to European Union Council decision 2017/2284,[100] to support Member States in Africa, Asia and the Pacific, and Latin America and the Caribbean to participate in possible future negotiations on a fissile material cut-off treaty.

The activities included three workshops for States in Western and Central Africa, Eastern and Southern Africa and Latin America, respectively. The Office also convened two expert meetings for Latin America and the Caribbean, and for Asia and Africa, targeting representatives from relevant regional organizations, academia and civil society organizations. The Office facilitated the first of six planned national round-table discussions in Peru, bringing together all relevant national agencies.

The project activities, funded by the European Union and carried out in cooperation with the Office's three regional centres, were aimed at facilitating dialogue at the regional and subregional levels among Member States and regional organizations on the implications of a future treaty and its relationship with existing regional and global disarmament and non-proliferation instruments. Participants were encouraged to share knowledge and information across regions on issues relevant to banning the production of fissile material for nuclear weapons or other nuclear explosive devices; exchange views and discuss challenges and ways ahead in relation to a future treaty; and build their knowledge on the structure and functions of relevant negotiation forums and procedures.

---

[100] European Union, Council Decision (CFSP) 2017/2284 of 11 December 2017, Official Journal of the European Union, L 328 (12 December 2017), pp. 32–37.

Annex I

Composition of the Group of Governmental Experts to consider the role of verification in advancing nuclear disarmament

Knut Langeland (Chair)
  Ambassador, Royal Embassy of Norway, Algiers

Djamel Moktefi
  Director of Legal Affairs, Ministry of Foreign Affairs of Algeria

María Jimena Schiaffino
  Counsellor, Permanent Mission of Argentina to the United Nations Office and other international organizations in Geneva

Marcelo Câmara
  Head of the Disarmament and Sensitive Technologies Division, Ministry of Foreign Affairs of Brazil

Alfredo Labbé
  Ambassador (ret.), Vice-President of the International Humanitarian Fact-Finding Commission, Chile

Wang Chang
  Counsellor and Division Director, Nuclear Affairs Division, Department of Arms Control and Disarmament, Ministry of Foreign Affairs of China (first and second sessions)

Zhang Shen
  Counsellor, Department of Arms Control and Disarmament, Ministry of Foreign Affairs of China (third session)

Pasi Patokallio
  Ambassador (ret.), Senior Adviser, Ministry of Foreign Affairs of Finland

Romain Le Floc'h
  Counsellor, Directorate for Strategic Affairs, Security and Disarmament, Ministry of Europe and Foreign Affairs of France

Louis Riquet
  Alternate Expert, Deputy Permanent Representative of France to the Conference on Disarmament

Michael Biontino
  Ambassador (ret.), Adviser, Federal Foreign Office of Germany

György Molnár
  Ambassador, Special Representative for Arms Control, Disarmament and Non-Proliferation, Hungary

Pankaj Sharma
> Ambassador and Permanent Representative of India to the Conference on Disarmament

Clemens T. Bektisukuma
> Permanent Mission of Indonesia to the United Nations Office and other international organizations in Geneva (first session)

Grata Werdaningtyas
> Director for International Security and Disarmament, Ministry of Foreign Affairs of Indonesia (second session)

Roy Martin Hasudungan
> Directorate of International Security and Disarmament, Directorate General of Multilateral Cooperation Affairs, Ministry of Foreign Affairs of Indonesia (third session)

Takeshi Nakane
> Special Assistant to the Minister for Foreign Affairs of Japan, Ambassador for Science and Technology Cooperation

Erlan Gadletovich Batyrbekov
> Director General of the Republican State Enterprise, National Nuclear Centre of the Republic of Kazakhstan

Jaime Aguirre Gómez
> Deputy Director General for Environmental Radiological Surveillance, Physical Security and Safeguards of the National Commission of Nuclear Safety and Safeguards, Mexico (first session)

Sandra Paola Ramírez Valenzuela
> Deputy Director General for Disarmament, Non-Proliferation and Arms Control, Directorate General for the United Nations, Ministry of Foreign Affairs of Mexico (third session)

Abdessamad Tajerramt
> Head of the Division of International Organizations, Ministry of Foreign Affairs and International Cooperation of Morocco

Tom Coppen
> Senior Policy Officer, Ministry of Foreign Affairs of the Netherlands

Abiodun Richards Adejola
> Deputy Head of Mission, Embassy of Nigeria to Ethiopia and Permanent Mission to the African Union and the Economic Commission for Africa, Addis Ababa

Usman Jadoon
> Counsellor, Permanent Mission of Pakistan to the United Nations Office and other international organizations in Geneva

Damian Przenioslo
> Minister-Counsellor, Head of the Weapons of Mass Destruction Non-Proliferation and Disarmament Unit, Ministry of Foreign Affairs of Poland

Vladimir Leontiev
> Deputy Director of Department for Non-Proliferation and Arms Control, Ministry of Foreign Affairs of the Russian Federation (first and second sessions)

Alexander Deyneko
> Alternate Expert, Deputy Representative, Permanent Mission of the Russian Federation to the United Nations Office and other international organizations in Geneva (third session)

Denis Davydov
> Alternate Expert, Counsellor, Permanent Mission of the Russian Federation to the United Nations Office and other international organizations in Geneva

Johann Kellerman
> Director, Disarmament and Non-Proliferation, Department of International Relations and Cooperation, South Africa

Benno Laggner
> Ambassador, Resident Representative to the International Atomic Energy Agency, Permanent Representative to the Preparatory Commission for the Comprehensive Nuclear-Test-Ban Treaty Organization, Permanent Mission of Switzerland to the United Nations (Vienna) (first session)

Reto Wollenmann
> Deputy Head Arms Control, Disarmament and Non-Proliferation Section, Division for Security Policy, Federal Department of Foreign Affairs of Switzerland (second and third sessions)

David Chambers
> Arms Control and Disarmament Research Unit, Foreign and Commonwealth Office of the United Kingdom

Michael Edinger
> Foreign Affairs Officer, Office of Multilateral and Nuclear Affairs, Bureau of Arms Control, Verification and Compliance, Department of State of the United States

chapter

II Biological and chemical weapons

High Representative for Disarmament Affairs Izumi Nakamitsu delivering a statement at the twenty-fourth session of the Conference of States Parties to the Chemical Weapons Convention. The Conference was held at the World Forum, The Hague, Netherlands, from 25 to 29 November 2019.

Photo: Organisation for the Prohibition of Chemical Weapons

Chapter II

Biological and chemical weapons

Ensuring accountability for a confirmed use of chemical weapons is our responsibility, not least to the victims of such attacks. A lack of accountability emboldens those who would use such weapons by providing them with the reassurance of impunity. This in turn further weakens the norm proscribing the use of chemical weapons and the international disarmament and non-proliferation architecture as a whole.

ANTÓNIO GUTERRES, SECRETARY-GENERAL OF THE UNITED NATIONS[1]

Developments and trends, 2019

A PERIOD OF INTENSE CHALLENGE to the international norm against chemical weapons use continued throughout 2019. In that context, the Organisation for the Prohibition of Chemical Weapons (OPCW) persisted in its efforts to broaden and strengthen the implementation of the Convention on the Prohibition of the Development, Production, Stockpiling and Use of Chemical Weapons and on Their Destruction (Chemical Weapons Convention).

At the international level, much of that work remained centred around allegations of chemical weapons possession and use in the Syrian Arab Republic. The Office for Disarmament Affairs continued to support the Secretary-General's good offices in furtherance of the implementation of Security Council resolution 2118 (2013) on the elimination of the Syrian chemical weapons programme.

OPCW continued to assist the Government of the Syrian Arab Republic in efforts to resolve all gaps, inconsistencies and discrepancies that had arisen from the initial declaration of its chemical weapons programme. The OPCW Fact-Finding Mission continued its work to establish the facts surrounding allegations of chemical weapons use in the Syrian Arab Republic. Pursuant to a 2018 decision[2] of the fourth special session of the Conference of the States Parties, the OPCW Technical Secretariat established the Investigation and Identification Team to identify the perpetrators of chemical weapons use in the country.

Separately, OPCW enhanced its efforts to build capacities among States parties to prevent the re-emergence of chemical weapons. Through its related work, OPCW sought to bolster cooperation with key stakeholders in the areas of promoting the peaceful uses of chemistry; advance scientific and technological

---

[1] Remarks to the Security Council, New York, 13 April 2018.
[2] OPCW, Conference of the States Parties decision C-SS-4/DEC.3 of 27 June 2018.

cooperation; counter threats posed by non-State actors; and expand partnerships with international organizations, non-governmental organizations (NGOs), the chemical industry and other entities. During the year, further progress was made in an ongoing project to upgrade the OPCW Laboratory and Equipment Store into the Centre for Chemistry and Technology (ChemTech Centre). Furthermore, OPCW continued its work to universalize the Chemical Weapons Convention, urging the remaining four States not party to the Convention to join without delay or preconditions.

While no incidents concerning the potential use of biological weapons were reported in 2019, States worked to further strengthen a decades-old global ban on those arms. The United Republic of Tanzania ratified the Convention on the Prohibition of the Development, Production and Stockpiling of Bacteriological (Biological) and Toxin Weapons and on Their Destruction (Biological Weapons Convention) on 14 August, becoming the 183rd State party. As at 31 December, four signatory States had not yet ratified the Convention, and 10 States had neither signed nor ratified it. In 2019, States parties held five intersessional Meetings of Experts in July and August and a Meeting of States Parties in December as part of a previously adopted intersessional programme for the years 2018 to 2020.

Chemical weapons

Twenty-fourth session of the Conference of the States Parties

The twenty-fourth session of the Conference of the States Parties to the Chemical Weapons Convention took place from 25 to 29 November in The Hague, Netherlands, drawing representatives of 154 States parties and one signatory State.[3] In addition, 87 civil society organizations—a record number—and representatives from the chemical industry and the scientific community participated in the Conference.[4]

The Conference reviewed the status of the Convention's implementation in all programme areas, including disarmament, prevention of the re-emergence of chemical weapons, assistance and protection, and international cooperation. Delegates were briefed on: (a) progress made by the last declared possessor State party, the United States of America, in its destruction operations over the previous year; and (b) the recovery and destruction of abandoned chemical weapons by Japan on the territory of China.[5] The Conference also considered and approved by vote the 2020 programme and budget, which would provide the necessary resources for the OPCW Technical Secretariat to implement its activities.

---

[3] For the report of the twenty-fourth session of the Conference and the list of States that attended, see OPCW, document C-24/5.

[4] For the lists of organizations, see OPCW, documents C-24/DEC.2, annex, and C-24/DEC.3, annex, respectively.

[5] OPCW, document C-24/4, paras. 1.3, 1.19.

For the first time since the entry into force of the Chemical Weapons Convention in 1997, the Conference adopted, by consensus, two decisions to update the Convention's annex on chemicals. Those decisions reflected two proposals—the first from Canada, the Netherlands and the United States, and the second from the Russian Federation—which were submitted in the context of an evolving threat from chemical weapons and their recent use that required OPCW to continually adjust its ability to respond. The annex on chemicals contains three schedules listing toxic chemicals and their precursors; both decisions called for technical changes to Schedule 1.[6] Those changes were to enter into force for States parties on 7 June 2020, following the timelines laid out in article XV of the Convention.

The Conference also considered efforts to foster international cooperation for peaceful purposes in the field of chemical activities, the further deepening of engagement with the chemical industry and the scientific community, the annual report by the OPCW Director-General on the implementation of the action plan on universality, the OPCW Programme to Strengthen Cooperation with Africa, and the activities of the Advisory Board on Education and Outreach.

Organisation for the Prohibition of Chemical Weapons

As at 30 November, 97.42 per cent (68,675 metric tons) of the total amount of Category 1 chemical weapons declared by States parties had been destroyed.

The destruction of all Category 1 chemical weapons stockpiles declared by six States parties had been completed previously.[7]

The aggregate amount of Category 2 chemical weapons destroyed stood at 1,811 metric tons, or 100 per cent of the total amount declared. Albania, India, Libya, the Russian Federation, the Syrian Arab Republic and the United States had completed the destruction of all declared Category 2 chemical weapons.

The United States continued to make progress in its efforts to destroy all of its declared chemical weapons. As at 30 November, the country had eliminated 93.44 per cent of its Category 1 chemical weapons and all of its Category 2 and Category 3 chemical weapons.

Meanwhile, China and Japan continued to cooperate on the recovery and destruction of abandoned chemical weapons on Chinese territory. At two trilateral meetings—held in Tokyo on 24 and 25 July, and in Beijing on 18 and 19 December—China, Japan and the Technical Secretariat discussed practical and technical issues regarding abandoned chemical-weapons-destruction projects.

---

[6] For the purpose of implementing the Convention, these schedules identify chemicals in respect of which special verification measures are applied in accordance with the provisions of the Convention's Verification Annex.

[7] The States concerned have been referenced as "a State Party, Albania, India, Libya, the Russian Federation and the Syrian Arab Republic". See OPCW, document C-22/DG.20, para. 50.

As at 31 December, OPCW had conducted, in accordance with article VI of the Convention, over 4,000 inspections, concerning toxic chemicals and their precursors for purposes not prohibited under the Convention, in more than 80 countries.

During the year, OPCW provided training to representatives of 25 States parties in its current Laboratory and Equipment Store. Meanwhile, planning continued for the construction of the Centre for Chemistry and Technology (ChemTech Centre), which would provide enhanced training and technological capabilities. As at the end of 2019, OPCW had received €28.9 million in financial contributions and pledges for that project from 28 States parties, the European Union and private donors. It was expected that the Centre would enable the OPCW to develop new and improved tools for verification, while also increasing international cooperation for training and capacity-building.

In March, August and September, the Technical Secretariat conducted workshops at the OPCW headquarters on operational mission planning. In addition, training exercises on reconnaissance and sampling took place in Serbia in April, in Slovakia in June and in Canada in July.

OPCW and the chemical industry continued efforts to strengthen their cooperation in accordance with the relevant recommendations of the third Review Conference. In March and September, OPCW and the International Council of Chemical Associations held meetings of the Chemical Industry Coordination Group to further discuss relevant issues of common interest. Those meetings covered matters such as improving the efficiency of industry inspections, capacity-building in chemical safety and security, the impact of industry revolution on the chemical sector and the Convention's implementation, and efforts to further increase cross-participation in the respective events of OPCW and the International Council of Chemical Associations.

In addition, the OPCW Advisory Board on Education and Outreach held its seventh and eighth sessions, as well as carried out intersessional activities in four working groups that focused on: (a) a history of chemical weapons use; (b) a new list of "other resources" for the education and outreach resources page on OPCW public website; (c) active learning approaches; and (d) the preparation of new education and outreach materials.

National implementation, assistance and protection against chemical weapons, and international cooperation on promoting peaceful uses of chemistry

OPCW Technical Secretariat continued to assist States parties towards achieving full and effective implementation of the Convention in the areas of national implementation, assistance and protection against chemical weapons, and international cooperation on promoting peaceful uses of chemistry. In 2019, the

Technical Secretariat conducted over 95 training courses, workshops, seminars and other capacity-building programmes that benefited 2,364 participants.

In the field of assistance and protection, the Technical Secretariat consolidated and applied its established capacity-building approaches and other training modalities. Through those tailored efforts, it supported States parties in their actions to enhance their capacity to respond promptly and effectively to emergencies involving chemical warfare agents or other toxic chemicals.

In 2019, a new capacity-development programme on the medical aspects of chemical emergency response under article X of the Convention was launched. Through the programme on Chemical Incident Preparedness for Hospitals, aimed at improving the resilience of medical facilities and enhance awareness of the importance of chemical incident readiness, a total of 1,014 first responders and chemical emergency response experts attended 35 training courses and workshops that the Technical Secretariat organized in 31 States parties.[8]

The Technical Secretariat also increased its assistance to States parties and stakeholders in the area of chemical safety and security, including by successfully initiating a pilot project to develop related tools. With support from OPCW, experts from Governments, industry, academia, the technical community, and regional and international organizations produced, for the first time, a non-binding document containing indicative guidelines on chemical safety and security management for small and medium-sized enterprises.

The Technical Secretariat further championed gender mainstreaming initiatives by organizing its fourth Symposium on Women in Chemistry, which focused on strengthening the role of women scientists for future generations. The event provided States parties with a platform to discuss and highlight the role of women both in implementing the Chemical Weapons Convention and in encouraging international solidarity and cooperation to develop human capital for the future of peaceful chemistry.

Mission to eliminate the Syrian chemical weapons programme

In 2019, OPCW continued its mission to verifiably eliminate the declared chemical weapons programme of the Syrian Arab Republic. Continuous monitoring systems previously installed in the Government's former underground production facilities underwent maintenance and continued to operate normally. As part of the yearly agreed verification activities, OPCW Technical Secretariat visited the five destroyed underground structures in November and verified the integrity of installed external and interior plugs.

---

[8] Algeria, Argentina, Bangladesh, Belarus, Brazil, China, Colombia, Côte d'Ivoire, Czechia, Fiji, Ghana, Indonesia, Italy, Jordan, Kenya, Malaysia, Mexico, Mozambique, Namibia, Pakistan, Panama, Peru, Poland, Portugal, Republic of Korea, Serbia, Singapore, Slovakia, Switzerland, Netherlands and Uganda.

The OPCW Fact-Finding Mission continued to gather all available information related to allegations of use of chemical weapons in the Syrian Arab Republic. In 2019, the Technical Secretariat issued one Fact-Finding Mission report[9] regarding the incident of alleged use of toxic chemicals as a weapon in Douma, Syrian Arab Republic, on 7 April 2018. In the report, the Fact-Finding Mission concluded that the evaluation and analysis of all the information it had gathered provided reasonable grounds for it to conclude that the use of a toxic chemical as a weapon had taken place. The Technical Secretariat also issued a summary update[10] of the activities carried out by the Fact-Finding Mission in the Syrian Arab Republic in 2019.

Pursuant to paragraph 11 of the OPCW Executive Council decision EC-83/DEC.5, dated 11 November 2016, the Technical Secretariat conducted two rounds of inspections in July and November 2019 at the Scientific Studies and Research Centre in the Syrian Arab Republic.

The Technical Secretariat's Declaration Assessment Team also continued working with the Syrian Arab Republic in order to ensure that all declaration-related requirements had been met in accordance with the Chemical Weapons Convention, as well as with relevant Security Council resolutions and decisions by the OPCW policymaking organs. In 2019, the Declaration Assessment Team conducted three rounds of consultations with the Syrian Arab Republic in March, April, and October. The outcomes of those consultations were reported to the regular sessions of the OPCW Executive Council in March, July and October, respectively.

Separately, in accordance with decision C-SS-4/DEC.3 of 27 June 2018, the Technical Secretariat established the Investigation and Identification Team in 2019 with the mandate to identify individuals or entities directly or indirectly involved in the use of chemical weapons in the Syrian Arab Republic, by investigating and reporting on all information potentially relevant to the origin of those weapons. The Investigation and Identification Team functions under the authority of the Director-General.

On the basis of a preliminary assessment of the relevant incidents, the Investigation and Identification Team focused its 2019 investigations on a non-exhaustive preliminary list of nine incidents.[11] After reaching out to States parties and other international, regional and local actors to gather information and conduct investigations and analysis, the Team began preparing a first report on certain incidents under its purview for submission to the OPCW Executive Council and the Secretary-General for their consideration.

---

[9] OPCW, document S/1731/2019.
[10] OPCW, document S/1798/2019.
[11] OPCW, document EC-91/S/3, annex 2.

Science and technology-related activities

The Technical Secretariat continued to engage with broad sectors of the global scientific community throughout the year, both to maintain strong ties with scientists and scientific societies and to keep fully abreast of developments in science and technology. In June, the OPCW Scientific Advisory Board met for its twenty-eighth session,[12] during which it initiated its next scientific review cycle for the period leading up to the fifth Review Conference of the Convention.

The Scientific Advisory Board's temporary working group on investigative science and technology held three meetings in 2019, in January, September and November.[13] At its fifth and final meeting, convened in November in Helsinki, the working group drafted a final report with recommendations drawing upon findings from an in-depth review of methods and technologies applicable to the Technical Secretariat's investigative work. The document was expected to be issued at the Scientific Advisory Board's twenty-ninth session in 2020.

In addition, OPCW shared experiences from its science advice process and its Advisory Board, making the information available to States parties of the Biological Weapons Convention at a Meeting of Experts in July and at the Meeting of States Parties in December.[14]

United Nations project on lessons learned from the Organisation for the Prohibition of Chemical Weapons–United Nations Joint Investigative Mechanism

In 2019, the Office for Disarmament Affairs convened the first two workshops of a project to identify lessons learned from the OPCW–United Nations Joint Investigative Mechanism (JIM), which was established by the Security Council in 2015 to identify the perpetrators of confirmed chemical-weapon attacks in the Syrian Arab Republic.[15] With JIM ceasing operations in 2017,[16] the workshops were designed to use the experiences in past investigations to better prepare

---

[12] See the report of the Scientific Advisory Board at its twenty-eighth session (OPCW, document SAB-28/1) and the response of the Director-General to that report (OPCW, document EC-92/DG.1).

[13] See the summaries of the third and fourth meetings—held in January and September, respectively—of the Scientific Advisory Board Temporary Working Group on Investigative Science and Technology (OPCW, documents SAB-28/WP.3 and SAB-29/WP.1).

[14] For the briefing to the Meeting of Experts, see OPCW, "Science for Diplomats at CSP-24 Presents: The Return of the Chemical Mystery". For the briefing to the Meeting of States Parties, see OPCW, "Scientific Advice for the Chemical Weapons Convention".

[15] JIM was mandated by Security Council resolution 2235 (2015) to identify, to the greatest extent feasible, individuals, entities, groups, or governments who were perpetrators, organizers, sponsors or otherwise involved in the use of chemicals as weapons, including chlorine or any other toxic chemical, in the Syrian Arab Republic, where the OPCW Fact-Finding Mission determines that a specific incident involved or likely involved the use of chemicals as weapons.

[16] The Security Council could not agree to further extend the mandate of JIM.

the United Nations and its partners to respond to future allegations of chemical weapons use, particularly with regard to attribution.

Thanks to voluntary contributions from two Member States,[17] the Office convened the first workshop in July in Glion, Switzerland, focusing on the internal organization and management of JIM. The second workshop was held in September in The Hague, Netherlands, with a focus on the investigations. During discussions at the workshops, participants identified several preliminary recommendations and lessons learned in those two thematic areas. The remaining workshops and the final report of the project will be completed in 2020.

Biological weapons

The Convention on the Prohibition of the Development, Production and Stockpiling of Bacteriological (Biological) and Toxin Weapons and on Their Destruction (Biological Weapons Convention) was opened for signature on 10 April 1972 and entered into force on 26 March 1975, becoming the first multilateral treaty banning an entire category of weapons. The Convention effectively prohibits the development, production, acquisition, transfer, stockpiling and use of biological and toxin weapons. As at the end of 2019, the Convention had 183 States parties and 109 signatory States.

Meetings of Experts to the Biological Weapons Convention

In 2019, States parties held five Meetings of Experts in which they addressed the following topics: cooperation and assistance, with particular focus on strengthening cooperation and assistance under article X of the Convention; review of developments in the field of science and technology related to the Convention; strengthening national implementation; assistance, response and preparedness; and institutional strengthening of the Convention. At the conclusion of each Meeting, States parties adopted a procedural report that included, in annex, a Chair's summary of considerations, lessons learned, perspectives, recommendations, conclusions and proposals drawn from the presentations, statements, working papers and interventions at the Meeting. The Chairs produced the summary reports on their own authority and initiative, in consultation with the States parties.[18]

---

[17] Canada and Switzerland.

[18] See the reports of the five Meetings of Experts (BWC/MSP/2019/MX.1/2, BWC/MSP/2019/ MX.2/2, BWC/MSP/2019/MX.3/2, BWC/MSP/2019/MX.4/2 and BWC/MSP/2019/MX.5/2) and their respective annexes for the summary reports of the Chairs.

Meeting of Experts on Cooperation and Assistance, with a Particular Focus on Strengthening Cooperation and Assistance under Article X

The Meeting of Experts on Cooperation and Assistance, with a Particular Focus on Strengthening Cooperation and Assistance under Article X[19] took place on 29 and 30 July in Geneva. The Meeting was chaired by Victor Dolidze (Georgia) and attended by representatives from 96 States parties, three signatory States and one State not party to the Convention. The national delegations were joined by officials from three United Nations entities, four specialized agencies/other international organizations, two guests[20] and 30 NGOs and research institutes.[21] The topics that the Meeting considered were listed in its agenda.[22]

During the Meeting, States parties discussed the low number of national reports submitted in accordance with article X for the biennial period 2018–2019 and, in that context, they considered options to improve voluntary reporting, such as providing guidelines or a reporting template. They also welcomed: (a) the work of the Convention's Implementation Support Unit to enhance the Assistance and Cooperation Database, in line with a request from the eighth Review Conference; and (b) the increased number of offers and requests listed in the Database.

In discussing obstacles to international cooperation, assistance and exchange, States parties referred to practical challenges that their programmes in those areas had faced.[23] While reiterating the importance of relevant innovative public-private partnerships for addressing cooperation and assistance needs under article X, States parties examined approaches and instruments that, through resource mobilization guidelines, could help meet such needs effectively and sustainably. In addition, in considering existing international and regional platforms for education, training, exchange and twinning programmes in the biological sciences, participants noted that such platforms were the strongest area of overlap between articles X and VII.[24] States parties reiterated that relevant international and regional organizations, such as the World Health Organization (WHO) and the World Organization for Animal Health, played an important role in disease surveillance, prevention, detection and response; participants saw merit in continuing coordination and cooperation with those entities to implement article X in accordance with their respective mandates.

---

[19] Under article X of the Convention, States parties undertake to facilitate and promote the peaceful uses of biology.

[20] "Guests of the Meeting" are identified in each of the reports of the Meetings of Experts, in which they participated.

[21] For the list of participants, see BWC/MSP/2019/MX.1/INF.1.

[22] BWC/MSP/2019/MX.1/1.

[23] Examples of those challenges included identifying specific requests from recipient States and ensuring the sustainability of assistance, as well as addressing staff turnover and projects of short duration.

[24] Article VII of the Convention addresses the provision of assistance in the event of the use of biological weapons.

Meeting of Experts on Review of Developments in the Field of Science and Technology Related to the Convention

The Meeting of Experts on Review of Developments in the Field of Science and Technology Related to the Convention took place on 31 July and 2 August in Geneva, with Yury Nikolaichik (Belarus) serving as Chair. The Meeting was attended by representatives from 96 States parties, three signatory States and one State not party to the Convention. The national delegations were joined by officials from three United Nations entities, five specialized agencies/other international organizations, three guests of the Meeting and 31 NGOs and research institutes.[25] The topics that the Meeting considered were listed in its agenda.[26]

States parties noted both the rapid scientific and technological advances in the field of life sciences and the growing "do-it-yourself bio" community. There was broad support to consider establishing, in the framework of the Convention, a systematic and structured science and technology review process to monitor relevant developments and assess their potential implications. In light of the continuous emergence of new technologies and novel technical capabilities in the life sciences, the importance of assessing their potential implications for the Convention in a timely manner was underlined. Participants emphasized that, while those technologies enabled various legitimate and beneficial applications, they also bore the risk of misuse for malign purposes and military applications. States parties also discussed the crucial importance of awareness-raising and education as complementary and effective measures to reduce risks regarding dual-use research of concern, with some participants remarking on the benefits of open online training and education material. States parties noted the rapid advances in the field of science and technology, including the increasing convergence of technologies from traditionally different scientific fields and disciplines. They discussed, in particular, the implications of the convergence between cyber technologies, artificial intelligence and biotechnologies, noting the huge impact of those implications on various sectors, such as health, medicine, industry or agriculture.

Meeting of Experts on Strengthening National Implementation

The Meeting of Experts on Strengthening National Implementation took place on 5 August in Geneva, chaired by Lebogang Phihlela (South Africa). The attendees included representatives from 96 States parties, three signatory States and one State not party to the Convention, as well as officials from three United Nations entities, six specialized agencies/other international organizations, one guest of the Meeting, and 31 NGOs and research institutes.[27] The topics that the Meeting considered were listed in its agenda.[28]

---

[25] For the list of participants, see BWC/MSP/2019/MX.2/INF.1.
[26] BWC/MSP/2019/MX.2/1.
[27] For the list of participants, see BWC/MSP/2019/MX.3/INF.1.
[28] BWC/MSP/2019/MX.3/1.

During the Meeting, States parties shared their views on measures related to article IV of the Convention,[29] noting that national implementation was a broad concept and required implementation of a wide range of measures at multiple levels. Participants mentioned, inter alia, development, harmonization and enforcement of comprehensive national legislation; adoption of effective national export control systems; and adoption and sustainment of robust national implementation measures.

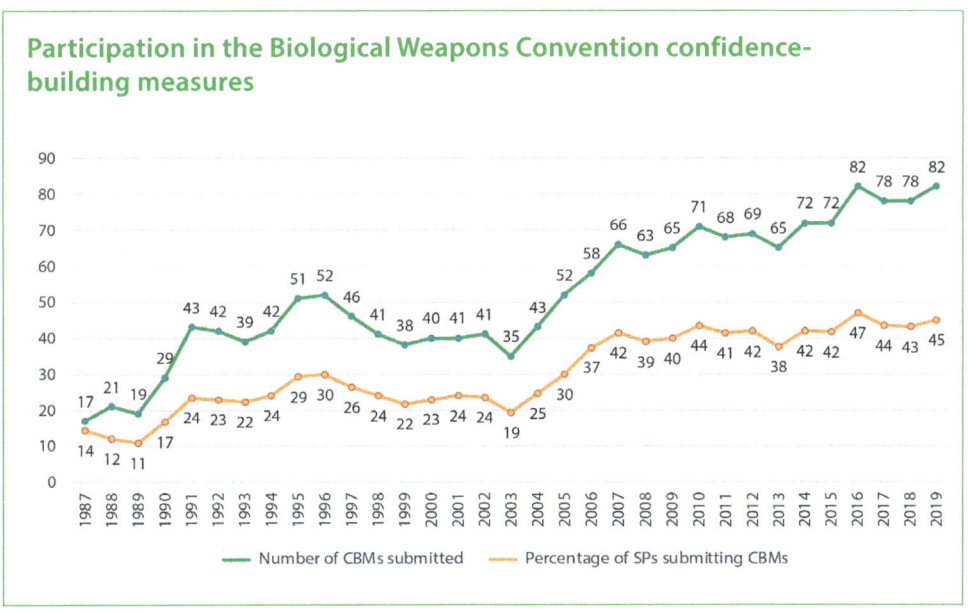

Participation in the Biological Weapons Convention confidence-building measures

Legend: Number of CBMs submitted — Percentage of SPs submitting CBMs

States reiterated that confidence-building measures were the only formal tool under the Convention for promoting transparency and building confidence among States parties and, as such, they played an important role in preventing and reducing ambiguities, doubts and suspicions. States parties expressed different views on the nature of confidence-building measures, some considering such measures to be politically binding and others viewing them as voluntary. Highlighting the importance of strengthening the quantity and quality of confidence-building measures under the Convention, they encouraged other States to develop and participate in the measures. Meanwhile, several participants made concrete proposals to enhance the utility and use of confidence-building measures.

States parties mentioned the linkage between article X and national implementation, noting that an incomplete understanding of existing national implementation measures was often hampering the fulfilment of offers of

---

[29] Under article IV, States commit to take any national measures necessary to implement the provisions of the Convention domestically.

assistance. It was therefore suggested that the Meeting consider concrete measures to improve reporting on those measures by States parties.

Participants also discussed issues related to article III,[30] including by exchanging views on its implementation and sharing proposals to strengthen effective export control measures.

Meeting of Experts on Assistance, Response and Preparedness

The Meeting of Experts on Assistance, Response and Preparedness took place on 6 and 7 August in Geneva, with Usman Iqbal Jadoon (Pakistan) as its Chair. It was attended by representatives from 96 States parties, three signatory States and one State not party to the Convention, as well as officials from five United Nations entities, eight specialized agencies/other international organizations, one guest of the Meeting, and 31 NGOs and research institutes.[31] The topics that the Meeting considered were listed in its agenda.[32]

In discussing practical challenges facing the implementation of article VII, as well as possible solutions, participants suggested: (a) the designation of a permanent facilitator or unit to coordinate responses to a deliberate biological release; and (b) enhanced financing for national pandemic preparedness. Some States parties stressed the critical importance of effective command and control for an article VII response, as well as the need to establish and test respective capabilities and plans before an event occurred. It was also suggested that the Secretary-General develop a plan aimed at ensuring that Member States, the Secretariat, the wider United Nations system and other partners respond in coordination to a deliberate release of a biological agent or toxin. Such a plan could include the time-bound appointment of a special representative of the Secretary-General.

The guidelines and formats for a potential assistance request under article VII featured prominently in the discussions and received considerable attention from many States parties, as in 2018. Some delegations suggested that the proposed guidelines could be deposited with the Biological Weapons Convention Implementation Support Unit and used on an interim basis prior to formal adoption. Another widely discussed issue concerned the development of an assistance database to support implementation of article VII by matching offers and requests for assistance. Separately, States parties discussed how they could use mobile biomedical units to contribute to the implementation of the Convention in many areas, including in the sphere of international cooperation and assistance under article X in the context of article VII and article VI. While exploring approaches to strengthening international response capabilities for

---

[30] Under article III, States parties commit not to transfer, or in any way assist, encourage or induce anyone else to acquire or retain biological weapons.

[31] For the list of participants, see BWC/MSP/2019/MX.4/INF.1.

[32] BWC/MSP/2019/MX.4/1.

infectious disease outbreaks, whether natural or deliberate in origin, some States parties stressed the importance of well-equipped national laboratories. While exploring means to prepare for, respond to and render assistance in case of possible hostile use of biological agents and toxins, States parties highlighted the need to strengthen attention beyond solely human-health aspects and also address threats to agriculture, plants, livestock and the environment. Some participants noted that attacks on those sectors could have an enormous impact on national economies, the environment and livelihoods.

Meeting of Experts on Institutional Strengthening of the Convention

The Meeting of Experts on Institutional Strengthening of the Convention took place on 8 August in Geneva, with Laurent Masmejean (Switzerland) serving as Chair. The Meeting was attended by representatives from 96 States parties, three signatory States and one State not party to the Convention, as well as officials from three United Nations entities, five specialized agencies/other international organizations, and 31 NGOs and research institutes.[33] The topics that the Meeting considered were listed in its agenda.[34]

States parties expressed strong support for strengthening the Convention and making progress in the framework of the Meeting of Experts. As in the previous year, States discussed approaches to strengthening the Convention, the importance of its universalization, challenges faced, additional legally binding measures in the Convention, verification, strengthening the Implementation Support Unit, and the Convention's financial stability and sustainability.

It was noted that the Convention faced a number of challenges, notably its operation in a highly dynamic environment with stakeholders including States, industry, academia and civil society. Participants also highlighted challenges related to the implications of rapid advances in life sciences and other relevant disciplines. In that context, States parties underlined the potential for misuse of advances in science and technology. Similarly, some expressed concern about the use or threat of use of biological agents and toxins as instruments of war or terror.

Meeting of States Parties to the Biological Weapons Convention

The 2019 Meeting of States Parties took place in Geneva from 3 to 6 December, with Yann Hwang (France) as its Chair, and Adrian Vierita (Romania) and Andreano Erwin (Indonesia) as the two Vice-Chairs. The Meeting was attended by representatives from 122 States parties, four signatory States and two States not party, as well as officials from four United Nations entities, 10 specialized agencies/other international organizations, and 27 NGOs and research institutes.[35]

---

[33] For the list of participants, see BWC/MSP/2019/MX.5/INF.1.
[34] BWC/MSP/2019/MX.5/1.
[35] For the list of participants, see BWC/MSP/2019/INF.1/Rev.1.

The 2019 Meeting of States Parties was mandated to consider the factual reports of the Meetings of Experts, a report[36] from the Chair on universalization activities and the annual report[37] of the Implementation Support Unit. It was also responsible for managing the intersessional programme, including by taking necessary measures with respect to budgetary and financial matters. The Meeting of States Parties also approved office-holders and dates for meetings planned for 2020.

The Meeting opened with a statement[38] from the High Representative for Disarmament Affairs, Izumi Nakamitsu, delivered by Anja Kaspersen, Director of the Geneva Branch of the Office for Disarmament Affairs. After adopting the agenda, programme of work[39] and rules of procedure,[40] the Meeting entered a general debate[41] in which 63 States parties,[42] three signatory States[43] and nine observer organizations[44] participated. At a subsequent informal session, the Meeting heard a joint statement[45] endorsed by 45 NGOs and individuals, as well as individual statements from nine NGOs.

The Meeting reviewed the report[46] prepared by the Chair on the overall financial situation of the Convention. The Implementation Support Unit gave a briefing on the status of contributions and the financial outlook. States parties welcomed the improvement of the financial situation in 2019, following the measures endorsed by the 2018 Meeting of States Parties, including the establishment of the working capital fund. Stressing the need to continue

---

[36] BWC/MSP/2019/3.

[37] BWC/MSP/2019/4.

[38] Statement of the High Representative for Disarmament Affairs to the 2019 Meeting of States Parties to the Convention, Geneva, 3 December 2019.

[39] BWC/MSP/2019/2.

[40] BWC/CONF.VIII/2.

[41] United Nations Office at Geneva, "2019 Meeting of States Parties" to the Biological Weapons Convention (Statements and presentations).

[42] Algeria, Argentina, Armenia, Australia, Austria, Azerbaijan (in its national capacity and, separately, on behalf of the Group of the Non-Aligned Movement and other State parties to the Convention), Belarus, Bosnia and Herzegovina, Brazil, Bulgaria, Canada, Chile, China, Colombia, Costa Rica, Cuba, Ecuador, Fiji, Germany, India, Indonesia, Iran (Islamic Republic of), Iraq (in its national capacity and, separately, on behalf of the Arab Group), Ireland, Italy, Japan, Jordan, Kazakhstan, Kenya, Kuwait, Lebanon, Libya, Malaysia, Mexico, Mongolia, Myanmar, Nepal, Netherlands, Nigeria, Norway, Pakistan, Panama, Peru, Philippines (in its national capacity and, separately, on behalf of the member States of the Association of Southeast Asian Nations), Poland, Qatar, Republic of Korea, Romania, Russian Federation, Saudi Arabia, South Africa, Spain, Sri Lanka, Sudan, Sweden, Switzerland, Thailand, Turkey, Ukraine, United Arab Emirates, United Kingdom, United States and Venezuela (Bolivarian Republic of).

[43] Egypt, Haiti and Somalia.

[44] African Union, Caribbean Community Secretariat, European Union, International Criminal Police Organization (INTERPOL), International Science and Technology Centre, Organization for the Prohibition of Chemical Weapons, United Nations Interregional Crime and Justice Research Institute, World Animal Health Organization and World Health Organization.

[45] United Nations Office at Geneva, joint statement to the Biological Weapons Convention Meetings of States Parties, Geneva, 4 December 2019.

[46] BWC/MSP/2019/5.

monitoring the Convention's financial situation, they requested the Chair-designate of the 2020 Meeting of States Parties to report on the matter in close consultation with the States parties, the Implementation Support Unit, the Office for Disarmament Affairs and the United Nations Office at Geneva.

The Chairs of each of the five Meetings of Experts orally introduced the reports[47] of those Meetings and offered their personal reflections for possible outcomes of the Meeting of States Parties. However, the Meeting of States Parties could not reach consensus on the deliberations the Meetings of Experts, including the possible outcomes.

States parties decided that, in 2020, the Meetings of Experts would be held in Geneva from 25 August to 3 September 2020 and that the Meeting of States Parties would be held in Geneva from 8 to 11 December 2020. They approved the nominations of Aliyar Lebbe Abdul Azeez (Sri Lanka) as Chair of the 2020 Meeting of States Parties, and of Robertas Rosinas (Lithuania) and Peter Beerwerth (Germany) as the two Vice-Chairs. Looking further ahead, the 2019 Meeting of States Parties considered arrangements for the ninth Review Conference, to be held in Geneva in November 2021.

The Meeting of States Parties considered progress towards universalization of the Convention. In that regard, States parties welcomed the increase in the number of ratifications and accessions. They also reaffirmed the particular importance of universalization, urging signatory States to ratify the agreement without delay and non-signatories to accede without delay. The Chair also introduced his report[48] on progress towards the Convention's universalization.

Work of the Implementation Support Unit

At the Meeting of States Parties, the Chief of the Implementation Support Unit[49] presented the Unit's annual report[50] containing a summary of its support for the administration, national implementation and universalization of the Convention; confidence-building measures; maintenance of the database for assistance requests and offers; and the sponsorship programme.

Regarding national implementation, the Unit continued to collect and update details of national points of contact for the Convention. The table below provides additional details about national contact points designated by States parties.

In the area of confidence-building measures, the Unit maintained capabilities for the electronic submission of reports by States parties, compiled and distributed

---

[47] BWC/MSP/2019/MX.1/2, BWC/MSP/2019/MX.2/2, BWC/MSP/2019/MX.3/2, BWC/MSP/2019/MX.4/2 and BWC/MSP/2019/MX.5/2.

[48] BWC/MSP/2019/3.

[49] At the sixth Review Conference of the Convention in 2006, States parties decided to establish the Implementation Support Unit within the Geneva Branch of the Office for Disarmament Affairs to provide, inter alia, support and assistance for administration, national implementation, confidence-building measures and obtaining universality.

[50] BWC/MSP/2019/4.

Biological Weapons Convention sponsorship programme

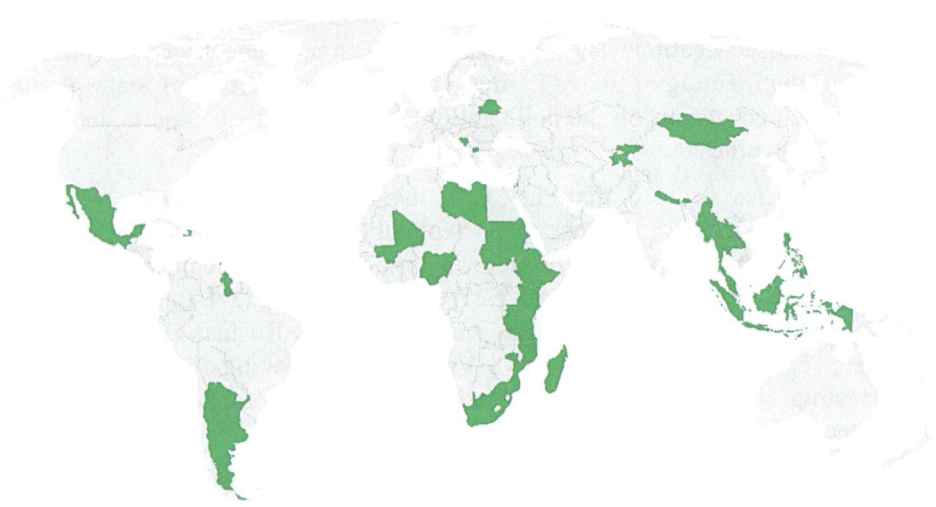

The Biological Weapons Convention was the first multilateral disarmament treaty to ban an entire category of weapons. Throughout the years since it entered into force in 1975, States parties have met at conferences organized every five years to review its operation. Between those review conferences, States parties have pursued various activities and initiatives to strengthen the effectiveness and improve the implementation of the Convention. Over the period from 2018 to 2019, States parties meet for five Meetings of Experts and one Meeting of States Parties.

In 2011, States that were party to the Convention established a sponsorship programme that they renewed at the Eighth Review Conference in 2016. Priority for sponsorship is given to those developing States Parties which have previously not participated in the meetings, or which have been unable to regularly send experts. Sponsorship may also be provided, depending on the availability of resources, to enhance the participation of States not party to the Convention, in order to promote its universalization. The Programme is funded through voluntary contributions from States parties in a position to make them.

Sponsorship programme participants in 2019: Argentina, Belarus, Bhutan, Bosnia and Herzegovina, Ethiopia, Guyana, Haiti, Indonesia, Kenya, Kyrgyzstan, Lao People's Democratic Republic, Libya, Madagascar, Malaysia, Maldives, Mali, Mexico, Mongolia, Mozambique, Myanmar, Nepal, Nigeria, North Macedonia, Philippines, South Africa, State of Palestine, Sudan, Tajikistan, Thailand, Trinidad and Tobago, and United Republic of Tanzania.

The boundaries and names shown and the designations used on this map do not imply official endorsement or acceptance by the United Nations. Final boundary between the Republic of Sudan and the Republic of South Sudan has not yet been determined.

Map source: United Nations Geospatial Information Section.

submissions, provided routine administrative assistance and advice, took part in or organized workshops on promoting confidence-building measures, and wrote to States parties reminding them of the deadline for submission of their reports. The table below shows the increase in the number of submissions relating to confidence-building measures over time.

The Implementation Support Unit continued to maintain and administer the Assistance and Cooperation Database and to facilitate contacts between States parties offering or requesting assistance.

The Unit also continued to administer the Convention's sponsorship programme which supports the participation of developing States parties in meetings of the Convention. In 2019, voluntary contributions to the sponsorship programme were received from one State party and a group of States parties.[51] Other States parties supported the sponsorship programme through bilateral arrangements. As a result, experts from 18 developing States parties and two signatory States were sponsored to attend the Meetings of Experts, and experts from 17 States parties and one signatory State were sponsored to attend the Meeting of States Parties.

During the year, several States parties provided voluntary contributions through the Office for Disarmament Affairs for specific activities in support of the implementation of the Convention:

- Canada provided a voluntary contribution of $665,000 to the Office for the second phase of a project on strengthening global mechanisms and capacities for responding to deliberate use of biological agents.

- France provided a voluntary contribution of €150,000 to the Office to organize two tabletop exercises on article VI.

- Japan provided two voluntary contributions to the Office. The first, totalling $80,000, for a training workshop for national contact points from South-East Asia on domestic implementation aspects of the Convention; the second, totalling $819,250 for improving the preparedness of the United Nations Secretariat and relevant international organizations to ensure a coordinated international response to the potential use of biological or chemical weapons.

The European Union continued to support the Convention through European Union Council decision 2019/97, by which it contributed €3,482,594 to the Office for Disarmament Affairs over three years to carry out Convention-related activities. In 2019, those funds enabled the Office to conduct a Universalization Workshop for the Pacific, in partnership with the Inter-Parliamentary Union and the Parliament of New Zealand; organize a workshop for young scientists from the Global South to discuss biosecurity diplomacy; and, in the margins of the 2019 Meeting of States Parties, bring together the lead organizers and researchers from regional science and technology workshops conducted in 2017 and 2018 to discuss the implications of developments in science and technology for the Convention.

---

[51] Canada and the European Union.

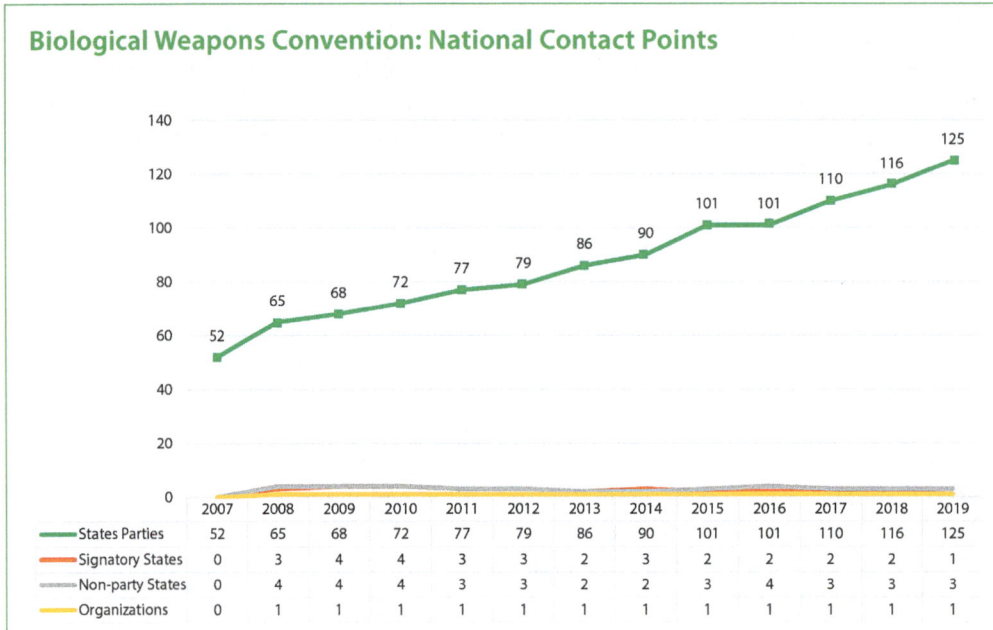

Biological Weapons Convention: National Contact Points

	2007	2008	2009	2010	2011	2012	2013	2014	2015	2016	2017	2018	2019
States Parties	52	65	68	72	77	79	86	90	101	101	110	116	125
Signatory States	0	3	4	4	3	3	2	3	2	2	2	2	1
Non-party States	0	4	4	4	3	3	2	2	3	4	3	3	3
Organizations	0	1	1	1	1	1	1	1	1	1	1	1	1

In 2006, States parties to the Biological Weapons Convention agreed to designate national contact points to coordinate national implementation of the Convention; communicate with other States parties and international organizations; and carry out other Convention-related activities. The number of States parties that have designated a national contact point has more than doubled since that time.

Also in 2019, the Office for Disarmament Affairs announced the selection of the beneficiary States that would receive capacity-development assistance to strengthen their national implementation of the Convention under the Extended Assistance Programmes set out in the decision, and to enhance their preparedness, prevention and response capacities in the event of a deliberate biological attack, through the National Preparedness Programmes.[52]

Secretary-General's Mechanism for Investigation of Alleged Use of Chemical and Biological Weapons

In 2019, the Office for Disarmament Affairs continued to carry out activities to maintain the Secretary-General's Mechanism for Investigation of Alleged Use of Chemical and Biological Weapons,[53] including training of experts on the

---

[52] The States selected under the Extended Assistance Programmes were Botswana, Jamaica, Papua New Guinea, State of Palestine and Viet Nam. The selected beneficiaries of the National Preparedness Programmes were Fiji, Nigeria, Sri Lanka and Sudan.

[53] By General Assembly resolution 42/37 of 30 November 1987, which the Security Council later reaffirmed in its resolution 620 (1988), the Secretary-General was requested to investigate,

A growing roster of experts

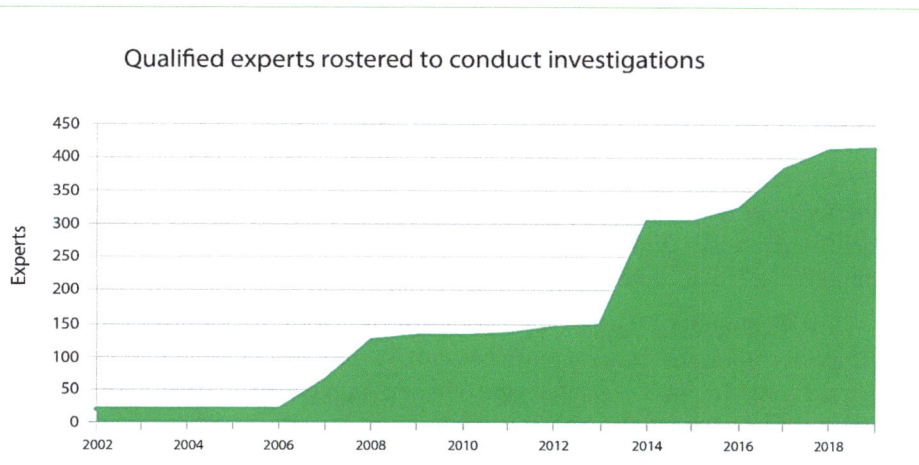

Qualified experts rostered to conduct investigations

The Secretary-General of the United Nations is mandated to carry out investigations when Member States bring to his attention the possible use of chemical or biological weapons. The United Nations relies on Governments to designate technical experts to deploy to the field on short notice to support such investigations. A group of experts was activated in 2013 to look into reports of chemical weapons use in the Syrian Arab Republic.

In the following years, the Office for Disarmament Affairs has built a growing roster of experts.

Qualified experts trained to conduct investigations (cumulative)

The Office for Disarmament Affairs facilitates the design and delivery of specialized training courses to ensure that investigators can operate efficiently as a team under challenging field conditions. Since 2009, financial and technical support from Member States has enabled the Office to maintain a growing roster of qualified experts trained in areas critical to conducting efficient field investigations into an alleged use of chemical and biological weapons.

The number of qualified experts who have taken all available training courses has grown along with the overall roster.

Mechanism's roster. As at 31 December, the roster maintained by the Office for Disarmament Affairs comprised 520 qualified experts, 39 expert consultants and 66 laboratories, nominated by Member States on a voluntary basis, whose services could be made available on short notice.

In 2019, the Office continued working with Member States to design and deliver training for rostered experts, giving particular focus to potential allegations of biological-weapon use.[54] That training incorporated lessons learned from the experience in the Syrian Arab Republic in 2013,[55] when the Mechanism was most recently activated, and it drew on a new training approach emphasizing the core competencies of an investigative team.[56]

In September, Germany provided Hazardous Environment Awareness training for qualified experts on the roster. Twenty experts learned: (a) how to deal effectively with risk-associated and challenging situations during deployment in hostile environments; and (b) how to work as a team member of an international field operation, irrespective of national or professional backgrounds. In October, Sweden organized a leadership training course for experts at the European CBRNE[57] Center at Umeå University. The course, which was the second of its kind offered in Sweden,[58] aimed at providing potential future heads of mission with a common basis for leadership skills required in the context of a Mechanism investigation, as well as a better understanding of different expert roles under the Mechanism.

---

upon request by any Member State, the possible use of chemical, biological and toxin weapons (see C, para. 4). For further information, see Office for Disarmament Affairs, "Secretary-General's Mechanism for Investigation of Alleged Use of Chemical and Biological Weapons".

[54] Following the entry into force of the Chemical Weapons Convention and the establishment in 1997 of the OPCW as its implementing body, and in the absence of an equivalent organization for the implementation of the Biological Weapons Convention, training activities relating to the Mechanism focused on investigating the alleged use of biological weapons. However, the Mechanism also continued to play a limited role with regard to chemical weapons, notwithstanding the implementation of the Chemical Weapons Convention. If there is an allegation of use of a chemical weapon in a State that is not party to the Convention, as was the case in 2013 in the Syrian Arab Republic, or in a territory not controlled by a State party, the Secretary-General may cooperate with OPCW in an investigation through the modalities set out in the 2012 Supplementary Arrangement to the 2001 Relationship Agreement between the United Nations and OPCW (A/55/988).

[55] On 19 March 2013, the Syrian Arab Republic requested the Secretary-General to investigate the alleged use of chemical weapons on its territory. Accordingly, the United Nations Mission to Investigate Allegations of the Use of Chemical Weapons in the Syrian Arab Republic was established on 21 March 2013 by the Secretary-General, based on the authority vested in him by the General Assembly and the Security Council. The Mission presented a final report in December 2013 (A/68/663-S/2013/735).

[56] That approach was in line with a commitment, contained in the Secretary-General's Agenda for Disarmament, for the Office for Disarmament Affairs to work to establish a minimal but effective operational capacity to conduct effective, credible and independent investigations into an alleged use of biological weapons (*Securing Our Common Future: An Agenda for Disarmament*, p. 26).

[57] CBRNE: Chemical, biological, radiological, nuclear and explosive.

[58] The first course took place from 28 September to 3 October 2016 in Umeå, Sweden.

Export controls

Australia Group

The 42 participating countries[59] of the Australia Group and the European Union met in Paris from 3 to 7 June for the Group's thirty-fourth plenary meeting.[60]

Participants reaffirmed their commitment to strengthening chemical and biological weapons-related counter-proliferation efforts and agreed, inter alia: (a) to reinforce efforts to stay ahead of potential proliferators by increasing awareness of emerging technologies and the potential exploitation of scientific developments; and (b) to share approaches to challenges posed by intangible technology transfers, proliferation financing, procurement, trans-shipment and broader proliferation networks, including through enhanced engagement with industry and academia.

At the invitation of the secretariat of the Group, several guest speakers from academia and research institutions addressed the plenary on topics such as cloud laboratories, counter-proliferation financing and additive manufacturing.

With a view to ensuring accountability for the use of chemical weapons and deterring such use by others, participants reaffirmed their support for the Director-General, the Technical Secretariat and the Investigation and Identification Team of the Organisation for the Prohibition of Chemical Weapons (OPCW).

In support of the Group's ongoing efforts to enhance engagement with non-members, the participants reinforced the importance of outreach to industry and academia. Recalling a relevant dialogue with Middle Eastern countries in Malta in March, the Group agreed to greater follow-up and to encourage all States, inter alia, to adopt the Group's export controls as the model for international best practice.

The member countries of the Group concluded that there would be value in holding an intersessional meeting before its next plenary meeting, in particular to discuss both the effective implementation of catch-all controls and the possible listing of precursors to the chemical agent Novichok. The participants accepted an offer by Slovakia to host an intersessional meeting in early 2020, as well as an offer by France to host the next plenary in Paris from 15 to 19 June 2020.

---

[59] Argentina, Australia, Austria, Belgium, Bulgaria, Canada, Croatia, Cyprus, Czechia, Denmark, Estonia, Finland, France, Germany, Greece, Hungary, Ireland, Iceland, India, Italy, Japan, Latvia, Lithuania, Luxembourg, Malta, Mexico, Netherlands, New Zealand, Norway, Poland, Portugal, Republic of Korea, Romania, Slovakia, Slovenia, Spain, Sweden, Switzerland, Turkey, Ukraine, United Kingdom and United States.

[60] See Australia Group, "Statement by the Chair of the 2019 Australia Group Plenary", 15 July 2019.

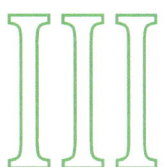

chapter

III Conventional weapons

Explosive remnants of war found close to the United Nations Mission in South Sudan compound in Juba for destruction by the United Nations Mine Action Service, 20 March 2019.

UN Photo/Nektarios Markogiannis

Conventional weapons

Thousands of civilian lives continue to be lost because of illicit small arms and the use in urban areas of explosive weapons designed for open battlefields. New weapon technologies are intensifying risks in ways we do not yet understand and cannot even imagine. We need a new vision for arms control in the complex international security environment of today.

ANTÓNIO GUTERRES, SECRETARY-GENERAL OF THE UNITED NATIONS[1]

Developments and trends, 2019

THE CHALLENGES POSED BY CONVENTIONAL ARMS—their illicit trade, their accumulation and their proliferation—persisted through 2019. Of equal significance were the immediate, direct impacts of addressing, or failing to address, those challenges. In the context of conventional arms, the international community's efforts to accomplish the Secretary-General's vision of "disarmament that saves lives" resulted in varying levels of progress, setbacks and stasis, as in previous years.

Global sales of arms and military services increased again in 2019, reaching a level almost 50 per cent higher than in 2002,[2] and an independent analysis found that arms flows to the Middle East had almost doubled over the previous five years.[3] While the global authorized small arms trade recorded its highest sales since 2001, the transparency of States in that area was in decline.[4]

Meanwhile, States parties to the Arms Trade Treaty focused on gender and gender-based violence as a priority theme for their sixth Conference. They also addressed continuing concerns about the timely submission of reports and unpaid contributions, as well as the need for the Treaty's universalization.

In the context of ammunition management, States continued to pay increased attention to the issue of conventional ammunition as a stand-alone matter of concern. During the year, the United Nations Institute for Disarmament

---

[1] Remarks to the Conference on Disarmament, Geneva, 25 February 2019.
[2] Stockholm International Peace Research Institute, "Global arms industry rankings: Sales up 4.6 per cent worldwide and US companies dominate the Top 5", 9 December 2019.
[3] Stockholm International Peace Research Institute, "Global arms trade: USA increases dominance; arms flows to the Middle East surge, says SIPRI", 11 March 2019.
[4] Michael Picard, Paul Holtom and Fiona Mangan, *Trade Update 2019: Transfers, Transparency, and South-east Asia Spotlight* (Geneva, Small Arms Survey, 2019).

Research (UNIDIR) organized informal consultations, regional outreach activities and seminars, which were convened to inform and facilitate the work of a new group of governmental experts on "problems arising from the accumulation of conventional ammunition stockpiles in surplus". The group was scheduled to begin work in January 2020. Building on informal consultations convened in 2018 in the framework of General Assembly resolution 72/55 of 4 December 2017,[5] States actively engaged in three informal consultations organized by Germany, the resolution's main sponsor. They were held in February, May and September 2019 at the United Nations Headquarters in New York.

In another development on the issue of ammunition, the United Nations Office for Disarmament Affairs and the Geneva International Centre for Humanitarian Demining established the Ammunition Management Advisory Team to provide technical assistance to interested States in accordance with the International Ammunition Technical Guidelines, including under the quick-response mechanism of the United Nations Safer*Guard Programme. The Advisory Team was established to enhance State and regional action on safe and secure management of ammunition and to facilitate effective and sustainable international cooperation and assistance.

The Security Council, for its part, remained seized of the issue of small arms and light weapons, including the role of weapons and ammunition management in support of peace operations. In December, the Secretary-General issued his sixth biennial thematic report[6] on small arms and light weapons to the Council, providing an overview of relevant trends and developments in that area over the previous two years. In that regard, particular emphasis was placed on the prioritization of "disarmament that saves lives", including a call for enhanced efforts on small arms and light weapons at the national level. The Secretary-General concluded that the destabilizing accumulation, illicit transfer and misuse of small arms and light weapons continued to initiate, sustain and exacerbate armed conflict and pervasive crime.

Reporting by Member States to the United Nations Register of Conventional Arms and in the United Nations Report on Military Expenditures trended downwards from the previous year, underscoring a decade of marked decline. Encouragingly, however, the proportion of States reporting transfers of small arms and light weapons as part of their reporting to the Register held generally steady, at 73 per cent. A recommendation on small arms and light weapons in that context

---

[5] By resolution 72/55, the General Assembly encouraged States to participate in open, informal consultations within the framework of the respective resolution, focusing on matters of conventional ammunition management within the United Nations system and beyond, and with a view to identifying urgent issues pertaining to the accumulation of conventional ammunition stockpiles in surplus on which progress could be made and that may constitute a basis for convening a group of governmental experts.

[6] S/2019/1011.

was, in fact, one of the key outcomes of the 2019 Group of Governmental Experts on the Register (for more information on the Group, see p. 105).

The increasing attention to the gender dimension of conventional arms issues represented a continuing and welcome trend in 2019. That was reflected in, for example, the strong gender-relevant language and discussions during the fifth Conference of States Parties to the Arms Trade Treaty, as well as in the framework of the Programme of Action to Prevent, Combat and Eradicate the Illicit Trade in Small Arms and Light Weapons. The focus has now shifted to supporting States in their implementation efforts of those international commitments. (For more information on gender and disarmament, see chapter VI.)

In addition, the Office for Disarmament Affairs partnered with the United Nations Development Programme (UNDP) to launch the Saving Lives Entity, a facility designed to support Member States in tackling illicit small arms and light weapons as part of a comprehensive approach to sustainable security and development. The aim was not only to address specific problems, but also to change cultural attitudes and perceptions regarding small arms, including resistance to women's involvement in decision-making and conflation of masculinity with gun ownership.[7] As at the end of 2019, work was under way to identify initial pilot activities to be carried out under the facility.

The continued development of the Modular Small-arms-control Implementation Compendium included planning for new modules and the translation of existing modules. The growing availability of modules in languages other than English continued to be seen as critical to the overall function of the Compendium by providing increased access to the best expert advice on small arms in succinct operational terminology.

Arms Trade Treaty

The Arms Trade Treaty, which was created to establish standards and restrictions on the international trade in conventional arms, continued to increase its membership. The fifth Conference of States Parties to the Treaty agreed upon a final report, including a series of decisions and recommendations.

In 2019, five States[8] expressed consent to be bound by the Arms Trade Treaty by depositing their instruments of ratification with the Secretary-General in his capacity as treaty depositary. Accordingly, the total number of States parties increased to 105, with an additional 33 States that had signed but not yet acceded to the Treaty.

---

[7] The Secretary-General committed to channelling at least 30 per cent of Saving Lives Entity funds to gender-related activities, while identifying gender equality as a principal programme objective.

[8] Palau (8 April), Lebanon (9 May), Botswana (7 June), Canada (19 June) and Maldives (27 September).

The Treaty's long-standing imbalance in terms of regional participation continued, albeit with slight improvements. As at the end of 2019, 9 of 54 States from the Asia-Pacific Group had joined the Treaty (an increase of 3 from the previous year); 26 of 31 States from the Western European and Others Group (an increase of 1 from 2018); 4 of 54 States from the African Group (also an increase of 1); and 18 of 23 States from the Eastern European Group.

Fifth Conference of States Parties

The fifth Conference of States Parties took place in Geneva from 26 to 30 August, presided over by Jānis Kārkliņš (Latvia). The Conference was attended by 86 States parties; 2 States that had ratified the Treaty but for which it had not yet entered into force; 15 States signatories; and 3 observer States, bringing the total number of participating States to 106.[9] In addition, 8 international and regional organizations[10] and 39 civil society organizations participated as observers.[11] As in 2018, the Conference itself was preceded by two informal preparatory meetings, one held in January and February and the other in April, as well as meetings of three working groups that the third Conference of States Parties had established in 2017.

The High Representative for Disarmament Affairs, Izumi Nakamitsu, opened the Conference with a statement[12] highlighting the decision taken to incorporate the theme of gender into the work of the Conference, including through a thematic discussion and panel on gender and gender-based violence.[13] Building on extensive discussion of that topic during the two informal preparatory meetings, participants in the thematic discussion and other parts of the Conference addressed the issue of gender balance in representation, the wider matter of the gendered impact of armed violence and conflict, and gender-based violence and risk assessment under articles 6 and 7 of the Arms Trade Treaty. As a result, in its final report,[14] the Conference welcomed the thematic discussion on gender and gender-based violence as the priority theme for the Conference and explored how that subject could be articulated in the context of the Treaty. Among its decisions and recommendations in that regard, the Conference stated the following:

---

[9] The two States that had ratified the Treaty but for which it had not yet entered into force were Botswana and Canada. Observer States were China, Fiji and Tonga.

[10] European Union, International Committee of the Red Cross (ICRC), International Criminal Police Organization (INTERPOL), Regional Centre on Small Arms, United Nations Institute for Disarmament Research (UNIDIR), United Nations Office for Disarmament Affairs, United Nations Office on Drugs and Crime (UNODC) and the Wassenaar Arrangement.

[11] ATT/CSP5/2019/SEC/535/Conf.PartList.

[12] The High Representative for Disarmament Affairs gave the keynote address at the fifth Conference of States Parties to the Arms Trade Treaty, Geneva, 26 August 2019.

[13] Christine Hoebes (Namibia); Gilles Carbonnier (ICRC); Andris Pelšsi; Fiorella Salazar Rojas; Nounou Booto Meeti (Centre for Peace and Development, Security and Armed Violence Prevention) also addressed the Conference during the opening session.

[14] ATT/CSP5/2019/SEC/536/Conf.FinRep.Rev1.

- States parties, signatory and observer States attending Arms Trade Treaty working groups, preparatory meetings and the Conference itself should strive for gender balance in their delegations;

- Gender-balanced panels should be encouraged in plenary sessions, side events and other forums. Event organizers should strive to achieve gender-balanced panels at an early stage in their planning;

- All working group Chairs and facilitators are encouraged to consider gender aspects in their sessions;

- States parties are encouraged to collect gender-disaggregated data within their national crime and health statistics, including gender-disaggregated data on victims of armed violence and conflict, and make that data publicly available.

In the report, the Conference also directed the Working Group on Effective Treaty Implementation to, inter alia:

- Encourage discussion on States' practices in interpreting the language and standards entailed in article 7 (4), including "serious", "facilitate" and "overriding" risk, to assist States parties in considering issues regarding gender-based violence in implementing the Treaty;

- Consider how to encourage States parties to provide information on their national practices in risk assessment with regard to gender-based violence to facilitate learning between States parties.

In addition, the Conference undertook a thorough review of the Treaty's general implementation, as well as transparency and reporting; efforts to promote its universalization; and financial matters. In particular, the Conference noted the importance of the Voluntary Trust Fund, established in 2016 pursuant to article 16 (3) of the Treaty as a mechanism to support States in implementing their obligations under the agreement. At the time of the Conference, the Voluntary Trust Fund had funded 44 implementation projects in different regions. The Conference reiterated the importance of the Trust Fund as a viable facility for assisting States in the practical implementation of the Arms Trade Treaty.

In addition to the decisions and recommendations related to gender and gender-based violence, the Conference adopted several other decisions and recommendations, including the following:

- Calling on all relevant stakeholders to advocate for reporting in line with the outreach strategy on reporting that was adopted at the Conference;

- Supporting the development of a system of voluntary practical bilateral and regional assistance with reporting (peer-to-peer);

- Endorsing the proposed amendments to voluntary guidance in the living document "Reporting Authorized or Actual Exports and Imports of

Global illicit arms seizures

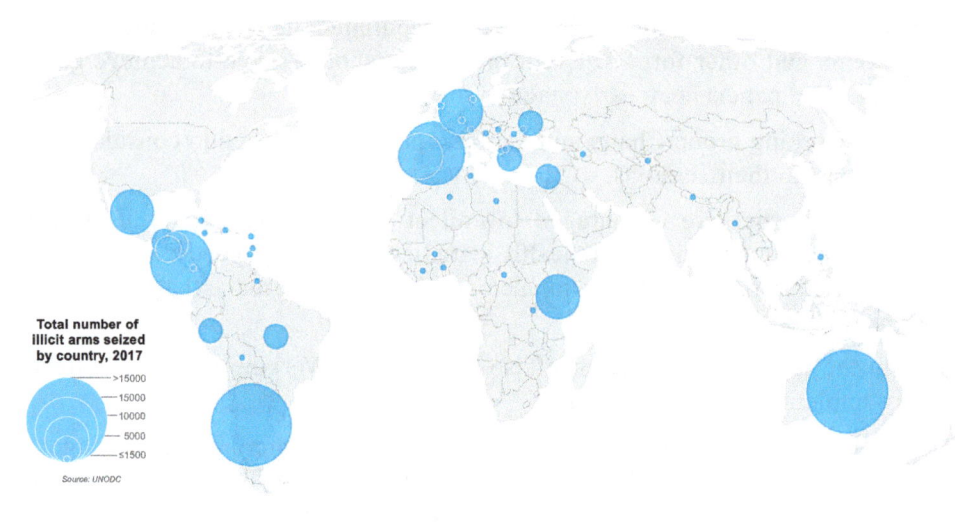

Total number of
illicit arms seized
by country, 2017

>15000
15000
10000
5000
≤1500

Source: UNODC

The negative correlation between areas afflicted by armed conflict, violence, and organized crime and illicit weapon seizures can be attributed to limited law enforcement capacities in those regions.

National rates of illicit arms seizure reflect law enforcement capacity, not the number of illicit arms in a given region. The figures provided are based on 2017 data.

The boundaries and names shown and the designations used on this map do not imply official endorsement or acceptance by the United Nations. Final boundary between the Republic of Sudan and the Republic of South Sudan has not yet been determined.

Map source: United Nations Geospatial Information Section.
Data source: UNODC, Small Arms Survey and United Nations Operations and Crisis (Centre Research and Liaison Unit).

Global firearms holdings

There are more than **1 billion firearms** in circulation in the world, the vast majority of which are in civilian hands. Civilian ownership is the fastest-growing category.*

Total firearms holdings by sector

Civilians (857 M)
Military (133 M)
Law enforcement (22.7 M)

Largest firearms holdings by region and sector

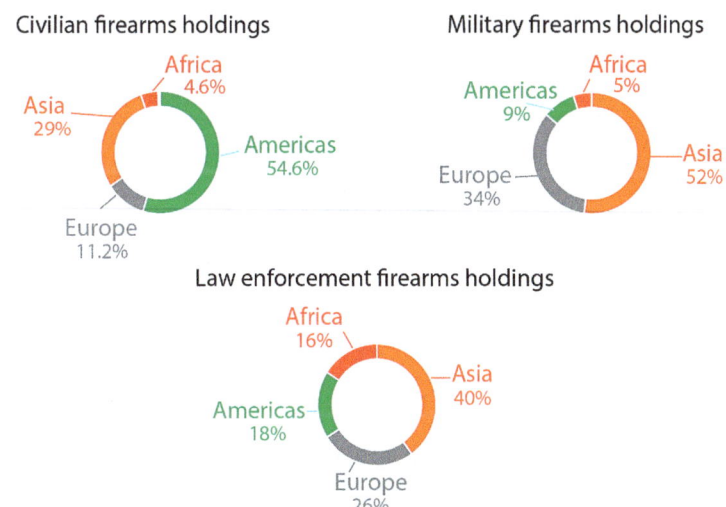

Civilian firearms holdings

Africa 4.6%
Asia 29%
Americas 54.6%
Europe 11.2%

Military firearms holdings

Africa 5%
Americas 9%
Asia 52%
Europe 34%

Law enforcement firearms holdings

Africa 16%
Asia 40%
Americas 18%
Europe 26%

Small arms and light weapons remain drivers of armed conflict and violence.

* The terms "firearms" and "small arms" are used interchangeably in this graphic. The figures provided are based on 2017 data. Uncertainty about any firearms data requires systematic estimation that relies on a broad spectrum of sources and makes approximation unavoidable.

Data source: Small Arms Survey.
Graphic courtesy of United Nations Operations and Crisis Centre (Research and Liaison Unit).

Death by firearms

Firearms were used to kill **more than 238,000 people** in 2017.*

Total homicides worldwide (2017)

97,183 victims	22%
104,341 victims	24%
238,804 victims	54%

> Shooting has long been the most common cause of death in homicide cases worldwide. !

Breakdown of homicides by mechanism and region (2017)

■ Africa   ■ Americas   ■ Asia   ■ Europe

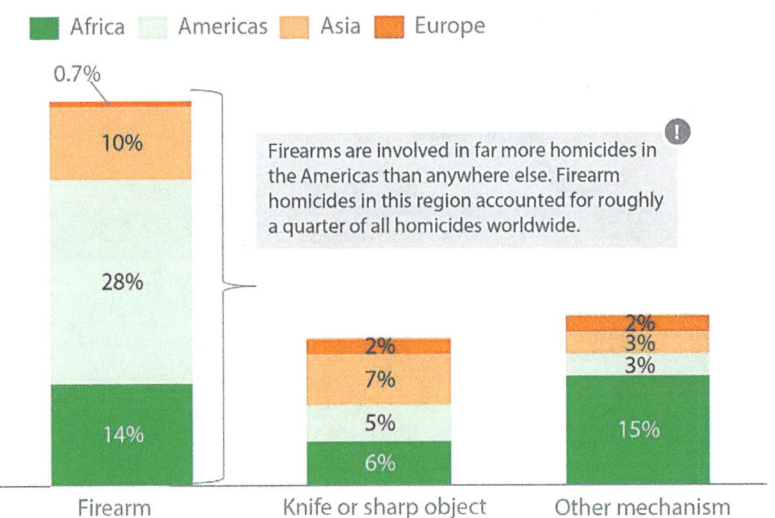

Firearm
- 0.7%
- 10%
- 28%
- 14%

> Firearms are involved in far more homicides in the Americas than anywhere else. Firearm homicides in this region accounted for roughly a quarter of all homicides worldwide. !

Knife or sharp object
- 2%
- 7%
- 5%
- 6%

Other mechanism
- 2%
- 3%
- 3%
- 15%

Firearms were involved in more than half of all homicides worldwide.

* The terms "firearms" and "small arms" are synonymous for the purposes of this graphic. Figures are from 2017.

Data source: UNODC, Global Study on Homicide 2019, booklet 3, pp. 77–88.
Graphic courtesy of United Nations Operations and Crisis Centre (Research and Liaison Unit).

Conventional Arms: Questions and Answers" to reflect the introduction of the online reporting tool;

- Welcoming the first informal meeting to discuss concrete cases of detected or suspected diversion that States parties and signatories are dealing or had dealt with as a solid basis for further exchanges, and taking note of the open session for all stakeholders;

- Adopting the Arms Trade Treaty Universalization Toolkit (annex A of the Co-Chairs' report[15]) and the Welcome Pack for New States Parties to the Arms Trade Treaty (annex B of the Co-Chairs' report) as living documents of a voluntary nature to be reviewed and updated regularly by the Working Group, as appropriate, and encouraging Treaty stakeholders to utilize the materials in their bilateral, multilateral and regional meetings and workshops, when appropriate;

- Requesting the Arms Trade Treaty Secretariat to continue to analyse the trends and pace of universalization of the Treaty and report annually to the Conference of States Parties;

- Expressing deep concern about the unpaid contributions of States and calling on States that had not done so to address their financial obligations in a prompt and timely manner;[16]

- Adopting the budget for the sixth Conference of States Parties;

- Electing, by acclamation, Kazakhstan, Latvia, Nigeria and Switzerland as the four Vice-Presidents for the sixth Conference of States Parties.

The Conference decided to hold the sixth Conference of States Parties—its next formal annual meeting—in Geneva from 17 to 21 August 2020. It elected, by acclamation, Carlos Foradori (Argentina) as the President of that meeting.

Small arms and light weapons

Programme of Action on Small Arms and Light Weapons

The Programme of Action to Prevent, Combat and Eradicate the Illicit Trade in Small Arms and Light Weapons in All Its Aspects and the International Tracing Instrument[17] continued to serve as the global framework for coordinated efforts to combat the illicit trade in small arms and light weapons.

---

[15] ATT/CSP5.WGTU/2019/CHAIR/532/Conf.Rep.

[16] The Conference also decided that no State shall be prejudiced by Financial Rule 8.1.d in applying for support from the Arms Trade Treaty Voluntary Trust Fund or the Arms Trade Treaty Sponsorship Programme until the sixth Conference of States Parties, when the matter will be considered (see ATT/CSP5/2019/SEC/536/Conf.FinRep.Rev1, para. 36).

[17] For more information, see Office for Disarmament Affairs, "Programme of Action on small arms and its International Tracing Instrument".

In 2019, Member States appointed Lazarus Ombai Amayo (Kenya) as Chair-designate of the seventh Biennial Meeting of States to Consider the Implementation of the Programme of Action, to be held from 15 to 19 June 2020. Pursuant to the outcome document[18] of the third Review Conference, held in 2018, as well as General Assembly resolution 74/60 adopted on 12 December 2019, the Meeting would consider: (a) the national, regional and global implementation of the Programme of Action; and (b) key challenges and opportunities relating to preventing and combating the diversion and the illicit international transfer of small arms and light weapons to unauthorized recipients.[19]

In preparation for the Meeting, States discussed in 2019 options to strengthen the implementation of the Programme of Action. Based on those exchanges and on an informal food-for-thought paper,[20] the Secretary-General issued an annual report[21] on the illicit trade in small arms and light weapons in all its aspects that included: (a) specific recommendations on a strengthened small arms process; and (b) possible elements for a supplementary annex to the International Tracing Instrument aimed at addressing recent developments in the manufacturing, technology and design of small arms and light weapons. Issues in those two areas were expected to be central to both the preparations for the seventh Biennial Meeting of States and the deliberations during the Meeting itself.

International cooperation and assistance were also expected to be addressed at the Meeting, as explained in the table on p. 83.

Also in the context of the Programme of Action,[22] the Office for Disarmament Affairs began implementing in 2019 a three-year project funded by the European Union[23] in support of gender-mainstreamed policies, programmes and actions in the fight against small arms trafficking and misuse, in line with the women, peace and security agenda. Through the project, the Office would assist States in mainstreaming gender considerations into their implementation efforts by providing training workshops on gender and small arms control for national authorities in 18 countries; developing training materials for the wider community

---

[18] A/CONF.192/2018/RC/3.

[19] The Meeting would also set the agenda for the eighth Biennial Meeting of States, to be held in 2022.

[20] Secretariat of the Arms Trade Treaty, "Advancing implementation of the Programme of Action on the illicit trade on small arms and light weapons", 23 October 2018.

[21] A/74/187.

[22] Member States agreed at the sixth Biennial Meeting of States in 2016 and the third Review Conference in 2018 to increase their understanding of the gender-specific impacts of the illicit trade in small arms and light weapons; to promote the meaningful participation and representation of women in related policymaking, planning and implementation processes; to collect sex-disaggregated data; and to ensure coordination between relevant national authorities involved in implementation and entities working on gender equality and women's affairs, including women's civil society organizations. See A/CONF.192/BMS/2016/2 and A/CONF.192/2018/RC/3.

[23] European Union, Council Decision (CFSP) 2018/2011 of 17 December 2018, *Official Journal of the European Union*, L 322 (18 December 2018), pp. 38–50.

Requests for small arms-related assistance

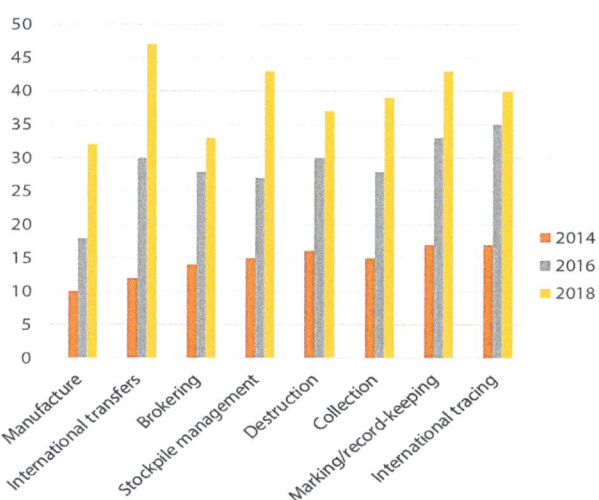

In 2001, States adopted by consensus the Programme of Action to tackle the scourge of illicit flows of small arms and light weapons. Four years later, the adoption of the International Tracing Instrument further strengthened the framework.

To implement both instruments fully and effectively, it is critical to enhance international cooperation and assistance. To that end, Governments of countries particularly affected by a challenging security situation have been sharing information on their need for assistance for small arms control through biennial national reports.*

A growing number of States are submitting those national reports as the result of remarkable improvements in how the contents are being put to work. With growing opportunities to match needs with available resources and improving capabilities to measure implementation progress, States are reaffirming their commitment to the Programme of Action process.

The number of requests for assistance has jumped since 2014, as growing concern about weapons diversion to black markets and unauthorized recipients has prompted a push for improved government control over international transfers, stockpile management, and marking and record-keeping. Implementation of the Arms Trade Treaty has scaled up in parallel, encouraging Governments to seek assistance on international arms transfers through synergies with the Programme of Action and the International Tracing Instrument. Meanwhile, requests related to weapons collection have increased amid efforts to gather data in support of target 16.4 of the 2030 Agenda for Sustainable Development.

* In reports on country-level implementation of the Programme of Action, national small arms authorities can make requests for relevant financial and technical assistance. Such requests are addressed to other Governments, intergovernmental and regional organizations, and international non-governmental organizations.

Arms-related provisions in peace operations mandated by the Security Council

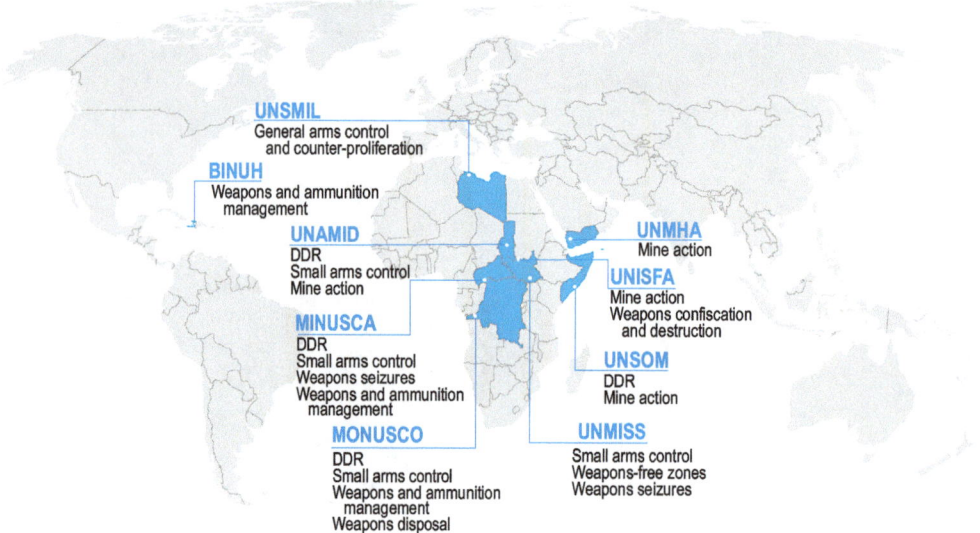

UNSMIL
General arms control
and counter-proliferation

BINUH
Weapons and ammunition
management

UNAMID
DDR
Small arms control
Mine action

UNMHA
Mine action

UNISFA
Mine action
Weapons confiscation
and destruction

MINUSCA
DDR
Small arms control
Weapons seizures
Weapons and ammunition
management

UNSOM
DDR
Mine action

MONUSCO
DDR
Small arms control
Weapons and ammunition
management
Weapons disposal

UNMISS
Small arms control
Weapons-free zones
Weapons seizures

The United Nations deploys peacekeeping and special political missions in support of a particular country or region, as mandated by the Security Council or General Assembly. Currently, there are more than a dozen United Nations peacekeeping operations that are helping States navigate the pathway to peace, while over 20 special political missions are engaging in conflict prevention, peacemaking and post-conflict peacebuilding.

An increasingly common feature of those missions is the inclusion of conventional weapons-related provisions in their mandates.

Whether through disarmament, demobilization and reintegration (DDR) technical support, mine action and clearance activities, weapons and ammunition management, or small arms and light weapons control, the United Nations has been increasingly asked to support national authorities in addressing various issues related to conventional weapons, including their illicit flow and circulation.

Weapons and ammunition management has become an especially critical component of United Nations peacekeeping operations. In settings where weaponry is not properly secured, there is greater potential for outbreaks of renewed conflict and endemic crime.

In mandating peacekeeping and special political missions, States have recognized the colossal negative consequences of the illicit circulation and misuse of conventional weapons. United Nations missions have been requested to support national authorities in a range of areas, from management and storage of weapons to destruction and disposal to identification and clearance of mines.

The boundaries and names shown and the designations used on this map do not imply official endorsement or acceptance by the United Nations. Final boundary between the Republic of Sudan and the Republic of South Sudan has not yet been determined.

Mandates as of 26 March 2020.

Abbreviations: BINUH=United Nations Integrated Office in Haiti; MINUSCA=United Nations Multidimensional Integrated Stabilization Mission in the Central African Republic; MONUSCO=United Nations Organization Stabilization Mission in the Democratic Republic of the Congo; UNAMID=African Union-United Nations Hybrid Operation in Darfur; UNISFA=United Nations Interim Security Force for Abyei; UNMHA=United Nations Mission to Support the Hudaydah Agreement; UNSMIL=United Nations Support Mission in Libya; UNMISS=United Nations Mission in South Sudan; and UNSOM=United Nations Assistance Mission in Somalia.

Map source: United Nations Geospatial Information Section.
Data source: United Nations Operations and Crisis Centre (Research and Liaison Unit).

of practice; and aiming to strengthen the linkages between small arms control and the women, peace and security agenda.

Security Council

In recent years, the Security Council has more frequently included conventional weapons-related provisions in mandates for peacekeeping and special political missions.

Throughout 2019, the Security Council remained seized of the issue of small arms and light weapons in the context of country-specific and thematic agenda items. Building on a trend of recent years, weapons and ammunition management featured prominently in peace operation contexts, specifically in the Central African Republic, the Democratic Republic of the Congo, Haiti and Mali. In June, the Security Council adopted an explicit mandate on a weapons and ammunition management advisory capacity for the United Nations Integrated Office in Haiti (BINUH).[24] Moreover, the Council continued to express serious concern over challenges arising from the illicit transfer, destabilizing accumulation and misuse of small arms and light weapons in conflict-affected settings such as the Abyei Area,[25] the Democratic Republic of the Congo,[26] Somalia,[27] South Sudan[28] and Yemen.[29]

Report of the Secretary-General

In December, the Secretary-General published his sixth report to the Security Council on small arms and light weapons,[30] concluding that the destabilizing accumulation, illicit transfer and misuse of small arms and light weapons continued to initiate, sustain and exacerbate armed conflict and pervasive crime. In his report, the Secretary-General outlined the efforts undertaken over the previous two years at the national, subregional, regional and global levels to strengthen control of small arms and light weapons, including through the third Review Conference of the Programme of Action. With regard to trends and developments, the Secretary-General underscored the role of illicit trade and diversion in fuelling conflict, terrorism and crime, including in fragile areas such as Haiti, Libya, the Sahel and South Sudan. The report also focused on the highly gendered nature of small arms and light weapons, including the relationship between the availability of small arms and light weapons and intimate-partner violence. To assist Security Council members in further mainstreaming considerations regarding small arms and light weapons across its work, the Secretary-General outlined several

---

[24] Security Council resolution 2476 (2019).
[25] Security Council resolution 2469 (2019).
[26] Security Council resolution 2463 (2019).
[27] Security Council resolutions 2472 (2019) and 2498 (2019).
[28] Security Council resolution 2459 (2019).
[29] Security Council resolution 2456 (2019).
[30] S/2019/1011. The previous reports were S/2008/258, S/2011/255, S/2013/503, S/2015/289 and S/2017/1025.

thematic areas of particular relevance, including the protection of civilians in armed conflict; peace operations; arms embargoes; women, peace and security; children and armed conflict; counter-terrorism; and transnational organized crime. In doing so, the Secretary-General provided specific recommendations on how the Council could effectively mainstream considerations regarding small arms and light weapons into discussions in those respective areas, both conceptually and concretely.

Terrorism

In the context of threats to international peace and security caused by terrorist acts, the Security Council adopted resolution 2462 (2019) in March, noting with grave concern that terrorists and terrorist groups raised funds through a variety of means, including the illicit trade in small arms and light weapons. The Council urged States to adopt and implement necessary legislative and other measures to criminalize the illegal manufacture, possession, stockpiling and trade of small arms and light weapons. It further reaffirmed that all States "shall ... refrain from providing any form of support to entities or persons involved in terrorist acts, including by eliminating the supply of weapons".

By its resolution 2482 (2019), adopted in July, the Security Council strongly condemned the continued flow of weapons, including small arms and light weapons, to and between Islamic State in Iraq and the Levant (also known as Da'esh), Al-Qaida, their affiliates and associated groups, illegal armed groups and criminals. In that context, the Security Council urged Member States to fully implement the Programme of Action and the International Tracing Instrument in order to prevent terrorists from acquiring small arms and light weapons, particularly in conflict and post-conflict areas. The dangers posed by illicit falsification, obliteration, removal or alteration of unique markings of small arms and light weapons were noted. In that regard, the Council called for implementation of the provisions contained in the International Tracing Instrument.

Women, peace and security

In the framework of the agenda item on women, peace and security, the Security Council adopted in April resolution 2467 (2019) on sexual violence in conflict, drawing a connection between the perpetration of such violence and the availability of illicit small arms and light weapons. By the resolution, the Council recalled with grave concern that the illicit transfer, destabilizing accumulation and misuse of small arms and light weapons fuelled armed conflicts and had a wide range of negative human rights, humanitarian, development and socioeconomic consequences, in particular on the security of civilians in armed conflict, including the disproportionate impact on violence perpetrated against women and girls and exacerbating sexual and gender-based violence in conflict. By the same resolution, the Council acknowledged the adoption of the Arms Trade Treaty and the provisions contained therein that obligated States parties, when undertaking export assessments, to take into account the risk of conventional arms, including small arms and light weapons, of being used to commit or facilitate serious acts of gender-based violence or serious acts of violence against women and children.

Weapons and ammunition management

The Security Council addressed weapons and ammunition management in a range of peace operation contexts throughout 2019, reflecting a growing understanding of the contribution of safe and secure management of stockpiles to building sustainable peace. Several resolutions adopted on country-specific situations demonstrated the priority placed by the Council on the safe and effective management, storage and security of stockpiles and ammunition.

With regard to the Central African Republic, the Security Council adopted two resolutions in January and November, respectively. In resolution 2454 (2019), adopted in January, the Council requested the Secretary-General to assess the progress achieved on key benchmarks it had established on arms embargo measures in the Central African Republic, including on weapons and ammunition management, and expressed its intention to review the arms-embargo measures in light of that assessment. The Secretary-General issued his assessment[31] in July, noting that the Central African Republic and its partners had demonstrated commitment to achieving the necessary progress against the benchmarks and that they should be encouraged to continue their efforts, although the needs of the Government were significant and that considerable challenges remained. Through the same resolution, the Council also requested that the Central African Republic authorities report on progress achieved in the management of weapons and ammunition. In November, the Security Council adopted resolution 2499 (2019), condemning cross-border criminal activities, such as arms trafficking, and stressing the threat posed to the Central African Republic's peace and stability by the illicit transfer, destabilizing accumulation and misuse of small arms and light weapons. By this resolution, the Council called upon national authorities to coordinate with the United Nations Multidimensional Integrated Stabilization Mission in the Central African Republic and international partners to ensure the safe and effective management, storage and security of stockpiles.

Regarding the situation in Mali, in June, the Security Council adopted resolution 2480 (2019), calling upon national authorities to address the proliferation and illicit trafficking in small arms and light weapons, including through effective stockpile management, in line with the Economic Community of West African States Convention on Small Arms and Light Weapons, Their Ammunition and Other Related Materials, as well as the Programme of Action on Small Arms and Light Weapons.

---

[31] S/2019/609.

The Security Council also adopted resolution 2476 (2019) in June, establishing a new special political mission in Haiti as the successor to the United Nations Mission for Justice Support in Haiti, whose mandate would expire in October. By the resolution, the Council requested the Secretary-General to establish BINUH beginning on 16 October to strengthen political stability and good governance, including the rule of law; advance a peaceful and stable environment; and protect and promote human rights. As part of the provision of BINUH advisory services to the Haitian national authorities, the Security Council requested establishment of a dedicated advisory unit on gang violence, community violence reduction and weapons and ammunition management.

Silencing the Guns in Africa

In February, the Security Council unanimously adopted resolution 2457 (2019) in support of the African Union "Silencing the Guns by 2020" initiative, during the presidency of Equatorial Guinea. The resolution addressed a wide range of challenges facing the African Continent—from governance to economics to security to development[32]—with multiple references to the effective implementation of relevant arms control instruments and regimes, in particular those related to small arms and light weapons.

In the preamble of the resolution, the Council expressed grave concern over the illicit trade, destabilizing accumulation and misuse of small arms and light weapons. In that context, it recalled relevant instruments, including the Programme of Action. Reference was also made to the designation of the month of September of each year until 2020 as "Africa Amnesty Month" for the surrender of illegally owned weapons.

Modular Small-arms-control Implementation Compendium

The Modular Small-arms-control Implementation Compendium (referred to as MOSAIC) is a series of modules providing voluntary, practical guidance on measures for small arms control, translating into practice the objectives of key global agreements[33] and supporting achievement of the Sustainable Development Goals.[34] As at the end of the year, the modules[35] had been used by over 110

---

[32] Various obstacles to peace and security in Africa were enumerated in the text, including border insecurity, insurgencies and rebellions, terrorism, illicit exploitation of natural resources, corruption and climate change. The important role of women and youth in peace was also highlighted.

[33] Such agreements include the Programme of Action on Small Arms and Light Weapons, the International Tracing Instrument, the Firearms Protocol, supplementing the United Nations Convention against Transnational Organized Crime and the Arms Trade Treaty. For further information, see www.un.org/disarmament/convarms/mosaic/.

[34] MOSAIC supports, in particular, Goal 16 to promote peaceful, just and inclusive societies and target 16.4, which includes significantly reducing illicit arms flows.

[35] Topics covered by MOSAIC modules, which were developed since 2009, include establishing a national small arms commission, setting up a national action plan on small arms and light weapons, stockpile management, and weapons marking. Designed for use by any Government

Member States and applied in the development of national controls covering the entire life cycle of small arms.

In 2019, the Office for Disarmament Affairs progressed towards finalizing a module on monitoring, evaluation and reporting, as well as three additional modules addressing control of small arms and light weapons in three respective contexts: disarmament, demobilization and reintegration; preventing armed violence; and security sector reform. Initial planning for the development of two further modules—on gun-free zones and on deactivation of small arms and light weapons, respectively—also took place during the year.

Meanwhile, the regional centres of the Office for Disarmament Affairs continued to incorporate MOSAIC modules into their training. The United Nations Regional Centre for Peace and Disarmament in Asia and the Pacific, based in Kathmandu, used MOSAIC modules in a training workshop on developing National Action Plans to reduce illegal arms flows.

In 2019, eight additional MOSAIC modules were translated into French. Several modules were previously available in languages other than English, including Arabic, French and Spanish, as well as Bosnian, Croatian, Montenegrin and Serbian.

In its resolution 74/60 on the illicit trade in small arms and light weapons, the General Assembly again noted the role of web-based tools developed by the Secretariat, including MOSAIC, and their utility in assessing progress made in the implementation of the Programme of Action on Small Arms and Light Weapons.

Coordinating Action on Small Arms mechanism

Three working meetings of the United Nations Coordinating Action on Small Arms[36] mechanism were held in 2019 in furtherance of its aim to foster coherent

---

or organization, the modules are based on good practices, codes of conduct and standard operating procedures developed at regional and subregional levels. They were developed and reviewed by technical experts from around the world, including an expert reference group of over 300 specialists.

[36] This inter-agency coordination mechanism comprises 24 United Nations partners that jointly address the issues of small arms, ammunition and the arms trade from a variety of perspectives, including economic and social development, human rights, disarmament, organized crime, terrorism, conflict prevention, peacekeeping, public health, environment, gender and children. The following United Nations entities participated in 2019: Counter-Terrorism Executive Directorate, Department for Economic and Social Affairs, Department of Global Communications, Department of Peace Operations, Department of Political and Peacebuilding Affairs, International Civil Aviation Organization, Office for Disarmament Affairs, Office for the Coordination of Humanitarian Affairs, Office of Counter-Terrorism, Office of the Special Adviser on Africa, Office of the Special Adviser on the Prevention of Genocide, Office of the Special Representative of the Secretary-General for Children and Armed Conflict, Office of the Special Representative of the Secretary-General on Violence against Children, Office of the United Nations High Commissioner for Human Rights, Office of the United Nations High Commissioner for Refugees, United Nations Children's Fund, United Nations Development Programme, United Nations Entity for Gender Equality and the Empowerment of Women

and cohesive policy and programming on small arms, ammunition and the arms trade within the United Nations system. At those meetings, the mechanism's members prepared the Secretary-General's report to the Security Council on the issue of small arms,[37] shared information on relevant United Nations funding mechanisms (e.g., the operation of the United Nations Trust Facility Supporting Cooperation on Arms Regulation), reviewed progress and support across the United Nations system for the African Union "Silencing the Guns by 2020" initiative, and discussed ongoing work on data collection and analysis related to indicator 16.4.2 of the 2030 Agenda for Sustainable Development.[38]

The members of the mechanism also followed relevant developments at the Human Rights Council, including the adoption of a new resolution on the impact of arms transfers on human rights (41/20).[39] In addition, the mechanism continued functioning as a forum to approve draft modules for use at the working level. The mechanism's members also coordinated the establishment of Saving Lives Entity, the new trust fund on armed violence prevention and reduction.

Protocol against the Illicit Manufacturing of and Trafficking in Firearms, Their Parts and Components and Ammunition

States parties to the United Nations Convention against Transnational Organized Crime and the Protocols thereto, including the Protocol against the Illicit Manufacturing of and Trafficking in Firearms, Their Parts and Components and Ammunition, started to implement the preparatory phase for a new mechanism to review the implementation of those instruments. The mechanism was adopted by the Conference of by the Parties to the United Nations Convention against Transnational Organized Crime and its supplementing Protocols in October 2018 and constitutes the first mandatory mechanism to review the implementation of their obligations under those instruments.

Ammunition

Throughout 2019, States actively engaged in multilateral deliberations on conventional ammunition with a view to supporting the work of a group of governmental experts on the topic to be convened in 2020. In that context, States continued to raise concerns over the dual risks of poorly managed ammunition: unintended explosions at munitions sites and diversion of ammunition.

(UN-Women), United Nations Environment Programme, United Nations Human Settlements Programme, United Nations Institute for Disarmament Research, United Nations Mine Action Service, United Nations Office on Drugs and Crime and World Health Organization.

[37] S/2019/1011.

[38] United Nations, "SDG Indicators".

[39] By this resolution, the Council highlighted the impact of arms on women and girls, especially in relation to gender-based violence.

The human cost of unplanned explosions at munitions sites

Casualties, 1979–2019

During the period January 1979 to December 2019, almost 30,000 deaths and injuries were recorded from unplanned explosions at munitions sites (UEMS). The highest number of casualties was recorded in 2002, mainly due to the devastating incident that occurred in Lagos, Nigeria. Similarly, the incident in Abadan, Turkmenistan, in 2011 and the one in Brazzaville, Congo, in 2012 contributed strongly to the spikes in 2011 and 2012.

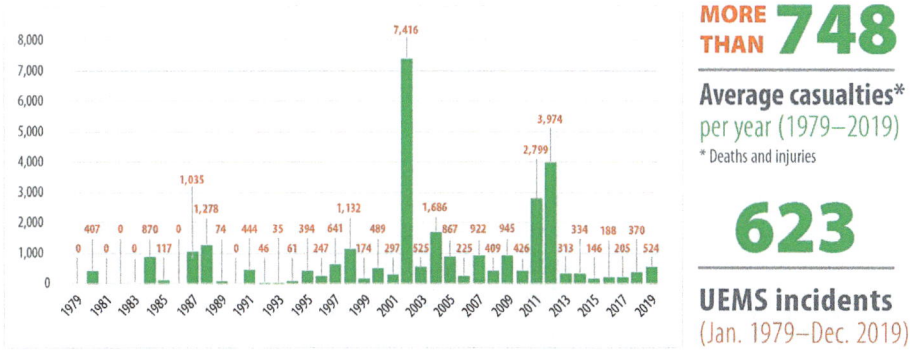

MORE THAN 748

Average casualties*
per year (1979–2019)
* Deaths and injuries

623

UEMS incidents
(Jan. 1979–Dec. 2019)

Ageing, unstable and excess ammunition stockpiles pose the dual hazards of illicit proliferation and accidental explosion, which have caused humanitarian disasters and destabilization in various global regions. In view of those challenges, the United Nations developed the **International Ammunition Technical Guidelines** in 2011 and established the **SaferGuard Programme** as the corresponding knowledge management platform, at the request of the General Assembly. The Guidelines constitute practical, modular guidance on the safe and secure management of ammunition, which benefits United Nations personnel in the field, interested States and other relevant stakeholders.

Source: Small Arms Survey

During the first half of 2019, according to a database maintained by the non-governmental organization Small Arms Survey, 14 unplanned explosions occurred at munitions sites.[40] The human cost of unplanned explosions at munitions sites is devastating. Over the prior five decades, more than 600 such explosions had occurred, affecting thousands of people in 101 countries.[41] Against that backdrop, the SaferGuard Programme, managed by the Office for Disarmament Affairs, maintained its emphasis on promoting and disseminating the International Ammunition Technical Guidelines to assist in enhancing the safety and security of ammunition stockpiles.

---

[40] Small Arms Survey, "Unplanned Explosions at Munitions Sites", October 2019.

[41] Ibid.

General Assembly

By resolution 74/65 of 12 December 2019, entitled "Problems arising from the accumulation of conventional ammunition stockpiles in surplus", the General Assembly reiterated the request to the Secretary-General contained in resolution 72/55 of 4 December 2017, to convene a group of governmental experts in 2020 on conventional ammunition. The Assembly also took note with appreciation of the series of informal consultations convened by the resolution's main sponsor, Germany, throughout 2018 and 2019. Building on three informal consultations held in 2018, Germany organized three additional consultations in February, May and September in New York to identify issues on which progress could be made and to inform the work of the 2020 Group of Governmental Experts.

The first consultation of the year, held on 20 February, addressed the life-cycle management of ammunition, with a view to preventing diversion. UNIDIR presented key findings from the first of a series of thematic seminars organized to support States in framing key issues and informing processes pertinent to the management of conventional ammunition. UNIDIR stressed the need, for example, to situate physical security and stockpile management within a wider supply-chain framework, including pre-transfer risk assessments and diversion monitoring and diagnostic activities. During the informal exchange of views, several States noted the importance of national applications of the International Ammunition Technical Guidelines to prevent diversion from ammunition stockpiles, while also acknowledging the need for a comprehensive approach to safe and secure management of ammunition to address all sources of diversion.

The subsequent consultation, convened on 21 May, focused on good-practice frameworks at the national, subregional, regional and global levels, addressing the safety and security challenges arising from conventional ammunition stockpiles. Discussing relevant global frameworks, the United Nations Office on Drugs and Crime and the Arms Trade Treaty Secretariat offered reflections on how ammunition was addressed in the Firearms Protocol, supplementing the United Nations Convention Against Transnational Organized Crime and in the Arms Trade Treaty, respectively. Regarding the regional level, the Inter-American Convention Against the Illicit Manufacturing of and Trafficking in Firearms, Ammunition, Explosives, and Other Related Materials was presented by the Organization of American States (OAS) as a useful model for further consideration. Switzerland reflected on the Forum for Security Cooperation of the Organization for Security and Co-operation in Europe, briefing participants on two security dialogues on conventional ammunition it had organized as Chair of the Forum in January and April. In addition, Ghana shared its national views and experience, highlighting the importance of the International Ammunition Technical Guidelines for improving national stockpile management.

A final consultation was held on 16 September, providing States an opportunity to discuss an informal non-paper presented by Germany that summarized the informal consultative process organized pursuant to resolution 72/55. The non-paper outlined potential priorities for the 2020 group of governmental experts, underscoring the dual concerns of safety and security and stressing the need for a comprehensive life-cycle management system to address safety of stockpiles and prevention of diversion.[42] During the open discussion, many States welcomed the informal consultative process organized by Germany in advance of the group of governmental experts session in 2020. The issue of applicable legal and normative frameworks was raised by several States, including with respect to the lack of a universally applicable framework to address ammunition. States noted the importance of international cooperation and assistance to support application of the International Ammunition Technical Guidelines at the national level. Participants also expressed support for devoting discussion in the group of governmental experts to the issues of diversion and illicit trafficking of ammunition.

To further enrich the informal consultative process, Germany convened a series of regional-level outreach events on conventional ammunition with interested States. Following discussions held in Abidjan and Addis Ababa in 2018, regional activities took place in Vienna in January, Bangkok in March, and Lima and Kingston in September.

International Ammunition Technical Guidelines and United Nations SaferGuard activities

Ammunition Management Advisory Team

In response to the growing demand for technical support in ammunition management, the Ammunition Management Advisory Team was established in January as a standing advisory mechanism aimed at enhancing State and regional action on safe and secure management of ammunition. A joint initiative of the Office for Disarmament Affairs and the Geneva International Centre for Humanitarian Demining, the Advisory Team will provide technical assistance in ammunition management to interested States in accordance with the International Ammunition Technical Guidelines. It was conceived to support the "Saving Lives" pillar of the Secretary-General's Agenda for Disarmament[43]—specifically, action 22 on securing excessive and poorly maintained stockpiles.

---

[42] Informal non-paper presented by Germany on the consultative process pursuant to General Assembly resolution 72/55 of 4 December 2017.

[43] António Guterres, *Securing Our Common Future: An Agenda for Disarmament* (United Nations publication, Sales No. E.18.IX.6).

Validation process

Under the Saf*er*Guard Programme, the Office for Disarmament Affairs continued to promote the global application of the International Ammunition Technical Guidelines, including through the Programme's validation process. In 2019, the Office sought to further refine that validation process in order to identify a diverse set of ammunition management experts with knowledge and skills compatible with the Guidelines. Building on pilot exercises in 2017 and 2018, the Office collaborated with the Ammunition Management Advisory Team to organize two validation exercises in 2019, one held in Austria in August and another—the first to be conducted in French—in Senegal in November. In total, 23 ammunition management experts—representing national authorities, United Nations entities and non-governmental organizations—passed the validation process and were placed on a roster of experts to support the Office and the Advisory Team in responding to State requests for ammunition management assistance, including through the Saf*er*Guard quick-response mechanism.[44]

Participants in the validation exercises completed an online e-learning programme on the International Ammunition Technical Guidelines, an individual technical exercise, round-table discussions and a scenario-based group exercise, strengthening their knowledge and skills related to the Guidelines and supporting the dissemination of the Guidelines across regions. Validated experts were invited to a dedicated online platform allowing rostered experts to interact informally, contributing to a network of ammunition management practitioners.

While the exercise in Austria enabled the Saf*er*Guard validation methodology and materials to be refined and finalized, the francophone exercise marked the launch of the validation process at the regional level, ensuring a geographically diverse pool of validated experts who possessed varied language skills and could provide advice on ammunition management based firmly on the Guidelines.

Technical Review Board

The United Nations Saf*er*Guard Technical Review Board, a group of ammunition technical experts who support the work of the Saf*er*Guard Programme by overseeing the technical updates of the International Ammunition Technical Guidelines, which is due made significant progress on a quinquennial update of the Guidelines, which is due for completion in 2020.[45] The Board also initiated a comprehensive review of the implementation support toolkit for the Guidelines. To

---

[44] The Saf*er*Guard quick-response mechanism allows ammunition experts to be deployed to assist requesting States in the management of ammunition stockpiles. It was first welcomed by General Assembly resolution 68/52 of 5 December 2013. To ensure the availability of technical expertise to respond to such requests, the Saf*er*Guard Programme initiated an expert validation process in 2016.

[45] The Technical Review Board members are national ammunition experts from Austria, Bangladesh, Brazil, Canada, China, Germany, Singapore, South Africa, Switzerland and United States.

support those activities, the Office for Disarmament Affairs convened an informal meeting of the Board from 9 to 12 July in New York, allowing members to hold required in-depth technical discussions on the Guidelines and online toolkit. From 13 to 15 November, the Board and the Strategic Coordination Group[46] held their annual meeting in Geneva. Based on recommendations from the informal meeting in July, members decided on: (a) various technical amendments to the Guidelines with a view to completing version 3 in 2020; and (b) technical requirements regarding further improvement of the implementation support toolkit.

Support guides

Under the Saf*er*Guard Programme, the Office continued to develop resources for the application of the International Ammunition Technical Guidelines with a view to promoting effective, safe and secure management of ammunition. Three implementation support guides—namely, the *Critical Path Guide to the International Ammunition Technical Guidelines*, the *Guide to Developing National Standards on Ammunition Management* and a UNIDIR publication entitled *Utilizing the International Ammunition Technical Guidelines in Conflict-Affected and Low Capacity Environments*—were released in March. To facilitate the comprehensive and sustainable application of the Guidelines, the Saf*er*Guard Programme issued Spanish and French versions of the guides in December.[47]

Improvised explosive devices

Improvised explosive devices remained a leading cause of death and injury in armed conflict throughout 2019, producing high levels of well-documented civilian casualties in conflicts in Iraq, the Syrian Arab Republic and Yemen. In Afghanistan, the use of improvised explosive devices in suicide and non-suicide incidents caused more than one third of the 3,800 civilian casualties recorded by the United Nations in the first six months of the year, making them the second leading cause of civilian casualties during that period.[48] In a summary of its research published in October 2019, the non-governmental organization Action on Armed Violence concluded that more than 164,000 casualties from improvised explosive devices had been recorded since 2010.[49]

Member States continued to grapple with the threat from improvised explosive devices across relevant contexts, including the Security Council and the Convention on Certain Conventional Weapons. In the framework of the Convention, the Group of Experts of the High Contracting Parties to Amended

---

[46] The Board receives inputs and guidance from the Strategic Coordination Group, which is composed of implementing partners.
[47] See the web pages of the publications for the translated versions..
[48] United Nations Assistance Mission in Afghanistan, "Midyear update on the protection of civilians in armed conflict: 1 January to 30 June 2019", 30 July 2019.
[49] "AOAV's research on Improvised Explosive Devices (IEDs)", 12 October 2019.

Protocol II continued discussions on improvised explosive devices during its annual meeting in August. General Assembly resolution "Countering the threat posed by improvised explosive devices" was not tabled for consideration in 2019, a break from the established practice of adopting it on an annual basis.[50]

The Security Council devoted further attention in 2019 to the use of improvised explosive devices by terrorist groups, with States continuing to express concern over the acquisition of related materials by Islamic State in Iraq and the Levant (also known as Da'esh), Al-Qaida, their affiliates and associated groups, illegal armed groups and criminals. By resolution 2482 (2019), adopted in July, the Security Council strongly condemned the flow of components for improvised explosive devices to and between these groups and entities. By the same resolution, the Council urged all States that had not already done so to criminalize the illegal manufacture, possession, stockpiling and trade of all types of explosives, whether military or civilian, that can be used to manufacture improvised explosive devices, including detonators, detonating cords and chemical components.

In the context of the situation in Somalia, the Security Council adopted resolution 2472 (2019) in May, authorizing the African Union Mission in Somalia to take action to mitigate the threat posed by improvised explosive devices. In November, the Council adopted resolution 2498 (2019), condemning the increased use by Al-Shabaab of improvised explosive devices and imposing a ban on their components. The Security Council decided that all States "shall prevent the direct or indirect sale, supply or transfer of specific items to Somalia from their territories, or by their nationals outside their territories, if there is sufficient evidence to demonstrate that the item(s) will be used, or a significant risk that they may be used, in the manufacture of improvised explosive devices".[51] By resolution 2498 (2019), the Council further called upon Member States to undertake appropriate measures to promote vigilance in the sale, supply, or transfer of explosive precursors and materials to Somalia that may be used in the manufacture of improvised explosive devices. States were urged to keep records of transactions and share information with Somali authorities to that end.

To better address the threat of improvised explosive devices, the United Nations continued to pursue a whole-of-system approach and to strengthen coordination on relevant threat responses, in line with the Secretary-General's Agenda for Disarmament.[52] In 2019, the United Nations Mine Action Service concluded a mapping exercise to identify and analyse responses to improvised

---

[50] The General Assembly previously adopted a version of the text as resolution 73/67 of 5 December 2018. The Assembly was expected to consider a new iteration in 2020, when it would also receive a report of the Secretary-General on the topic.

[51] Annex C of the resolution detailed the particular explosive materials, explosive precursors, explosive-related equipment and technology that would be subject to the decision, including ammonium nitrate fuel oil, sodium chlorate and nitric acid.

[52] Through the Agenda for Disarmament, the United Nations committed to enhance the Organization's response to improvised explosive devices.

explosive devices across the United Nations system. The mapping exercise confirmed that attacks and incidents involving improvised explosive devices adversely affected programme and mandate delivery of the United Nations, especially in the contexts of the protection of civilians and the provision of humanitarian assistance. In tandem with the mapping, the United Nations Mine Action Service initiated development of the Smart Improvised Explosive Device Threat Mitigation Technology Roadmap to compile, in a searchable database, the latest information on related threats, including technologies and commercial equipment.

Amended Protocol II of the Convention on Certain Conventional Weapons

States also took up the issue of improvised explosive devices at two meetings held in the framework of the Protocol on Prohibitions or Restrictions on the Use of Mines, Booby Traps and Other Devices as amended on 3 May 1996,[53] also known as Amended Protocol II to the Convention on Certain Conventional Weapons (for more information on relevant activities under Amended Protocol II, see pp. 113–116).

United Nations Mine Action Service activities

Pursuant to the Secretary-General's Agenda for Disarmament, the United Nations Mine Action Service completed a mapping exercise to chart the responses of United Nations entities to improvised explosive devices with a view to developing a coherent, whole-of-system approach to addressing the threat. Based on the findings of that exercise, the United Nations Mine Action Service continued work to harmonize operational, programmatic, policy and doctrinal responses of the United Nations to improvised explosive devices. In a round of initial consultations for the exercise, stakeholders highlighted a need to deepen information-sharing and data collection, as well as to eliminate siloed approaches, in order to enhance United Nations responses in areas such as staff safety and security, strategic planning, security assessments, policy development, humanitarian and protection responses, and implementation of operational mandates.

In July, the United Nations Mine Action Service finished the development of two specialized operator-level training courses—on the disposal of conventional munitions and of improvised explosive devices, respectively—following broad consultations with Member States to ensure the inter-operability of explosive ordnance disposal forces working in United Nations peace operations. The courses drew upon the United Nations Improvised Explosive Device Disposal Standards,

---

[53] The 2019 discussions were held in accordance with the decisions taken at the twentieth Annual Conference of High Contracting Parties to Amended Protocol II. See CCW/AP.II/CONF.20/5, para. 29.

the United Nations Explosive Ordnance Disposal Unit Manual and the United Nations Explosive Ordnance Disposal Standardized Training Material.

To support the adoption of those standardized training courses, the United Nations Mine Action Service began preparing to establish a mobile response and training team that would: (a) coordinate the integration of the courses into the work of regional training centres; and (b) respond to urgent capacity-building requests from Member States. The team is expected to begin delivering training in 2020 in Entebbe, including synchronized training at the United Nations Regional Service Centre in Entebbe.

Meanwhile, in view of the evolving threat from improvised explosive devices and the related challenges posed to humanitarian mine action, the International Mine Action Standards Review Board, under the chairmanship of the United Nations Mine Action Service, completed an addition to the International Mine Action Standards entitled "Improvised Explosive Device Disposal", published in February.[54] The standard includes sections on relevant terminology; competencies for improvised explosive device disposal, including in urban settings; and guidance for clearing improvised explosive devices for humanitarian purposes where active hostilities have ceased.

Through its field programmes, the United Nations Mine Action Service continued working with Member States and troop-contributing countries in support of capacity-building activities addressing improvised explosive devices. By providing training and technical equipment, as well as through mentoring and advisory support, the United Nations Mine Action Service also helped national authorities to develop technical capacity to safely manage improvised explosive devices, coordinate mitigation responses and comply with relevant international standards.

Explosive weapons in populated areas

Throughout 2019, Member States, civil society and United Nations entities further focused their efforts on addressing the devastating harm caused by the use of explosive weapons in populated areas. As that persisted in conflicts in Afghanistan, the Syrian Arab Republic, Yemen and elsewhere, States responded through various multilateral tracks, including an international conference on protecting civilians in urban warfare convened in Vienna in October, as well as the initiation of a Geneva-based process to develop a political declaration. A number of additional processes contributed to the growing momentum, including discussions in the Security Council on the protection of civilians in armed conflict; deliberations in the framework of the Convention on Certain Conventional Weapons; and the development of methodologies for supplying data, including on arms, under the 2030 Agenda for Sustainable Development.

---

[54] International Mine Action Standards 09.31.

Use of explosive weapons in populated areas devastates lives

70% of all deaths and injuries from explosive weapons were civilians

Total reported deaths and injuries: 32,110
Total civilian deaths and injuries: 22,342

Populated areas

90% of all deaths and injuries from explosive weapons used in populated areas were civilians

Non-populated areas

20% of deaths and injuries from explosive weapons used in non-populated areas were civilians

Civilian deaths and injuries by weapon-launch method

42%	15%	32%	11%

Improvised explosive devices	Ground-launched	Air-launched	Combinations or unclear

When explosive weapons are used in populated areas, civilians bear the brunt.

In the Agenda for Disarmament, the Secretary-General places special emphasis on addressing the use of explosive weapons in populated areas and has committed to supporting Member States in their efforts to develop a political declaration as well as appropriate limitations, common standards and operational policies, in conformity with international humanitarian law.

Data source: 2018 English-language media reports and Action on Armed Violence, 2018 Explosive Violence Monitor Report, pp. 5–6.

In line with the commitments contained in the Secretary-General's Agenda for Disarmament, the United Nations system continued support States in the development of a political declaration, appropriate limitations, common standards and operational policies, in conformity with international humanitarian law; raise awareness on the impact of explosive weapons in populated areas; facilitate the sharing of practice and policy among States; and support casualty recording and data collection with a view to reducing civilian casualties.

At the seventy-fourth session of the General Assembly First Committee, in October, the issue of explosive weapons in populated areas continued to receive heightened attention. In a joint statement[55] delivered by Ireland, a cross-regional group of 71 States reaffirmed their grave concern about the humanitarian harm caused during active hostilities in populated areas and, in particular, by the use of explosive weapons with wide-area effects. The States acknowledged the devastating impact on civilians and civilian objects, as well as the long-term humanitarian harm resulting from the use of explosive weapons in populated areas, which has impacted recovery and development of affected communities. The authors also welcomed the high priority that the Secretary-General had accorded to the issue in his Agenda for Disarmament, called for strengthened compliance with international humanitarian law, encouraged States to engage in efforts towards a political declaration in 2020, and recognized the value of sharing good policy and practice to prevent civilian harm caused by the use of explosive weapons in populated areas. A number of other Governments separately addressed the matter in their national statements.

High-level advocacy on the issue also intensified in 2019. In September, on the occasion of the high-level segment of the seventy-fourth session of the General Assembly, the Secretary-General and the President of the International Committee of the Red Cross (ICRC) issued a joint appeal on the use of explosive weapons, calling for an end to the devastation and civilian suffering caused by their use in cities.[56] They emphasized that, when cities were bombarded by explosive weapons, whether by air strikes, rockets, artillery or improvised explosive devices, civilians overwhelmingly bore the brunt. Recalling incidents of explosive weapons use in population centres in Afghanistan, Iraq, the Syrian Arab Republic and Ukraine, the authors urged parties to conflict to recognize that using explosive weapons with wide-area effects in populated areas, such as cities, towns and refugee camps, placed civilians at high risk of indiscriminate harm.

The joint appeal included calls for several specific measures. Notably, the Secretary-General and the President of ICRC supported the efforts of States to develop a political declaration, as well as appropriate limitations, common standards and operational policies, in conformity with international humanitarian law, relating to the use of explosive weapons in populated areas. The authors also

---

[55] "Explosive Weapons in Populated Areas Thematic Debate on Conventional Weapons UNGA 74 – First Committee Joint Statement".

[56] Press release (SG/2251), 18 September 2019.

urged States and other stakeholders to strengthen the collection of data on civilian casualties. They further encouraged States to identify and share good practices for mitigating the risk of civilian harm in urban armed conflict, including restrictions and limitations on the use of heavy explosive weapons in populated areas. In addition, they called on all parties to armed conflicts to employ strategies and tactics that took combat outside populated areas. Finally, they appealed to States to adopt policies and practices that would enhance the protection of civilians when warfare took place in populated areas, including policies and practices to avoid the use of explosive weapons with a wide impact area, due to the significant likelihood of indiscriminate effects.

In his 2019 report[57] to the Security Council on the protection of civilians in armed conflict, the Secretary-General reaffirmed concern over the challenges posed by urban warfare, including the use of explosive weapons, and called for protective measures in that regard. He underscored, in particular, the acute impact on civilians and civilian objects of fighting in populated areas when explosive weapons were involved. He noted that more than 17,000 conflict-related incidents had been reported in Yemen the previous year, including widespread accounts of explosive-weapons use resulting in deaths, injuries and damage to agricultural sites, schools, hospitals and water sites. The Secretary-General repeated his call for States to avoid the use of explosive weapons with wide-area impacts in populated areas, owing to the immediate and cumulative, complex and long-term harm resulting from such use.

Vienna Conference and development of a political declaration

On 1 and 2 October, Austria hosted the "Vienna Conference on Protecting Civilians in Urban Warfare", where participants sought to develop a common understanding of the various forms of harm caused by the use of explosive weapons in populated areas, the legal context of their use, and good examples of military practice and policy in mitigating civilian harm. Delegations representing 133 States, United Nations entities, international organizations and civil society entities took part.

Building on momentum generated since 2015, the Vienna Conference was the first international event at which all States were invited to address the protection of civilians in urban warfare and the devastation caused to civilians by the use of explosive weapons in populated areas. Thematic panel discussions took place on, inter alia, the direct and indirect humanitarian effects of the use of explosive weapons in populated areas, the characteristics of explosive weapons and challenges in the urban context, restrictions posed by international humanitarian law on the use of explosive weapons in populated areas, and military practice and policy. The final session included an exchange of views on the development of a political declaration as a concrete action to mitigate civilian harm. Many States

---

[57] S/2019/373.

affirmed the need for urgent action and emphasized that the process to develop a political declaration should be open, transparent and inclusive. Participating delegations also noted that a political declaration could serve as a future vehicle or framework for exchanging best practices and for dialogue to monitor implementation of the political commitment.

Building on the Vienna Conference outcome, Ireland convened the first round of an informal consultative process to elaborate a political declaration for adoption in 2020. More than 200 participants attended the consultations on 18 November in Geneva, including States, international organizations, United Nations entities and civil society organizations. Stakeholders largely focused their interventions on concrete proposals for the development of a political declaration. Proposals addressed various aspects of the use of explosive weapons in populated areas, including humanitarian impacts, compliance with international humanitarian law, data collection, victims' assistance and humanitarian access, and the role of non-State actors. A general consensus emerged among participating delegations on the need to express concern over the devastating humanitarian consequences caused by the use of explosive weapons in populated areas. States, civil society organizations and ICRC contributed working papers in support of the consultation.[58]

The United States of America, along with Germany and the United Kingdom of Great Britain and Northern Ireland, presented a draft document on practical measures to strengthen the protection of civilians during military operations in armed conflict, outlining measures to strengthen implementation of international humanitarian law and civilian protection in military operations, and highlighting specific good practices in that regard. Similarly, France presented examples of good practice implemented by the French Armed Forces in contributing to better protection of civilians during the conduct of hostilities in urban contexts. A technical compilation of practical measures was submitted on behalf of Belgium, France, Germany, the United Kingdom and the United States.

Ireland announced its intention to circulate a draft declaration text ahead of the next round of informal consultations to take place in early 2020.

Relevant discussions under the Convention on Certain Conventional Weapons

In 2019, differences of opinion persisted on whether the use of explosive weapons in populated areas should be discussed in the framework of the Convention on Certain Conventional Weapons, which was adopted in 1980 with the aim of banning or restricting the use of specific types of weapons considered to cause unnecessary or unjustifiable suffering to combatants or to affect civilians

---

[58] Ireland, Department of Foreign Affairs and Trade, "Protecting Civilians in Urban Warfare: Towards a political declaration to address the humanitarian harm arising from the use of explosive weapons in populated areas".

indiscriminately (for more information on relevant activities in the framework of the Convention, see pp. 116–117).

Data collection and civilian casualty recording

Under the leadership of the Office of the United Nations High Commissioner for Human Rights (OHCHR), United Nations entities continued to develop and implement casualty-recording mechanisms in United Nations peace operations and other missions, including reporting on the types of arms used, with a view to supporting parties to conflict in their efforts to reduce civilian casualties.

Those efforts also contributed to Sustainable Development Goal target 16.1 to "significantly reduce all forms of violence and related death rates everywhere". In March, the Inter-Agency and Expert Group on the Sustainable Development Goal Indicators approved the conceptual, methodological and data collection framework for indicator 16.1.2, which envisages the collection of data on conflict-related deaths per 100,000 population, disaggregated by sex, age and cause. OHCHR developed the framework in consultation with relevant entities that included the Office for Disarmament Affairs, which provided advice related to recording the "cause" of conflict-related deaths, including categories of weapons.

In December, OHCHR launched its *Guidance on Casualty Recording,*[59] intended to standardize methodology for casualty recording in the United Nations system and beyond. The Guidance provides a "how to" guide for actors who operate or may establish a casualty-recording system, as well as readers who wish to better understand the nature and purpose of casualty recording. Based on a review of casualty-recording practices inside and outside the United Nations, the Guidance is aimed at a wide audience, with a view to, inter alia, expanding available data providers for casualty recording.

Transparency in conventional arms transfers and military expenditures

United Nations Register of Conventional Arms

In support of transparency in international conventional-arms transfers, Member States continued to voluntarily report to the United Nations Register of Conventional Arms their imports and exports of conventional arms during the previous year in seven categories: (a) battle tanks; (b) armoured combat vehicles; (c) large-calibre artillery systems; (d) combat aircraft and unmanned combat aerial vehicles; (e) attack helicopters; (f) warships; and (g) missiles and missile launchers. Member States were also encouraged to report on imports and exports of small arms and light weapons, and they were invited to provide, as background

---

[59] HR/PUB/19/1 (United Nations publication, Sales No. E.20.XIV.1).

information, additional data on procurement through national production, military holdings and national policies on arms transfers.

Follow-up to the 2016 Group of Governmental Experts

In 2019, action continued to be taken to implement General Assembly resolution 71/44 of 5 December 2016, entitled "Transparency in armaments". In addition, a group of governmental experts on the Register, convened every three years, held three meetings to further discuss the Register's operation and continuing development.

In February, the Office for Disarmament Affairs circulated its annual note verbale calling upon all Member States to submit their national reports to the Register. In line with the recommendations of the 2016 Group of Governmental Experts, Member States were encouraged to provide, on a trial basis, information on their international transfers of small arms and light weapons, in parallel with the seven categories of the Register.[60] The Office also requested Member States to complete a questionnaire developed by the 2016 Group to better understand the reasons for the decline in reporting and to gather data on how Member States viewed the desirability and implications of including small arms and light weapons as an eighth category of the Register, on a par with the major conventional arms systems covered through categories I to VII.[61] As at the end of 2019, 18 Member States had forwarded a completed questionnaire to the Office.[62]

Meanwhile, the Office for Disarmament Affairs conducted one briefing for Member States, as part of its activities to promote the Register, familiarize Member States with the electronic database and online reporting tool, and encourage States to submit their national reports.

Annual report

In 2019, 37 States submitted reports on transfers of conventional arms that had taken place in 2018. Of the national reports received by the Office for Disarmament Affairs, 33 were included in the relevant report[63] of the Secretary-General and all were made available in the Register's electronic database. The number of reports received in 2019 represented a decrease from 2018.

Four of the 37 reports received in 2019 were "nil reports", in which the submitting States indicated that they had no transfers of weapons under the Register's seven categories in 2018. Of the other reports, 24 contained information on exports and 17 contained information on imports in the seven categories. In

---

[60] A/71/259, para. 83.

[61] Ibid., annex V.

[62] Argentina, Bhutan, Brazil, Canada, China, Dominican Republic, Finland, Germany, Italy, Japan, Madagascar, Netherlands, Romania, Russian Federation, Singapore, Slovakia, Turkey and Ukraine.

[63] A/74/201. Late submissions do not figure in the report, but are included in the Register's database.

addition, 12 States provided background information on military holdings, 7 on procurement through national production and 27 on international transfers of small arms and light weapons.

The rate of participation by Member States differed significantly from region to region, as in previous years, and the reporting rate of each region also showed little change in 2019. The number of reports submitted by African States decreased from 3 in 2018 to 2 in 2019, while the number of reports by States in Latin America and the Caribbean increased slightly, from 4 to 5 reports.

The reporting rate of Western European and other States reflected a notable decrease, from 24 in 2018 to 14 in 2019. While reporting by States in Asia and the Pacific also fell significantly, from 11 to 4, States notably agreed at a meeting of the Association of Southeast Asian Nations Defence Ministers to share information on national submissions to the Register as a confidence-building measure.[64] Meanwhile, the 12 reports submitted by Eastern European States in 2019 represented another sharp decrease, down from 18 in the previous year.

Database

The data provided by States were made available on the Register's interactive, map-based information platform, "The Global Reported Arms Trade". The site presents information submitted to the Register since 1992 and allows comparisons of data, including details submitted by exporting and importing States on any transfer.

2019 Governmental Group of Experts

Further to General Assembly resolution 71/44 and in keeping with the practice of undertaking triennial reviews of the Register, the 2019 Group of Governmental Experts on the Register held three meetings—two in Geneva and one in New York—and adopted a report by consensus.[65] It was the first instance of gender parity in the Group's 25-year history: 8 of the 15 participating experts were women.

Significantly, and for the first time, the Group agreed on a recommendation that Member States should report international transfers of small arms and light weapons in addition to reporting on the seven categories of weapons systems already covered by the Register. The reporting of information on transfers of small arms and light weapons had previously been undertaken only on a trial basis in an approach referenced by the Group as the "seven-plus-one" formula. Furthermore, the Group's 2019 report was the first to include a section dedicated to the use of the Register as a tool for confidence-building among States.

---

[64] Association of Southeast Asian Nations (ASEAN), "ASEAN Defense Ministers' Meeting (ADMM) three (3)-year work programme", para. 3.2.1.3.

[65] A/74/211.

Objective information on military matters, including transparency of military expenditures

United Nations Report on Military Expenditures

The General Assembly established the United Nations Report on Military Expenditures in 1980 with the aim of increasing transparency in military spending. In the resolution entitled "Objective information on military matters, including transparency of military expenditures", Member States are called upon to voluntarily provide information on their military expenditures for the latest fiscal year for which data are available. Member States are further encouraged to provide such information in the templates developed by the United Nations[66] or, for those Member States that do not have military expenditures, to provide nil reports. A "single-figure" form, adopted following a recommendation of the 2016–2017 Group of Governmental Experts to review the Report, may be used by Member States that wish to report only the total amount of their military expenditure. The United Nations makes the submitted information publicly available through the publication of reports of the Secretary-General and an online database.

Annual report on military expenditures

In accordance with the General Assembly's most recent resolution[67] on objective information on military matters, including transparency of military expenditures, the Office for Disarmament Affairs sent a note verbale in February to all Member States calling for the submission by 30 April of reports on military expenditures. In response, the Office received 28 reports from States, including one nil report, which were all included in the report[68] of the Secretary-General on the matter. The national reports can be found in the above-mentioned online database. Seven fewer reports were submitted in 2019 than in 2018, when 35 reports were submitted.

In 2019, as in previous years and as was the case with the Register, the rate of participation varied greatly across regions. The regional distribution of States that reported in 2019 was as follows: none from Africa (unchanged since 2016); 3 from Asia and the Pacific (compared with 2 in 2018); 1 from Latin America and the Caribbean (down from 5 in 2018); 11 from Eastern Europe (down from 14 in 2018); and 13 from Western Europe and other States (compared with 14 in 2018).

---

[66] Standardized and simplified forms were developed for this purpose.
[67] General Assembly resolution 72/20 of 4 December 2017.
[68] A/74/155.

Export controls

Wassenaar Arrangement

In 2019, the Participating States of the Wassenaar Arrangement continued to promote transparency and responsibility in the transfer of conventional arms and dual-use goods and technologies with a view to preventing destabilizing accumulations and to ensuring effective control of proliferation-sensitive exports. To that end, the Arrangement updated its control lists, namely, the List of Dual-Use Goods and the Technologies and Munitions List, in order to improve their structure and clarity for licensing authorities and exporters. Through an ongoing systematic and comprehensive review of those control lists, Participating States prioritized the ongoing relevance of the lists while bearing in mind the consequences of international and regional security developments, technological change and market trends. The Participating States also gave further attention to proliferation risks related to small arms and light weapons.

The twenty-fifth Wassenaar Arrangement plenary meeting took place on 4 and 5 December in Vienna. In a statement[69] for the meeting, the Chair outlined the relevant 2019 activities of Participating States, including the following: the adoption of new export controls and further clarification of existing ones in areas such as cyberwarfare software, communications, monitoring, digital investigative tools, suborbital aerospace vehicles, ballistic protection, optical sensors and ball bearings; a review of the criteria used to select items for the List of Dual-Use Goods and Technologies, as well as the Sensitive List and the Very Sensitive List; the sharing of experiences in licensing and enforcement practice; and the discussion of how to strengthen national export control implementation. It was announced that the next Wassenaar Arrangement plenary meeting would take place in Vienna in December 2020 with Croatia as its Chair.

The Arrangement updated two documents in 2019: "Best Practices for Exports of Small Arms and Light Weapons", previously amended in 2007; and "Best Practices for Disposal of Surplus/Demilitarised Military Equipment", originally adopted in 2000. Participating States also identified other existing guidelines to potentially update in 2020, as appropriate, as part of a regular review cycle. Furthermore, the plenary Chair, the Experts Group Chair and several Participating States undertook a technical outreach mission to Israel.

Meanwhile, the Wassenaar Arrangement continued its communication and public outreach activities. The Arrangement's secretariat maintained technical contacts with the Missile Technology Control Regime and the Nuclear Suppliers Group on control list issues, while also expanding the web page of the Arrangement to feature content in French, German, Russian and Spanish. In

---

[69] "Statement issued by the plenary Chair on 2019 outcomes of the Wassenaar Arrangement on export controls for conventional arms and dual-use goods and technologies", Vienna, 5 December 2019.

addition, the secretariat took part in relevant conferences and events, such as the fifth Conference of States Parties to the Arms Trade Treaty and the United Nations Disarmament Fellowship Programme.[70]

United Nations Trust Facility Supporting Cooperation on Arms Regulation

In 2019, the United Nations Trust Facility Supporting Cooperation on Arms Regulation continued to provide a flexible mechanism for funding quick-impact, short-term and small-scale projects on controlling conventional arms. As at the end of 2019, the Trust Facility had drawn upon the financial and policy support of 13 donors[71] to allocate $11 million in support of 80 projects, benefiting 140 countries. The selected projects began as proposals submitted by civil society groups, regional and subregional organizations, and United Nations entities.

During the year, the Trust Facility strengthened its efforts to match available resources with needs for assistance in implementing global frameworks for arms control, including the Programme of Action on Small Arms and Light Weapons. Its implementing partners carried out 16 projects with a view to prioritizing, inter alia, the promotion of gender considerations, the application of relevant technical guidance and support for the 2030 Agenda for Sustainable Development. Those projects included the following:

- Marking of police-owned weapons to prevent diversion
- Developing an arms-transfer database and related technical solutions for the Economic Community of West African States
- Drafting of laws and procedures to regulate manufacture and trade of military goods, including licensing for import, export and transit
- Capacity-building of the national authority for effective stockpile management
- Supporting women parliamentarians in addressing illicit trade in small arms and light weapons
- Developing national systems for small arms–related indicators, in accordance with the 2030 Agenda
- Awareness-raising to enhance civil society's support for the United Nations small arms process.

Meanwhile, the Trust Facility received 57 applications in 2019 following an annual call for proposals, up from 40 in 2017 and 53 in 2018. The applications in 2019 closely reflected the assistance needs of States as articulated in their

---

[70] Ibid.

[71] Australia, Canada, Cyprus, Denmark, Finland, Germany, Ireland, Japan, Netherlands, Spain, Sweden, Switzerland and United Kingdom.

respective national reports on the Programme of Action, and 14 of the proposals were selected to receive a total of $1.5 million in implementation assistance in 2020. Implementing partners of the selected proposals had committed to delivering specific outputs related to the following:

- Promotion of the 2030 Agenda
- Application of and compliance with the Modular Small-arms-control Implementation Compendium and the International Ammunition Technical Guidelines
- Implementation of the Secretary-General's Agenda for Disarmament, particularly with regard to actions 21, 22, 35, 36 and 38
- Support for the women, peace and security agenda.

The Trust Facility also continued to ensure effective and efficient monitoring and evaluation, as well as coordination among stakeholders. Implementing partners submitted more than 30 coordination plans in consultation with recipient countries, regional organizations, United Nations system entities and civil society organizations supporting implementation in the field. Such coordination plans help to maximize the impact of project outcomes and avoid duplication of efforts. In this regard, administrators of the Trust Facility consulted on a regular basis with the Arms Trade Treaty Voluntary Trust Fund and relevant European Union programmes.

Confidence-building measures in the field of conventional arms

The Secretary-General, in his Agenda for Disarmament, recognized the development of military confidence-building measures as an essential tool for preventing and resolving conflict; averting accidental military escalation; and reducing arms competition and excessive military spending. In accordance with the biennial General Assembly resolution entitled "Information on confidence-building measures in the field of conventional arms",[72] the Office for Disarmament Affairs continued to engage with interested States and regional organizations on developing and advancing military confidence-building measures, strengthening understanding of this topic and providing substantial and procedural advice and assistance. The Office also maintained and expanded its online repository of military confidence-building measures in the areas of communication and coordination, observation and verification, military constraint, training and education, and cooperation and integration. In 2019, information on confidence-

---

[72] By resolution 73/51 of 12 December 2018, the General Assembly requested the Secretary-General to assist Member States, at their request, in the organization of seminars, courses and workshops aimed at enhancing developments in this field.

building measures was provided by several Member States[73] through voluntary submissions that the Office made available in a related database.[74]

Convention on Certain Conventional Weapons

The Convention on Certain Conventional Weapons[75] (1980) entered into force in 1983 with the aim of banning or restricting the use of specific types of weapons considered to cause unnecessary or unjustifiable suffering to combatants or to affect civilians indiscriminately. The Convention's structure provides unique flexibility to address future developments in the means and methods of warfare, specifically by allowing the negotiation of additional protocols addressing new types of weapons or developments in the conduct of armed conflict.[76] It had 125 High Contracting Parties as at the end of 2019.

The Convention's financial difficulties persisted through the year, posing ongoing complications for related activities. While all of its planned meetings were held, the continued shortage of funds allowed for only partial and temporary staffing of its Implementation Support Unit.[77] The Chair of the 2019 Meeting of the High Contracting Parties, Khalil Hashmi (Pakistan), cooperated with the United Nations Office at Geneva, the Office for Disarmament Affairs and the High Contracting Parties to further stabilize the secretariat's support to the Convention and to ensure the Convention's financial sustainability.

Group of Governmental Experts on Emerging Technologies in the Area of Lethal Autonomous Weapons Systems

The Group of Governmental Experts on Emerging Technologies in the Area of Lethal Autonomous Weapons Systems held its third session in Geneva from 25 to 29 March, and from 20 to 21 August in the framework of the Convention on

---

[73] Armenia, Colombia, Georgia, Honduras, Lebanon, Qatar and Spain.

[74] "Military Confidence-building" (Information received from Member States).

[75] The Convention on Prohibitions or Restrictions on the Use of Certain Conventional Weapons Which May Be Deemed to be Excessively Injurious or to Have Indiscriminate Effects entered into force with its first three protocols (on fragments undetectable by X-ray, landmines and other devices, and incendiary weapons) on 2 December 1983. Protocol IV on blinding laser weapons entered into force in 1998 and Protocol V on explosive remnants of war in 2006. In 2014, the High Contracting Parties to the Convention began discussions on questions related to emerging technologies in the area of lethal autonomous weapon systems. The Convention's text and adherence status are available at the Disarmament Treaty Database of the Office for Disarmament Affairs.

[76] To be able to deal with different types of conventional weapons, each of which may require a different approach, the Convention has a unique structure, whereby issues regarding each weapon are addressed in a separate protocol annexed to an umbrella treaty, which sets the legal framework under which the protocols operate. Although each protocol is integral to the Convention, each is also a stand-alone legal instrument with its own membership. In adhering to the Convention, a State should join the umbrella convention and at least two of its protocols.

[77] For the decision on the establishment of the Convention's Implementation Support Unit and its core tasks, see CCW/MSP/2009/5, para. 36.

Certain Conventional Weapons.[78] The Group achieved consensus on a substantive report,[79] in which it provided a set of conclusions; identified areas for further clarification or review under the five substantive items on its agenda;[80] and identified an additional eleventh guiding principle concerning human-machine interaction and ensuring compliance with international law.

Acting in November on the basis of the Group's recommendations, the 2019 Meeting of the High Contracting Parties to the Convention endorsed the 11 guiding principles identified by the Group.[81] The Meeting also decided that the Group should continue to meet, in 2020 and 2021, with a mandate to consider the following: (a) the guiding principles, which it might further develop and elaborate; (b) the work on the legal, technological and military aspects; and (c) the conclusions of the Group, as reflected in its reports of 2017, 2018 and 2019. This consideration was to be used as a basis for the clarification, consideration and development of aspects of the normative and operational framework on emerging technologies in the area of lethal autonomous weapon systems.

Meanwhile, Member States worked to build high-level political support for work in that area. The Alliance for Multilateralism, launched on 2 April by the Foreign Ministers of Germany and France, included the issue of lethal autonomous weapon systems as one of six initiatives it presented to the high-level segment of the General Assembly in September. Specifically, the Alliance presented a declaration[82] on lethal autonomous weapon systems in which it affirmed the 11 guiding principles and called on all States to contribute actively to the clarification and development of an effective and comprehensive normative and operational framework for such systems.

---

[78] The Group was established by the fifth Review Conference of the High Contracting Parties to the Convention on Certain Conventional Weapons. See the decisions contained in the final document of the Fifth Review Conference (CCW/CONF.V/10). For the list of participants, see CCW/GGE.1/2019/INF.1/Rev.1.

[79] CCW/GGE.1/2019/3.

[80] The Group considered the following items:
  (a) An exploration of the potential challenges posed by emerging technologies in the area of Lethal Autonomous Weapons Systems to International Humanitarian Law
  (b) Characterization of the systems under consideration in order to promote a common understanding on concepts and characteristics relevant to the objectives and purposes of the Convention
  (c) Further consideration of the human element in the use of lethal force; aspects of human-machine interaction in the development, deployment and use of emerging technologies in the area of lethal autonomous weapon systems
  (d) Review of potential military applications of related technologies in the context of the Group's work
  (e) Possible options for addressing the humanitarian and international security challenges posed by emerging technologies in the area of lethal autonomous weapon systems in the context of the objectives and purposes of the Convention without prejudging policy outcomes and taking into account past, present and future proposals.

[81] CCW/MSP/2019/9, annex III.

[82] Alliance for Multilateralism, "Declaration by the Alliance for Multilateralism on Lethal Autonomous Weapons Systems (LAWS)", 2 April 2019.

The Secretary-General separately continued drawing attention to related concerns. In a message[83] delivered to the Group of Governmental Experts on 25 March by the Director-General of the United Nations Office at Geneva, the Secretary-General reiterated his prior assertion that "machines with the power and discretion to take lives without human involvement are politically unacceptable, morally repugnant and should be prohibited by international law". In an interview[84] with the magazine *Wired* published on 25 November, he stressed that position again while noting that there was still no worldwide consensus about how to regulate the technology.

Protocol V: Meeting of Experts and thirteenth Conference of the High Contracting Parties

Protocol V on Explosive Remnants of War[85] was adopted in 2003 to prevent and minimize the humanitarian impact of unexploded ordnance and abandoned explosive weapons, including through provisions on the clearance and destruction of explosive remnants of war, the protection of civilians, recording of the use of explosive ordnance, and international cooperation and assistance. It had 96 High Contracting Parties as at the end of 2019.

In preparation for the thirteenth Annual Conference of the High Contracting Parties to Protocol V, a Meeting of Experts took place on 23 August, addressing universalization efforts; national reporting; the clearance of explosive remnants of war in urban contexts; the recording, retaining and transmission of information according to article 4; and cooperation and victim assistance. Before the Annual Conference, the President-designate, Terhi Hakala (Finland), issued a brief summary report of the Meeting as an official document.

The thirteenth Annual Conference took place on 11 November, chaired by Terhi Hakala (Finland). In accordance with decisions taken in 2018,[86] the Conference considered, inter alia, article 4 of the Protocol, entitled "Recording, retaining and transmission of information"; national reporting; and victim assistance. It concluded with the consideration and adoption of a final document.[87]

Of the 96 High Contracting Parties to Protocol V, 64 participated in the Conference, as well as 9 High Contracting Parties to the Convention, 1 signatory State and 3 observer States. Other participants included the United Nations Mine Action Service (on behalf of the United Nations Inter-Agency Coordination Group

---

[83] Secretary-General's message delivered by Michael Møller, Geneva, 25 March 2019.
[84] *Wired*, "UN Secretary-General: US-China Tech Divide Could Cause More Havoc Than the Cold War", 25 November 2019.
[85] The text and adherence status of Protocol V are available at the Disarmament Treaty Database of the Office for Disarmament Affairs.
[86] CCW/P.V/CONF/2018/5.
[87] CCW/P.V/CONF/2019/5.

on Mine Action), the European Union, ICRC, the Geneva International Centre for Humanitarian Demining and four other civil society organizations.[88]

In considering the goal of universalization, the Conference welcomed the consent of Benin to be bound by Protocol V, bringing the number of High Contracting Parties to the Protocol to 96.

On the issue of article 4, the Conference decided that, under the overall responsibility of the President-designate, High Contracting Parties should, on a voluntary basis and subject to national policies on protecting sensitive information, continue to share national best practices on implementing the article and generic preventive measures. The Conference also requested the Office for Disarmament Affairs to publish the compilations of national best practices on its website to inform future consideration of the article's implementation.

Pursuant to the implementation mechanism established at the first Conference of the High Contracting Parties to Protocol V[89] and established practice, the Conference decided to nominate two new Coordinators, one on victim assistance and another on clearance and technical assistance. The President-designate of the fourteenth Annual Conference was expected to identify these coordinators, who would be tasked with preparing and chairing relevant work of the next Meeting of Experts and reporting back to the fourteenth Annual Conference.

While the Conference agreed to hold the next Meeting of Experts for "a duration of up to one-and-a-half days", the 2019 Meeting of High Contracting Parties later decided to reduce the duration of that meeting to one day.[90] The Conference nominated Yury Ambrazevich (Belarus) as President-designate of the fourteenth Annual Conference, as well as a representative of the Western European and Others Group and a representative of the Non-Aligned Movement as Vice-Presidents-designates.

Amended Protocol II: Group of Experts and twenty-first Annual Conference of the High Contracting Parties

The Protocol on Prohibitions or Restrictions on the Use of Mines, Booby Traps and Other Devices as amended on 3 May 1996, also known as Amended Protocol II to the Convention on Certain Conventional Weapons, was designed to limit the indiscriminate harm caused by such weapons. It requires the High Contracting Parties to take all feasible precautions to protect civilians from their use. The Protocol had 106 High Contracting Parties as at the end of 2019.

On 22 August, a meeting of a Group of Experts was held in preparation for the twenty-first Annual Conference of the High Contracting Parties to the Protocol. The Coordinators on improvised explosive devices, Colombia and France, issued

---

[88] For the list of participants, see CCW/P.V/CONF/2019/INF.1.

[89] CCW/P.V/CONF/2007/1, para. 38.

[90] CCW/MSP/2019/9.

a report[91] on relevant discussions held in the framework of that meeting. Building on its work on the issue since 2009, the Group held discussions that consisted of: (a) a general exchange of views; and (b) updates by the Coordinators on the compilation of existing guidelines and best practices and the questionnaire on international cooperation to counter that threat. During three thematic panel discussions, the following issues were addressed: challenges posed by improvised explosive devices in specific contexts, as well as an exchange of information on general features and new types, methods of humanitarian clearance and measures to protect civilians; prevention and risk education, including an exchange of information by delegations on national, regional or international risk education methods, campaigns or practices and prevention measures; and threat mitigation, with a focus on humanitarian clearance and deployed capacities.

Throughout the expert discussions, delegations expressed their concern over the continued widespread use of improvised explosive devices and their detrimental impact on civilians due to their indiscriminate use and effects. Delegations stressed the severe humanitarian implications of improvised explosive devices and their negative effects on security, stability and socioeconomic development. Furthermore, many delegations underscored the importance of a comprehensive approach to countering the various aspects of the threat and, in that regard, a large number highlighted the need to continue raising awareness on its scope and characteristics, as well as the need for increased international cooperation and coordination. Accordingly, participants commended the ongoing discussions and the exchange of information in the framework of the Group of Experts as important contributions towards those ends. Several delegations also welcomed the resolutions of the General Assembly entitled "Countering the threat posed by improvised explosive devices" for having helped to raise awareness at the global level about the threat and about the fundamental importance of a comprehensive approach to countering it.[92] The ongoing efforts by the United Nations to strengthen inter-agency coordination and to ensure a whole-of-system approach to addressing improvised explosive devices, as laid out in the Secretary-General's Agenda for Disarmament, were also welcomed.

On 12 November, Zbigniew Czech (Poland) presided over the twenty-first Annual Conference. In accordance with decisions taken the prior year,[93] the Conference continued to focus on (a) the operation and status of the Protocol, under the overall responsibility of the President-designate; and (b) improvised explosive devices, under the overall responsibility of the Coordinators, France and Colombia.

---

[91] CCW/AP.II/CONF.21/2.
[92] General Assembly resolution 73/67 of 5 December 2018.
[93] CCW/AP.II/CONF.20/5.

With Benin expressing consent to be bound by Amended Protocol II, the total number of High Contracting Parties to the Protocol reached 106.[94] Of those States, 67 participated in the twenty-first Conference, as well as 5 other High Contracting Parties to the Convention, 2 signatory States and 4 observer States. UNIDIR, the United Nations Mine Action Service (on behalf of the United Nations Inter-Agency Coordination Group on Mine Action), the European Union, ICRC, the Geneva International Centre for Humanitarian Demining and nine other civil society organizations[95] also participated.

The Conference decided to continue the discussions on improvised explosive devices. Setting its mandate for the coming year, the Conference requested further updates to the compilation of existing guidelines and best practices addressing the diversion or illicit use of related materials. It also decided that the Group of Experts would continue to share information on risk education, new types of improvised explosive devices, methods of clearance with a focus on urban environments and methods to protect civilians. The High Contracting Parties agreed to the revision of the questionnaire on relevant international cooperation in accordance with changes to the mandate on improvised explosive devices in the Convention's framework. The Conference also referred in its report to the importance of having a balanced involvement of women and men in the Group of Experts in 2020. In its final document,[96] the Conference decided that, in 2020, the Group of Experts would continue considering measures to increase both the rate of national reporting and the consistency of the Protocol's reporting methodology. The Conference further developed the mandate on improvised explosive devices for 2020, deciding that the information exchange during the next meeting of the Group would, inter alia, focus on new types of improvised devices and methods of clearance with an added focus on urban environments. The Conference also mandated the Coordinators to revise the questionnaire on International Cooperation in Countering Improvised Explosive Devices,[97] adopted in 2015, and to present the suggested revisions for approval by the Group of Experts. Furthermore, the Conference decided to include in the mandate on improvised explosive devices a reference to the importance of balanced involvement by women and men in the Group of Experts.

Separately, the Conference heard a report by the President on his consultations with delegations on the possibilities to include discussions on good practices in implementing the Protocol with respect to mines other than anti-personnel mines, in particular for the protection of civilians.[98] Delegations expressed divergent views on the need to continue the consideration of mines

---

[94] The text and adherence status of Amended Protocol II are available at the Disarmament Treaty Database of the Office for Disarmament Affairs.

[95] For the full list of participants, see CCW/AP.II/CONF.21/INF.1.

[96] CCW/AP.II/CONF.21/5.

[97] CCW/AP.II/CONF.17/WP.1.

[98] These consultations took place pursuant to paragraph 34 of the final document of the twentieth Conference (CCW/AP.II/CONF.20/5).

other than anti-personnel mines in the framework of Amended Protocol II, and the Conference reflected those differences in its final report.

The Conference proposed convening its next Meeting of Experts for "a duration of up to one-and-a-half-days" in 2020, and the 2019 Meeting of the High Contracting Parties later set the duration for that full period.[99]

The Conference nominated a representative of the Non-Aligned Movement as President-designate of the twenty-second Annual Conference and representatives of China, the Netherlands and the Eastern European Group as Vice-Presidents-designates. The Movement appointed Maria Teresa T. Almojuela (Philippines) as President-designate in February 2020.

Meeting of the High Contracting Parties to the Convention on Certain Conventional Weapons

The 2019 Meeting of the High Contracting Parties[100] took place in Geneva from 13 to 15 November under the chairmanship of Khalil Hashmi (Pakistan).[101] The Meeting drew participants from 87 High Contracting Parties, two signatory States and seven States not party. Also taking part in its work were three United Nations entities, three international organizations and 23 non-governmental organizations and other entities.[102]

The Meeting of the High Contracting Parties took note of the conclusions and recommendations[103] of the Group of Governmental Experts on Emerging Technologies in the Area of Lethal Autonomous Weapons Systems. The Meeting further decided that the Group would meet in Geneva twice in 2020, first from 22 to 26 June and then from 10 to 14 August. The 2019 Meeting also agreed that the Group would be chaired by Jānis Kārkliņš (Latvia) (for more information on the Group of Governmental Experts, see p. 105).

Under its agenda item "Other matters, including the preparation of the sixth Review Conference expected to take place in 2021", the Meeting decided to convene the meeting of the Preparatory Committee for the Review Conference from 23 to 25 August 2021 and the Review Conference from 13 to 17 December 2021.

Under the agenda item "Emerging issues in the context of the objectives and purposes of the Convention", participants expressed divergent views about whether or not the Convention was the right framework to address the use of explosive weapons in populated areas. Several States expressed the view that

---

[99] CCW/MSP/2019/9.

[100] For the Meeting's final report, see CCW/MSP/2019/9.

[101] The Chair was elected *ad personam* through a silence procedure following the departure of his predecessor, Farukh Amil (Pakistan), who had been elected by the 2018 Meeting of the High Contracting Parties.

[102] For the list of participants, see CCW/MSP/2019/INF.1.

[103] CCW/GGE.1/2019/3.

the Convention, centred around the prohibition or the regulation of certain types of weapons, was not the right forum to discuss the use of explosive weapons in populated areas. However, other States disagreed in light of the Convention's objective to protect civilians from unnecessary suffering; the expertise assembled within its framework; and its flexible design, which was tailored to further development of international humanitarian law. The view was also expressed that curtailing the use of explosive weapons in populated areas could incentivize non-State actors to use the civilian population as human shields.

Several States welcomed the Secretary-General's 2019 report on the protection of civilians and the joint appeal by the Secretary-General and the President of ICRC. In addition, Germany submitted under the agenda item "Emerging issues in the context of the objectives and purposes of the Convention" a working paper entitled "Practical measures to improve policies and practices to reduce civilian harm from explosive weapons in urban conflict".[104] The working paper drew upon the research carried out in 2019 by UNIDIR on military policy and practice to reduce civilian harm from explosive weapons in urban conflict.[105] The Meeting decided to keep the item on emerging issues on the agenda for 2020, and it reiterated the invitation to the High Contracting Parties to submit working papers on any emerging issues in the context of the objectives and purposes of the Convention.

In relation to the agenda item "Status of implementation of and compliance with the Convention and its Protocols", the Meeting called for the full implementation of Protocol III and its provisions, as well as for its universalization.

On financial issues, the 2019 Meeting decided to enhance the stability of the Convention's Implementation Support Unit by establishing a voluntary Working Capital Fund, whose functioning would undergo review at the Sixth Review Conference in 2021. The Meeting also decided, inter alia, that: (a) arrears should remain the amount of the initial assessed contribution corresponding to the year in question; and (b) the United Nations Secretariat should maintain the annual expenditures below the average year-end collection rate of the three preceding years. Stressing the importance of the Implementation Support Unit for the operational continuity of the Convention, the Meeting requested the incoming Chair to hold a consultation for the High Contracting Parties and the United Nations Secretariat in March 2020 to discuss the prioritization of funding to ensure the Convention's effective implementation.

The Meeting elected Robbert Jan Gabriëlse (Netherlands) as Chair of the 2020 Meeting of the High Contracting Parties to the Convention.

---

[104] CCW/MSP/2019/WP.1.
[105] Roger Lane, Larry Lewis and Himayu Shiotani, *Opportunities to Improve Military Policies and Practices to Reduce Civilian Harm From Explosive Weapons in Urban Conflict: An Options Paper* (Geneva, UNIDIR, 2019).

Work of the Implementation Support Unit of the Convention on Certain Conventional Weapons

In accordance with the request of the 2018 Meeting of the High Contracting Parties for the Office for Disarmament Affairs to provide temporary staff support to the Implementation Support Unit of the Convention,[106] the Unit was partially staffed for the last seven months of 2019. While all meetings of the Convention for 2019 took place as decided by the 2018 Meeting of the High Contracting Parties, only those in the second half of the year received support from the Unit with the Office's assistance.

In 2019, the Unit engaged in five areas of work, aided by the Office for Disarmament Affairs: (a) secretariat support to meetings; (b) communication and information management; (c) coordination; (d) universalization; and (e) outreach and public information. With regard to secretariat support, the Unit prepared draft briefs for the Chair, prepared cost estimates, provided advice to the Chair on procedural issues and liaised with regional groups to organize informal consultations and identify office holders for upcoming meetings.[107] The Unit also managed the Convention's website, including its databases of national annual reports on compliance with the Convention,[108] Amended Protocol II[109] and Protocol V.[110]

In addition, the Implementation Support Unit coordinated within the United Nations Office at Geneva to contribute to prudent planning, effective organization and regular monitoring of the Convention's activities. Its activities included tracking related developments in the framework of the First Committee to ensure consistency and continuity with activities under the Convention.

In the area of universalization, the Implementation Support Unit conveyed a letter of the Secretary-General to 66 States inviting them to join the Convention. The Unit also provided information on the Convention directly to non-High Contracting Parties and supported the universalization efforts of office holders. Furthermore, the Unit assisted the coordinator of the Convention Sponsorship Programme[111] in collaboration with the Geneva International Centre for

---

[106] The Implementation Support Unit of the Convention on Certain Conventional Weapons was established by the 2009 Meeting of the High Contracting Parties to the Convention.

[107] The Unit endeavoured to deliver information and documents to High Contracting Parties and non-governmental representatives and to respond to their requests in a timely manner, especially with regard to budget and payment.

[108] United Nations Office at Geneva, "The Convention on Certain Conventional Weapons", Compliance Annual Reports Database.

[109] United Nations Office at Geneva, "CCW Amended Protocol II", Database of National Annual Reports.

[110] United Nations Office at Geneva, "CCW Protocol V on Explosive Remnants of War", Protocol V Database.

[111] The Sponsorship Programme was developed in 2005 and 2006 to support the participation of the representatives of High Contracting Parties in Convention-related activities, in particular States that are affected by landmines and explosive remnants of war and have limited resources.

Humanitarian Demining. In 2019, delegates from five States and four experts were sponsored to participate in Convention meetings.

Cluster munitions

The Convention on Cluster Munitions entered into force in 2010, prohibiting the use, development, production, transfer or stockpiling of cluster munitions under any circumstances. It also created a framework for clearance of contaminated areas and destruction of stockpiles, as well as risk-reduction education in affected communities. As at the end of 2019, the Convention had 107 States parties.[112]

Ninth Meeting of States Parties to the Convention on Cluster Munitions

Pursuant to General Assembly resolution 70/54 of 7 December 2015 and the decision of the Convention's first Review Conference, the Secretary-General convened the ninth Meeting of States Parties from 2 to 4 September in Geneva. Aliyar Lebbe Abdul Azeez (Sri Lanka) presided over the Meeting, in which 84 States participated, including 6 signatory and 20 non-signatory States.[113] The observers in attendance included the United Nations Mine Action Service, the European Union, ICRC, the Geneva International Centre for Humanitarian Demining, the Cluster Munitions Coalition, the Regional Mine Action Center of the Association of Southeast Asian Nations, the British Columbia Aboriginal Network on Disability Society, the Center for International Stabilization and Recovery of James Madison University, the Mines Advisory Group and the Halo Trust. The Office for Disarmament Affairs served as secretariat of the Meeting.

Anja Kaspersen, Director of the Geneva Branch of the Office for Disarmament Affairs, delivered a message on behalf of the High Representative for Disarmament Affairs. The participants also heard addresses[114] by Félix Baumann (Switzerland); Gilles Carbonnier, Vice-President of ICRC; and Hector Guerra, Director of the Cluster Munition Coalition.

During the thematic discussion, the Meeting welcomed the accession by the Gambia and the Philippines and reiterated the importance of universalization efforts with the aim of reaching 130 States parties by the second Review Conference in 2020, a goal set forth in the Dubrovnik Action Plan. In addition, the Meeting expressed strong concern regarding recent incidents and evidence of cluster munitions use in different parts of the world and condemned any use by any actor, in accordance with article 21.

---

[112] The Convention's text and adherence status are available at the Disarmament Treaty Database of the Office for Disarmament Affairs.

[113] CCM/MSP/2019/13, paras. 13–18.

[114] See Convention on Cluster Munitions, "Ninth Meeting of States Parties" (Opening of the Meeting).

The Meeting also welcomed continued progress in stockpile destruction over the previous year, which had seen the number of States parties with obligations in that area fall from 10 to 5. In particular, it congratulated Botswana and Switzerland for having complied with their article 3 obligations ahead of their respective deadlines. It also took note of a significant increase in the number of initial reports submitted in 2019 relative to previous years.[115]

After assessing a request from Bulgaria for an extension of its deadline to complete the destruction of all its cluster munitions stockpiles in accordance with article 3.2, the Meeting granted an extension of 12 months to 1 October 2020. The Meeting also assessed separate requests from Germany and the Lao People's Democratic Republic for five additional years to complete clearance and destruction of cluster munitions remnants in accordance with article 4.1, and granted each country the requested extensions to 1 August 2025. Furthermore, the Meeting considered and adopted the methodology[116] for requests of deadline extensions under articles 3 and 4 of the Convention.

Meanwhile, expressing deep concern about the financial situation caused by arrears in payment of assessed contributions, the Meeting underlined the importance of ensuring full compliance with article 14 obligations and called upon all States parties and States not party to address issues arising from outstanding dues. In that context, it considered the document "Possible measures to address the financial predictability and sustainability of the Convention on Cluster Munitions"[117] and requested the President of the second Review Conference to conduct consultations with a view to presenting a proposal for a decision.

The Meeting adopted its final report[118] by consensus and appointed new coordinators[119] to guide the intersessional work programme in 2019 and 2020, including in the thematic areas of national reporting and national implementation measures. The Meeting designated Félix Baumann (Switzerland) as President of the second Review Conference, which it decided would be held from 16 to

---

[115] See United Nations Office at Geneva, "Convention on Cluster Munitions", Article 7 Database.

[116] CCM/MSP/2019/12.

[117] CCM/MSP/2019/5.

[118] CCM/MSP/2019/13.

[119] The appointed coordinators were: working group on the general status and operation of the Convention—Zambia (until the end of the second Review Conference) working with Namibia (until the end of the tenth Meeting of States Parties); working group on universalization—Chile (until the end of the second Review Conference) working with the Philippines (until the end of the tenth Meeting of States Parties); working group on clearance and risk reduction—Sweden (until the end of the second Review Conference) working with Afghanistan (until the end of the tenth Meeting of States Parties); working group on stockpile destruction and retention—Austria (until the end of the second Review Conference) working with Australia (until the end of the tenth Meeting of States Parties); and working group on cooperation and assistance—Netherlands (until the end of the second Review Conference) working with Montenegro (until the end of the tenth Meeting of States Parties). The Meeting also welcomed the coordinators to lead on the following thematic areas: reporting—Iraq; and national implementation measures—New Zealand.

20 November 2020. It also designated Aidan Liddle (United Kingdom) as President of the tenth Meeting of States Parties.

Anti-personnel mines

The 1997 Convention on the Prohibition of the Use, Stockpiling, Production and Transfer of Anti-Personnel Mines and on Their Destruction entered into force on 1 March 1999, prompting deadlines for the destruction of existing mine stocks and the clearance of all contaminated areas, promoting relevant cooperation and assistance, and establishing a strong victim-assistance framework. As at the end of 2019, the Convention had 164 States parties.[120]

Intersessional activities and the fourth Review Conference of the States Parties to the Anti-Personnel Mine Ban Convention

Pursuant to article 12 of the Anti-Personnel Mine Ban Convention and the relevant decisions of its third Review Conference[121] and its seventeenth Meeting of the States Parties,[122] the fourth Review Conference took place in Oslo from 26 to 29 November 2019. It followed two preparatory meetings and a set of informal intersessional meetings held in Geneva earlier in the year, as well as meetings carried out by the Convention committees.[123]

At the first preparatory meeting, held on 24 May, participating States parties focused on procedural and other organizational matters.[124] The meeting considered, inter alia, a concept note[125] submitted by the President to support the development of three substantive documents for the Review Conference: (a) the review of the general status and operation of the Convention; (b) a draft Oslo Action Plan for the five-year period following the Review Conference; and (c) a draft political declaration.[126] The second preparatory meeting, held on 18 September, approved the agenda[127] and provisional programme of work[128] of the Conference, while

---

[120] The Convention's text and adherence status are available at the Disarmament Treaties Database of the Office for Disarmament Affairs.

[121] APLC/CONF/2014/4.

[122] APLC/MSP.17/2018/12.

[123] In addition, the fourth International Pledging Conference was held in Geneva on 26 February, pursuant to the relevant decision of the fourteenth Meeting of the States Parties (APLC/ MSP.14/2015/L.1), with the aim of further securing the financial stability of the Convention's Implementation Support Unit. For a summary of the Conference, see Convention on the Prohibition of the Use, Stockpiling, Production and Transfer of Anti-Personnel Mines and on Their Destruction, "Fourth Annual Pledging Conference for the Implementation of the Anti-Personnel Mine Ban Convention: Tuesday, 26 February 2019".

[124] See the procedural report of the first preparatory meeting (APLC/CONF/2019/PM.1/4).

[125] APLC/CONF/2019/PM.1/3.

[126] The meeting also recommended, per established practice, that the outgoing members of the Convention's Committees—namely, Belgium, Colombia, Mozambique, Netherlands, Poland, Sweden, Thailand and Zambia—serve as Vice-Presidents of the fourth Review Conference.

[127] APLC/CONF/2019/1.

[128] APLC/CONF/2019/2.

also noting and expressing general satisfaction with the documents submitted in preparation for the fourth Review Conference.[129] The meeting further called upon the States participating in the Meetings of the States Parties and Review Conferences to ensure prompt and full payment of their respective assessed contributions and compliance with their obligations pursuant to article 14 of the Convention. In addition, the meeting took note of the proposed dates and structure of the 2020 Convention implementation machinery.

The informal intersessional meetings,[130] held from 22 to 24 May under the overall responsibility of the President-elect of the fourth Review Conference, Hans Brattskar (Norway), considered updates to the activities and the preliminary observations of the four Convention committees, as well as to the mandate of the President.[131]

Those intersessional meetings also included, on 23 May, thematic discussions intended to inform and provide impetus for the development of a strong Oslo Action Plan.[132] Held under the chairmanship of the President-elect of the Review Conference, the discussions focused on six thematic areas: (a) mine clearance and completion deadlines; (b) new use of anti-personnel mines and national reporting; (c) risk education and protection of civilians; (d) victim assistance; (e) integrating a gender perspective in mine action; and (f) cooperation and assistance.

Meanwhile, the four substantive committees of the Convention held regular meetings throughout 2019, accomplishing the following:

- The Committee on Article 5 Implementation communicated and exchanged information with: (a) States parties[133] reporting a need to request extensions of their article 5 deadlines in 2019; (b) States parties[134] with article 5 deadlines in 2021; and (c) States parties implementing their article 5 obligations. The Committee later presented analyses[135] and observations[136] on the extension requests to the fourth Review Conference.

---

[129] See the procedural report of the second preparatory meeting (APLC/CONF/2019/PM.2/2).

[130] For the statements during the meetings, see Convention on the Prohibition of the Use, Stockpiling, Production and Transfer of Anti-Personnel Mines and on Their Destruction, Intersessional Work Programme, May 2019, "Summary and Statements: Wednesday 22 May and Friday 24 May".

[131] The mandate of the President covers the areas of universalization, stockpile destruction and national reporting (APLC/CONF/2014/4, para. 24).

[132] For concept notes on each of these thematic discussions, including the organizations represented in each, see Convention on the Prohibition of the Use, Stockpiling, Production and Transfer of Anti-Personnel Mines and on Their Destruction, Intersessional Work Programme, May 2019, "Thematic Discussions".

[133] Argentina, Cambodia, Chad, Eritrea, Ethiopia, Tajikistan and Yemen.

[134] Bosnia and Herzegovina, Colombia, Democratic Republic of the Congo, Senegal and South Sudan.

[135] APLC/CONF/2019/WP.8-9, WP.12, WP.15-16 and WP.26.

[136] APLC/CONF/2019/WP.28.

- The Committee on Cooperative Compliance continued its cooperative dialogue with States parties[137] confronted with allegations of use of anti-personnel landmines.

- The Committee on the Enhancement of Cooperation and Assistance focused on: (a) strengthening partnerships; and (b) promoting information sharing. In particular, the Committee continued its work in support of the individualized approach.[138]

- The Committee on Victim Assistance continued efforts to improve the implementation of relevant commitments by States parties with significant numbers of landmine survivors. The Committee conducted those activities in line with three core priorities it had identified for 2019: (a) continuing efforts to increase quality and quantity of reports by affected States; (b) strengthening synergies with relevant stakeholders outside the Convention; and (c) increasing collaboration between office holders taking the lead on victim-assistance matters.

In addition, the Coordinating Committee held regular meetings throughout the year to manage work flowing from and related to formal and informal events of the States parties, as well as to implement its responsibilities related to the accountability of the Implementation Support Unit.

The fourth Review Conference of the States Parties to the Convention was chaired by Hans Brattskar (Norway), with Belgium, Colombia, Mozambique, Netherlands, Poland, Sweden, Thailand and Zambia serving as Vice-Presidents.

The Conference began with an opening ceremony featuring Crown Prince Haakon of Norway; the Minister of Foreign Affairs of Norway, Ine Eriksen Søreide; the Minister of International Development of Norway, Dag-Inge Ulstein; the Mayor of Oslo, Marianne Borgen; the United Nations High Representative for Disarmament Affairs, Izumi Nakamitsu, who conveyed a message[139] from the Secretary-General; the United Nations High Commissioner for Refugees, Filippo Grandi; the Vice-President of ICRC, Gilles Carbonnier; the Special Adviser to the United Nations Children's Fund, Geert Cappelaere; the Special Envoys of the Convention, Princess Astrid of Belgium and Prince Mired Raad Al-Hussein of Jordan; Selma Guso from Bosnia and Herzegovina; and Alex Munyambabazi from Uganda, representing landmine survivors; and Fay Wildhagen, a Norwegian artist.

As reflected in its final report,[140] the Conference took stock of the current status of implementation of the Convention and the progress made since the third

---

[137] Sudan, Ukraine and Yemen.

[138] The individualized approach provides a platform under the Convention for affected States parties to strengthen partnerships towards completion of their obligations, in particular those under article 5.

[139] Secretary-General's message to the fourth Review Conference of the States Parties to the Convention on the Prohibition of the Use, Stockpiling, Production and Transfer of Anti-Personnel Mines, Oslo, 25 November 2019.

[140] APLC/CONF/2019/5 and Add.1.

Review Conference in 2014, condemned the use of anti-personnel mines by any actor, and reaffirmed the determination of the States parties to put an end to the suffering and casualties caused by anti-personnel mines, and their aspiration to meet the goals of the Convention to the fullest extent possible by 2025. The Conference also adopted the Oslo Declaration on a Mine-Free World, the Oslo Action Plan for 2020 to 2024, and the review of the operation and status of the Convention for 2014 to 2019.[141]

Furthermore, the Conference assessed and granted the extension requests of six States parties[142] for completing the destruction of anti-personnel mines in mined areas.[143] In considering its extension request, the Conference asked Eritrea to submit a new request in accordance with the established process by 31 March 2020.

With regard to the operation and status of the Convention and its meeting programme and machinery, the Conference decided to keep the current implementation mechanism with several adjustments. Specifically, the Conference strengthened the mandate of the President to: (a) lead on matters related to assessed contributions received pursuant to article 14 of the Convention; and (b) to propose, if deemed necessary, one or more members of the Coordinating Committee to provide support on any issue of the President's mandate that may require particular attention, including on financial matters. The Conference also amended the Committees' mandates, calling for the review of relevant information provided by States parties on the implementation of commitments contained in the Oslo Action Plan, as well as for the consideration of matters related to gender and the diverse needs and experiences of people in affected communities. Furthermore, the Conference amended the Committees' working methods to: (a) include appointing a focal point for each Committee to advise on gender mainstreaming; and (b) increase and strengthen coordination among the Committees, both for more holistic monitoring of implementation by States parties and for consideration of potential joint conclusions on the status of the Convention's implementation. In addition, the Committee on Cooperative Compliance was mandated to: (a) address all matters under article 1.2 of the Convention in cases where a State party has not submitted an article 7 report detailing progress in implementing relevant obligations each year; (b) support States parties in their efforts to implement and report on matters contained in article 9 of the Convention; and (c) encourage States parties to submit annual article 7 reports.

Separately, States parties noted again with concern the financial situation of the Convention owing to late payment and arrears of assessed contributions. In that connection, the Conference requested States in arrears to pay outstanding amounts in full at the earliest possible date, and it underlined the importance of ensuring full compliance with article 14 obligations.

---

[141] APLC/CONF/2019/5/Add.1.

[142] Argentina, Cambodia, Chad, Ethiopia, Tajikistan and Yemen.

[143] The Conference granted the extensions in accordance with the agreed process for the preparation, submission and consideration of requests for extensions to deadlines pursuant to article 5 of the Convention. See APLC/MSP.7/2016/L.3 and APLC/MSP.7/2006/5, para. 27.

In considering the status of assessed contributions pursuant to article 14 of the Convention, based on the recommendations contained in the document[144] submitted by the President on financial predictability and sustainability of United Nations assessed contributions, the Conference agreed to continue to implement, inter alia, the inclusion of a 15-per-cent contingency line in the cost estimates of the Meetings of States Parties and Review Conferences; the publication of monthly financial status reports on the website of the United Nations Office at Geneva; the inclusion of an agenda item entitled "Status of assessed contributions received pursuant to Article 14 of the Convention" in all Convention-related meetings; and issuance by the Office for Disarmament Affairs of regular notices to States and updates to the Coordinating Committee on the financial situation.

The Conference also took additional measures aimed at securing financial predictability and sustainability of the Convention's finances, including requesting the United Nations to close the accounts for each financial period within 12 months of its conclusion, send individualized digital invoices to States and prepare a two-year cost estimate for approval by States parties. The Conference also: decided that arrears for unpaid contributions would remain the amount initially invoiced to the relevant State party for the year in question, unless the expenditures were higher than initial cost estimates; encouraged each State whose contributions were in arrears for two or more years to enter into a payment schedule with the President, supported by the United Nations; requested States in a position to do so to notify the President at the beginning of the year when they expected to pay their contributions; and requested the President, for the purpose of financial planning over the year, to contact States that did not pay their assessed contributions by 30 April to ask those in a position to do so to clarify when they would submit payment.

The fourth Review Conference decided to hold the eighteenth Meeting of the States Parties in Geneva during the week of 16 November 2020, under the chairmanship of Osman Abufatima Adam Mohammed (Sudan), and the nineteenth Meeting of the States Parties in 2021 in the Netherlands, under the chairmanship of Robbert Jan Gabriëlse (Netherlands). The 2020 intersessional meetings were scheduled to take place from 30 June to 2 July 2020. The Conference also decided on the new membership of the Convention Committees.[145]

---

[144] APLC/CONF/2019/WP.17.

[145] The new members of the Committees were as follows: Committee on Victim Assistance— Chile and Italy until the end of the eighteenth Meeting of States Parties, and Sweden and Thailand until the end of the nineteenth Meeting of States Parties; Committee on Article 5 Implementation—Austria and Canada until the end of the eighteenth Meeting of States Parties, and Norway and Zambia until the end of the nineteenth Meeting of States Parties; Committee on the Enhancement of Cooperation and Assistance—Turkey and the United Kingdom until the end of the eighteenth Meeting of States Parties, and Colombia and Germany until the end of the nineteenth Meeting of States Parties; Committee on Cooperative Compliance—Iraq and Switzerland until the end of the eighteenth Meeting of States Parties, and Panama and Poland until the end of the nineteenth Meeting of States Parties.

Annex I

Composition of the Group of Governmental Experts on the continuing operation of the United Nations Register of Conventional Arms and its further development

Mariela Fogante (Chair)
Director, Ministry of Foreign Relations and Worship of Argentina

Maria Cecilia B. Cavalcante Vieira
Deputy Head, Division for Disarmament and Sensitive Technologies, Ministry of Foreign Relations of Brazil

Eden Clabuchar Martingo
Second Secretary, Special Representation of Brazil to the Conference on Disarmament, Geneva (third session)

Danhui Song
Director, Department of Arms Control and Disarmament, Ministry of Foreign Affairs of China

Andreja Petkovic
First Committee Expert, Permanent Mission of Croatia to the United Nations, New York

Pascal Levant
Military Adviser, Permanent Mission of France to the Conference on Disarmament

Regis Lamarque
Lieutenant Colonel, Ministry of Armed Forces of France (second session)

Julien Fort
Export Control Expert, Directorate General for International Relationships and Strategy, Ministry of Armed Forces of France

Tarmo Dix
Deputy Head, Division for Export Control of Conventional Arms and Dual-Use Goods, Federal Foreign Office of Germany

Tripuresh Dhar Diwivedi
Director Air II, Ministry of Defence of India

Yoko Owatari
First Secretary, Delegation of Japan to the Conference on Disarmament, Geneva

Sachi Claringbould
Deputy Permanent Representative, Permanent Mission of the Netherlands to the Conference on Disarmament, Geneva

Vladislav Antonyuk
> Deputy Director, Department for Non-Proliferation and Arms Control, Ministry of Foreign Affairs of the Russian Federation

Cheikh Ahmadou Bamba Gaye
> Counsellor, Permanent Mission of Senegal to the United Nations, New York

Seow Peng Yeo
> Director, Association of Southeast Asian Nations and International Affairs Defence Policy Office, Ministry of Defence of Singapore

Johann Kellerman
> Director for Disarmament and Non-Proliferation, Department of International Relations and Cooperation of South Africa

Eleonora Saggese
> Disarmament and Arms Control Attaché, Permanent Mission of the United Kingdom of Great Britain and Northern Ireland to the United Nations Office at Geneva and other international organizations in Geneva

Guy Pollard
> Head of Strategic Export Compliance, Rolls-Royce, United Kingdom

William B. Malzahn
> Representative to the Arms Trade Treaty Conference, Bureau of International Security and Non-Proliferation, Department of State of the United States of America

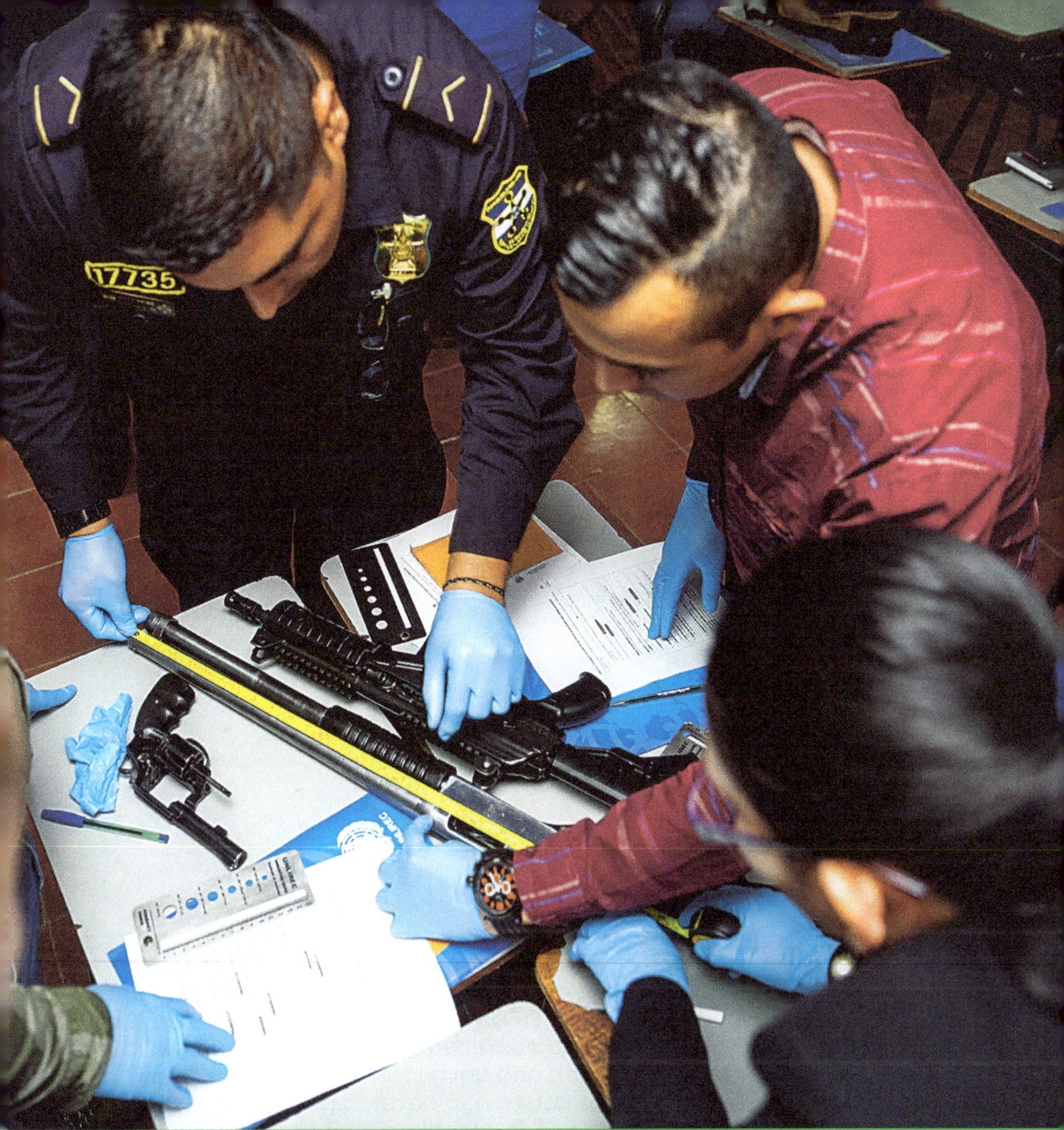

chapter

IV Regional disarmament

At the Firearms and Ammunition Evidence Management Course at La Paz, El Salvador, from 2 to 4 December 2019, where 25 participants received theoretical and practical training in firearm and ammunition identification and guidelines. The course also covered good practices for ensuring the competent management of crime scenes, evidence processing and analysis, as well as the correct utilization of the chain-of-custody system, among other useful tools to strengthen the investigation process and intelligence related to cases involving firearms and ammunition.

Photo: United Nations Regional Centre for Peace, Disarmament and Development in Latin America and the Caribbean

Chapter IV

Regional disarmament

Serious deliberations on a Middle East zone free of nuclear, chemical and other weapons of mass destruction would be an opportunity for the States of the region to engage in direct dialogue on arrangements that could address their security requirements.

ANTÓNIO GUTERRES, UNITED NATIONS SECRETARY-GENERAL[1]

Developments and trends, 2019

THE YEAR 2019 saw the continuation of many regional activities in support of disarmament, non-proliferation and arms control, with goals ranging from preventing the proliferation of weapons of mass destruction to countering the illicit manufacturing of and trade in conventional arms, particularly small arms, light weapons and their ammunition. In support, the United Nations engaged, coordinated and facilitated cooperation with States, regional and subregional organizations, relevant international organizations and civil society, including through exchanges and dialogues, capacity-building projects and information campaigns.

Meanwhile, the ongoing deterioration of the global security environment cast dark shadows over already-complex geopolitical realities at the regional and subregional levels. In the Middle East and North-East Asia, ongoing conflicts hampered progress in addressing pressing disarmament and non-proliferation issues. In addition, the gradual erosion of the disarmament and international security architecture contributed further to fears of a new arms race between major powers, with negative implications for regional and international security.[2]

Notwithstanding, significant progress was made at the regional and subregional levels in adherence by Member States to multilateral treaties and regional conventions.

---

[1] Remarks at the Conference on the Establishment of a Middle East Zone Free of Nuclear Weapons and Other Weapons of Mass Destructions, New York, 18 November 2019.

[2] In that regard, two particularly important developments were the demise of the 1987 Treaty between the United States of America and the Union of Soviet Socialist Republics on the Elimination of Their Intermediate-Range and Shorter-Range Missiles (Intermediate-Range Nuclear Forces Treaty) and the impending potential expiration of the 2011 Treaty between the United States of America and the Russian Federation on Measures for the Further Reduction and Limitation of Strategic Offensive Arms (New START Treaty). For more information on those developments, see chap. I.

In the field of weapons of mass destruction, 21 States ratified or signed the Treaty on the Prohibition of Nuclear Weapons. In Latin America and the Caribbean, the Treaty was ratified by eight States and signed by five, including two States that also ratified it.[3] In Africa, the Treaty was ratified by two States and signed by three, including one State that also ratified it.[4] In Asia and the Pacific, the Treaty was ratified by four States and signed by two.[5] Separately, Zimbabwe ratified the Comprehensive Nuclear-Test-Ban Treaty in February, while Montenegro and Thailand ratified the International Convention for the Suppression of Acts of Nuclear Terrorism in February and May, respectively. In August, the United Republic of Tanzania ratified the Biological Weapons Convention.

In the area of conventional weapons, a degree of progress was made in the adherence by States to relevant global and subregional treaties. That was particularly the case in Africa, where Botswana ratified the Arms Trade Treaty in June and, in December, Equatorial Guinea became a State party of the Central African Convention for the Control of Small Arms and Light Weapons, Their Ammunition and All Parts and Components That Can Be Used for Their Manufacture, Repair and Assembly (Kinshasa Convention, 2010).[6] In Latin America and the Caribbean, the Plurinational State of Bolivia subscribed in May to the Protocol against the Illicit Manufacturing of and Trafficking in Firearms, Their Parts and Components and Ammunition (Firearms Protocol) of the United Nations Convention against Transnational Organized Crime. In Asia and the Pacific, the Philippines ratified the Convention on Cluster Munitions in January, and Maldives acceded to the Convention in September.

Pursuant to General Assembly decision 73/546 of 22 December 2018, the Secretary-General convened the first annual session of the Conference on the Establishment of a Middle East Zone Free of Nuclear Weapons and Other Weapons of Mass Destruction at the United Nations Headquarters from 11 to 22 November. That meeting represented the beginning of an annual process expected to continue until concluding the elaboration of a legally binding treaty establishing such a zone in that region.

In the meantime, States within existing nuclear-weapon-free zones continued efforts to strengthen those zones in 2019 by enhancing cooperation within and between them, thus contributing to the global nuclear disarmament

---

[3] In 2019, Dominica and Trinidad and Tobago signed and ratified the Treaty on the Prohibition of Nuclear Weapons; Antigua and Barbuda, Bolivia (Plurinational State of), El Salvador, Panama, Saint Vincent and the Grenadines, and Santa Lucia ratified it; and Grenada and Saint Kitts and Nevis signed it.

[4] In 2019, Maldives signed and ratified the Treaty on the Prohibition on Nuclear Weapons; South Africa also ratified it; and Botswana, Lesotho and Zambia signed it.

[5] In 2019, Bangladesh, Kazakhstan, Kiribati and the Lao People's Democratic Republic ratified the Treaty on the Prohibition on Nuclear Weapons, and Cambodia and Nauru signed it.

[6] The text and adherence status of the Kinshasa Convention are available from the Disarmament Treaty Database of the Office for Disarmament Affairs. The Convention entered into force on 8 March 2017.

and non-proliferation regime at the regional level. In particular, States in nuclear-weapon-free zones worked together to ensure full implementation of their respective treaties by building the capacities of their implementation agencies and fully utilizing their consultation mechanisms. They also enhanced cooperation between and among the zones, including by jointly planning the fourth Conference of Nuclear-Weapon-Free Zones and Mongolia, to be held in 2020. Furthermore, those States continued engaging with nuclear-weapon States to resolve outstanding issues regarding assurances against the use or the threat of use of nuclear weapons. In the case of the Treaty on the Southeast Asia Nuclear-Weapon-Free Zone, States parties continued dialogues and discussions with five nuclear-weapons States to obtain their signatures or ratifications of the relevant protocol of the Treaty.

Meanwhile, in line with the Secretary-General's Agenda for Disarmament, the Office for Disarmament Affairs and its three regional centres expanded their engagement with regional and subregional organizations to explore new opportunities and strengthen existing platforms for regional dialogue on security and arms control. As part of that effort, the centres assisted States and regional organizations to accede to and implement multilateral and regional treaties and conventions, as well as to build their capacities to manage conventional weapons and ammunition and combat their illicit manufacturing and trade. For instance, the United Nations Regional Centre for Peace, Disarmament and Development in Latin America and the Caribbean, in partnership with the Caribbean Community's Implementation Agency for Crime and Security, launched the Caribbean Firearms Roadmap, aimed at accelerating efforts to prevent and combat the illicit proliferation of firearms and ammunition in the region by 2030.

Furthermore, regional and subregional organizations deepened their activities to advance a range of disarmament goals. The United Nations supported those organizations by, for example, bolstering its support to the African Union flagship initiative on "Silencing the Guns in Africa by 2020", particularly after the Security Council adopted a resolution[7] on the matter in February. Other regional and subregional organizations also benefited from high-level political engagements, such as the Security Council's consideration of United Nations cooperation with the League of Arab States in June and the Secretary-General's participation in its summit in Tunis in March, as well as his participation in a high-level political dialogue with the Pacific Islands Forum leaders in Fiji in May. Furthermore, the European Union, the North Atlantic Treaty Organization and the Organization for Security and Co-operation in Europe expanded their partnerships with the Office for Disarmament Affairs and its regional centres to carry out capacity-building projects and dissemination activities at the regional and subregional levels, providing further opportunities for cross-regional synergies.

---

[7] Security Council resolution 2457 (2019).

Nuclear-weapon-free zones

Nuclear-weapon-free zones continued to provide a regional approach to strengthening global nuclear non-proliferation and disarmament norms, while also promoting peace and security at both regional and international levels. The legal foundation for such zones rests with the Charter of the United Nations and its language concerning "regional arrangements or agencies" to deal with the maintenance of international peace and security. Their importance is recognized in article VII of the Treaty on the Non-Proliferation of Nuclear Weapons (Nuclear Non-Proliferation Treaty), stating, "nothing in this Treaty affects the right of any group of States to conclude regional treaties in order to assure the total absence of nuclear weapons in their respective territories".

As at the end of 2019, more than 100 States were parties or signatories to nuclear-weapon-free zone treaties, representing nearly 60 per cent of the membership of the United Nations. Five regional nuclear-weapon-free zones had been established under the following treaties: (a) the Treaty for the Prohibition of Nuclear Weapons in Latin America and the Caribbean (Treaty of Tlatelolco, 1969); (b) the South Pacific Nuclear Free Zone Treaty (Rarotonga Treaty, 1986); (c) the Treaty on the Southeast Asia Nuclear Weapon-Free Zone (Bangkok Treaty, 1997); (d) the African Nuclear-Weapon-Free Zone Treaty (Pelindaba Treaty, 2009); and (e) the Treaty on a Nuclear-Weapon-Free Zone in Central Asia (2009). In 2018, the General Assembly reaffirmed Mongolia as a self-declared, single-State nuclear-weapon-free zone in its biennial resolution entitled "Mongolia's international security and nuclear-weapon status" (73/44), first adopted in 1998.

During its seventy-fourth session, the General Assembly adopted the traditional resolution entitled "Nuclear-weapon-free southern hemisphere and adjacent areas" (74/48), reaffirming the role of nuclear-weapon-free zones in promoting nuclear disarmament and non-proliferation, as well as their contribution to peace and security, at the regional and global level.

In the lead-up to the fourth Conference of Nuclear-Weapon-Free Zones and Mongolia planned for April 2020, a number of States parties and signatories to the nuclear-weapon-free zone treaties and other stakeholders met in Nur-Sultan, Kazakhstan, on 28 and 29 August for the Seminar on Fostering Cooperation and Enhancing Consultation Mechanisms Among the Existing Nuclear-Weapon-Free Zones. Jointly organized by the Office for Disarmament Affairs and Kazakhstan, the seminar drew representatives from all existing nuclear-weapon-free zones and Mongolia, as well as relevant international organizations and observers from State parties and signatories to the treaty protocols. Kazakhstan, as the host country, produced a set of recommendations[8] aimed at revitalizing and systematizing

---

[8] Office for Disarmament Affairs, "Chair's summary at the conclusion of the Seminar on Fostering Cooperation and Enhancing Consultation Mechanisms Among the Existing Nuclear-Weapon-Free Zones", 29 August 2019.

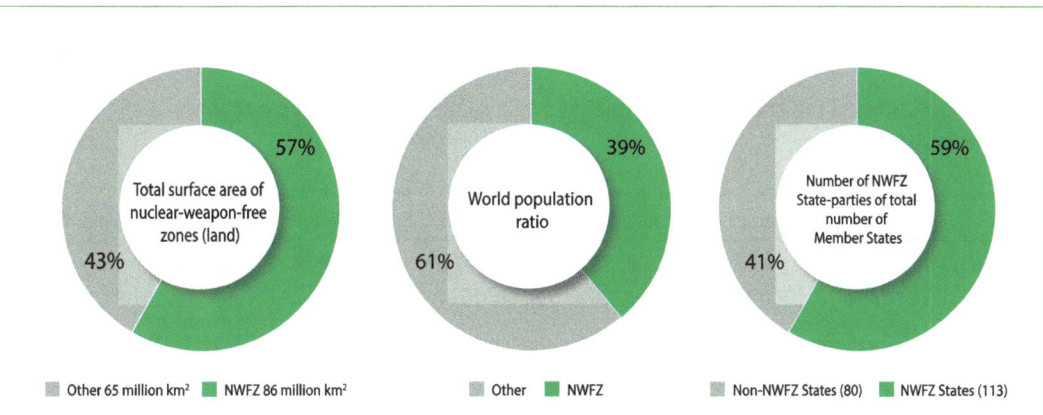

Nuclear-weapon-free zones strengthen the global nuclear non-proliferation regime, advance the case for global nuclear disarmament, and strengthen both regional and international peace and security. In parallel, nuclear-weapon-free zones are "landmark instruments" that cover roughly half the world's land mass (86 million square kilometres), include 60 per cent of the United Nation's membership (113 Member States) and represent more than a third of the world population as of 2019.

cooperation between the zones in alignment with Action 5 of the Secretary-General's Agenda for Disarmament.[9]

In 2019, the nuclear-weapon States of the Nuclear Non-Proliferation Treaty maintained varying positions concerning adherence to the above-mentioned treaties. Under relevant protocols to each of the treaties, the States committed to respecting the nuclear-weapon-free status of the respective specified areas and undertake not to use or threaten to use nuclear weapons against States parties. All five nuclear-weapon States adhered to Additional Protocol II to the Treaty of Tlatelolco. In prior years, four of the nuclear-weapon States had ratified Protocols 1, 2 and 3 to the Rarotonga Treaty, Protocols I and II to the Pelindaba Treaty, and the Protocol to the Treaty on a Nuclear-Weapon-Free Zone in Central Asia. The United States of America had signed all those protocols but had not yet ratified them.

Meanwhile, none of the five nuclear-weapon States had signed the Protocol to the Bangkok Treaty. France expressed its intent to continue dialogue with member countries of the Association of Southeast Asian Nations (ASEAN) with a view to making progress on the signature of the Protocol,[10] while the Russian Federation expressed its readiness to sign it in the near future.[11]

---

[9] Office for Disarmament Affairs, "Securing Our Common Future: An Agenda for Disarmament" (Status of Steps and Activities, Action 5).

[10] M. Yann Hwang, Permanent Representative of France to the Conference on Disarmament, statement at the seventy-fourth session of General Assembly First Committee, New York, 22 October 2019.

[11] Statement by the delegation of the Russian Federation at the Conference for Disarmament, 2019 session. See also the statement by the delegation of the Russian Federation at the third session of the Preparatory Committee for the 2020 Review Conference of the Parties to The Treaty on the Non-Proliferation of Nuclear Weapons, New York, 3 May 2019.

See the following table for the status of adherence to the protocols that provide negative security assurances.

Status of ratification of the protocols to the treaties establishing nuclear-weapon-free zones as at 1 December 2019

Protocol	Status	China	France	Russian Federation	United Kingdom	United States
Additional Protocol II to the Treaty of Tlatelolco	Signed	21 Aug. 1973	18 July 1973	18 May 1978	20 Dec. 1967	1 Apr. 1968
	Ratified	12 June 1974	22 Mar. 1974	8 Jan. 1979	11 Dec. 1969	12 May 1971
Protocol 2 to the Treaty of Rarotonga	Signed	10 Feb. 1987	25 Mar. 1996	15 Dec. 1986	25 Mar. 1996	25 Mar. 1996
	Ratified	21 Oct. 1988	20 Sep. 1996	21 Apr. 1988	19 Sep. 1997	—[a]
Protocol to the Bangkok Treaty	Signed	–	–	–	–	–
	Ratified	–	–	–	–	–
Protocol I to the Pelindaba Treaty	Signed	11 Apr. 1996	11 Apr. 1996	5 Nov. 1996	11 Apr. 1996	11 Apr. 1996
	Ratified	10 Oct. 1997	20 Sep. 1996	5 Apr. 2011	12 Mar. 2001	—[b]
Protocol to the Treaty on a Nuclear-Weapon-Free Zone in Central Asia	Signed	6 May 2014	6 May 2014	6 May 2014	6 May 2014	6 May 2014
	Ratified	17 Aug. 2015	17 Nov. 2014	22 June 2015	30 Jan. 2015	—[c]

Note: The status of signature and ratification of the treaties and protocols are available from the Disarmament Treaties Database of the Office of Disarmament Affairs.

[a] The Protocol was submitted on 2 May 2011 to the United States Senate for its consent to ratification. See United States, *Message from the President of the United States transmitting Protocols 1, 2, and 3 to the South Pacific Nuclear Free Zone Treaty, signed on behalf of the United States at Suva on March 25, 1996* (Washington, D.C., United States Government Printing Office, 2011).

[b] The Protocol was submitted on 2 May 2011 to the United States Senate for its consent to ratification. See United States, *Message from the President of the United States transmitting Protocols I and II to the African Nuclear-Weapon-Free Zone Treaty, signed on behalf of the United States at Cairo, on April 11, 1996, including a Third Protocol Related to the Treaty* (Washington, D.C., United States Government Printing Office, 2011).

[c] The Protocol was submitted on 27 April 2015 to the United States Senate for its consent to ratification. See United States, *Message from the President of the United States Transmitting the Protocol to the Treaty on a Nuclear-Weapon-Free Zone in Central Asia, signed at New York on May 6, 2014* (Washington, D.C., United States Government Printing Office, 2015).

Treaty for the Prohibition of Nuclear Weapons in Latin America and the Caribbean (Treaty of Tlatelolco)

The year 2019 marked the fifty-second anniversary of the Treaty of Tlatelolco and the fiftieth anniversary of its main implementing body, the Agency for the Prohibition of Nuclear Weapons in Latin America and the Caribbean. To mark that occasion, the Agency issued a communiqué[12] on 14 February in which it highlighted the full implementation of the Treaty and its contribution towards nuclear disarmament.

---

[12] Agency for the Prohibition of Nuclear Weapons in Latin America and the Caribbean (OPANAL), document Inf.02/2019Rev.8.

The Agency engaged in activities at the regional and international levels throughout the year. In February, the Agency participated in an extraordinary session of the African Commission of Nuclear Energy in Algiers, its first official participation in an event of the Commission.[13] Then, in April, the Agency participated and delivered a statement[14] during the third session of the Preparatory Committee for the 2020 Nuclear Non-Proliferation Treaty Review Conference.

On the occasion of the International Day for the Total Elimination of Nuclear Weapons on 26 September, the Agency's member States issued a declaration[15] in which they demanded that nuclear weapons not be used again, under any circumstances, by any actor. Those States also reiterated the call upon all States, in particular nuclear-weapon States, to eliminate the role of nuclear weapons in their security and defence doctrines and policies, as well as to comply fully with their legal obligations and unequivocal commitments to accomplish the total elimination of nuclear weapons without further delay. The Agency's member States also reiterated their continued commitment to promoting dialogue and cooperation between the nuclear-weapon-free zones, including Mongolia, through plans to conduct the fourth Conference of Nuclear-Weapon-Free Zones and Mongolia in 2020.

In its capacity as President of the Agency's Council, Argentina delivered a statement[16] on 16 October during the general debate of the General Assembly's First Committee. The following week, the President made remarks[17] on behalf of the Agency's Secretary-General during the exchange[18] with the United Nations High Representative for Disarmament Affairs and briefings by other high-level officials in the field of arms control and disarmament.[19] In addition, 31 States introduced the traditional resolution entitled "Treaty for the Prohibition of Nuclear Weapons in Latin America and the Caribbean (Treaty of Tlatelolco)", which the General Assembly later adopted (General Assembly resolution 74/27), as in previous years.

On 7 November, the Agency held the twenty-sixth session of its General Conference in Mexico City. The Conference adopted 16 resolutions, including one on the election, by acclamation, of Flavio Roberto Bonzanini (Brazil) as the Agency's next Secretary-General for the period 2020–2021.

---

[13] OPANAL, document Inf.18/2019.

[14] OPANAL, document Inf.11/2019.

[15] OPANAL, document C/17/2019.Rev8.

[16] OPANAL, document Inf.22/2019.

[17] OPANAL, "OPANAL reaffirmed the commitment of its Member States to nuclear disarmament and non-proliferation at the High-Level Panel of the First Committee of the 74th United Nations General Assembly", 24 October 2019.

[18] United Nations Web TV, "Disarmament and International Security Committee-Exchange with the High Representative for Disarmament Affairs and briefings by other high-level officials in the field of arms control and disarmament (24 October 2019)" (video), 24 October 2019.

[19] The Argentinian presidency was represented, respectively, by Ezequiel Sabor and by Martin García Moritán in the two interventions referenced.

The Agency's other activities included continued efforts in the area of disarmament and non-proliferation education. In 2019, it organized two training courses in Guatemala and Nicaragua on disarmament and non-proliferation of nuclear weapons.

South Pacific Nuclear Free Zone (Rarotonga Treaty)

The Rarotonga Treaty entered into force in 1986, following its adoption the previous year by leaders of the Pacific Islands Forum.

At the fiftieth Pacific Islands Forum,[20] held in Tuvalu from 13 to 16 August, the leaders endorsed the Boe Declaration Action Plan, including two actions and associated measures of success related to disarmament. For the first of those actions, "Strengthening the progression and reporting of Sustainable Development Goal 16 across Forum Members", the Forum decided to measure success by the support provided to member countries in becoming parties to United Nations disarmament treaties and conventions, such as the Arms Trade Treaty, the Chemical Weapons Convention and the Biological Weapons Convention. Regarding the second action, "Support universalisation across the region of relevant international security treaties and conventions including Security Council resolutions as espoused under the Honiara Declaration and the Nasonini Declaration", the Forum would measure success by any increases in the number of member countries that had signed, ratified and implemented relevant Security Council resolutions and disarmament treaties. Notably, the leaders also urged the four member States that had not already done so to sign and ratify the Comprehensive Nuclear-Test-Ban Treaty,[21] which would achieve its universalization in the region.

The leaders also stressed the importance of upholding the objects of the South Pacific Nuclear Free Zone established under the Rarotonga Treaty. In that regard, they highlighted two key actions: (a) operationalizing Treaty mechanisms; and (b) commissioning a scientific body to undertake an independent assessment of radioactive contamination in the Pacific. To take those tasks forward, the Forum secretariat considered the potential to convene a "consultative committee" meeting of States parties in 2020—the thirty-fifth year since the Treaty's entry into force—to endorse and initiate the necessary activities.

Meanwhile, the Forum's member States planned to take advantage of the 2020 Nuclear Non-Proliferation Treaty Review Conference as a critical opportunity for the Pacific and other regions to project a strong stance on non-proliferation and disarmament. In light of the close relationship between key provisions of the Rarotonga Treaty and the Nuclear Non-Proliferation Treaty, as well as the potential for modifications to the latter instrument to affect

---

[20] Pacific Islands Forum, "Fiftieth Pacific Islands Forum, Tuvalu, 13–16 August 2019: Forum communiqué".

[21] All but four of the Forum's 18 member States had signed and ratified the Comprehensive Nuclear-Test-Ban Treaty as at the end of the year. Papua New Guinea, Solomon Islands and Tuvalu had signed but not ratified the Treaty, while Tonga had neither signed nor ratified it.

the implementation of the regional nuclear-weapon-free zone agreement, the Forum secretariat planned to consult closely with member States to coordinate a collective regional position in preparation for the Review Conference.

Also in 2019, the leaders called for further support of bilateral, regional and multilateral action to assist the Marshall Islands in efforts to meaningfully engage with the United States on achieving the full, fair and just resolution of all outstanding nuclear testing legacy issues. The Forum intended to join other regional organizations in the Pacific in helping Kiribati and the Marshall Islands to address ongoing impacts of nuclear testing, including in the areas of human rights, health and the environment.

Treaty on the Southeast Asia Nuclear Weapon-Free Zone (Bangkok Treaty)

The Bangkok Treaty remained the only one of the five above-mentioned treaties without legally binding negative security assurances in force.

In the framework of the ASEAN Regional Forum, the eleventh Inter-Sessional Meeting on Non-Proliferation and Disarmament in April took note of efforts to promote peaceful uses of nuclear technology and regional cooperation in nuclear energy in the region. Regarding such efforts, the Meeting received updates on the ASEAN Network of Regulatory Bodies on Atomic Energy, the Bangkok Treaty and the Treaty on the Prohibition of Nuclear Weapons. The Meeting also exchanged views on the way forward for the 2020 Nuclear Non-Proliferation Treaty Review Conference, as well as on non-proliferation challenges and prospects in the region.

ASEAN held its thirty-fourth and thirty-fifth summits in Bangkok on 23 June and 3 November, respectively.[22] The Heads of State and Government of member countries reiterated their commitment to preserving the South-East Asia as a zone free of nuclear weapons and all other weapons of mass destruction, as enshrined in the Bangkok Treaty and the ASEAN Charter. They also reaffirmed their commitment to engage continuously with the nuclear-weapon States and to intensify the ongoing efforts of all parties to resolve all outstanding issues in accordance with the objectives and principles of the Bangkok Treaty.

On 30 July, during the meeting of the Commission for the Southeast Asia Nuclear Weapon-Free Zone held as part of the Association's fifty-second Foreign Ministers' Meeting, the member States underscored the importance of the Bangkok Treaty's full and effective implementation, including under the Plan of Action to Strengthen the Implementation of the Treaty on the Southeast Asia Nuclear Weapon-Free Zone (2018–2022).[23] The Association's foreign ministers

---

[22] See ASEAN, "Chairman's Statement of the 34th ASEAN Summit, Bangkok, 23 June 2019, Advancing Partnership for Sustainability" and "Chairman's Statement of the 35th ASEAN Summit, Bangkok/Nonthaburi, 3 November 2019, Advancing Partnership for Sustainability".

[23] ASEAN, "Plan of action to strengthen the implementation of the Treaty on the Southeast Asia Nuclear Weapon -Free Zone (2018–2022)", 4 August 2017.

agreed to explore ways to bridge differences, including potential expert-level engagement with nuclear-weapon States on the possibility of those States signing and ratifying the Protocol to the Bangkok Treaty, achieving the full formalization of a South-East Asia free of nuclear weapons.[24]

At the seventy-fourth session of the General Assembly First Committee, Myanmar delivered a statement[25] during the general debate on behalf of the ASEAN member States and Bangkok Treaty States parties. However, only a technical decision under the agenda item "Treaty on the South-East Asia Nuclear-Weapon-Free Zone (Bangkok Treaty)" (74/510) was introduced instead of a substantive resolution, as in 2017.

African Nuclear-Weapon-Free Zone Treaty (Pelindaba Treaty)

In 2019, the African Commission on Nuclear Energy achieved significant progress in operationalizing its role as the main implementing body of the African Nuclear-Weapon-Free-Zone Treaty. The Commission, inter alia, began actively developing partnerships with international organizations and other nuclear-weapon-free zones to consolidate and strengthen efforts in nuclear disarmament, non-proliferation and peaceful applications of nuclear science and technology, particularly through enhanced South-South cooperation.[26]

The Commission also continued to prioritize the implementation and operationalization of national State systems to account for and control nuclear material for nuclear safeguards, which would allow African States parties to fulfil their obligations under their comprehensive safeguards agreements with the International Atomic Energy Agency (IAEA). In that connection, the Commission joined the IAEA Department of Safeguards to organize the first joint Regional Workshop on Strengthening and Establishing the State System of Accounting for and Control of Nuclear Material in African States Parties to the Pelindaba Treaty, held in June 2019. The organizers planned to hold several more workshops on that topic in 2020.[27]

On 27 August, the Commission and the International Science and Technology Center, based in Nur-Sultan, signed a memorandum of understanding for cooperation in strengthening nuclear safety, security and safeguards in African

---

[24] ASEAN, "Joint Communique of the 52nd ASEAN Foreign Ministers' Meeting Bangkok, 31 July 2019".

[25] Kyaw Moe Tun, Permanent Representative of the Republic of the Union of Myanmar to the United Nations at Geneva, statement on behalf of ASEAN at the seventy-fourth session of the United Nations General Assembly, New York, 7 October 2019.

[26] African Union, "Communique: Adopted by the Peace and Security Council at its 837th meeting held on 4 April 2019 on international disarmament, with a focus on the Anti-Personnel Mine Ban Convention (APMBC) and the Treaty on the Prohibition of Nuclear Weapons (TPNW)", document PSC/PR/COMM.(DCCCXXXVII).

[27] Messaoud Baaliouamer, Executive Secretary of the African Commission on Nuclear Energy, statement to the sixty-third General Conference of the International Atomic Energy Agency (16–20 September 2019), Vienna.

countries. Through the memorandum, the two organizations aimed to establish a framework for interacting in areas of common interest, including scientific, technological and innovation-based research, and capacity-building programmes. Furthermore, the organizations could use the memorandum as a framework to survey the difficulties of individual African countries in complying with their international obligations, as well as to facilitate the provision of external assistance, as appropriate.

Separately, on the margins of the IAEA General Conference in September, the Commission and the IAEA signed practical arrangements on strengthening the cooperation in safe and secure implementation in Africa of peaceful nuclear applications.

In addition, senior officials of the Commission participated in the second African Youth Nuclear Summit, held in Centurion, South Africa, from 7 to 11 October, with the theme "Unlocking the Potential of Nuclear Science and Technology Applications in Africa". The event brought together young experts in the field of nuclear energy and security from across the African continent to share expert knowledge, as well as scientific skills and technology.

At the General Assembly First Committee, Zambia delivered a statement[28] on behalf of the African Group in which its members underscored the tenth anniversary of the Pelindaba Treaty's entry into force, while also reiterating their collective commitment to the disarmament and non-proliferation norms of the agreement that established the African nuclear-weapon-free zone. The traditional resolution entitled "African Nuclear-Weapon-Free Zone Treaty" (74/26) was introduced to the General Assembly and adopted without a vote, similar to previous years.

Treaty on a Nuclear-Weapon-Free Zone in Central Asia

On 11 April, the States parties to the Treaty on a Nuclear-Weapon-Free Zone in Central Asia gathered in Nur-Sultan for a regular annual consultative meeting, with Kazakhstan succeeding Uzbekistan as Chair/Coordinator for the 2019–2020 cycle. During the meeting, the States parties identified the following main priorities for the 2019–2020 period: (a) preparation for the 2020 Nuclear Non-Proliferation Treaty Review Conference; (b) strengthening the coordination within the zone; and (c) further elaboration of the draft of a "Treaty on cooperation in preventing illicit trafficking in nuclear materials and combating nuclear terrorism among the State Parties to the Central Asian Nuclear-Weapon-Free Zone Treaty".

On 29 April, during the third session of the Preparatory Committee for the 2020 Nuclear Non-Proliferation Treaty Review Conference, Kazakhstan

---

[28] Lazarous Kapambwe, Permanent Representative of the Republic of Zambia to the United Nations, statement on behalf of the African Group at the seventy-fourth session of the United Nations General Assembly, general debate on disarmament and international security of the First Committee, New York, 8 October 2019.

delivered a joint statement,[29] on behalf of the States parties to the Treaty on a Nuclear-Weapon-Free Zone in Central Asia, highlighting the tenth anniversary of the Treaty's entry into force, as well as the continuing commitment of Central Asian States to the voluntary and unequivocal ban of the production, acquisition and deployment of nuclear weapons on their territories.

Also, in 2019, the Central Asian States promised to continue holding regular consultations with the United States regarding the Protocol on negative assurances. As at the end 2019, all five nuclear-weapons States had signed the Protocol and all but the United States had ratified it.

Establishment of a Middle East zone free of nuclear weapons and other weapons of mass destruction

First session of the Conference on the Establishment of a Middle East Zone Free of Nuclear Weapons and Other Weapons of Mass Destruction

In 2018, the General Assembly adopted decision 73/546, entrusting the Secretary-General to convene in 2019 a conference on the establishment of a Middle East zone free of nuclear weapons and other weapons of mass destruction. By decision 73/546, the Assembly also requested the Secretary-General to convene annual one-week sessions of the conference at the United Nations Headquarters until the conference concluded the elaboration of a legally binding treaty establishing a Middle East zone free of nuclear weapons and other weapons of mass destruction.

Pursuant to that decision, the first session of the Conference was held from 18 to 22 November 2019 at the United Nations Headquarters. Twenty-two States[30] from the region participated, while four other States[31] and three relevant international organizations or entities[32] attended as observers.

Jordan was elected by acclamation as President of the first session of the Conference, and Sima Sami I. Bahous (Jordan) was invited to preside over it. The Secretary-General and the President of the General Assembly of the seventy-fourth session made statements[33] at the opening session. Other Member States, relevant

---

[29] Yerzhan Ashikbayev, Deputy Minister of Foreign Affairs of the Republic of Kazakhstan, joint statement, New York, 29 April 2019.
[30] Algeria, Bahrain, Comoros, Djibouti, Egypt, Iran (Islamic Republic of), Iraq, Jordan, Kuwait, Lebanon, Libya, Mauritania, Morocco, Oman, Qatar, Saudi Arabia, State of Palestine, Sudan, Syrian Arab Republic, Tunisia, United Arab Emirates and Yemen.
[31] China, France, Russian Federation and United Kingdom.
[32] International Atomic Energy Agency, Organisation for the Prohibition of Chemical Weapons and Biological Weapons Convention Implementation Support Unit.
[33] António Guterres, Secretary-General, remarks at the Conference, New York, 18 November 2019; and Tijjani Muhammad Bande, President of the seventy-fourth session of the General Assembly, statement to the Conference, New York, 18 November 2019.

international organizations, United Nations entities and non-governmental organizations were invited to attend the opening meeting.

During the general debate, 17 participating States, 4 observer States and the Biological Weapons Convention Implementation Support Unit made statements. In the ensuing thematic debate, representatives of participating States had an initial exchange of views on a range of issues related to a future legally binding treaty on establishing the Middle East zone, including the principles and objectives, general obligations regarding nuclear weapons, general obligations regarding other weapons of mass destruction, peaceful uses and international cooperation, institutional arrangements, and other aspects.

After five days of deliberation, the first session of the Conference successfully concluded with the adoption of its report and a Political Declaration.[34] In the Political Declaration, the participating States conveyed their intent and solemn commitment to pursue in accordance with relevant international resolutions, and in an open and inclusive manner with all invited States, the elaboration of a legally binding treaty to establish a Middle East zone free of nuclear weapons and other weapons of mass destruction, on the basis of arrangements freely arrived at by consensus by the States of the region. They also expressed the belief that the Conference, through the elaboration of a legally binding treaty establishing a Middle East zone free of nuclear weapons and other weapons of mass destruction, could contribute to building regional and international confidence therein and that the establishment of a verifiable Middle East zone free of nuclear weapons and other weapons of mass destruction would greatly enhance regional and international peace and security.

The Conference adopted several decisions[35] on organizational matters, including for future sessions. In that regard, it decided to hold future annual sessions for a duration of one week, starting on the third Monday of November of each year in New York. The Conference also decided that the presidency shall be rotated among the participating States for a period of one year, following the English alphabetical order of States' names, starting from Jordan as the President of the first session.

Participating States agreed to continue to consult among themselves on the rules of procedure of the Conference to reach agreement as early as possible. In that regard, the President stated, inter alia, that the participating States agreed that, pending the final agreement on the text of the Conference's rules of procedure, consensus would be the only method of decision-making on procedural and substantive issues, except rulings by the President on procedural motions related to points of order and suspension or adjournment of the meeting.

---

[34] A/CONF.236/6 and its annex.
[35] Office for Disarmament Affairs, "First Session of the Conference – 18 to 22 November 2020" (Official Documents, Decisions).

The Conference agreed that the President, in consultation with participating States, should undertake efforts to prepare for the second session. It was agreed that representatives of existing nuclear-weapon-free zones organizations should be invited to share good practices and lessons learned concerning the implementation of treaties establishing such zones before the second session of the Conference.

The success of the first session of the Conference marked an important step forward by the States in the Middle East and the international community in their decades-long effort towards a Middle East region free of nuclear weapons and other weapons of mass destruction. The establishment of such a zone will represent a valuable contribution to the global disarmament and non-proliferation effort and enhance regional peace and security.

The Secretary-General welcomed the successful conclusion of the first session of the Conference by congratulating the participating States, in particular on the adoption of a political declaration, and pledged his continuous support for the efforts to pursue, in an open and inclusive manner, the establishment of a zone free of nuclear weapons and other weapons of mass destruction in the Middle East.

United Nations Office for Disarmament Affairs regional centres

United Nations Regional Centre for Peace and Disarmament in Africa

Throughout 2019, the United Nations Regional Centre for Peace and Disarmament in Africa maintained its support for African Member States, as well as regional and subregional organizations, in their efforts to promote disarmament, non-proliferation and arms control. By further strengthening the capacities of those entities and supplying them with technical, legal and substantive assistance, the Centre contributed towards sustainable peace and security in support of the 2030 Agenda for Sustainable Development, the Secretary-General's Agenda for Disarmament and Security Council resolution 2457 (2019).[36]

During the year, the Centre supported the 11 member States of the Economic Community of Central African States (ECCAS)[37] in developing a guide to advance the implementation of the Kinshasa Convention. Drawing on financial support from the United Nations Peace and Development Trust Fund and assistance from both the Regional Centre and the United Nations Regional Office for Central Africa, ECCAS surveyed each of its member States on the impact of small arms and light weapons on the security of those States and their populations. The findings became the basis for a draft guide that relevant stakeholders endorsed

---

[36] By resolution 2457 (2019), the Council welcomed the determination of the African Union to rid Africa of conflicts and create conditions favourable for the growth, development and integration of the continent as encapsulated in its goal for Africa of "Silencing the Guns by 2020".

[37] Angola, Burundi, Cameroon, Central African Republic, Chad, Congo, Democratic Republic of the Congo, Equatorial Guinea, Gabon, Rwanda and Sao Tome and Principe.

through a series of national validation workshops held in all 11 of the ECCAS member States. Each of those workshops brought together 20 participants from institutions that included national commissions to combat the proliferation of small arms and light weapons; ministries of security, defence and foreign affairs; non-governmental organizations; and community and religious groups. Upon completion, the guide was expected to support relevant national authorities in establishing and strengthening national commissions on small arms and light weapons, as well as in facilitating the adoption of national action plans to implement the Kinshasa Convention.

The Regional Centre convened two additional meetings in 2019 to support the Convention's implementation in the framework of the same project. The first of those was a subregional technical capacity-building workshop that the Centre organized in Yaoundé from 24 to 26 April. That workshop brought together 40 participants, including 7 women, and included presentations on the following: the state of international, regional and subregional arms control instruments; collection and recording of data on small arms and light weapons and indicators of progress; and the roles of the ECCAS secretariat and of national commissions on small arms and light weapons in implementing the Kinshasa Convention.

That event was followed by a subregional legal workshop held in Malabo from 25 to 27 September. That second workshop drew 46 participants, including 6 women, and provided presentations on the Convention's legal obligations, the Modular Small-arms-control Implementation Compendium (MOSAIC) and experiences and good practices for updating national legislative texts on arms control. In one notable result of those advocacy efforts, Equatorial Guinea ratified the Kinshasa Convention on 24 December.

Meanwhile, the Centre partnered with the United Nations Institute for Training and Research to co-organize two events during the year. The first was a high-level regional methodological workshop on election security in Africa at the Centre's premises in Lomé on 24 and 25 June, which brought together senior officials from the security and defence forces of nine countries,[38] as well as representatives of United Nations agencies. The participants considered election security in the contexts of human security and the rule of law, giving attention to the current dynamics affecting election security in their respective countries. The second was held from 15 July to 9 August, whereby the Centre offered its premises to the Institute to host a training programme with participation by the Alioune Blondin Bèye Peacekeeping School in Bamako and the Ministry of Security and Civil Protection of Togo. The aim of that programme was to prepare formed police units to deploy to United Nations peacekeeping missions.

Separately, with financial support from Japan, the Regional Centre implemented a project in two countries to strengthen the physical security and stockpile management of small arms and light weapons, as well as their

---

[38] Benin, Burundi, Cameroon, Côte d'Ivoire, Gabon, Guinea, Guinea-Bissau, Madagascar and Togo.

ammunition. In Madagascar, the Centre trained 100 representatives of relevant national authorities at a technical capacity-building workshop held from 6 to 18 May, concluding the event with the handover of two arms-marking machines to the country's authorities. After providing similar training to 35 officials in Togo from 8 to 12 July, the Centre delivered a separate pair of arms-marking machines to the country's authorities on 14 August. As a separate activity of the project, Togo destroyed seized and obsolete weapons and ammunition at an event to mark the International Day of Peace on 21 September.

To support the implementation of Security Council resolution 1540 (2004), the Centre helped organize a capacity-building workshop for Togolese stakeholders involved in the strategic trade in and management of sensitive products. Held in Lomé from 23 to 25 January through a collaboration with Togo, the World Customs Organization and the Group of Experts of the Security Council Committee established pursuant to resolution 1540 (2004) (1540 Committee), the workshop drew 25 participants from various technical services to learn how the resolution was interlinked with a number of export control regimes.

Furthermore, from 10 to 15 February, the Regional Centre participated in an intensive course held in Accra on nuclear non-proliferation and security for women in science, technology, engineering and mathematics. The Centre delivered a presentation on the international disarmament machinery as a contribution to that course, which was co-organized by the African Center for Science and International Security and the James Martin Center for Nonproliferation Studies of the Middlebury Institute of International Studies at Monterey.

The Regional Centre also held two regional workshops on a potential treaty banning the production of fissile material for nuclear weapons or other nuclear explosive devices, one in Equatorial Guinea on 5 and 6 February and the other in South Africa on 22 and 23 May. Those workshops provided an opportunity for representatives from 22 African States, as well as the Economic Community of West African States and the African Commission on Nuclear Energy, to learn and exchange views about the relevant technical and political aspects of such a potential treaty. The European Union funded both of the events, which the Centre organized in cooperation with the Geneva Branch of the Office for Disarmament Affairs and the respective host Governments.

At the request of Youth Awake, a non-governmental organization, the Centre provided capacity-building assistance to 20 young people at a seminar entitled "African youth, the main actor of peace and sustainable development", held from 15 to 19 May in Kara, Togo. The seminar aimed to foster discussions among participants from Togo's five regions on peace, conflict management, social security for sustainable national cohesion and entrepreneurship.

Ministerial meetings of the United Nations Standing Advisory Committee on Security Questions in Central Africa

The United Nations Standing Advisory Committee on Security Questions in Central Africa held two ministerial meetings in 2019, both to examine continuing and emerging peace and security challenges in the region and to assist Member States in collectively addressing those issues. Countries assessed progress in the implementation of recommendations emanating from previous sessions, while also sharing information and analysis on the geopolitical and security situation in Central Africa.

During its forty-eighth meeting, held in Kinshasa from 27 to 31 May, the Committee discussed, inter alia, the following: activities of terrorist groups in the subregion, including Boko Haram and the Lord's Resistance Army; mercenaries and transnational organized crime; maritime piracy in the Gulf of Guinea; illicit trafficking in natural resources; free movement of people; security sector reform; and impacts on security from conflicts related to transhumance and pastoralism. Transhumance-related security issues were also the focus of a workshop held on 26 and 27 May on the meeting's margins.

In addition, the Committee reported on a field visit by its Bureau to the Democratic Republic of the Congo from 25 to 29 March, providing the basis for recommendations to Member States, the United Nations Secretariat and the Economic Community of Central African States on peace and security issues in the country's northeast that were associated with transhumance and related matters, in particular the subjects of poaching and trafficking in small arms and light weapons.

At its forty-ninth meeting, held in Luanda from 25 to 29 November, the Committee continued to review regional security and peace trends with an emphasis on the situation in the Central African Republic and the Lake Chad Basin, as well as the matter of piracy in the Gulf of Guinea. In that context, the Committee stressed the importance of advancing further towards a subregional regulatory framework on transhumance. Member States also discussed impacts on peace and security from phenomena related to climate change that were increasingly affecting the Central African subregion. In addition, the Committee examined the implementation of measures on revitalizing its work, basing the review on recommendations from its forty-fourth meeting.

The Committee continued to urge its members to swiftly ratify the Kinshasa Convention and deposit relevant instruments with the Secretary-General. It further encouraged its members to establish national small arms and light weapons control commissions, in accordance with the Kinshasa Convention, and to sign and ratify the Arms Trade Treaty.

United Nations Regional Centre for Peace, Disarmament and Development in Latin America and the Caribbean

In 2019, the United Nations Regional Centre for Peace, Disarmament and Development in Latin America and the Caribbean continued to support Latin American and Caribbean States, at their request, with the implementation of international instruments related to conventional arms and weapons of mass destruction, as well as with adherence to international standards and norms.

In addition to lending its technical and policy support capacities to improve the control of conventional arms, the Regional Centre focused heavily throughout 2019 on advancing dialogue among States on conventional ammunition management at the national and subregional levels. The Centre also provided support throughout the year to Member States in investigating firearms-related crime scenes, assisting national authorities in their efforts to manage small arms within the private security sector, marking and tracing arms and ammunition, interdicting weapons at entry and exit points, strengthening physical security and stockpile management, and addressing firearms use and possession in school settings. The Centre likewise focused on building States' technical capacity to implement instruments on the non-proliferation of weapons of mass destruction, most notably Security Council resolution 1540 (2004).

To help States combat illicit trafficking in arms and ammunition, as well as their parts and components, the Regional Centre delivered specialized training to 180 officials working at entry and exit points in countries across the region to improve the detection and interdiction of weapons using innovative X-ray identification tools. After the training, two Governments[39] reported the successful interdiction of ammunition in luggage at airports in their respective countries in 2019. Furthermore, private security companies in Costa Rica and the Dominican Republic received Centre-led training on managing arms and ammunition stockpile facilities and on countering risks of weapons diversion for illicit use.

To help States develop adequate policy responses to combat illicit ammunition trafficking, the Centre led a series of national workshops for policymakers that addressed the ammunition management life cycle and national-level control measures that were in accordance with the International Ammunition Technical Guidelines. Those workshops, which targeted officials in Colombia, Costa Rica and Peru, were complemented by two Centre-led subregional seminars on those topics for Latin American and Caribbean audiences, held in Lima on 5 and 6 September and in Kingston on 10 and 11 September. Those seminars took place in the lead-up to the first session, scheduled in 2020, of the Group of Governmental Experts on problems arising from the accumulation of conventional ammunition stockpiles in surplus (for more information, see p. 105).

---

[39] Costa Rica and Paraguay.

Meanwhile, to help support the implementation of the Firearms Protocol, the Centre provided national control entities in Costa Rica in March with technical assistance and training on international marking obligations, standards and best practices of small arms and ammunition.

The Regional Centre also continued to deliver on-site training to officials from the Dominican Republic and Paraguay in support of their efforts to implement the Arms Trade Treaty. In that regard, the Centre was acting in its role as the main partner of those States in carrying out activities supported through the Arms Trade Treaty Voluntary Trust Fund.

In addition, the Centre expanded its efforts to help Caribbean States build their forensic ballistic capabilities to combat illicit firearms trafficking in line with the International Tracing Instrument. In addition to providing those States with expert training on the proper handling of firearms-related evidence at crime scenes, the Centre collaborated with the Caribbean Community Implementation Agency for Crime and Security to host a stakeholder meeting on preventing illicit arms trafficking through improvements to forensic ballistics capacity. The meeting was held to facilitate information-sharing among the Caribbean States, and its conclusions fed into a document entitled "Recommended Caribbean priority actions on addressing illicit firearms trafficking", subsequently adopted by the Caribbean Community secretariat and Caribbean Heads of State.

In support of the United Nations youth, peace and security agenda, the Centre teamed up with the municipality of Lima to conduct a forum for local teachers, school directors and youth networks on the impact of armed violence on young people, as well as policies and approaches for preventing such violence. The Centre also led the first Regional Seminar on Firearms in Schools, held in Peru on 22 and 23 October to promote regional dialogue and the exchange of experiences on the use and possession of firearms in schools in the region. In that context, the Centre developed a working paper on that subject that facilitated in-depth discussions on its main manifestations, impact and challenges, as well as on initiatives aimed at ensuring that schools remain free of violence.

Throughout 2019, the Centre also continued to engage with beneficiary States to advance the women, peace and security agenda by incorporating gender-responsive programming into armed violence reduction measures (for more information, see chap. VI).

Furthermore, the Regional Centre continued assisting States in the region in their implementation of Security Council resolution 1540 (2004). The Centre's assistance to Peru, for example, included technical support in drafting legislation to bring the country's legal code into closer alignment with its obligations under the Biological Weapons Convention. In Suriname, pursuant to the Government's voluntary national action plan to implement the resolution, the Centre partnered with the International Maritime Organization to organize a series of practical tabletop exercises to help national officials more effectively tackle proliferation-related issues in the area of maritime and port security. The Centre also led two training courses in Santo Domingo to assist national authorities of the Dominican Republic in implementing resolution 1540 (2004); the first course ran from 1 to 4 October and addressed strategic trade controls and dual-use goods, while the second training took place on 13 December and covered biosecurity and biosafety measures that could help the country bolster its implementation of resolution 1540 (2004), as well as the Biological Weapons Convention. In Belize, the Centre organized a subregional seminar on 6 and 7 November to promote dialogue on the importance of implementing resolution 1540 (2004) in the Caribbean region, as well as to reflect on the role of customs agencies in countering weapons of mass destruction proliferation with an emphasis on licensing protocols, risk assessments and operational focus lists.

In 2019, the Centre carried out close to 80 activities in total to respond to official requests for assistance from Member States, reaching close to 1,600 national representatives and participants.

United Nations Regional Centre for Peace and Disarmament in Asia and the Pacific

The United Nations Regional Centre for Peace and Disarmament in Asia and the Pacific continued to assist Member States of the region in strengthening their national implementation of the United Nations Programme of Action to Prevent, Combat and Eradicate the Illicit Trade in Small Arms and Light Weapons in All Its Aspects (Programme of Action on Small Arms and Light Weapons), the Arms Trade Treaty and the women, peace and security agenda. The Centre also organized events on various issues related to a potential treaty banning the production of fissile material for nuclear weapons and other nuclear explosive devices, safe and secure ammunition management, Security Council resolution 1540 (2004), and responsible innovation for emerging technologies.

In March, the Centre organized the Regional Outreach Seminar on Trade and Trafficking of Illicit Conventional Ammunition for South-East Asia, held in Bangkok with funding from Germany. Held from 20 to 22 March, the seminar brought together representatives of Governments and security forces from 10 South-East Asian States[40] to, inter alia, examine synergies between the Programme of Action on Small Arms and Light Weapons, the Arms Trade Treaty, the Firearms Protocol and other instruments in relation to illicit trafficking of ammunition. The event also featured a day of open discussions on national experiences, challenges and effective practices related to conventional ammunition, an area that would be addressed by the Group of Governmental Experts on problems arising from the accumulation of conventional ammunition stockpiles in surplus, scheduled to convene in 2020.

---

[40] Brunei, Cambodia, Indonesia, Lao People's Democratic Republic, Malaysia, Myanmar, Philippines, Thailand, Timor-Leste and Viet Nam.

Meanwhile, with financial support from the Arms Trade Treaty Voluntary Trust Fund, the Centre partnered with Kazakhstan to hold the Arms Trade Treaty Universalization and Implementation Workshop in Nur-Sultan on 3 and 4 July. The 32 national participants, representing Member States in Central Asia and Mongolia, discussed the main provisions and obligations of the Arms Trade Treaty, rationales and potential benefits for joining the Treaty, regional priorities and concerns, practical measures related to implementing the Treaty, and relevant tools for assistance.

The Centre conducted the Baseline Assessment for Disarmament Education in nine States in the region[41] from March to November, interviewing representatives of Government ministries, United Nations entities, academic institutes and non-governmental organizations. Through quantitative and qualitative surveys, the Centre found that perceptions about arms among participants appeared to be linked with their views on the importance of a responsible and trustworthy State security apparatus. Most participants agreed that when individuals do not feel that a State can maintain their security or safety, people will arm themselves with legal, illegal or homemade weapons, depending on access and means. The Baseline Assessment, which was funded by the non-governmental organization Rissho Kosei-kai, would form the basis of the Centre's future work in the area of peace and disarmament education.

The Centre's activities also included organizing a training programme on MOSAIC for five ASEAN member States,[42] as well as Timor-Leste. The training—carried out in Bangkok from 1 to 4 October and funded by Germany—supported 18 officials from ministries of defence, foreign affairs and interior in their efforts to either develop or update national action plans for their respective countries to effectively implement the United Nations Programme of Action on Small Arms and Light Weapons. Participants also benefited from interactive scenario-based training on cross-cutting issues, including gender and youth considerations in the control of small arms and light weapons.

Furthermore, the Centre coordinated with the Solomon Islands to organize a national round-table meeting on strengthening the country's national capacity to implement Security Council resolution 1540 (2004). The event, held from 29 to 30 October in Honiara, was intended to assist the Solomon Islands in preparing its first national report on the resolution's implementation.

The Centre also undertook a number of activities related to responsible innovation. Those efforts included co-organizing—with the ASEAN Foundation, under its Data Science Explorers programme, and the private company Systems, Applications and Products in Data Processing—a workshop in Bangkok on 10 October to examine the topic of responsible innovation for peace and security.

---

[41] Bangladesh, Indonesia, Kyrgyzstan, Myanmar, Nepal, Philippines, Solomon Islands, Sri Lanka and Tajikistan.
[42] Cambodia, Lao People's Democratic Republic, Myanmar, Thailand and Viet Nam.

Subsequently, in Kathmandu on 6 November, the Centre convened a second workshop with the same focus in partnership with the Robotics Association of Nepal, a local non-governmental organization. Those meetings enabled a total of 24 young science, technology, engineering and mathematics students from 11 countries[43] to critically examine, through scenario-based exercises, ethical issues around emerging technologies and the role of such technologies in advancing the 2030 Agenda for Sustainable Development.

The eighteenth United Nations-Republic of Korea Joint Conference on Disarmament and Non-proliferation Issues took place in Seoul on 13 and 14 November, drawing 30 participants from Governments, particularly of countries in the region, as well as research institutes, academia and non-governmental organizations. In line with the meeting's thematic focus on the Nuclear Non-Proliferation Treaty Review Conference, the participants discussed prospects and building blocks for the Review Conference, as well as ways to reinvigorate the Treaty's review process. The attendees also considered regional non-proliferation issues, particularly on the Korean Peninsula.

From 12 to 15 November, the Centre organized a workshop in Suva funded by the European Union, as part of the wider Centre's project on "Gun Violence and Illicit Small-Arms Trafficking from a Gender Perspective" in the Asia-Pacific region (for more information, see pp. 224–225).

Meanwhile, during the same month, the Centre completed the first phase of a technical and legal support project with Timor-Leste, made possible through funding from the United Nations Trust Facility Supporting Cooperation on Arms Regulation. After meeting with Government stakeholders and conducting a series of site visits, the Centre produced a detailed report providing clear recommendations to facilitate Timor-Leste's further implementation of the Programme of Action on Small Arms and Light Weapons, as well as to support its possible future accession to the Arms Trade Treaty.

On 17 and 18 December, in cooperation with the United Nations Regional Centre for Peace and Disarmament in Africa and the Geneva Branch of the Office for Disarmament Affairs, the Centre organized in Bangkok a cross-regional meeting of scientific experts from Africa and Asia to contribute to future negotiations on a treaty banning the production of fissile material for nuclear weapons and other nuclear explosive devices. The workshop, which was part of a project implemented by the Office for Disarmament Affairs and funded by the European Union, brought together experts from nine States,[44] including members of scientific and academic institutions and representatives of regional organizations participating in the ASEAN Regional Forum and meetings of the African Commission on Nuclear Energy.

---

[43] Brunei, Cambodia, Indonesia, Lao People's Democratic Republic, Malaysia, Myanmar, Nepal, Philippines, Singapore, Thailand and Viet Nam.

[44] Algeria, Canada, India, Japan, Kazakhstan, Namibia, Pakistan, South Africa and United States.

Disarmament and arms regulation at the regional level

Africa

Economic Community of West African States

Activities related to arms control

In a step to establish arms-tracing systems in its region, the Commission of the Economic Community of West African States (ECOWAS) collaborated with Conflict Armament Research, a non-governmental organization, to conclude the operationalization of article 19 of the ECOWAS Convention on Small Arms and Light Weapons, Their Ammunition and Other Related Materials (Convention on Small Arms and Light Weapons).[45] That effort, which was funded by the United Nations Trust Facility Supporting Cooperation on Arms Regulation, resulted in the development of tracing guidelines, also known as standard operating procedures, that were piloted in countries including Benin, Burkina Faso, the Niger and Nigeria. In line with the guidelines, the participating States documented the recovery of illicit weapons and sought to trace the previous movements of those arms back to their points of diversion.

Meanwhile, with support from the tenth European Development Fund, ECOWAS assessed the compliance of armouries in its member States with international standards and best practices for physical security and stockpile management. That mission, which was based on the ECOWAS Roadmap on Physical Security and Stockpile Management, took place to establish a baseline for the compliance of the facilities. In support of the effort, ECOWAS procured equipment for record-keeping and arms destruction that it delivered to participating member States.

Activities related to peace, security and disarmament

During the year, ECOWAS developed and validated, a baseline study report and accompanying action plan to guide the integration of gender perspectives into the implementation of regional- and national-level interventions for small arms and light weapons control. That effort took place with support from the European Union Regional Indicative Programme of the tenth European Development Fund.

It also supported two initiatives to help its member States exchange their experiences in fighting proliferation. With financial support from Germany, ECOWAS convened a technical review meeting in Niamey to review successes, challenges and lessons learned from efforts over the previous decade to implement its Convention on Small Arms and Light Weapons. That discussion, which was held in September, prompted calls for the next 10-year implementation plan to be more robust, including through the development of performance indicators.

---

[45] Convention on Small Arms and Light Weapons, Their Ammunition and Other Related Materials, article 16.

Then, in November, ECOWAS hosted the eleventh annual meeting of national commissions on small arms in Monrovia, where participants shared updates on relevant initiatives and challenges.

Furthermore, ECOWAS partnered with the United Nations Institute for Disarmament Research to complete baseline assessments on weapons and ammunition in Ghana and Sierra Leone.

ECOWAS also undertook several arms-related initiatives aimed at making peacekeeping more effective. In that regard, it collaborated with Small Arms Survey, an independent research institute, on the following activities: (a) developing a training module on weapons and ammunition management in peace support operations; (b) holding a pilot training for front line officers; and (c) developing new standard operating procedures for troop- and police-contributing countries on adhering to their obligations under article 11 of its Convention on Small Arms and Light Weapons, including by reporting on the deployment and life cycle of all small arms and light weapons, ammunition and related materiel in peacekeeping operations.

Economic Community of Central African States

Disarmament and arms regulation in Central Africa

In 2019, the ECCAS States members made tangible progress in combating the proliferation of small arms and light weapons in the region through the implementation of the Kinshasa Convention.

That progress included movement towards achieving the Convention's universalization in the region. Equatorial Guinea became a State party in December, bringing the number of States parties to eight.[46]

In addition, the ECCAS General Secretariat worked with the United Nations Regional Centre for Peace and Disarmament in Africa and the United Nations Regional Office for Central Africa to conduct a project entitled "Supporting African States towards the vision of silencing the guns in Africa by 2020: capacity-building in Central Africa". That project included two capacity-building workshops—the first, held in Yaoundé in April, focused on establishing national commissions on small arms and light weapons, while the second, held in Malabo in September, addressed harmonizing relevant national legislation. In the same context, ECCAS partnered with the United Nations Office on Drugs and Crime to convene a regional conference in Kinshasa on 10 and 11 November to discuss the harmonization of national legislation related to the Kinshasa Convention or the Firearms Protocol.

---

[46] Angola, Cameroon, Central African Republic, Chad, Congo, Equatorial Guinea, Gabon, and Sao Tome and Principe. Furthermore, the Democratic Republic of the Congo had finalized a domestic ratification law in 2018 and was expected to deposit its instrument of ratification with the United Nations Secretary-General of the United Nations, the depositary of the Convention, in 2020.

Meanwhile, in its capacity as a coordination mechanism for the Kinshasa Convention at the subregional level, the General Secretariat continued efforts aimed at establishing national commissions in member States. In that regard, it deemed that the Congo, Cameroon and Chad had achieved sufficient progress in creating their respective national bodies during the year.

Furthermore, in a major success for ECCAS, 10 of its member States[47] adopted an action plan developed by its Secretary-General for implementing the Kinshasa Convention from 2020 to 2024.

Regional Centre on Small Arms in the Great Lakes Region and the Horn of Africa

During the year, the Regional Centre on Small Arms in the Great Lakes Region and the Horn of Africa continued executing its mandate to coordinate the implementation of the Nairobi Protocol[48] by its member States. It undertook that effort with support both from those States and a number of development partners—namely, the African Development Bank, the United States Department of State, the United Nations Trust Facility Supporting Cooperation on Arms Regulation, the Foreign and Commonwealth Office of the United Kingdom of Great Britain and Northern Ireland, the Multinational Small Arms and Ammunition Group, the German Federal Foreign Office, and the Bonn International Center for Conversion.

As at the end of 2019, the Regional Centre had supported physical security and stockpile management through the following activities funded through the Weapons Removal and Abatement Grant of the Department of State of the United States:

- Constructing four armouries in the United Republic of Tanzania for the safe storage of firearms and ammunition in Dar es Salaam, Moshi, Zanzibar and Dodoma

- Providing training on physical security and stockpile management to 120 police and military law enforcement personnel in Rwanda, Kenya, Uganda and the United Republic of Tanzania

- Supplying 105 steel arms boxes to Rwanda, 90 to Kenya, 80 to Uganda and 90 to the United Republic of Tanzania

- Supplying Rwanda and the United Republic of Tanzania each with 40 gun racks

---

[47] Only Sao Tome and Principe was not represented.
[48] The treaty text and status of adherence are available from Regional Centre on Small Arms in the Great Lakes Region and the Horn of Africa, "Nairobi Protocol for the Prevention, Control and Reduction of Small Arms and Light Weapons in the Great Lakes Region, the Horn of Africa and Bordering States".

- Procuring 10 arms-marking machines with corresponding accessories and delivering them to the Democratic Republic of the Congo in support of an arms-marking process in the country's east

- Destroying 130 tons of obsolete unexploded ordinance in Uganda.

Under Phase II of the African Development Bank project entitled "Strengthening Regional and National Institutions for Reduction of Proliferation of Small Arms", the Regional Centre undertook the following activities:

- Helping build the capacity of national institutions responsible for managing and controlling small arms and light weapons in the Central African Republic and South Sudan

- Supporting the rapid assessment of national action plans to control and manage small arms and light weapons in Burundi, Kenya, Rwanda, Uganda and the United Republic of Tanzania

- Providing training on physical security and stockpile management to 80 law enforcement personnel based in the Central African Republic, 80 in the Democratic Republic of the Congo, 40 in Somalia and 80 in South Sudan

- Supporting high-level consultative meetings with selected Regional Centre member States, including the Democratic Republic of the Congo, Rwanda, South Sudan, the Sudan, Uganda and the United Republic of Tanzania.

Under a separate project financed by the Foreign and Commonwealth Office of the United Kingdom, the Regional Centre engaged in the following activities:

- Supporting work on national baseline assessments for civilian disarmament initiatives and practices in Kenya, South Sudan and Uganda

- Assisting in the implementation of national campaigns to raise awareness about civilian disarmament activities in selected areas of Kenya, South Sudan and Uganda.

In partnership with the Bonn International Center for Conversion and the Multinational Small Arms and Ammunition Group, the Regional Centre carried out activities that included the following:

- Supporting the training of 26 police and military personnel of the Sudan on physical security and stockpile management

- Providing assistance for training on physical security and stockpile management and a related high-level meeting in South Sudan

- Supporting regional "train the trainer" activities in Kenya, educating 36 officers on issues related to physical security and stockpile management

- Assisting in the implementation of a high-level executive training course on small arms control and management in Germany, bringing together attendees from the Regional Centre's secretariat, as well as focal points on small arms and light weapons from Kenya, the Sudan and the United Republic of Tanzania.

Furthermore, through a project funded by the United Nations Trust Facility Supporting Cooperation on Arms Regulation, the Regional Centre supported a regional awareness-raising workshop on ratifying or acceding to the Arms Trade Treaty. That event brought together senior Government officials and delegates from selected civil society organizations from the Democratic Republic of the Congo, Kenya, Rwanda, South Sudan, the Sudan, Uganda and the United Republic of Tanzania.

Americas

Organization of American States

Inter-American Convention Against the Illicit Manufacturing and Trafficking in Firearms, Ammunition, Explosives and Other Related Materials

The Organization of American States, through its Technical Secretariat of the Inter-American Convention Against the Illicit Manufacturing and Trafficking in Firearms, Ammunition, Explosives and Other Related Materials,[49] noted that 31 of its 35 member States were party to that Convention as at the end of 2019.

On 5 April, the Organization convened the nineteenth Regular Meeting of the Convention's Consultative Committee at its headquarters in Washington. Chaired by Mexico, the Meeting focused on advancing the Convention's objectives through collaboration between the Organization of American States, international and regional organizations, other relevant mechanisms and instruments, and civil society. On the same day, in accordance with its resolution AG/RES. 2925 (XLVIII-O/18) of 2018, the Organization of American States celebrated the first Inter-American Day for Counteracting the Illicit Manufacturing of and Trafficking in Firearms.

Countering the illicit proliferation and trafficking of small arms, light weapons and ammunition, and their impact in Latin America and the Caribbean

Through its Department of Public Security and with support from the European Union, the Organization launched a three-year initiative to support 18 member States in the following activities: (a) strengthening physical security and management systems for national military and other institutional stockpiles; (b) strengthening national capacity to destroy small arms, light weapons and ammunition that are confiscated, unsafe or held in excess; (c) enhancing national capacity to mark and trace small arms and light weapons, while also encouraging

---

[49] The Technical Secretariat was a joint operation of the Department against Transnational Organized Crime and the Department of Public Security, two offices of the organization's Secretariat for Multidimensional Security.

regional cooperation to trace seized arms and ammunition; (d) advancing national legislation, border controls and regional coordination to improve mechanisms for transferring small arms and light weapons; and (e) promoting socially responsible behaviours in selected communities with an emphasis on groups severely affected by armed violence.

From May until the end of the year, the above-mentioned initiative strengthened the national capacities of Costa Rica, El Salvador, Guatemala and Honduras to record, mark and destroy small arms and light weapons. In Costa Rica, it enabled training for 21 officials to identify and destroy small arms, light weapons and ammunition, and it supported the confiscation of 1,109 small arms and light weapons and the destruction 5.4 tons of small-calibre ammunition. Officials from El Salvador, Guatemala and Honduras also received training to mark and record such arms. Furthermore, a regional training on best practices for physical security and stockpile management took place in Guatemala, drawing 18 officials from 7 member States,[50] and a separate training on advanced explosive ordnance disposal was held in collaboration with the Ministry of Defense of Spain, reaching 14 officials from 9 member States.[51]

Humanitarian demining

Through its programme entitled "Comprehensive Action against Anti-personnel Mines", the Organization of American States supported Colombia's land release process by providing accreditation support, external monitoring, and quality assurance and control for all demining activities. During 8,531 monitoring visits conducted to humanitarian demining organizations during the year, the programme employed non-technical and technical surveys to strengthen confidence that cancelled and cleared areas in Colombia were safe for use. In 2019, such demining organizations cleared a total of 2,274 square kilometres of land in the country.

Through the same programme, the Organization of American States provided mine risk education to 12,254 women, men, girls and boys in 242 communities of 40 different municipalities of Colombia affected by landmines. In addition, it provided physical and psychosocial rehabilitation and socioeconomic reintegration to 103 landmine survivors in Colombia, while also continuing to assist in logistical and administrative aspects of demining activities in the Colombian departments of Sucre and Bolivar.

Support for the implementation of Security Council resolution 1540 (2004)

In 2019, the secretariat of the Inter-American Committee against Terrorism of the Organization of American States provided several of its member States with

---

[50] Costa Rica, Dominican Republic, Ecuador, El Salvador, Honduras, Guatemala and Peru.
[51] Costa Rica, Dominican Republic, Ecuador, El Salvador, Guatemala, Honduras, Mexico, Panama and Peru.

legislative and technical assistance in adapting their legal codes to obligations contained in Security Council resolution 1540 (2004). It also supported such States in drafting relevant national action plans and in conducting two regional 1540 peer review exercises.

The Committee also participated in consultations of the 1540 Committee, joining various international, regional and subregional organizations in doing so. The Committee also co-organized a high-level side event on the resolution's implementation during the General Assembly First Committee. Similarly, it organized a regional workshop in Mexico, a subregional workshop in Colombia and several national workshops on implementing the resolution.

Asia

Association of Southeast Asian Nations

The Bangkok Treaty was signed on 15 December 1995 by the 10 ASEAN member States. In 2019, it remained the most important instrument of ASEAN on disarmament and non-proliferation (for more information on the Bangkok Treaty, see pp. 139–140).

At the fifty-second ASEAN Foreign Ministers' Meeting, held in Bangkok on 31 July, participants underscored the importance of the Treaty's full and effective implementation, including under the Plan of Action to Strengthen the Implementation of the Treaty on the Southeast Asia Nuclear Weapon-Free Zone (2018–2022).[52] The Ministers also agreed, inter alia, to explore ways to bridge the differences with nuclear-weapon States, including through possible engagement.[53]

At the thirty-fifth ASEAN Summit, held in Bangkok in November, the ASEAN leaders reiterated their commitment to preserving South-East Asia as a region free of nuclear weapons and all other weapons of mass destruction, as enshrined in the Bangkok Treaty and the ASEAN Charter. The leaders further reiterated their commitment to engaging the nuclear-weapon States and intensifying efforts to resolve all outstanding issues in accordance with the Treaty's objectives and principles.[54]

The ASEAN member States maintained steady progress in implementing the five-year Plan of Action to Strengthen the Implementation of the Treaty on the Southeast Asia Nuclear Weapon-Free Zone (2018–2022).[55] Other relevant

---

[52] ASEAN, "Plan of Action to Strengthen the Implementation of the Treaty on the Southeast Asia Nuclear Weapon-Free Zone (2018-2022)", 4 August 2017.

[53] ASEAN, "Joint communiqué of the 52nd ASEAN Foreign Ministers' Meeting", 31 July 2019.

[54] ASEAN, "Chairman's Statement of the 35th ASEAN Summit", 3 November 2019.

[55] The Plan of Action was adopted by the Southeast Asia Nuclear-Weapon-Free Zone Commission in August 2017 to provide a framework for the ASEAN member States to fulfil their obligations under the Bangkok Treaty. It comprised four areas of work: (a) compliance with the undertakings in the Bangkok Treaty; (b) the Protocol to the Bangkok Treaty; (c) cooperation with IAEA and other partners; and (d) institutional arrangements. Implementation of and compliance with the Treaty continued to be overseen by the Commission for the Southeast Asia

ASEAN sectoral bodies, including its Nuclear Energy Cooperation Sub-Sector Network[56] and its Network of Regulatory Bodies on Atomic Energy,[57] also made important contributions to that end. For example, the Nuclear Energy Cooperation Sub-Sector Network continued contributing towards the eventual development of a nuclear safety regime for the region's energy sector.

ASEAN also finalized practical arrangements with IAEA, paving the way for closer cooperation in the areas of nuclear safety, security and safeguards, as well as nuclear technologies and their applications. The ASEAN Secretary-General and the IAEA Acting Director-General signed those practical arrangements in Vienna on 16 September.

In addition, the eleventh Inter-Sessional Meeting on Non-Proliferation and Disarmament—held in April 2019 under the ambit of the ASEAN Regional Forum—took note of efforts to promote peaceful uses of nuclear technology and regional cooperation related to nuclear energy in the region, including through the ASEAN Network of Regulatory Bodies on Atomic Energy and within the framework of the Bangkok Treaty. Furthermore, the Meeting noted developments related to the Treaty on the Prohibition of Nuclear Weapons, and participants exchanged views on the way forward both for the Nuclear Non-Proliferation Treaty Review Conference and for non-proliferation challenges and prospects in the region.

Pacific Islands Forum

Boe Declaration on Regional Security

At the fiftieth Pacific Islands Forum, held in Tuvalu from 13 to 16 August, Forum leaders endorsed an action plan[58] to implement the Boe Declaration on Regional Security (2018). That plan called, inter alia, for the following: (a) strengthening progress and reporting under Sustainable Development Goal 16 by Forum member States; and (b) supporting universalization across the region of relevant international security treaties and conventions, as well as Security Council resolutions as espoused under the Honiara Declaration and the Nasonini Declaration. Meanwhile, the Forum Sub-Committee on Regional Security held its inaugural meeting in October 2019. Tasked in part with reviewing the implementation of activities under the Boe Declaration Action Plan, the

---

Nuclear-Weapon-Free Zone, made up of foreign ministers from the ASEAN member States, and by the Zone's Executive Committee, made up of senior officials of the Association.

[56] The Nuclear Energy Cooperation Sub-Sector Network provided the Association's main platform to promote cooperation among its member States in the area of peaceful nuclear energy through exchange of information and technical assistance on safe and sustainable civilian nuclear power programmes.

[57] The Network of Regulatory Bodies on Atomic Energy served as the Association's primary platform for its member States to discuss nuclear safety, security and safeguards, as well as for their national nuclear regulatory bodies to share information and experiences.

[58] Pacific Islands Forum, "Action Plan to Implement the Boe Declaration on Regional Security".

Sub-Committee was intended as a vehicle to harmonize regional security efforts, including in the context of disarmament and non-proliferation.

Operationalizing mechanisms of the Rarotonga Treaty

The Pacific Islands Forum continued to regard the Rarotonga Treaty as its primary contribution to the global disarmament and non-proliferation regime (for more information on the Rarotonga Treaty, see pp. 138–139). In 2019, the fiftieth Forum stressed the importance of upholding the objects of the South Pacific Nuclear Free Zone established under the Treaty. It highlighted two key actions in that regard: (a) operationalizing the Treaty's mechanisms; and (b) commissioning a scientific body to undertake an independent scientific assessment of radioactive contamination in the Pacific.

To take those tasks forward, the Forum secretariat considered, among other steps, potentially holding a meeting in 2020 for States parties to endorse and initiate activities to operationalize mechanisms under the Treaty, while also marking the agreement's thirty-fifth anniversary.

Deepening cooperation with other nuclear-weapon-free zones

On 28 and 29 August, the Forum secretariat, as depositary for the Rarotonga Treaty, participated in a seminar for nuclear-weapon-free-zones co-hosted by the Office of Disarmament Affairs and the Ministry of Foreign Affairs of Kazakhstan. The event coincided with the International Day against Nuclear Tests.

Comprehensive Nuclear-Test-Ban Treaty

At their 2019 meeting in Tuvalu, leaders urged member States to sign and ratify the Comprehensive Nuclear-Test-Ban Treaty.[59] As at the end of the year, all except four of those States had ratified the Treaty.[60]

Security Council resolution 1540 (2004)

From 18 to 20 September, the New Zealand House of Representatives and the Inter-Parliamentary Union hosted a regional seminar on engaging parliaments of the Pacific region in the implementation of Security Council resolution 1540 (2004). Parliamentarians from 10 States[61] attended the event in Wellington, issuing a joint statement[62] in which they, inter alia, highlighted the synergies between resolution 1540 (2004) and the Sustainable Development Goals, as well as recognized the value of the resolution's implementation in achieving relevant

---

[59] Pacific Islands Forum, "Communiqué, Fiftieth Pacific Islands Forum, 13–16 August 2019".
[60] Papua New Guinea, Solomon Islands and Tuvalu had signed but not ratified the Treaty, while Tonga had neither signed nor ratified it.
[61] Fiji, Kiribati, New Zealand, New Caledonia (France), Niue, Samoa, Solomon Islands, Timor-Leste, Tonga and Vanuatu.
[62] Inter-Parliamentary Union, *Engaging parliaments of the Pacific region in the implementation of UN Security Council resolution 1540*, p. 14, September 2019.

actions under the Boe Declaration and other regional and global priorities for sustainable development, health, safety and security. Acknowledging the value in contextualizing the fulfilment of obligations under resolution 1540 (2004), the participants emphasized the benefits of maximizing efficiencies and strengthening existing governance and enforcement structures, as well as legislative frameworks, in implementing the resolution.

Biological Weapons Convention

As at the end of 2019, all except three[63] of the Forum's member States had signed the Biological Weapons Convention. To support efforts to universalize the Convention in the Pacific region, the House of Representatives of New Zealand and the Office for Disarmament Affairs jointly held a workshop for Pacific parliamentarians in Wellington on 21 September.

Model Provisions on Counter Terrorism and Transnational Organised Crime and targeted financial sanctions relating to proliferation financing and terrorism financing

The Forum also considered relevant obligations under disarmament treaties and resolutions in the context of developing regional model laws, leading to forthcoming model provisions on targeted financial sanctions related to proliferation and terrorism financing, as well as preparations for an update to its Model Provisions on Counter Terrorism and Transnational Organised Crime (2002).[64]

The Forum secretariat also continued to collaborate with member States and specialized agencies, such as the United Nations Office on Drugs and Crime and the Asia/Pacific Group on Money Laundering, to review the Forum's Model Provisions on Counter Terrorism and Transnational Organised Crime, given the evolving nature of the terrorist threat and the transnational nature of criminal activity. They identified a number of specific areas for focused technical review, particularly regarding targeted sanctions concerning terrorism, proliferation or related financing. Both sets of model provisions were being finalized for endorsement in 2020.

Nuclear legacy issues

The leaders also called for further bilateral, regional and multilateral assistance to the Marshall Islands in engaging with the United States to seek a full, fair and just resolution of all outstanding nuclear-testing legacy issues. Furthermore, regional organizations in the Pacific planned to continue supporting Kiribati and the Marshall Islands in addressing ongoing impacts from nuclear

---

[63] Federated States of Micronesia, Kiribati and Tuvalu.

[64] For example, the model provisions on targeted financial sanctions were expected to address obligations under resolution 1540 (2004).

testing, including its effects on human rights, environmental contamination and health.

Europe

European Union

The European Union continued throughout 2019 to be guided by its Global Strategy for Foreign and Security Policy,[65] unveiled three years earlier. The Strategy acknowledged the growing threat of the proliferation of weapons of mass destruction and their delivery systems, while also reaffirming the Union's strong commitment to the universality, full implementation and enforcement of multilateral disarmament, non-proliferation and arms control treaties and regimes.

Activities related to weapons of mass destruction, including the implementation of Security Council resolution 1540 (2004)

The European Union continued to refer to its Strategy against Proliferation of Weapons of Mass Destruction[66] in undertaking relevant activities.

In line with its view that the Nuclear Non-Proliferation Treaty remained the cornerstone of the global nuclear non-proliferation regime, the Union continued to support all three of the Treaty's pillars, along with efforts to advance the agreement's universalization and implementation. On 15 April, the Council of the European Union adopted a decision[67] providing the Office for Disarmament Affairs with €1.3 million to organize thematic and regional consultations in the run-up to the Review Conference of the Treaty, aiming to help facilitate both a successful Conference outcome and the development of realistic and feasible actions and recommendations that could enjoy consensus. Under the new Council decision, the Union financially supported over 18 months the organization of three thematic seminars for all States parties, each dedicated to one pillar of the Treaty.[68] By the same Council decision, the Union also financially supported the organization of four regional meetings that would each cover all three of the Treaty's pillars through the lens of regional priorities and concerns.[69] Those activities were

---

[65] European Union, "A Global Strategy for the European Union's Foreign and Security Policy", 15 December 2016.

[66] European Union, document 15708/03.

[67] European Union, Council decision (CFSP) 2019/615 of 15 April 2019, *Official Journal of the European Union*, L 105 (16 April 2019), pp. 25–30.

[68] The first meeting, on the peaceful uses of nuclear energy, was held in Vienna on 20 and 21 November 2019. The following meeting, addressing nuclear disarmament, was scheduled to be held in Geneva on 29 and 30 January 2020 and the final meeting, on nuclear non-proliferation, in New York on 2 and 3 March 2020.

[69] The first meeting, for Asia and the Pacific, took place in Bangkok on 3 and 4 December 2019. The second meeting, for Africa, was held in Addis Ababa on 29 and 30 August 2019. Two additional meetings—for the Middle East and for Latin America and the Caribbean, respectively—were planned for 2020.

organized to highlight the many benefits already provided by the Treaty, as well as the need to preserve those benefits.

The European Union also continued to support IAEA in carrying out its responsibilities in the areas of non-proliferation; nuclear energy, safety and security; and technical cooperation. Comprehensive safeguards agreements, together with additional protocols, constituted the current verification standard, and the Union continued to call for universal adherence to those instruments. Meanwhile, IAEA continued to effectively and efficiently implement safeguards within the European Union through close cooperation between the European Atomic Energy Community.[70] The Union continued to disburse €325 million it had allocated for the period 2014–2020 to promote nuclear safety, radiation protection the application of efficient and effective safeguards in non-member countries. The European Union also constituted, with its member States, the second-largest donor to the IAEA Nuclear Security Fund.

In addition, the European Union continued to pursue the early entry into force and universalization of the Comprehensive Nuclear-Test-Ban Treaty, in line with its Strategy against Proliferation of Weapons of Mass Destruction and the Secretary-General's Agenda for Disarmament. Its contributions in that regard included the following: (a) diplomatic outreach aimed at soliciting commitments from all remaining annex II and non-annex II countries to ratify the Treaty; (b) financial support for the Preparatory Commission for the Comprehensive Nuclear-Test-Ban Treaty Organization, as outlined in the relevant 2018 decision of the European Council;[71] (c) technical support and advice to a subsidiary body of the Preparatory Commission, as well as various workshops and seminars, to help maintain and strengthen the Treaty's verification regime; and (d) active participation in the Preparatory Commission's two working groups, respectively devoted to budgetary and administrative matters and verification issues.

Furthermore, at the invitation of the Preparatory Commission's Executive Secretary, the High Representative of the European Union for Foreign Affairs and Security Policy participated in the eleventh Conference on Facilitating the Entry into Force of the Treaty, held on 25 September at the United Nations Headquarters in New York. Earlier in the year, during the "Comprehensive Nuclear-Test-Ban Treaty: Science and Technology 2019 Conference" in Vienna, the European Union organized an event on 25 June about its cooperation with the Preparatory Commission.

---

[70] The Union and its member States attached high importance to the worldwide implementation and continuous improvement of nuclear safety. In that regard, the Union had given legal force to the objectives of the Vienna Declaration on Nuclear Safety through its amended Nuclear Safety Directive (2009/71/EURATOM and 2014/87/EURATOM). The Union and its member States also continued their strong support for the IAEA Technical Cooperation Programme, for which they together ranked among the highest contributors.

[71] European Union, Council decision (CFSP) 2018/298 of 26 February 2018, *Official Journal of the European Union*, L 56 (28 February 2018), pp. 34–45.

The European Union also continued to promote two landmark treaties—the International Convention for the Suppression of Acts of Nuclear Terrorism and the Amendment to the Convention on the Physical Protection of Nuclear Material— as fundamental elements of the global nuclear security and anti-terrorism architecture. In that regard, the United Nations Office on Drugs and Crime and the Office of Counter-Terrorism began implementing a decision[72] that the Council adopted in 2018 to support the universalization and effective implementation of the Convention and Amendment. Meanwhile, the European Union continued to actively support the Global Initiative to Combat Nuclear Terrorism in its mission to strengthen the international community's capacity to prevent, detect and respond to nuclear terrorism. That support included participation by the Union and its member States in all areas of the Initiative's work, including nuclear detection, nuclear forensics and response, as well as mitigation.

In line with its commitment to verifiable treaty-based nuclear disarmament and arms control, the European Union stressed the need to renew multilateral efforts and revitalize multilateral negotiating bodies. The Union placed particular focus on the Conference on Disarmament, where its long-standing priority was to immediately commence negotiations on a treaty banning the production of fissile material for nuclear weapons or other nuclear explosive devices, based on document CD/1299 and the mandate contained therein. In accordance with a decision[73] taken by the European Council in 2017 to advance that priority, the Union continued providing financial support to the Office for Disarmament Affairs to facilitate the participation of African, Asian, Latin American and Caribbean countries in consultations and other activities related to such a treaty.

During the year, the European Union also marked the third anniversary of the Implementation Day of the Joint Comprehensive Plan of Action, under which the Union's High Representative for Foreign Affairs and Security Policy serves as Coordinator of the Joint Commission, established by the Plan, to provide oversight. With its aim of providing the international community with the necessary assurances on the exclusively peaceful nature of the nuclear programme of the Islamic Republic of Iran, the Plan of Action remained a key element of the global nuclear non-proliferation architecture and crucial for regional, European and international security. Its full implementation remained essential. During the year, the European Union repeatedly expressed its resolute commitment to and continued support for the Plan of Action, as well as its determination to continue working with the international community to preserve that important multilateral achievement, which the Security Council unanimously endorsed in resolution 2231 (2015). Furthermore, the Union planned to continue to fully support IAEA

---

[72] European Union, Council decision (CFSP) 2018/1939 of 10 December 2018, *Official Journal of the European Union*, L 41 (11 December 2018), pp. 41–46.

[73] European Union, Council decision (CFSP) 2017/2284 of 11 December 2017, *Official Journal of the European Union*, L 32 (12 December 2017), pp. 32–37.

in its monitoring and verification of nuclear commitments of the Islamic Republic of Iran.

In line with its Council decision of 2017,[74] the European Union continued to support the implementation of resolution 1540 (2004) through related training, capacity-building and facilitation of assistance to help enhance relevant national and regional efforts and capabilities. In undertaking those efforts, the Union sought close coordination among its separate programmes, as well as with other actors involved in the resolution's implementation, ensuring synergies and complementarity. The projects also contributed towards the practical implementation of specific recommendations from two comprehensive reviews on implementation, respectively conducted in 2009 and 2016.[75]

The European Union also continued its support for the Hague Code of Conduct against Ballistic Missile Proliferation, to which all of its member States had subscribed. Further to the Council's 2017 decision[76] in support of the Code, the Union continued to ensure financial and political support for the Code's universalization and full implementation, including through targeted outreach activities. In 2019, it held four regional outreach seminars: for member States of the South Asian Association for Regional Cooperation (Sri Lanka, 15 January); for French-speaking Western African countries (Togo, 4 February); for States in the Southern African Development Community (Zambia, 9 July); and for Eastern African countries (Djibouti, 26 September). Moreover, the Union organized three expert missions: in Malaysia on 11 March; in Indonesia on 17 July; and in Côte d'Ivoire on 12 December. Furthermore, the European Union funded three outreach events carried out by the independent Fondation pour la recherche stratégique: in Geneva on 29 May, during the Space Security Conference organized by the United Nations Institute for Disarmament Research; in Vienna on 3 June, on the margins of the Code's annual regular meeting; and in New York on 9 October, during the seventy-fourth session of the General Assembly's First Committee.

Separately, the European Union continued pursuing the universalization and full and effective implementation of the Biological Weapons Convention. As at the end of the year, the Union had devoted more than €9 million since 2006 to promoting national implementation, universalization and intersessional programmes of the Convention, as well as regional and national awareness on the impact of science and technology on biosafety and biosecurity. Throughout 2019, the European Union adopted the following decisions related to biological weapons, safety or security:

---

[74] European Union, Council decision (CFSP) 2017/809 of 11 May 2017, *Official Journal of the European Union*, L 39 (12 May 2017), pp. 39–44.

[75] S/2010/52 and S/2016/1038.

[76] European Union, Council decision (CFSP) 2017/2370 of 18 December 2017, *Official Journal of the European Union*, L 28 (19 December 2017), pp. 28–33.

- Council decision 2019/97 of 21 January,[77] providing €3 million in support of the Biological Weapons Convention for the period 2019–2022

- Council decision 2019/1296 of 31 July,[78] making €1.9 million available to strengthen biological safety and security in Ukraine, in line with Security Council resolution 1540 (2004)

- Council decision 2019/2108 of 9 December,[79] providing €2.7 million for biological safety and security in Latin America, in line with resolution 1540 (2004).

The Union also continued its support for the Chemical Weapons Convention. As at the end of 2019, the Union had contributed €34.5 million since 2004 for efforts by the Organisation for the Prohibition of Chemical Weapons (OPCW) to promote the Convention's universalization, as well as related verification and international cooperation and assistance. In 2019, the Union adopted the following decisions in that area:

- Council decision 2019/538 of 1 April,[80] providing €11.6 million in support of OPCW key activities from 2019 to 2022, including the establishment of a new Centre for Chemistry and Technology

- Council decision 2019/1092 of 26 June,[81] extending the implementation of a 2017 decision[82] that provided €3 million in support of OPCW assistance in clean-up operations at the former chemical weapons storage site in Libya

- Council decision 2019/2112 of 9 December,[83] extending the implementation of a 2017 decision[84] on allowing the delivery of satellite imagery to OPCW to support the implementation of Security Council resolution 2118 (2013) and OPCW Executive Council decision EC-M-33/DEC.1.

Activities related to conventional weapons

In line with its Strategy against illicit firearms adopted the previous year,[85] the European Union continued its political and financial assistance to counter the illicit trade and excessive accumulation of small arms, light weapons and their ammunition. In that regard, the Union adopted the following decisions in 2019:

---

[77] *Official Journal of the European Union*, L 19 (22 January 2019), pp. 11–19.
[78] *Official Journal of the European Union*, L 204 (2 August 2019), pp. 29–35.
[79] *Official Journal of the European Union*, L 318 (10 December 2019), pp. 123–133.
[80] *Official Journal of the European Union*, L 93 (2 April 2019), pp. 3–14.
[81] *Official Journal of the European Union*, L 173, 27.6.2019, pp. 47–48.
[82] European Union, Council decision (CFSP) 2017/2302 of 12 December 2017, *Official Journal of the European Union*, L 49 (13 December 2017), pp. 49–54.
[83] *Official Journal of the European Union*, L 318 (10 December 2019), pp. 159–160.
[84] The 2017 decision provided €1 million for that purpose. See European Union, Council decision (CFSP) 2017/2303 of 12 December 2017, *Official Journal of the European Union*, L 55 (13 December 2017), pp. 55–60.
[85] European Union, document 13581/2018.

- Council decision 2019/1298 of 31 July,[86] supporting an Africa-China-Europe dialogue and cooperation on preventing the diversion of arms and ammunition in Africa

- Council decision 2019/2009 of 2 December,[87] assisting Ukraine in efforts to combat illicit trafficking in weapons, ammunition and explosives, in cooperation with the Organization for Security and Co-operation in Europe (OSCE)

- Council decision 2019/2111 of 9 December,[88] seeking to reduce the threat of illicit small arms and light weapons and their ammunition in South-East Europe by supporting activities of the South Eastern and Eastern Europe Clearinghouse for the Control of Small Arms and Light Weapons

- Council decision 2019/2191 of 19 December,[89] supporting a global mechanism for reporting illicit small arms and light weapons, as well as other illicit conventional weapons and ammunition, to reduce the risk of their illicit trade.

In addition, the European Union also continued its efforts to counter illicit small arms, light weapons and ammunition through several other projects with a global scope: the Illicit Arms Records and Tracing Management System, implemented by the International Criminal Police Organization (INTERPOL); an initiative of the United Nations Office on Drugs and Crime on implementing the Firearms Protocol; a project undertaken in the Western Balkans by the United Nations Development Programme and the South Eastern and Eastern Europe Clearinghouse for the Control of Small Arms and Light Weapons; and relevant activities efforts undertaken in Africa by the African Union, ECOWAS and the United Nations Regional Centre for Peace and Disarmament in Africa.

Furthermore, in accordance with the European Union's long-standing support for the Arms Trade Treaty—a landmark instrument for enhancing responsibility and transparency in the trade of weapons—the Union issued a series of demarches in 2019 to promote the Treaty's universalization and effective implementation. In addition to those diplomatic efforts, the Union had supported an implementation support programme for the Treaty by contributing €8 million in funds and providing, over three years, technical assistance aimed at strengthening national systems in Latin America, Africa, Central and South-East Asia, and Eastern Europe and the Caucasus in line with the Treaty's requirements.

The European Union also continued to support mine action and implementation of the Convention on the Prohibition of the Use, Stockpiling, Production and Transfer of Anti-Personnel Mines and on Their Destruction. In that regard, its institutions and member States supported mine clearance, stockpile

---

[86] *Official Journal of the European Union*, L 204 (2 August 2019), pp. 37–43.
[87] *Official Journal of the European Union*, L 312 (3 December 2019), pp. 42–54.
[88] *Official Journal of the European Union*, L 318 (10 December 2019), pp. 147–158.
[89] *Official Journal of the European Union*, L 330, 20.12.2019, pp. 53–70.

destruction, assistance to victims, awareness-raising, advocacy, and research and development for the detection and clearance of mines for humanitarian and development purposes.

In 2019, the Union also became a supporter of 10 actions under the Secretary-General's Agenda for Disarmament: (a) Action 4: Bring the Comprehensive Nuclear-Test-Ban Treaty into force; (b) Action 7: Conclude a treaty banning fissile materials for nuclear weapons; (c) Action 8: Develop nuclear disarmament verification; (d) Action 9: Restore respect for the global norm against chemical weapons; (e) Action 10: Enhance readiness to investigate alleged use of biological weapons; (f) Action 22: Secure excessive and poorly maintained stockpiles; (g) Action 34: Ensure the financial stability of treaty support mechanisms; (h) Action 35: Increase engagement with regional organizations; and (i) Actions 36 and 37, on full and equal participation of women in decision-making processes.

Other relevant activities or institutional developments

The European Union Non-Proliferation Consortium of think tanks continued to benefit from support provided in the framework of Council decision 2018/299 of 26 February 2018,[90] covering the period 2018–2021. That financial assistance helped the Consortium to organize the eighth European Union Non-Proliferation and Disarmament Conference, which was held in Brussels on 13 and 14 December.

North Atlantic Treaty Organization

In the London Declaration of the North Atlantic Treaty Organization (NATO), Heads of State and Government participating in the meeting of the North Atlantic Council on 4 December reaffirmed their commitment to disarmament, non-proliferation and arms control. They noted, in particular, their strong commitment to the full implementation of the Nuclear Non-Proliferation Treaty in all its aspects, including nuclear disarmament, non-proliferation and the peaceful uses of nuclear energy.

At the fifteenth Annual Conference on Weapons of Mass Destruction, Arms Control, Disarmament and Non-Proliferation, held in Brussels on 23 October, the NATO Secretary General presented an agenda for enhancing its contribution to disarmament, non-proliferation and arms control.[91] That agenda included four elements: strengthening and preserving the Nuclear Non-Proliferation Treaty; engaging Allies in disarmament verification; modernizing the Vienna Document 2011; and considering new rules to address emerging technologies, including advanced missile technologies.

---

[90] *Official Journal of the European Union*, L 56, 28.2.2018, pp. 46–59.
[91] Jens Stoltenberg, NATO Secretary General, speech at the High-level NATO Conference on Arms Control and Disarmament, Brussels, 23 October 2019.

Allies issued two statements during the year on violations of the Intermediate-Range Nuclear Forces Treaty.[92] In those texts, they expressed full support for the decision of the United States to withdraw from the Treaty in light of the Russian Federation's refusal to credibly respond to its concerns, as well as Russian unwillingness to take demonstrable steps towards returning to full and verifiable compliance. They stated that the Russian Federation bore sole responsibility for the Treaty's demise.

Within OSCE, Allies led efforts both to modernize the Vienna Document 2011 on Confidence- and Security-Building Measures and to address compliance issues related to the Open Skies Treaty. In October, Allies and partners presented the most substantive proposal to update the Vienna Document since 1994, with jointly developed measures to strengthen transparency, risk reduction and arrangements for verification and annual exchanges of military information. Allies also remained concerned by the Russian Federation's selective approach to implementing its arms control obligations, as well as its violation of the principles of the Helsinki Final Act.

Separately, NATO remained a strong, committed partner for the implementation of the Programme of Action on Small Arms and Light Weapons. In that regard, NATO continued supporting activities to effectively control small arms and light weapons, to store them safely and securely, and to combat their illicit trafficking. As at December 2019, NATO had destroyed 626,000 small arms and light weapons, 5.65 million anti-personnel mines and 46,750 tons of ammunition, while also clearing 4,120 hectares of contaminated land.

Other NATO activities in 2019 included advising policymakers and practitioners on addressing gender dimensions of arms control and disarmament issues, including through the publication of relevant guidelines. NATO also continued to promote regional security by building the capacity of its partners to defend against chemical, biological, radiological and nuclear threats, both through programmes with its regional centres and through cooperation with the European Union and the United Nations.

Organization for Security and Co-operation in Europe

Non-proliferation of weapons of mass destruction

In 2019, OSCE continued to assist participating States in implementing Security Council resolution 1540 (2004). With funding from the United States, for example, OSCE helped States across Central Asia to develop and carry out national action plans to implement the resolution, as well as to build foundations through national legislation for controlling dual-use exports. Such efforts allowed

---

[92] NATO, "Statement on Russia's failure to comply with the Intermediate-Range Nuclear Forces (INF) Treaty", Brussels, 1 February 2019; and NATO, "Statement by the North Atlantic Council on the Intermediate-Range Nuclear Forces Treaty", 2 August 2019.

OSCE and the Office for Disarmament Affairs to strengthen their cooperation in support of the 1540 Committee and its Group of Experts.

Small arms, light weapons and stockpiles of conventional ammunition

OSCE participating States continued working in 2019 to streamline and update norms, best practices and mechanisms to effectively combat the proliferation of small arms and light weapons, while also seeking to strengthen the safety and security of stockpiles of conventional ammunition. They undertook those efforts in response to actions suggested the previous year, during the third Review Conference of the Programme of Action on Small Arms and Light Weapons.

A number of participating States also continued to exchange information on small arms and light weapons in accordance with an OSCE document[93] on implementing various commitments in that area, in particular those related to the Programme of Action. Responding to a drop over several years in the number of States providing relevant data—particularly regarding imports, exports and destruction of small arms and light weapons—OSCE and the Office for Disarmament Affairs continued their joint promotion of a previously launched online tool to report such information to both organizations at once. The tool aimed to decrease the reporting burden on participating States and encourage a coordinated approach to reporting.

In 2019, OSCE also mobilized financial resources and developed and implemented projects to help eight participating States to fulfil their commitments to address security and safety risks from small arms, light weapons and stockpiles of conventional ammunition. Such targeted assistance involved destroying surplus conventional ammunition, explosive material and detonating devices; disposing of rocket fuel components; improving physical infrastructure and practices in the field of physical security and stockpile management; clearing and disposing of explosive remnants of war and landmines; and combating illicit trafficking of small arms and light weapons in all its aspects.

Activities related to general security and disarmament

In 2019, OSCE focused its Structured Dialogue process on military transparency, risk reduction and incident prevention.[94] In political- and expert-level meetings, participants discussed military exercises and case studies of potential military incidents in the OSCE region and on the high seas.

---

[93] OSCE, "OSCE Document on Small Arms and Light Weapons" (document FSC.DOC/1/00/Rev.1).

[94] Recognizing the need to reverse negative developments concerning conventional arms control and Europe's architecture of confidence- and security-building measures, OSCE established the "Structured Dialogue" process in 2016 to help foster understanding on security issues that could serve as a common basis for a way forward. Its launch followed the adoption that year of the OSCE declaration on the twentieth anniversary of the framework for arms control.

Meanwhile, the OSCE and the Office for Disarmament Affairs jointly conducted their second nine-week training programme entitled "Disarmament and Non-Proliferation Education Partnership for the OSCE Area". That initiative, which received the OSCE Gender Champions Award for 2019,[95] was aimed at empowering women in the field of disarmament, non-proliferation and arms control, as well as contributing towards the creation of equal opportunities for young professionals in that field, with particular focus on increasing women's participation in relevant policymaking, planning and implementation processes. The training reached young professionals from 52 OSCE participating States and 10 Partners for Co-operation, contributing to their knowledge and raising their awareness both about the relevant contributions of various institutions and about issues related to peace, confidence- and security-building. The programme also provided numerous networking opportunities, facilitating women's career development and engagement in that field. Of its 100 participants, 50 took part in additional in-person training in Vienna. (For more information on the Scholarship for Peace and Security, see chap. VIII.)

Separately, OSCE participating States remained consistent in their implementation of agreed confidence- and security-building measures, with no major changes to the extent of military information they were exchanging. OSCE also continued to support the implementation of the agreement on subregional arms control[96] through assistance to its four States parties.

South Eastern and Eastern Europe Clearinghouse for the Control of Small Arms and Light Weapons

Activities related to conventional arms

In 2019, the South Eastern and Eastern Europe Clearinghouse for the Control of Small Arms and Light Weapons[97] further advanced its efforts to build the capacities of national stakeholders to control and reduce the proliferation of small arms and light weapons in South-East Europe. Drawing on crucial support from the European Union, Germany and the United States, the Clearinghouse sought to assist authorities in the Western Balkans in implementing a previously

---

[95] The OSCE Scholarship for Peace and Security was recognized for encompassing gender equality as a key element for conflict prevention and comprehensive security and as an outstanding initiative to support young women in the security sector. In addition to the qualities for which it received the award, the programme supported the following: resolutions of the Security Council on women, peace and security and on youth, peace and security; the 2030 Agenda for Sustainable Development, in particular Goal 5 on gender equality and Goal 17 on building partnerships; and the Secretary-General's Agenda for Disarmament.

[96] "Measures for Sub-Regional Arms Control" in "General Framework Agreement for Peace in Bosnia and Herzegovina" (A/50/790-S/1995/999), attachment, annex 1-B, article IV.

[97] The Clearinghouse is a joint initiative of the United Nations Development Programme and the Regional Cooperation Council.

agreed regional road map[98] for small arms and light weapons control, including by organizing regular local- and regional-level meetings, periodically measuring progress with key performance indicators and establishing a multi-partner trust fund to support related projects.

The Clearinghouse's activities in 2019 included the following:

- Increasing policy and operational regional cooperation and knowledge-sharing in Southeast Europe through existing regional platforms, bringing together representatives of small arms and light weapons commissions, as well as participants in the South-East Europe Firearms Experts Network

- Further harmonizing legal frameworks to control small arms, light weapons and explosives with relevant directives of the European Union, including through gap analyses and workshops on legal harmonization

- Enhancing the development of evidence-based policies through the Armed Violence Monitoring Platform—a web-based platform collecting daily reports on firearm-related incidents from the region—and by conducting surveys on the distribution, impact and perception of small arms and light weapons in Albania, Bosnia and Herzegovina, Kosovo,[99] Montenegro, North Macedonia, the Republic of Moldova and Serbia

- Increasing transparency in arms exports through the publication of its eleventh regional arms export report,[100] covering Albania, Bosnia and Herzegovina, Montenegro, North Macedonia and Serbia

- Contributing towards stronger gender-responsive small arms and light weapons policies by implementing a "gender coach programme" with the head of Albania's small arms and light weapons commission, as well as by carrying out related training and developing several knowledge products[101]

- Reducing stockpiles throughout the region by destroying 21,358 small arms and light weapons and 54,111 pieces of ammunition

- Enhancing capacities for physical security and stockpile management across the region through upgrades to the security infrastructure of several arms and ammunition storage locations and evidence rooms, as well as through specialized training

- Strengthening forensics capacities to trace and investigate firearms through specialized equipment and training.

---

[98] South Eastern and Eastern Europe Clearinghouse for the Control of Small Arms and Light Weapons, "Roadmap for a sustainable solution to the illegal possession, misuse and trafficking of Small Arms and Light Weapons", 1 February 2018.

[99] References to Kosovo shall be understood to be in the context of Security Council resolution 1244 (1999).

[100] South Eastern and Eastern Europe Clearinghouse for the Control of Small Arms and Light Weapons, *Regional Report on Arms Exports in 2017* (Belgrade, 2019).

[101] South Eastern and Eastern Europe Clearinghouse for the Control of Small Arms and Light Weapons, "Gender and SALW" (Publications).

Activities related to peace, security and disarmament in general

In 2019, the Clearinghouse initiated a new effort to strengthen regional cooperation aimed at integrating gender considerations into security sector reform activities in the Western Balkans. Supported by Norway and Slovakia, that initiative represented the second phase of the Clearinghouse's Gender Equality in the Military project, under which it had closely cooperated with ministries of defence and armed forces in the Western Balkans from 2012 to 2016.

In the project's next phase, the Clearinghouse continued supporting those entities through two unique regional platforms: (a) "gender equality mechanisms" bringing together relevant decision-makers; and (b) the Regional Network of Gender Military Trainers, established in 2014 by the Clearinghouse and armed forces of the region. Those platforms enabled participants to raise awareness, share information and exchange knowledge on integrating gender perspectives into defence policies and practices, thus contributing towards Sustainable Development Goal 16 on peace, justice and strong institutions, as well as Sustainable Development Goal 5 on gender equality.

In addition, the Clearinghouse implemented a gender coach programme with high-level defence officials in Montenegro and in Bosnia and Herzegovina. To assist those countries in advancing gender equality within their defence ministries and in the practical implementation of Security Council resolution 1325 (2000) on women, peace and security, the Clearinghouse helped launch the development of a regional manual on combating gender-based discrimination in the security sector. Through that programme, the Clearinghouse also supported the defence ministries in undertaking several small-scale projects on promoting gender equality and combating gender-based discrimination.

Regional Arms Control Verification and Implementation Assistance Centre-Centre for Security Cooperation

Throughout 2019, the Regional Arms Control Verification and Implementation Assistance Centre-Centre for Security Cooperation continued its work to foster dialogue and provide leadership on confidence- and security-building measures, including in the areas of arms control treaties and agreements, physical security and stockpile management, weapons of mass destruction and nuclear security.[102] It brought together experts from diverse military, political, diplomatic and academic backgrounds to discuss arms control issues and collectively tackle possible challenges and developments with political and security implications.

The Centre organized seven activities during the year, drawing 207 experts and participants to take part in lectures and presentations, discussions

---

[102] The Centre was established in 2000 as a regionally owned entity with a diplomatic status under the Vienna Convention of 1961.

and exchanges of experience, and practical applications. Its work included the following:

- Convening the Centre's Countering Weapons of Mass Destruction Network for two meetings to examine the benefits of regional cooperation in countering the proliferation of weapons of mass destruction, as well as various mechanisms and tools for acting within the regional cooperation framework. Alongside those discussions, the Centre supported a number of national table-top exercises aimed at validating national strategies and response plans for countering threats from weapons of mass destruction.

- Organizing a workshop on the Chemical Weapons Convention with particular focus on chemical safety and security. Notably, that workshop included the Centre's first table-top exercise on national chemical asset, threat, vulnerability and risk assessment, aimed at identifying risks based on the severity of harm and the likelihood of occurrence.

- Holding a training course on adhering to and verifying compliance with the Vienna Document 2011

- Planning an orientation course on the Agreement on Sub-Regional Arms Control (Dayton Agreement, article IV)

- Organizing an arms control symposium to reveal new perspectives on confidence-building measures in Europe and recent significant global trends in the field of non-proliferation

- Holding, in cooperation with IAEA, the fifth "Regional Pilot Workshop on Evaluation of Nuclear Security Detection Architecture", aimed at enabling participants to evaluate the effectiveness of nuclear security detection architecture through the use of performance management tools.

In addition, as a member of the Regional Approach to Stockpile Reduction Steering Committee, the Centre co-organized the Committee's eleventh workshop on conventional weapons and munitions, funded by the European Union.

Middle East

League of Arab States

In 2019, the League of Arab States took several actions pursuant to one of its primary responsibilities: coordinating and elaborating a unified regional and international position among its 22 member States on issues related to disarmament and arms control.

Activities addressing weapons of mass destruction

In 2019, the League convened seven meetings of its Arab Senior Officials Committee in Charge of Nuclear Weapons and other issues related to weapons of mass destruction. Based on the Committee's recommendations, the Ministerial Council adopted resolutions 8363 and 8479, in which it addressed, inter alia, preparations for the Nuclear Non-Proliferation Treaty Review Conference and its third Preparatory Committee; action for implementing General Assembly decision 73/546, entitled "Convening a conference on the establishment of a Middle East zone free of nuclear weapons and other weapons of mass destruction"; coordination during the sixty-third IAEA General Conference; and dangers of the nuclear reactor in Bushehr, Islamic Republic of Iran. The League also participated in the third session of the Preparatory Committee of the Nuclear Non-Proliferation Treaty Review Conference, held from 29 April to 10 May in New York.

Activities addressing conventional arms

In cooperation with the European Union, the League co-organized a conference in Cairo entitled "Combating the Illicit Trade in and Proliferation of Small Arms and Light Weapons in the member States of the League of Arab States", drawing officials and experts from 19 Arab States. The meeting took place from 23 to 27 June at the League's headquarters with technical support from INTERPOL, the World Customs Organization and the Small Arms Survey.

Other relevant activities or institutional development

The League's Department for Arms Control and Disarmament partnered with the Office for Disarmament Affairs to organize a second workshop on advancing confidence- and security-building measures, following up on discussions held the previous year. Convened at the League's headquarters on 1 October, the meeting brought together 13 department directors from different sectors of the League to learn about the experiences of the United Nations in the area of confidence- and security-building measures. Participants also considered how the League could contribute in that area, particularly as a regional organization familiar with the needs of its member States and the characteristics of its region.

United Nations Development Programme

In 2019, the United Nations Development Programme (UNDP) and the Office for Disarmament Affairs launched the Saving Lives Entity, a funding facility dedicated to helping Member States tackle illicit small arms and light weapons as part of a comprehensive approach to sustainable security and development. By supporting activities that accelerate the integration of small arms control measures in development and security efforts, the Saving Lives Entity was intended to address the multi-faceted nature of the illicit proliferation of small arms and light weapons, including root causes of armed violence. UNDP and the Office for Disarmament Affairs aimed to raise at least $12 million each year for the funding facility to support countries and territories most affected by illicit small arms. (For more information about the Saving Lives Entity, see chap. III.)

Meanwhile, in Côte d'Ivoire, UNDP continued to support the national commission on small arms and light weapons in carrying out disarmament and community response activities. After the voluntary surrender of 1,044 weapons following awareness-raising activities in six localities,[103] UNDP helped incentivize 526 of the handovers by facilitating income-generating activities in the agricultural sector (e.g., supplying agricultural kits, crushers and sprayers) and in small trades (e.g., providing tarpaulins and supplies for hairdressing and sewing and chair rentals). Furthermore, in cooperation with the secretariat of Côte d'Ivoire's National Security Council, UNDP helped community members build confidence with the country's Defence and Security Forces through the following activities: (a) co-organizing 10 socio-security dialogues; (b) subsequently establishing civil-military cells in 10 localities;[104] and (c) strengthening the capacities of existing cells. UNDP also facilitated training sessions on human rights, environmental protection, community security, civil protection and professional ethics to 574 ex-combatants integrated into the country's Penitentiary Guards Corps, Water and Forestry Service and Civilian Fire Brigade. Those initiatives supported the sustainable reintegration of ex-combatants into their public administration roles while broadly improving their professional conduct.[105]

In West Africa, UNDP continued supporting the implementation of a small arms project undertaken by ECOWAS and the European Union. Within the framework of disarmament, demobilization and reintegration, UNDP trained and integrated 235 former Boko Haram fighters after their demobilization in the Niger's Diffa region.[106] In Nigeria, UNDP conducted activities for the disassociation, disengagement and training of former Boko Haram associates and vigilantes. For example, 1,100 former vigilantes of the Civilian Joint Task Force[107] attended a vocational training session to acquire skills to build sustainable livelihoods.

UNDP also collaborated with ECOWAS to conduct and validate the first comprehensive mapping of stakeholders and interventions on small arms and light weapons in West Africa. The study provided a basis for ensuring coherent responses aimed at preventing the proliferation of such weapons, controlling their flow and addressing their use in conflict. The study also provided critical evidence and country-specific information on actors, arms dynamics, interventions, successes, impacts and lessons learned to feed into the ECOWAS Conflict Prevention Framework Database and its Prevention of Violent Extremism programme for the region.

---

[103] Boundiali, Dianra, Kani, Morondo, Séguéla and Tiemé.

[104] Abengourou, Aboisso, Adzopé, Bondoukou, Bouaflé, Boundiali, Daoukro, Dimbokro, Katiola and Man.

[105] For example, the Civilian Fire Brigade held no strikes in 2019, unlike in previous years. The Director of the Bouaké Penal Camp, where 12 officers benefited from the training, described the change in the attitude and performance of ex-combatants: "Today, this training has improved their professionalism; they understand their missions better and now do a better job. This has led me to make them my very close collaborators."

[106] The training and integration also paved the way for the Niger to commemorate the tenth anniversary of the ECOWAS Convention on Small Arms and Light Weapons.

[107] The former vigilantes included 37 young women and represented the states of Adamawa, Borno and Yobe.

In Kosovo,[108] UNDP helped the Ministry of Internal Affairs and local law enforcement to systematically destroy seized small arms and light weapons. In total, they destroyed 589 confiscated firearms and 754 "cold" weapons, melting them down to create manhole covers. UNDP also donated 36 computers to Kosovo Police stations and 4 computers to the relevant firearms focal points for use in efforts to control small arms and light weapons. In addition, UNDP cooperated with the Ministry of Internal Affairs and the Kosovo Police to support local stakeholders in raising awareness about the importance of small arms and light weapons control. They organized six information sessions in regional police directorates.[109] UNDP also partnered with the Kosovo Police to organize a round-table session with approximately 80 parents, teachers and pupils to mark the International Day for the Elimination of Violence against Women, as well as the 16 Days of Activism against Gender-Based Violence Campaign. Their participation in that international campaign helped underscore the message, "Violence against women and girls is not inevitable—and it is preventable."

United Nations Office on Drugs and Crime

Through its Global Firearms Programme, the United Nations Office on Drugs and Crime continued in 2019 to promote the ratification and implementation of the Firearms Protocol to the United Nations Convention Against Transnational Organized Crime. It also provided technical assistance to countries in the Balkans, in Latin America and in West and Central Africa through that Programme, contributing towards achieving target 16.4 of the Sustainable Development Goals.

The Office's legal and policy activities during the year included a legislative workshop and other meetings to promote the Plurinational State of Bolivia's accession to the Firearms Protocol. Following that engagement with authorities in the country's criminal justice system and its Plurinational Legislative Assembly, the Government adopted a national law that laid the foundation for it to join the Protocol. Similarly, the Office provided tailored legislative support to the Central African Republic, Côte d'Ivoire, Montenegro and North Macedonia, enhancing the capacities of those countries to enact comprehensive legal frameworks on firearms. At a regional workshop held in Kinshasa for Central African States, participants focused on how the Firearms Protocol and the relevant regional instrument, the Kinshasa Convention, complemented and supported one another.

To strengthen capacities for effectively implementing the Firearms Protocol, the Office continued in 2019 to provide training on detecting, investigating and prosecuting cases of firearms trafficking, reaching 200 practitioners from Bosnia and Herzegovina, Burkina Faso, the Central African Republic, Chad, Mali, Montenegro, the Niger and Serbia. Furthermore, the Office partnered with INTERPOL to organize a law enforcement operation targeting people and

---

[108] References to Kosovo shall be understood to be in the context of Security Council resolution 1244 (1999).

[109] Gjilan/Gnjilane, Ferizaj/Uroševac, Gjakova/Đakovica, Pejë/Peč, Prishtinë/Priština and Prizren.

networks responsible for illicit firearms trafficking in Burkina Faso, Côte d'Ivoire and Mali, as well as to support an initial meeting to plan a related joint operation in Latin America. In addition, the Office assisted the European Border and Coast Guard Agency in developing a a handbook for border guards and customs officers on detecting firearms, while also continuing to develop training material on firearms in the context of its Education for Justice initiative.

Meanwhile, the Office continued efforts to promote regular exchanges among firearms-control and criminal-justice experts through its community of practitioners. From 5 to 7 June, it brought together experts from Argentina, Brazil, Colombia and Mexico for a meeting in Mexico City entitled "Strengthening regional cooperation in Latin America to prevent and combat the illicit trafficking in firearms and related crimes". Through that "quadrilateral initiative", as well as through similar meetings it held during the year for a broader range of countries in the Americas, the Office reached 100 experts, 35 of whom were women.

Separately, the Office collected data from more than 100 countries and territories on seized and trafficked firearms and associated items in the context of its Monitoring Illicit Arms Flows initiative, which entered its second data collection cycle in May 2019. Under that initiative, the Office continued a series of regional meetings on firearms trafficking flows and related data-collection efforts, developed guiding templates and an information video to link the data-collection exercise to firearms-related investigations, and provided technical assistance to Argentina,[110] Bosnia and Herzegovina, Burkina Faso, Cameroon, Côte d'Ivoire, the Niger and Senegal. The findings also helped inform analysis from the Office, including its *Global Study on Firearms Trafficking 2020*.[111]

In addition, to enhance cooperation with national authorities on the fight against firearms trafficking and related forms of crime, the Office carried out assessment missions in the Plurinational State of Bolivia, the Central African Republic, El Salvador, Guatemala, Honduras, the Niger and Nigeria. Notably, a number of those missions led to the development of joint road maps for ongoing and future cooperation.

At the policy level, the Office pursued new initiatives with stakeholders working on the crime-terror nexus. Those activities included organizing, with Wilton Park,[112] an international conference aimed at developing a strategy to address firearms trafficking in the context of other forms of organized crime and terrorism. The Office also continued to engage in that area with INTERPOL, the Office of Counter-Terrorism and the United Nations Institute for Disarmament Research, particularly on the topics of law enforcement operations, preventing terrorists from acquiring weapons and ammunition control.

---

[110] Province of Córdoba.

[111] United Nations publication, Sales no. E.20.IV.1. The Global Study on Firearms Trafficking and additional analytical outputs were scheduled for launch in 2020.

[112] Wilton Park is a not-for-profit executive agency of the United Kingdom Foreign and Commonwealth Office.

chapter

V Emerging, cross-cutting and other issues

A view of the panellists at the United Nations Institute for Disarmament Research 2019 Innovations Dialogue, themed "Digital Technologies and International Security", which was held in Geneva on 19 August.

UN Photo/Violaine Martin

CHAPTER V

Emerging, cross-cutting and other issues

New weapon technologies are intensifying risks in ways we do not yet understand and cannot even imagine.

ANTÓNIO GUTERRES, SECRETARY-GENERAL OF THE UNITED NATIONS[1]

Developments and trends, 2019

IN 2019, THE INTERNATIONAL COMMUNITY sought through various international processes and new initiatives to keep ahead of emerging challenges, especially those related to developments in science and technology and their implications for international peace and security.

Governments encountered mixed results in efforts to develop new measures for ensuring the security and the non-weaponization of outer space. The Group of Governmental Experts on Further Practical Measures for the Prevention of an Arms Race in Outer Space concluded its work without agreeing on a substantive report, despite achieving important convergences in its efforts to elaborate elements of a legally binding instrument. As the United Nations Disarmament Commission could not convene its substantive session, Member States were able to pursue only informal work on the preparation of recommendations for the practical implementation of transparency and confidence-building measures in outer space activities with the goal of preventing an arms race in outer space. In addition, the Committee on the Peaceful Uses of Outer Space addressed issues relevant to international security in the guidelines that it had adopted for the long-term sustainability of outer space activities.

Work also commenced within two intergovernmental processes, established by the seventy-second session of the General Assembly, on information and communications technologies in the context of international security. One took place in the framework of the Open-ended Working Group on Developments in the Field of Information and Telecommunications in the Context of International Security, which held its first substantive session in September with a general debate and exchange on all substantive items on its agenda. It also held an informal intersessional consultative meeting in December with participation by businesses, non-governmental organizations and academia. The second process was led by the Group of Governmental Experts on Advancing Responsible State

---

[1] Remarks to the Conference on Disarmament, Geneva, 25 February 2019.

Behaviour in Cyberspace in the Context of International Security, which held its first substantive session in December.

The Group of Governmental Experts on Emerging Technologies in the Area of Lethal Autonomous Weapons Systems—initially convened in 2016 under the Convention on Certain Conventional Weapons—recommended endorsing 11 guiding principles.[2] It also agreed to a new two-year mandate, which is expected to serve as a basis for the clarification, consideration and development of aspects of the normative and operational framework on those matters. Member States and the Secretary-General also continued to draw attention to concerns about developing such systems.

In the area of missiles, various actors undertook new efforts to seek multilateral approaches in response to several developments—including the demise of the Treaty between the United States of America and the Union of Soviet Socialist Republics on the Elimination of Their Intermediate-Range and Shorter-Range Missiles (Intermediate-Range Nuclear Forces Treaty) of 1987, the testing and deployment of advanced new missile types, and the continued proliferation and use of conventional ballistic missiles. In that connection, Germany launched the Missile Dialogue Initiative, intended to facilitate expert discussions on possible arms-control approaches. The Office for Disarmament Affairs and the United Nations Institute for Disarmament Research also continued work to facilitate greater understanding of the peace and security implications of hypersonic weapons.

The work of the United Nations also extended to other emerging-weapons challenges. With regard to armed uncrewed aerial vehicles, the Office for Disarmament Affairs engaged in informal dialogue aimed in part at exploring various means to take forward multilateral efforts to enhance relevant transparency, accountability and oversight. Separately, to address concerns raised by recent developments in manufacturing, technology and design of small arms and light weapons, the Secretary-General made a recommendation on elements that could be provided in a supplementary annex to the International Tracing Instrument.

With respect to cross-cutting issues, the Office for Disarmament Affairs continued efforts in support of the implementation of the 2030 Agenda for Sustainable Development. Those included the commencement of data collection under Sustainable Development Goal Indicator 16.4.2, which is the "Proportion of seized, found or surrendered arms whose illicit origin or context has been traced or established by a competent authority in line with international instruments". The Office also contributed towards the finalization of a methodology for Indicator 16.1.2, "Conflict-related deaths per 100,000 population, by sex, age and cause", by providing input for the collection of data on arms used.

---

[2] CCW/GGE.1/2019/3, annex IV.

Emerging issues

Outer space

Prevention of an arms race in outer space

The Group of Governmental Experts on Further Practical Measures for the Prevention of an Arms Race in Outer Space[3] concluded its work in 2019 without reaching agreement on a substantive report, despite achieving important progress through its discussions.

As mandated by the General Assembly, the Chair of the Group convened a two-day open-ended intersessional informal consultative meeting, from 31 January to 1 February at the United Nations Headquarters in New York, so that all Member States could engage in interactive discussions and share their views on the basis of a report on the work of the Group provided by the Chair in his own capacity.[4] As part of that meeting, the Chair organized a series of informal panels to facilitate engagement and interaction between Member States and the broader outer space community, including representatives of national space agencies, the commercial sector and civil society. Notably, that multi-stakeholder engagement reflected progress in a step towards implementing Action 12 of the Secretary-General's Agenda for Disarmament.[5]

The Group held its second session in Geneva from 18 to 29 March. In accordance with its mandate, the Group considered recommendations on substantial elements of an international legally binding instrument on the prevention of an arms race in outer space, including on the prevention of the placement of weapons in outer space. It discussed the following: (a) the international security situation in outer space; (b) the existing legal regime applicable to the prevention of an arms race in outer space; (c) the application of the right to self-defence in outer space; (d) general principles; (e) general obligations; (f) definitions; (g) monitoring, verification and transparency and confidence-building measures; (h) international cooperation; and (i) final provisions, including institutional arrangements.

During its discussions, the Group achieved important convergences on several aspects of the issues it discussed. Those issues included the following:

- The applicability of international law in outer space, including the right to self-defence

---

[3] Convened pursuant to General Assembly resolution 72/250 of 24 December 2017. The following Member States nominated experts to participate in the Group: Algeria, Argentina, Australia, Belarus, Brazil, Canada, Chile, China, Egypt, France, Germany, India, Iran (Islamic Republic of), Italy, Japan, Kazakhstan, Malaysia, Nigeria, Pakistan, Republic of Korea, Romania, Russian Federation, South Africa, United Kingdom and United States.

[4] For materials from that meeting, see Office for Disarmament Affairs, "Group of Governmental Exerts on further effective measures for the prevention of an arms race in outer space".

[5] Action 12.3 is as follows: The Office for Disarmament Affairs will facilitate the engagement of the private sector and non-governmental organizations in United Nations deliberations on outer space security.

- Near unanimity on the applicability of international humanitarian law in outer space, notwithstanding concerns that a statement to such effect could be understood as authorizing or legitimizing the use of force in space
- The need to address three scenarios of space-related threats: space-to-space attacks, ground-to-space attacks and space-to-earth attacks
- A link between the strength of any general obligations, the nature of the threat and the verifiability of the relevant provision
- The challenges of multilateral verification in outer space and the benefits of pursuing greater cooperation in the area of space situational awareness
- The role of mandatory transparency and confidence-building measures in any legally binding instrument on this matter.

The Group considered several drafts of a substantive report but reached no consensus on a final text. By its resolution 74/34 of 12 December, the General Assembly welcomed the deliberations of the Group, emphasized that its work constituted an important contribution to international efforts to conclude a legally binding instrument and recommended that its work be taken into account in the search for further practical measures for the prevention of an arms race in outer space, in particular in the course of future negotiations at the Conference on Disarmament.

Transparency and confidence-building measures in outer space activities

Owing to unresolved procedural issues, the United Nations Disarmament Commission could not convene its substantive session. However, the Chairs of the two working groups were able to convene informal meetings during which they facilitated further deliberations on the substantive items before the Commission. In that connection, Jeroen Cooreman (Belgium) convened a number of informal meetings to consider recommendations to promote the practical implementation of transparency and confidence-building measures in outer space activities with the goal of preventing an arms race in outer space. Further to these discussions, the Chair circulated a draft text on 18 April and a revised text on 23 April.

The African Group submitted a working paper[6] under the outer space agenda item in which it, inter alia, annexed the final version of the non-agreed draft report circulated at the Group of Governmental Experts on Further Practical Measures for the Prevention of an Arms Race in Outer Space. The United States submitted a working paper[7] in which it, inter alia, expressed regret "that one State has decided to publish a working paper containing the non-consensus report of the Group of Governmental Experts on further practical measures for the prevention of an arms race in outer space". The United States further specified that it could

---

[6] A/CN.10/2019/WP.1.
[7] A/CN.10/2019/WP.2.

not support the submission or consideration of a working paper that included the non-consensus work of the Group.

Long-term sustainability of outer space activities

At its sixty-second session, the Committee on the Peaceful Uses of Outer Space adopted the preamble and 21 guidelines for the long-term sustainability of outer space activities.[8] The Committee encouraged States and international intergovernmental organizations to voluntarily take measures to ensure that the guidelines were implemented to the greatest extent feasible and practicable. A number of the agreed guidelines[9] effectively elaborate and implement measures that were recommended in the 2013 report[10] of the Group of Governmental Experts on Transparency and Confidence-building Measures in Outer Space Activities. In addition, a number of the agreed and non-agreed guidelines also address matters relevant to international security and, more specifically, to the prevention of an arms race in outer space.

The Committee decided to establish a new working group on the long-term sustainability of outer space activities of the Scientific and Technical Subcommittee, under a five-year workplan. The working group would agree to its own terms of reference, methods of work and workplan while guided by the following framework: (a) identifying and studying challenges and considering possible new guidelines for the long-term sustainability of outer space activities, which could be done by taking into consideration existing documents;[11] (b) sharing experiences, practices and lessons learned from voluntary national implementation of the adopted guidelines; and (c) raising awareness and building capacity, in particular among emerging space nations and developing countries.

Joint panel discussion of the First and Fourth Committees

On 31 October, the First and Fourth Committees convened a joint panel discussion on possible challenges to space security and sustainability, in

---

[8] A/AC.105/C.1/L.366. See also A/74/20, paras 163–168.
[9] Those include the following guidelines:
  6. Enhance the practice of registering space objects
  11. Provide updated contact information and share information on space objects and orbital events
  12. Improve accuracy of orbital data on space objects and enhance the practice and utility of sharing orbital information on space objects
  14. Perform conjunction assessment during all orbital phases of controlled flight
  15. Develop practical approaches for pre-launch conjunction assessment
  16. Share operational space weather data and forecasts
  17. Develop space weather models and tools and collect established practices on the mitigation of space weather effects
  28. Investigate and consider new measures to manage the space debris population in the long term.
[10] A/68/189.
[11] The relevant existing documents include A/AC.105/C.1/L.367 and A/AC.105/2019/CRP.16.

accordance with General Assembly resolutions 73/72 and 73/91 and on the basis of a concept note prepared by the Office for Outer Space Affairs and the Office for Disarmament Affairs.[12] The Committees heard presentations from invited panellists drawn from the broader space community, including academia, civil society and government. Participants in the interactive meeting also included delegations from 11 Member States and the European Union. Following the conclusion of the meeting, the Co-Chairs circulated a summary of the international dialogue among Member States.

Developments in the field of information and telecommunications in the context of international security

In 2019, work commenced within two intergovernmental processes on information and communications technologies in the context of international security. One took place within the framework of the Open-ended Working Group established pursuant to General Assembly resolution 73/27 of 5 December 2018, which held its first substantive session, as well as an informal intersessional consultative meeting with interested parties. The Group of Governmental Experts, established by General Assembly resolution 73/266 of 22 December 2018, held a series of regional consultations, followed by an informal consultative meeting and, finally, the Group's first substantive session. In addition, the Office for Disarmament Affairs continued its work to promote a greater understanding of the challenges to international security posed by the use of information and communications technologies.

Open-ended Working Group

The Open-ended Working Group on Developments in the Field of Information and Telecommunications in the Context of International Security held its organizational session on 3 June, during which it elected Jürg Lauber (Switzerland) as its Chair and adopted its provisional agenda and organization of work.[13]

At its first substantive session from 9 to 13 September, delegations held a general debate and then considered the substantive issues contained in paragraph 5 of General Assembly resolution 73/27. According to the language in that paragraph, the Group was mandated with several tasks: to further develop the rules, norms and principles of responsible behaviour of States listed in paragraph 1 of the resolution, and the ways for their implementation, and, if necessary, to introduce changes to them or elaborate additional rules of behaviour. By the same paragraph, the Group was also mandated to study the possibility of establishing regular institutional dialogue with broad participation under the auspices of the United Nations. Furthermore, the Group was also mandated to continue to study,

---

[12] A/C.1/74/CRP.4.

[13] For the documents of the Open-ended Working Group, see Office for Disarmament Affairs, "Open-ended Working Group".

with a view to promoting common understandings, (a) existing and potential threats in the sphere of information security and possible cooperative measures to address them; (b) how international law applies to the use of information and communications technologies by States; (c) confidence-building measures; (d) capacity-building; and (e) the concepts referred to in paragraph 3 of the resolution.

From 2 to 4 December, the Chair held, in accordance with the Group's mandate, an informal intersessional consultative meeting in New York with interested parties—namely, businesses, non-governmental organizations and academia—to share views on the issues within the mandate. It was chaired by David Koh, Chief Executive of the Cyber Security Agency of Singapore. Over 100 Member States and 100 interested parties participated in the meeting.[14]

Group of Governmental Experts

In 2019, the Group of Governmental Experts on Advancing Responsible State Behaviour in Cyberspace in the Context of International Security commenced its work with the election of Guilherme Patriota (Brazil) as its Chair.[15]

In accordance with resolution 73/266, the Office for Disarmament Affairs organized consultations between the Experts of the Group and member States of the African Union, the European Union, the Organization of American States, the Organization for Security and Co-operation in Europe, and the Association of Southeast Asian Nations and its Dialogue Partners. Those regional consultations provided an opportunity to share views on the issues within the mandate of the Group, as well as to learn from regional organizations and their member States about their experiences with measures and policies aimed at promoting a peaceful and secure regional and global environment for information and communications technology.

On 5 and 6 December, the Chair held an informal consultative meeting, open to all Member States, in accordance with the Group's mandate. At the meeting, delegations engaged in interactive discussions and shared their views, which the Chair conveyed to the Group for consideration.

The Group held its first substantive session from 9 to 13 December, during which it agreed on its working methods, while also reflecting both on its consultations with regional organizations and on the informal consultative meeting. In accordance with its mandate, the Group subsequently, commenced its task to study, with a view to promoting common understandings and effective implementation, possible cooperative measures to address existing and potential threats in the sphere of information security, including norms, rules and principles

---

[14] For the list of participating organizations, see Chair's letter to the participants of the meeting, annex.

[15] For the documents of the Group of Governmental Experts, see Office for Disarmament Affairs, "Group of Governmental Experts".

of responsible behaviour of States, confidence-building measures and capacity-building, as well as how international law applies to the use of information and communications technologies by States.

Awareness-raising, promoting understanding

Also in 2019, the Office for Disarmament Affairs launched an e-learning programme it developed in partnership with the Cyber Security Agency of Singapore. The course, entitled "Cyberdiplomacy: Furthering the peaceful use of information and communications technologies", was intended to provide interested Member States, researchers and students with a greater understanding of the challenges that the use of information and communications technologies presented to international security, as well as the work that had been done at the international level to address those challenges. Building on the training course, the Office for Disarmament Affairs and the Cyber Security Agency of Singapore co-organized a norms-awareness workshop in July with member States of the Association of Southeast Asian Nations. During the workshop, held in Singapore, participants explored ways to implement the voluntary, non-binding norms of responsible State behaviour in the region, as well as the capacities required to do so.

Missiles

Renewing multilateral dialogue

On 18 October, the Minister of Foreign Affairs of Germany, Heiko Mass, launched the Missile Dialogue Initiative at an event in Berlin.[16] In his address, the Foreign Minister referred to various developments, including the proliferation of intercontinental ballistic missiles, the development of a nuclear-powered cruise missile, the testing of anti-satellite missiles, and drone and cruise-missile strikes on civil installations in the Middle East. Under the initiative, a worldwide independent network of experts would discuss the future of arms control in all of its facets and advise policymakers and practitioners on an informal basis. The aim was for decision makers to be better prepared for modern-day challenges. The International Institute for Strategic Studies, an independent research institute based in the United Kingdom, was named as the initiative's implementing agency.

Developments in long-range conventional weapons, including hypersonic technologies

The Office for Disarmament Affairs and the United Nations Institute for Disarmament Research continued to work on facilitating greater understanding on the peace and security implications of long-range conventional weapons, including those using hypersonic technologies, in accordance with Action 13 of the Secretary-General's Agenda for Disarmament.

---

[16] See also his speech at the opening of the first Missile Dialogue Initiative, Berlin, 18 October 2019.

In February, the Office for Disarmament Affairs and the United Nations Institute for Disarmament Research published a study entitled *Hypersonic Weapons: A Challenge and Opportunity for Strategic Arms Control.*[17] Observing that the development of novel long-range strike options had received little attention in multilateral disarmament discussions despite their potentially negative consequences for security, arms control and disarmament, the authors sought to raise awareness about those implications. They recommended possible ways to address hypersonic weapons in a multilateral context, while also noting that "a significant amount of groundwork needs to take place before any such formal process could be initiated". On 16 May, the United Nations Institute for Disarmament Research addressed the matter by convening a Geneva panel event, which also included discussion of a 2017 study on hypersonic weapons by the RAND Corporation.[18]

On 19 September, the Office for Disarmament Affairs and the Institute held a tabletop exercise in Geneva to explore if and how hypersonic systems might impact various fictitious crisis scenarios and interrelate with other strategic technologies. The participants included 16 government representatives and seven independent experts.[19]

The outcome of the exercise resonated with the findings of the February study and could be summarized as follows: (a) hypersonic weapons have the potential to contribute to an arms race dynamic; (b) the military utility of such weapons remains unproven and therefore uncertain; (c) such weapons have the potential to contribute to strategic miscalculation or unintended escalation due to ambiguity about the nature of their payload; (d) such weapons present a challenge at a time when the arms-control and disarmament architecture is already strained; and (e) various existing arms-control approaches—including creating launch notifications, establishing export controls and addressing such systems as part of existing strategic arms control processes—can address issues raised by such weapons.

Armed uncrewed aerial vehicles

From 20 to 22 February, the Office for Disarmament Affairs, with financial support from Germany, convened an informal high-level meeting at the Greentree Estate in Manhasset, New York, to develop common objectives and understandings on the priority issues under the "Disarmament that Saves Lives" pillar of the Secretary-General's Agenda for Disarmament. The meeting addressed, inter

---

[17] John Borrie, Amy Dowler and Pavel Podvig (New York, United Nations Office for Disarmament Affairs and the United Nations Institute for Disarmament Research, 2019).

[18] Richard H. Speier, George Nacouzi, Carrie Lee and Richard M. Moore, *Hypersonic Missile Nonproliferation: Hindering the Spread of a New Class of Weapons* (Santa Monica, California, United States, RAND Corporation, 2017).

[19] See also John Borrie and Daniel Porras, *The Implications of Hypersonic Weapons for International Stability and Arms Control: Report on a UNIDIR-UNODA Turn-based Exercise*, (Geneva, United Nations Institute for Disarmament Research, 2019).

alia, enhancing transparency, accountability and oversight with respect to armed uncrewed aerial vehicles.

In that area, participants expressed concerns that included (a) the need to ensure respect for international humanitarian law and international human rights law, (b) cross-border use and international stability, and (c) proliferation and use of such vehicles by non-State actors. The interface between international humanitarian and human rights law was seen as a particular challenge, as some participants argued that the unique characteristics of armed uncrewed aerial vehicles were driving some actors to reinterpret the law. There was support for developing common standards for the transfer, holding and use of such vehicles in order to ensure accountability, transparency and oversight. Various ideas for dialogue were discussed, among them the establishment of a new group of governmental experts and the pursuit of informal discussion on a new agenda item of the Disarmament Commission from 2021 onwards.

On 8 July, during its presidency of the Security Council, Peru held an informal interactive dialogue on armed uncrewed aerial vehicles with briefings from the Office for Disarmament Affairs and the United Nations Institute for Disarmament Research. The meeting underscored a common understanding of the problems in relation both to humanitarian issues, including the protection of civilians, and to international peace and security. There was broad acceptance among participants of exploring new measures, especially in the area of transparency on use and transfers, while many called for adherence to the Arms Trade Treaty and for participation in the United Nations Register of Conventional Arms to be part of any solution.

Emerging technologies relevant to small arms and light weapons

In 2019, States continued to consider how new developments in design, technology and manufacture of small arms and light weapons may affect efforts to combat the illicit arms trade, particularly those developments that may have an impact on marking, tracing and record-keeping. In the context of the implementation of the Programme of Action to Prevent, Combat and Eradicate the Illicit Trade in Small Arms and Light Weapons in All Its Aspects and the International Tracing Instrument, States continued to highlight challenges and opportunities resulting from recent trends, especially the use of polymer material and modular design. (For more information on the Programme of Action, see chap. III).

In its annual resolution entitled "The illicit trade in small arms and light weapons in all its aspects" (74/60), the General Assembly highlighted both the opportunities and challenges posed by such trends with regard to effective marking, record-keeping and tracing. By the same resolution, the Assembly explicitly recognized the need for timely action in addressing new developments associated with polymer and modular weapons.

Against that backdrop and pursuant to the request of the General Assembly by its prior resolution on the matter (73/69), the Secretary-General provided concrete recommendations to Member States for addressing recent developments in manufacturing, technology and design of small arms and light weapons. The recommendations—offered in the framework of the Secretary-General's report to the General Assembly entitled "The illicit trade in small arms and light weapons in all its aspects and assistance to States for curbing the illicit traffic in small arms and light weapons and collecting them"[20]—included possible elements to include in a potential supplementary annex to the International Tracing Instrument. Those elements concerned, inter alia, general considerations, definitions, marking and record-keeping and follow-up measures. The non-exhaustive list of elements was intended to help take forward a recommendation made by the Secretary-General in 2014 for States to consider a document supplementary to the International Tracing Instrument that would reflect the implications of recent technical developments, while ensuring the full effectiveness of the Instrument moving forward.[21] In his 2019 report, the Secretary-General noted that the agreed schedule of meetings on the Programme of Action could guide discussions on such a document, beginning with the seventh Biennial Meeting of States in June 2020.

Cross-cutting issues

Relationship between disarmament and development

On 12 December 2019, the General Assembly adopted its annual resolution entitled "Relationship between disarmament and development" (74/57). As in past years, the resolution had been tabled by Indonesia on behalf of the Non-Aligned Movement.[22]

As in previous iterations of the resolution, the Assembly called for the international community to devote to economic and social development some of the resources made available by the implementation of disarmament and arms-limitation agreements in the service of allowing greater resources to be devoted to development needs. In that regard, the preambular paragraphs retained a reference to the "symbiotic" relationship between disarmament and development.

---

[20] A/74/187.

[21] A/CONF.192/BMS/2014/1, para. 60.

[22] The resolution served to highlight and underscore the link between disarmament and development—a link made plain in the 2030 Agenda for Sustainable Development and its target 16.4 on reducing illicit arms flows. In 2019, the Office for Disarmament Affairs and the United Nations Office on Drugs and Crime continued to serve as co-custodians for indicator 16.4.2, "Proportion of seized, found or surrendered arms whose illicit origin or context has been traced or established by a competent authority in line with international instruments."

Military spending cuts can help achieve the 2030 Agenda for Sustainable Development

Annual expenditures

$1,917
BILLION

Global military spending in 2018

Eliminate extreme **poverty and hunger** ≈ **13%** of military spending

Achieve primary and early secondary **education** ≈ **3%** of military spending

Extending basic **water, sanitation & hygiene** to unserved populations ≈ **2%** of military spending

Despite a clear, global commitment in the Charter of the United Nations for the "least diversion of the world's economic and human resources to armaments", world military expenditure is rising and arms competition remains a largely unchecked global problem. In 2019, military expenditure worldwide rose to $1.9 trillion, the highest level since the end of the cold war.

The 2030 Agenda for Sustainable Development acknowledges the link between peace and development: achieving the 17 Sustainable Development Goals requires a substantial financial investment, and redirecting funds from militaries to economic and social development can make a key contribution. It has been estimated that the cost of achieving quality universal primary and early secondary education for all (Goal 4) would be just over 3 per cent of global annual military spending. Eliminating extreme poverty and hunger (Goals 1 and 2) would cost about 13 per cent of annual military spending, and extending basic water, sanitation and hygiene (Goal 6) to unserved populations would cost less than 2 per cent of annual military spending.

Sources: SIPRI, UN Food and Agriculture Organization and UNESCO.

The Assembly also took note of a report submitted by the Secretary-General further to the resolution's predecessor (73/37).[23] In the report, the Secretary-General noted that the United Nations continued to strengthen its role regarding the relationship between disarmament and development, in particular through coordinated efforts towards achieving the Sustainable Development Goals. In particular, the role of the 25-member Coordinating Action on Small Arms mechanism was highlighted as the most relevant inter-agency mechanism for the

---

[23] The report of the Secretary-General (A/74/116), issued on 20 June 2019, contained replies by five Member States and the European Union to a note verbale, sent in February 2019 to all Member States, in which the Office for Disarmament Affairs called for the submission of information in accordance with resolution 73/37. For the reply of a sixth Member State submitted after the deadline, see Office for Disarmament Affairs, "Seventy-Fourth Session of the General Assembly" (Late Submission to the Secretary-General's Report.)

issue of disarmament and development. The Secretary-General also recalled that, in accordance with Article 26 of the United Nations Charter, all Member States had committed themselves to the least diversion for armaments of the world's human and economic resources, not only to determine trends in military spending, but also in setting the conditions for development through disarmament.

Meanwhile, the Office for Disarmament Affairs provided input on the collection of arms-related data under indicator 16.1.2, "Conflict-related deaths per 100,000 population, by sex, age and cause". That included the incorporation of terms and definitions from United Nations disarmament and arms-control instruments, thereby maximizing synergies between data collection related to the 2030 Agenda for Sustainable Development and the application of that data for broad arms-control process and policy discussions. The methodology for that indicator was approved in early 2019.

The relationship between disarmament and development was reflected in the establishment of the Saving Lives Entity, a new United Nations funding facility dedicated to supporting Member States in tackling illicit small arms and light weapons as part of a comprehensive approach to sustainable security and development. (For more information on the Saving Lives Entity, see chap. III).

Terrorism and disarmament

The United Nations supported counter-terrorism efforts in 2019 with a focus on weapons of mass destruction, conventional arms and improvised explosive devices.

As part of its work to address potential threats of terrorism involving weapons of mass destruction, the Office for Disarmament Affairs continued to maintain a roster of experts and laboratories provided by Member States in support of the Secretary-General's Mechanism for Investigation of Alleged Use of Chemical and Biological Weapons. Under the Mechanism, the Secretary-General could call upon the rostered experts to carry out fact-finding activities concerning reports of the alleged use of chemical and biological weapons, including by non-State actors. (For more information on the Mechanism, see chap. II.)

On 19 December, the General Assembly adopted without a vote a new iteration of its resolution on measures to prevent terrorists from acquiring weapons of mass destruction (74/43). As in prior versions, the Assembly emphasized the urgent need for progress in the area of disarmament and non-proliferation in order to maintain international peace and security and to contribute to global efforts against terrorism. It also urged all Member States to take and strengthen national measures, as appropriate, to prevent terrorists from acquiring weapons of mass destruction, their means of delivery and materials and technologies related to their manufacture.

Throughout the year, the Security Council continued to express concern over terrorists' acquisition of weapons, including small arms and light weapons and materials that could be used in the manufacture of improvised explosive devices. The Council also continued to condemn the flow of weapons, including small arms and light weapons, to and between Islamic State in Iraq and the Levant (Da'esh), Al-Qaida, their affiliates, and associated groups, illegal armed groups and criminals. By its resolution 2462 (2019) adopted in March, the Council noted with grave concern that terrorists and terrorist groups raise funds through a variety of means, including the illicit trade in small arms and light weapons.

The Security Council continued drawing attention to the use of improvised explosive devices by terrorist groups. In particular, the Security Council expressed concern over the acquisition of related materials by Islamic State in Iraq and the Levant, Al-Qaeda, their affiliates and associated groups, illegal armed groups and criminals. (For more information on efforts to address conventional weapons, see chap. III.)

Work of the United Nations Global Counter-Terrorism Coordination Compact

Following its launch in December 2018 by the Secretary-General, the United Nations Global Counter-Terrorism Coordination Compact entered into operation in 2019 under the leadership of the United Nations Office of Counter-Terrorism. Through its aim to promote and support a balanced implementation of the United Nations Global Counter-Terrorism Strategy and relevant General Assembly and Security Council resolutions, the Compact brought together 40 United Nations entities, as well as the International Criminal Police Organization (INTERPOL), the World Customs Organization and the Inter-Parliamentary Union, resulting in one of the largest coordination frameworks in the United Nations system.

In 2019, a new inter-agency structure was established to enhance the coordination and coherence of United Nations counter-terrorism work through the Compact. Under that structure, the Coordination Committee chaired by the Under-Secretary-General for Counter-Terrorism undertook the responsibility of steering the implementation of commitments under the Compact by adopting its first joint programme of work, covering the years 2019 and 2020. Additionally, the Committee established and maintained oversight of eight revitalized working groups aligned with the Strategy's four pillars. The Coordination Committee met three times in 2019, and its working groups held a total of 38 meetings during the year.

In the area of disarmament, non-proliferation and arms control, the revitalized Working Group on Border Management and Law Enforcement relating to Counter-Terrorism provided a forum for strategic and practical discussions on, inter alia, the illicit spread of weapons and the nexus between terrorism and transnational organized crime. The working group also developed a joint project for 2020, with catalytic funding from the Office of Counter-Terrorism, called "Developing Guidelines for Member States to Facilitate the Implementation of Security Council Resolution 2370 (2017) and the Relevant International Standards and Good Practices on preventing terrorists from acquiring weapons".

Meanwhile, the Working Group on Emerging Threats and Critical Infrastructure Protection provided a forum to discuss policy considerations and operational issues related to the protection of critical infrastructure, vulnerable targets, and chemical, biological, radiological and nuclear (CBRN) materials. In 2019, the Working Group launched a joint project called "Enhancing Knowledge About Advances in Science and Technology to Combat Weapons of Mass Destruction Terrorism", which the United Nations Counter Terrorism Centre, located in the Office of Counter-Terrorism, funded and co-led with the United Nations Interregional Crime and Justice Research Institute. The Centre also partnered with the Organisation for the Prohibition of Chemical Weapons (OPCW) to initiate a third phase of the joint working group project "Ensuring Effective Interagency Interoperability and Coordinated Communication in Case of Chemical and/or Biological Attacks".

Work of the United Nations Office of Counter-Terrorism and its United Nations Counter-Terrorism Centre

The prospect of non-State actors, including terrorist groups and their supporters, gaining access to and using weapons of mass destruction or CBRN materials remained a serious threat to international peace and security throughout 2019. Over the years, terrorist groups have tested new ways and means to acquire and use more dangerous weapons—including weapons using CBRN materials—to maximize damage and inspire terror. With technological advancements and the expansion of legal and illegal commercial channels, including on the dark web, some of those weapons have become increasingly accessible.

Through the United Nations Counter-Terrorism Centre, the Office of Counter-Terrorism continued the multi-year programme "Preventing and Responding to [Weapons of Mass Destruction]/CBRN Terrorism" in 2019. Launched the previous year in line with the Office's mandate to strengthen the ability of the United Nations to deliver counter-terrorism capacity-building assistance to Member States, the programme was aimed at (a) advancing the understanding of Member States and international organizations about the level of that terrorism threat and (b) supporting the prevention, preparedness and response efforts of those entities. Through the programme, the Office also sought to strengthen partnerships contributing to the international community's existing capacity-building efforts and to provide additional capacity-building support in areas such as border and export control, strategic trade control, illicit trafficking, protection of CBRN materials and critical infrastructure, incident response and crisis management, and related forensics.

The United Nations Counter-Terrorism Centre worked closely with INTERPOL in 2019 to develop a global study aimed at advancing knowledge and understanding of the threat of terrorist groups potentially accessing weapons of mass destruction or CBRN materials to use in attacks. The authors planned to divide the study into five phases, each assessing a different region for threats it faced from non-State actors in relation to such materials.

The Centre also delivered capacity-building activities at the global, regional and national levels, including international workshops on countering nuclear terrorism in Africa and the Middle East, national trainings on countering biological and chemical terrorism in Iraq, and national workshops on responding to CBRN terrorism in Jordan. In working to raise awareness about the threat of terrorism involving weapons of mass destruction or CBRN materials, the Centre partnered with the European Union, the Global Initiative to Combat Nuclear Terrorism, the North Atlantic Treaty Organization and the United Nations Office on Drugs and Crime.

Additionally, the United Nations Counter-Terrorism Centre coordinated activities and collaborated with a number of international organizations and initiatives, including the Security Council Committee established pursuant to resolution 1540 (2004) (1540 Committee), the Office for Disarmament Affairs, the Office of Legal Affairs, the International Atomic Energy Agency and the World Health Organization, as well as the Global Partnership Against the Spread of Weapons and Materials of Mass Destruction, the Nuclear Security Contact Group and the Nuclear Threat Initiative.

The Centre also tackled threats from weapons of mass destruction and CBRN materials through two projects it developed and co-implemented within the framework of the Global Counter-Terrorism Coordination Compact's Working Group on Emerging Threats and Critical Infrastructure Protection. In that regard, the Centre joined with the United Nations Interregional Crime and Justice Research Institute to launch one of those projects, focused on security and technology, with an expert workshop on 16 and 17 October in Geneva. Meanwhile, the Centre collaborated with OPCW to make preparations for the second project, which was scheduled for launch in 2020.

Work of the United Nations Office on Drugs and Crime on the prevention and suppression of chemical, biological, radiological and nuclear terrorism

In line with its General Assembly mandate to promote adherence to, and implementation of, the international legal instruments against terrorism,[24] the United Nations Office on Drugs and Crime launched a three-year joint project in 2019 with the European Union and the Office of Counter-Terrorism on promoting the universalization and effective implementation of the International Convention for the Suppression of Acts of Nuclear Terrorism. With support from Canada, the

---

[24] Those instruments include seven that deal with chemical, biological, radiological and/or nuclear terrorism. The Office's mandate in the area of CBRN terrorism was most recently reiterated and reinforced by the General Assembly in its resolution 74/175, "Technical assistance provided by the United Nations Office on Drugs and Crime related to counter-terrorism", adopted on 18 December 2019 without a vote.

Office also continued to implement a project on promoting the universalization and effective implementation of that Convention, as well as other nuclear-security legal instruments, including the Convention on the Physical Protection of Nuclear Material and its amendment of 2005.

In June, the Office conducted a regional workshop in Panama for selected countries in Latin America and the Caribbean on promoting the universalization and effective implementation of the three above-mentioned international legal instruments. It also conducted two national visits during the year to Angola and Togo, where it promoted the universalization and effective implementation of such instruments. Separately, the Office delivered a workshop for Libyan national authorities on nuclear terrorism, hosted in Morocco and organized in close collaboration with the Moroccan Agency for Nuclear and Radiological Safety and Security.

Also in 2019, the Office held two expert group meetings to develop a mock trial featuring the International Convention for the Suppression of Acts of Nuclear Terrorism. Intended as an opportunity to train judges and prosecutors on the specificities associated with the Convention, the mock trial would serve to demonstrate the benefits of being party to the Convention and having the adequate national legislation in place for implementation.

With a view to countering CBRN terrorism threats, the Office developed an e-learning tool on the international legal framework against CBRN terrorism, available in Arabic, English, French, Russian and Spanish.

The Office also cooperated regularly with the Office for Disarmament Affairs, the Office of Counter-Terrorism, the 1540 Committee and its Group of Experts, the International Atomic Energy Agency, the Organisation for the Prohibition of Chemical Weapons, the Global Initiative to Combat Nuclear Terrorism, the Nuclear Security Contact Group, the Global Partnership Against the Spread of Weapons and Materials of Mass Destruction, the Nuclear Threat Initiative and others, as appropriate. In addition to inviting such entities to its relevant activities, the Office on Drugs and Crime contributed its expertise to numerous activities organized by the aforementioned stakeholders.

Contribution of the Organisation for the Prohibition of Chemical Weapons to global counter-terrorism efforts

The OPCW Executive Council's Open-Ended Working Group on Terrorism continued to highlight where OPCW could work productively to advance its contribution to global counter-terrorism efforts. In that regard, it focused on sharing information among States parties on incidents involving non-State actors carrying out acts prohibited by the Convention, chemical-security regulations, cooperation with other international organizations active in countering chemical terrorism and new capacity-building programmes initiated by the Secretariat in that area.

Expanding on its efforts from the previous year, OPCW provided specific counter-terrorism capacity-building support to the States parties. It organized a pilot workshop for Asia, held in Malaysia in April, on addressing threats from non-State actors through national legislation on implementing the Chemical Weapons Convention. The workshop featured the participation of a number of other international organizations, including the United Nations Office on Drugs and Crime, INTERPOL, the 1540 Committee Group of Experts, and the World Customs Organization. OPCW also carried out capacity-building for chemical-emergency response, focusing on major events and hospital preparedness.

In support of international cooperation on counter-terrorism, OPCW served in 2019 as a Vice-Chair of the United Nations Global Counter-Terrorism Coordination Compact's newly established Working Group on Emerging Threats and Critical Infrastructure Protection, with INTERPOL serving as Chair and the Office for Disarmament Affairs and the United Nations Interregional Crime and Justice Research Institute as other Vice-Chairs. Participants in the Working Group jointly developed a project proposal for the third phase of a project, expected to begin in 2020, on enhancing inter-agency interoperability and public communications in the event of a chemical or biological attack. OPCW led the work on that proposal, with input from the United Nations Office for the Coordination of Humanitarian Affairs, the World Health Organization, INTERPOL, the United Nations Interregional Crime and Justice Research Institute and the Biological Weapons Convention Implementation Support Unit.

Promotion of multilateralism in the area of disarmament and non-proliferation

In its resolution 74/55 of 12 December, the General Assembly called upon all Member States to renew and fulfil their individual and collective commitments to multilateral cooperation as an important means of pursuing and achieving their common objectives in the area of disarmament and non-proliferation. In addition, the Assembly requested the Secretary-General to seek the views of Member States on the issue of the promotion of multilateralism in the area of disarmament and non-proliferation and to submit a report on the matter to the Assembly at its seventy-fourth session. Pursuant to resolution 73/41 of 5 December 2018, the Secretary-General submitted to the Assembly at its seventy-fourth session his report[25] on the subject, with replies from seven Governments.

Developments in science and technology and their potential impact on international security and disarmament efforts

In accordance with General Assembly resolution 73/32, the Secretary-General issued an update[26] to his 2018 report on recent developments in science and technology and their potential impact on international security and

---

[25] A/74/96.
[26] A/74/122 and Add.1.

disarmament efforts, with an annex containing submissions from Member States giving their views on the matter. The report included information on developments since the previous report in the areas of autonomous technologies, uncrewed aerial vehicles, biology and chemistry, advanced missile technologies, space-based technologies, materials technologies, and information and communications technologies, as well as on non-technology-specific discussions.

Observance of environmental norms in the drafting and implementation of agreements on disarmament and arms control

Emphasizing the importance of observing environmental norms in the preparation and implementation of disarmament and arms limitation agreements and mindful of the detrimental environmental effects of the use of nuclear weapons, the General Assembly adopted without a vote resolution 74/52 on 12 December. In the resolution, the Assembly called upon States to pursue unilateral, bilateral and multilateral measures to ensure the application of scientific and technological progress in international security, disarmament and other related spheres without detriment to the environment or to attaining sustainable development. The Assembly also invited Member States to communicate to the Secretary-General the measures they had adopted to promote objectives envisaged in its language, and it requested that he submit a report containing that information to the General Assembly at its seventy-fourth session. For the seventy-fourth session, the Secretary-General included replies received from eight Governments in his report[27] submitted to the General Assembly pursuant to resolution 73/39 of 5 December 2018.

Implementation of Security Council resolution 1540 (2004)

Status of implementation

On 24 December, the Security Council Committee established pursuant to resolution 1540 (2004) (1540 Committee) submitted to the Security Council its review[28] of the implementation of the resolution for 2019. The 1540 Committee, chaired by Dian Triansyah Djani (Indonesia), continued to facilitate and monitor the implementation of resolution 1540 (2004) by States, with the Office for Disarmament Affairs providing administrative and substantive support.

The review addressed all aspects of the Committee's work, which had been facilitated by its four working groups on monitoring and national implementation, assistance, cooperation with international organizations, and transparency and media outreach.

---

[27] A/74/99.
[28] S/2019/986.

Monitoring and national implementation

In 2019, the Committee systematically reviewed and updated all country-specific matrices containing details on each Member State's implementation of resolution 1540 (2004). It took that step in preparation for the next comprehensive review of the status of implementation of the resolution, mandated by resolution 1977 (2011) to take place every five years. The ongoing review, due for completion before 25 April 2021, is the third review of its kind.

In its resolution 2325 (2016), the Security Council called upon all States that had not yet done so to submit a first report to the 1540 Committee without delay. In support of its ongoing effort to achieve universal reporting, the Committee continued to encourage the submission of such reports. In that context, the Central African Republic and Solomon Islands submitted their first reports in 2019, bringing the total number of States that had provided such a report to 184.

By the same resolution, the Security Council encouraged States to provide additional information on their implementation of resolution 1540 (2004), including through their laws, regulations and effective practices. During the reporting period, 23 States[29] provided the required additional information.

In resolution 2325 (2016), the Council also encouraged States to develop, on a voluntary basis, national implementation action plans mapping out their priorities and plans for implementing the key provisions of resolution 1540 (2004). In 2019, four Member States[30] submitted such plans, bringing to 35 the total number of States that had submitted national implementation action plans to the Committee since 2007.

The Security Council, in its resolution 2325 (2016), recognized the importance of the Committee continuing to engage actively in dialogue with States on their implementation of resolution 1540 (2004), including through visits to States at their invitation. In 2019, the Committee undertook visits to Chile, Kuwait, Madagascar and Togo.

By resolution 2325 (2016), the Council also encouraged States to inform the Committee of their points of contact for resolution 1540 (2004). In 2019, the number of Member States that had provided such information reached 119.

In its eighteenth programme of work, the Committee encouraged initiatives to strengthen the capacity of national points of contact for resolution 1540 (2004) and the continuation of training courses conducted at the regional level. In that regard, a training course for English-speaking African countries took place in March in Addis Ababa, supported by the African Union. An additional training

---

[29] Argentina, Austria, Bahrain, Brunei Darussalam, Bulgaria, Cuba, Czechia, El Salvador, Honduras, India, Kyrgyzstan, Luxembourg, Madagascar, Monaco, Paraguay, Senegal, Singapore, Sweden, Togo, Tunisia, Turkey, Uruguay and Zambia,

[30] Madagascar, Paraguay, Suriname and Uzbekistan.

course was held in September in Bridgetown with support from the Caribbean Community, and a third was completed in October in Xiamen, China.

In its programme of work, the Committee also recognized the need to promote the sharing of experience through peer reviews and other means to evaluate and reinforce effective practices and lessons learned regarding States' efforts to implement resolution 1540 (2004). In 2019, two peer review processes[31] took place with the support of the 1540 Committee, the Organization of American States and the Office for Disarmament Affairs.

Assistance

In 2019, 12 States submitted new requests for assistance[32] to the 1540 Committee. The Committee also received letters from States and international organizations indicating their readiness to consider assistance requests, while also informing the Committee about current activities or possible areas in which assistance could be offered.[33] The Committee relayed those responses to the States concerned for their action.

Cooperation with international, regional and subregional organizations

In 2019, the 1540 Committee continued to enhance its collaboration with relevant international, regional and subregional organizations, as well as other relevant United Nations bodies. In that context, the Committee collaborated with and participated in relevant meetings of the African Union, the Organization of American States, the Organization for Security and Co-operation in Europe, the Commonwealth of Independent States, the Southern African Development Community, the Caribbean Community, the International Atomic Energy Agency, OPCW, the Implementation Support Unit of the Biological Weapons Convention, INTERPOL, the World Customs Organization, the United Nations Office on Drugs and Crime, the Financial Action Task Force and the Office for Disarmament Affairs.

In addition, the Committee and its Group of Experts continued to cooperate with the Counter-Terrorism Committee and with the Security Council Committee established pursuant to resolutions 1267 (1999), 1989 (2011) and 2253 (2015) concerning Islamic State in Iraq and the Levant (Da'esh), Al-Qaida and associated individuals, groups, undertakings and entities. In that regard, the Committee participated in the joint briefing of those entities to the Security Council in May.

---

[31] Dominican Republic and Panama; Paraguay and Uruguay.
[32] Algeria, Chile, Dominican Republic, Kuwait, Madagascar, Malawi, Mexico, Panama, Paraguay, Solomon Islands, Togo and Uruguay.
[33] International Maritime Organization, World Customs Organization, OPCW and World Organization for Animal Health.

Transparency and outreach

In 2019, the Committee participated in 58 outreach events to support transparency and help foster greater cooperation and awareness among States, parliamentarians, relevant international, regional and subregional organizations, and civil society, including academia and industry, regarding the obligations set out in resolution 1540 (2004) and their implementation.

With respect to the private sector, the Committee participated in two events that directly engaged industry and provided opportunities to work with and provide information regarding its obligations under national laws. The first of those events took place in May, when Zambia hosted a regional industry outreach conference for the Southern African Development Community with support from the Office for Disarmament Affairs and in cooperation with Germany. The second event was the sixth international industry outreach conference on resolution 1540 (2004) "Industry Engagement in Strategic Trade Controls Resolution 1540 (2004)", hosted by the Government of Germany in Wiesbaden in November.

In addition, the 1540 Committee engaged academia on ways to improve the implementation of resolution 1540 (2004) at a September event that the Government of Germany hosted in Berlin.

chapter

VI Gender and disarmament

Mine clearance in Mozambique by the Norwegian People's Aid, 6 November 2019.

Photo: Norwegian People's Aid / Ministry of Foreign Affairs, Oslo

CHAPTER VI

Gender and disarmament

Gender equality is not only a moral imperative and fundamental human right, but also a powerful tool for accelerating progress in all areas of the United Nations' work, including peace and security. Strengthening the role of women and diversity of voices in disarmament will advance our collective goals in disarmament, non-proliferation and arms control.

IZUMI NAKAMITSU, UNITED NATIONS HIGH REPRESENTATIVE FOR DISARMAMENT AFFAIRS[1]

Developments and trends, 2019

IN THE YEAR LEADING UP TO THE TWENTIETH ANNIVERSARY of Security Council resolution 1325 (2000) on women, peace and security, a growing number of Member States demonstrated interest and support in promoting the inclusion of gender perspectives in disarmament and arms control processes in order to achieve more sustainable and effective outcomes.

Women remained significantly underrepresented in multilateral disarmament forums and decision-making during the year, according to findings[2] by the United Nations Institute for Disarmament Research. Calls for women's full and equal participation increased, as did the understanding that women's participation needs to be meaningful. The General Assembly prioritized women's equal participation in multiple contexts, including for the first time in ammunition management policy, in the framework of the Convention on the Prohibition of the Development, Production and Stockpiling of Bacteriological (Biological) and Toxin Weapons and on Their Destruction (Biological Weapons Convention) and for the groups of governmental experts on nuclear disarmament verification. Women's participation was also prioritized across the world in relevant trainings, courses and other activities, contributing towards gender equality and women's empowerment in the field of disarmament, non-proliferation and arms control.

While gender considerations were featured prominently in multilateral small arms control processes and forums, there was increased recognition that additional in-depth research and policymaking efforts were necessary to ensure

---

[1] Remarks at the event with the theme "When participation becomes meaningful: advancing the conversation on gender diversity in the NPT" held on the margins of the 2019 session of the Nuclear Non-Proliferation Treaty Preparatory Committee, New York, 3 May 2019.

[2] Renata Hessmann Dalaqua, Kjølv Egeland and Torbjørn Graff Hugo, *Still Behind the Curve* (Geneva, United Nations Institute for Disarmament Research, 2019).

gender-responsive approaches to addressing weapons of mass destruction and new and emerging technologies. That growing recognition was informed, in part, by a growing awareness of the differential impacts of weapons on women, men, girls and boys.

In 2019, new projects, capacity-building measures, and initiatives were implemented at the community, national and regional levels to support gender-responsive commitments, including in the fight against small-arms trafficking and misuse; armed-violence reduction; disarmament, demobilization and reintegration; security sector reform; and mine action. Member States strengthened the formal recognition of linkages between arms control and the prevention of gender-based violence, including through resolutions of the General Assembly and Human Rights Council, and they expressed support for national arms control efforts aimed at preventing such violence. At the fifth Conference of States Parties to the Arms Trade Treaty, where gender and gender-based violence were the thematic priority, participants agreed on recommendations and actions to, inter alia, improve the gender balance in future conferences and promote an increased understanding of the gendered impact of armed violence in the context of the Treaty.

Meanwhile, various stakeholders made efforts throughout the year to promote a systematic gendered approach in the area of disarmament. Member States and the United Nations Institute for Disarmament Research organized a number of events to that end, including in the frameworks of the Biological Weapons Convention and the Treaty on the Non-Proliferation of Nuclear Weapons. In an op-ed written for the online magazine *Europe's World*, the High Representative for Disarmament Affairs called for gender to be placed "at the heart of arms policy", and the International Gender Champions Disarmament Impact Group issued new resources on the relevance of gender perspectives to the field as a whole.

The United Nations system also undertook further efforts to achieve the equal participation of women and men in disarmament processes and to address the gendered impacts of arms. The seventy-fourth session of the General Assembly First Committee adopted 17 resolutions containing references to equal gender representation or participation, gender considerations, the gendered impact of weapons or gender-based violence. Of those resolutions, four contained such language for the first time. In addition, a range of entities within the United Nations system implemented gender-sensitive approaches and trainings within disarmament-related areas of work.

Integrating gender perspectives

In 2019, the international community achieved considerable progress in strengthening linkages between multilateral disarmament frameworks and broader agendas aimed at promoting gender equality. In that regard, Member States and United Nations entities continued efforts to promote the inclusion of gender perspectives and the equal participation of men and women in the lead-up to the

Gender language in United Nations disarmament resolutions, 2017–2019

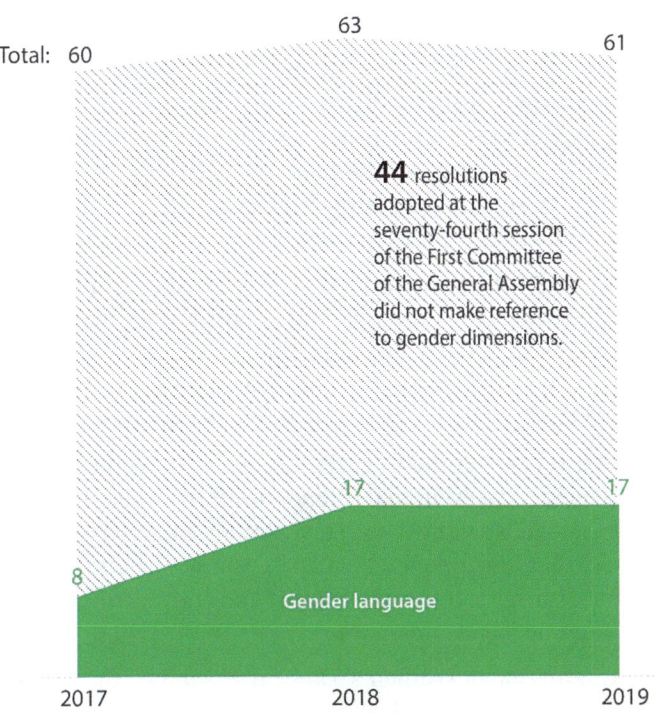

Total: 60   63   61

44 resolutions adopted at the seventy-fourth session of the First Committee of the General Assembly did not make reference to gender dimensions.

17   17

8

Gender language

2017   2018   2019

Successfully tackling gender-related disarmament issues—for example, the different impacts of weapons on women and men, as well as the need to ensure women's equal and meaningful participation in disarmament—requires addressing and integrating those considerations in many areas of work. Since first adopting resolution 65/69 of 8 December 2010, "Women, disarmament, non-proliferation and arms control", the General Assembly has referenced gender and women's participation in a growing number of disarmament-related resolutions.

Of the 61 resolutions that the General Assembly First Committee adopted at its seventy-fourth session in 2019, 17 included language on gender and 4 of those did so for the first time and 2 updated formulations on gender. This marked an increase since 2017, when the Committee adopted eight resolutions with references to gender or women.

Of the resolutions containing gender language in 2019, 10 referred to the equal participation of women and men in disarmament and 4 referenced their equal representation. Additionally, four of the resolutions mentioned the gendered impact of weapons, 2 referred to the contribution or role of women in disarmament and 3 referenced the mainstreaming of gender dimensions in the field.

Also in 2019, Member States removed relevant language from one resolution.

twentieth anniversary of Security Council resolution 1325 (2000) on women, peace and security and the twenty-fifth anniversary of the Beijing Declaration and Platform for Action[3] in 2020.

At the seventy-fourth session of the General Assembly First Committee, Trinidad and Tobago delivered a joint statement on gender and the disarmament machinery on behalf of 79 States, an increase from the 60 States that supported a similar message in 2018.[4] The new statement called for improved gender balance in the disarmament machinery and expressed support for gender considerations in disarmament and arms control processes. It further highlighted the gendered impact of weapons and the importance of applying a gender lens for the development of more sustainable, impactful and inclusive policy solution points that 39 individual States and four regional groups echoed in their own statements.

Meanwhile, civil society continued to play a central role in addressing gender perspectives in disarmament. In a joint statement[5] to the First Committee, 14 civil society organizations called on Member States "to push beyond the boundaries of the binary in work on gender and disarmament", changing perceptions and understandings to make concrete progress in building a peaceful world for all.

In his annual report[6] to the Security Council on women, peace and security, the Secretary-General stressed that global military spending continued to rise in contrast with social spending and investment in, inter alia, gender equality. He further noted that the repeated calls of women's civil society groups and peacebuilders for disarmament, arms control and the shifting of military spending to social investment had gone unanswered.

To mark International Women's Day on 8 March, the High Representative for Disarmament Affairs, Izumi Nakamitsu, authored an opinion piece entitled, "Let's Not Forget: Gender Must Be at the Heart of Arms Policy". Writing for the online magazine *Europe's World*, the High Representative highlighted the value of gender considerations in disarmament discussions and called for greater participation of women in disarmament, non-proliferation and arms-control negotiations. In addition, she noted the importance of collaborating at the national and community levels to promote a systematic, gendered approach to empowering women to take their seats at the decision-making table.

---

[3] The Beijing Declaration and Platform for Action on the empowerment of women is the outcome of the Fourth World Conference on Women, held in Beijing, China, in September 1995.

[4] For the text and the list of States, see the statement of Trinidad and Tobago in A/C.1/74/PV.21, pp. 9–10.

[5] Statement of the Women's International League for Peace and Freedom, delivered on behalf of 14 organizations, on gender and disarmament to the First Committee, New York, 18 October 2019.

[6] S/2019/800.

Also in 2019, the Geneva-based International Gender Champions Disarmament Impact Group[7] produced the publication entitled *Gender and Disarmament Resource Pack for Multilateral Practitioners.*[8] That reference provided information on the relevance of gender perspectives to arms control, non-proliferation and disarmament, as well as practical ideas for diplomats to apply a gender lens to their work. Separately, the United Nations Institute for Disarmament Research produced a short animated film entitled "How does gender relate to arms control and disarmament?" (10 October 2019), as well as a gender and disarmament online hub with additional reference materials.

Equal participation

Ensuring the equal, full and effective participation of women in disarmament, non-proliferation and arms-control processes remained both a priority of the Secretary-General, as stated in his Agenda for Disarmament (Actions 36 and 37), and a prerequisite to promoting and attaining sustainable peace and security, including through the achievement of the 2030 Agenda for Sustainable Development and Goal 5 on gender quality. The Office for Disarmament Affairs continued to monitor and analyse gender balance and women's participation in disarmament bodies and meetings throughout the year, finding that women remained underrepresented in multilateral disarmament meetings and conferences.[9] In the four groups of governmental experts mandated by the General Assembly that were active in 2019, only 28 per cent of participants were women.[10]

During the year, the United Nations Institute for Disarmament Research, under its gender and disarmament programme, conducted an extensive quantitative and qualitative analysis of women's participation and gender balance in arms control and disarmament that it published in a new report entitled *Still Behind the Curve.*[11] The authors affirmed that women were still significantly underrepresented

---

[7] The Group is co-chaired by the Director of the United Nations Institute for Disarmament Research and the Ambassadors of Canada, Ireland, Namibia and the Philippines.

[8] The publication was released in January 2020.

[9] First Committee (33 per cent women), Conference on Disarmament (36 per cent women), Biological Weapons Convention Meeting of States Parties (36 per cent women), Meeting of the High Contracting Parties to the Convention on Certain Conventional Weapons (32 per cent women), Preparatory Committee for the 2020 Review Conference of the Parties to the Treaty on the Non-Proliferation of Nuclear Weapons (30 per cent women), Meetings of States Parties to the Convention on Cluster Munitions (33 per cent women), Annual Conference of the High Contracting Parties to Amended Protocol II of the Convention on Certain Conventional Weapons (31 per cent women).

[10] The following is the breakdown by Group of Governmental Experts (GGE): GGE on Further Practical Measures for the Prevention of an Arms Race in Outer Space (16 per cent), GGE to Consider the Role of Verification in Advancing Nuclear Disarmament (8 per cent), GGE on the Continuing Operation of the United Nations Register of Conventional Arms and its Further Development (53 per cent) and GGE on Advancing Responsible State Behavior in Cyberspace in the Context of International Security (44 per cent).

[11] Hessmann Dalaqua, Egeland and Graff Hugo, *Still Behind the Curve.*

Gender in the General Assembly First Committee and other disarmament forums

2019 General Assembly First Committee

33%
of delegations were women

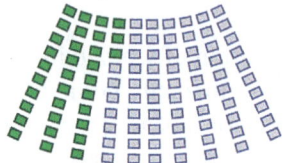

32% of heads of delegations were women

45 delegations included no women and
10 delegations had no men

1 in 4 statements were delivered by women and
7% of the Rights to Reply (total: 67) were made by women

2019 Preparatory Committee for the 2020 Review Conference of the Nuclear Non-Proliferation Treaty

30%
of delegations were women

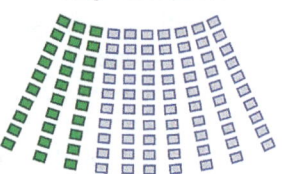

25% of heads of delegations were women

2019 Conference on Disarmament

36%
of delegations were women

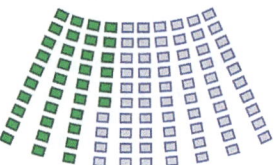

23% of heads of delegations were women

2019 Biological Weapons Convention Meeting of States Parties

36%
of delegations were women

20% of heads of delegations were women

Active Groups of Governmental Experts

Ensuring women's equal, full and effective participation in disarmament, non-proliferation and arms control is a priority within the Secretary-General's Agenda for Disarmament. Moreover, United Nations officials, Member States, regional organizations and civil society have repeatedly called for concerted action to promote gender equality in disarmament as a contribution towards sustainable peace and security, as well as the achievement of Goal 5 on gender-equality of the 2030 Agenda for Sustainable Development.

Despite growing attention to the issue, however, the year 2019 saw no significant progress towards achieving women's equal participation in multilateral disarmament meetings. Female delegates generally made up only about one third of the diplomats accredited to arms control and disarmament conferences, and even fewer women led their delegations. Although the proportion of women members in groups of governmental experts increased in 2019 as gender considerations were more systematically introduced into selection criteria, women still made up only about a quarter of all experts in such groups active during the year.

Prevailing data suggests that continued, concerted efforts by all stakeholders will be necessary to attain gender parity within disarmament, non-proliferation and arms control mechanisms and decision-making processes.

in multilateral forums dealing with weapons, making up only a third of diplomats accredited to arms control and disarmament conferences. In smaller, more specialized forums, the average proportion of women dropped to 20 per cent.

The report echoed calls in 2019 by United Nations officials, Member States, regional organizations and civil society for concerted action to promote gender equality in disarmament. In her remarks to the fifth Conference of States Parties to the Arms Trade Treaty, the High Representative for Disarmament Affairs called on all Member States to ensure that gender balance would be mentioned as an important selection criterion when drafting, sponsoring and negotiating resolutions that established groups of governmental experts. In a notable milestone, gender parity was included for the first time as a selection criterion for a disarmament-related group of governmental experts.[12]

Meanwhile, broader processes to improve women's inclusion in disarmament benefited from reinforcing, complementary approaches aimed at advancing the involvement and role of youth. By its resolution 74/64 of 12 December on youth, disarmament and non-proliferation, the General Assembly recalled the equal, full and effective participation of both women and men as one of the essential factors for the promotion and attainment of sustainable peace and security.

In 2019, the first woman Secretary-General of the Conference on Disarmament was appointed,[13] adding to the leadership positions held by women in the Office for Disarmament Affairs. Those posts included the Under-Secretary-General and High Representative for Disarmament Affairs, the Deputy Under-Secretary-General of the Conference on Disarmament and Director of the Office's Conference on Disarmament Secretariat and Conference Support Branch, and the Director of the United Nations Institute for Disarmament Research.

The Office for Disarmament Affairs also continued its efforts to support gender equality and parity among its staff at all levels, including by issuing new guidance on advancing a conducive and enabling work environment. Additionally, the United Nations Institute for Disarmament Research updated its Gender and Diversity Action Plan, adding new goals and objectives for 2019–2020.

The United Nations Programme of Fellowships on Disarmament also continued to encourage participation by women diplomats. Of the 25 Fellows who participated in the 2019 Programme, 16 were women. As a result, an increasing number of women were receiving training on multilateral disarmament, further strengthening their qualifications to hold important disarmament-related posts within their Governments.

---

[12] By its resolution on nuclear disarmament verification (74/50), the General Assembly requested equitable representation of women and men in the group of governmental experts to consider the role of verification in advancing nuclear disarmament for 2021 and 2022.

[13] See Tatiana Valovaya, Secretary-General of the Conference on Disarmament and Director-General of the United Nations Office at Geneva, remarks to the Conference on Disarmament, Geneva, 14 August 2019.

Disarmament Fellowship Programme, 2019

The United Nations Programme of Fellowships on Disarmament provides specialized training to an annual class of diplomats. Of the 25 Fellows who participated in the Programme in 2019, 16 were women. The increasing number of women being trained can contribute to more equal participation by women and men in disarmament-related positions within Governments and to gender balance in multilateral disarmament meetings.

64%   36%

Conventional weapons

The highly gendered nature of small arms and light weapons featured prominently in the Secretary-General's report[14] on small arms and light weapons to the Security Council. In the report, the Secretary-General concluded that armed conflict continued to have detrimental humanitarian impacts on civilians, including women and girls. In that context, he underscored that gender had not been sufficiently integrated into policies regulating small arms and light weapons. Noting the prominence of gender considerations in multilateral small-arms-control processes and forums, the Secretary-General highlighted gender as a critical element in discussions related to small arms, while also encouraging women's equal and meaningful participation to ensure that all views would be reflected in decision-making processes. Such inclusion would help ensure sustainable, successful policymaking. With a view to further integrating small arms and light weapons considerations in the Security Council's work, the Secretary-General recommended enhanced cross-referencing of small-arms issues in resolutions and discussions related to women, peace and security, including in the context of gender-based and sexual violence. He also encouraged Council members to support the collection and disaggregation of all data regarding small arms and light weapons by sex and age as the basis for sound gender analysis and policy design.

In 2019, the Human Rights Council adopted a resolution on the impact of arms transfers on human rights (41/20). By that text, the Council (a) expressed deep concern at the fact that the diversion of arms and unregulated or illicit arms transfers by States and non-State actors might seriously undermine the human rights of individuals, especially women, children, the elderly, persons with disabilities and vulnerable groups and (b) noted with alarm that such diversion of

---

[14] S/2019/1011.

Death by firearms: Gender dimensions

Global violent deaths in 2018: Firearms

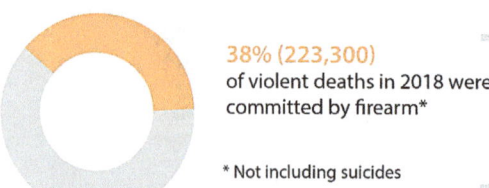

38% (223,300)
of violent deaths in 2018 were
committed by firearm*

* Not including suicides

Of these,
92% (206,100) of victims were men;
8% (17,200) were women

Armed conflict and armed violence affect women and men differently.

In 2018, firearms were used to kill about 223,300 people—38 per cent of all victims of lethal violence, including from direct conflict and intentional homicide. Men represent the vast majority of those deaths, an estimated 92 per cent. (Small Arms Survey, Global Violent Deaths Database)

But for women, guns and violence between intimate partners often form a deadly combination. In homicides perpetrated by an intimate partner or family member in several countries, killings are more likely to be carried out with a firearm when the victim is female (United Nations Office on Drugs and Crime, Global Study on Homicide, 2019).

arms and unregulated or illicit arms transfers can have a severely negative impact on women's and girls' full enjoyment of all human rights, including increasing the risk of sexual and gender-based violence. The Council also requested the Office of the United Nations High Commissioner for Human Rights to prepare a report, in consultation with States, United Nations agencies and other relevant stakeholders, on the impact of the diversion of arms and unregulated or illicit arms transfers on the human rights of women and girls and to present it to the Human Rights Council at its forty-fourth session.

Meanwhile, women's participation was a priority of the General Assembly in multiple conventional arms–related contexts. In its annual resolution on the illicit trade in small arms and light weapons in all its aspects (74/60), the Assembly recognized the need for strengthened women's participation in decision-making and implementation processes related to the Programme of Action, while also reaffirming the need for States to incorporate gender dimensions in their implementation efforts. By its resolution 74/65 of 12 December on problems arising from the accumulation of conventional ammunition stockpiles in surplus, the Assembly recognized for the first time the need to encourage the full involvement of both men and women in ammunition management practice and policy. Additionally, in the First Committee, Member States advocated for women's equal participation, welcomed the greater integration of gender perspectives in conventional-arms control, and highlighted the gendered impact of conventional weapons.

To help States implement their global commitments to include gender dimensions in their efforts to prevent, combat and eradicate the illicit trade in small arms and light weapons in all its aspects,[15] the Office for Disarmament Affairs in April launched a multi-year project advancing gender-mainstreamed policies, programmes and actions in the fight against small-arms trafficking and misuse, in line with the women, peace and security agenda and with funding from the European Union.[16] Under the project, the Office partnered with the International Action Network on Small Arms to supports States in designing and implementing policies for gender-responsive small arms control. Based on the Modular Small-arms-control Implementation Compendium (MOSAIC), a set of voluntary, practical guidance on small-arms control developed by the United Nations, the project includes workshops, training sessions and assistance programmes for national authorities and civil society to address gender issues in their small arms control-related work. The project's other activities include the development of a handbook for trainers, an online training course on gender-responsive small-arms control, a workshop for staff from regional organizations to exchange practice in advancing gender-responsive arms control, and initiatives to promote linkages in implementing the small arms and the women, peace and security agendas, as well as synergies with the 2030 Agenda for Sustainable Development.

Separately, the Office made efforts to help Member States include disarmament and arms-control components in their national action plans on women, peace and security. To increase the share of national action plans containing such elements, which stood at 30 per cent in 2019,[17] the Office for Disarmament Affairs developed an internal guidance note on better connecting those action plans with disarmament. In November, the United Nations Regional Centre for Peace and Disarmament in Asia and the Pacific launched an effort to support Nepal in including relevant references in its national action plan.

Incorporating gender considerations in conventional arms control was an aim of the United Nations Trust Facility Supporting Cooperation on Arms

---

[15] See the report of the third United Nations Conference to Review Progress Made in the Implementation of the Programme of Action to Prevent, Combat and Eradicate the Illicit Trade in Small Arms and Light Weapons in All Its Aspects (A/CONF.192/2018/RC/3) adopted in 2018.

[16] Council Decision (CFSP) 2018/2011 of 17 December 2018 in support of gender mainstreamed policies, programmes and actions in the fight against small arms trafficking and misuse, in line with the Women, Peace and Security agenda (ST/14645/2018/INIT), *Official Journal of the European Union*, L 322, 18 December 2018, p. 38–50.

[17] In total, 41 per cent of the 193 Member States had adopted national action plans on women, peace and security.

Regulation, a flexible small-scale funding mechanism administered by the Office for Disarmament Affairs. The Trust Facility required all applicants to develop gender-responsive project designs and closely monitored the implementation of all selected projects in that regard, with a view to supporting the implementation of the Secretary-General's Agenda for Disarmament and the achievement of the 2030 Agenda for Sustainable Development, specifically Goal 5. In 2019, one of the five thematic focus areas for the Trust Facility was to "promote implementation of Security Council resolutions on women, peace and security". Of 14 projects selected during the year to receive funding, 8 included outcomes and outputs directly related to implementation of the women, peace and security agenda.

Gender perspectives also had a foundational role in the Saving Lives Entity fund, including through newly finalized terms that emphasized gender equality.[18] In that regard, the fund would support national initiatives through a holistic and transformative approach, in particular by applying a gender lens and working upon the basis that the use, misuse and effects of small arms are gendered and that, accordingly, the gender dimension of small arms would be addressed as part of the activities carried out under its auspices. To that end, the fund would allocate 30 per cent of its spending to activities in direct pursuit of gender equality and women's empowerment.

In addition, gender and gender-based violence were the thematic priority of the fifth Conference of States Parties to the Arms Trade Treaty, held in Geneva from 26 to 30 August under the presidency of Latvia. The theme was a key focus of several side events and, in the final report[19] of the Conference, States agreed to recommendations and actions to improve the gender balance of future conferences, to promote an increased understanding of the gendered impact of armed violence in the context of the Treaty, to strengthen the ability of States parties to apply the risk-assessment criteria for gender-based violence and to review progress on an ongoing basis. In her remarks[20] at a thematic discussion on gender and gender-based violence and in a separate keynote address,[21] the High Representative for Disarmament Affairs highlighted the need to invest in inclusive decision-making, deepen the understanding of gender-responsive arms control and advance the full and effective implementation of gender-responsive arms-control measures. The Conference also encouraged States parties and others to consider work on gender and gender-based violence in projects funded by the Arms Trade Treaty Voluntary Trust Fund. The General Assembly, by its resolution on the Arms

---

[18] For more information on the Saving Lives Entity, see chapter III. The Saving Lives Entity is a fund designed to catalyse more comprehensive approaches to small arms and armed violence reduction in priority countries.

[19] Arms Trade Treaty Secretariat, document ATT/CSP5/2019/SEC/536/Conf.FinRep.Rev1.

[20] Izumi Nakamitsu, High Representative for Disarmament Affairs, statement at the Thematic Discussion on Gender and Gender Based Violence of the Fifth Conference of States Parties to the Arms Trade Treaty, Geneva, 26 August 2019.

[21] Izumi Nakamitsu, High Representative for Disarmament Affairs, keynote address to the Fifth Conference of States Parties to the Arms Trade Treaty, Geneva, 26 August 2019.

Trade Treaty (74/49) adopted later in the year, welcomed the adoption of action-oriented decisions on gender and gender-based violence, while also encouraging States parties to ensure the full and equal participation of men and women in implementation.

Meanwhile, the High Contracting Parties to Amended Protocol II of the Convention on Certain Conventional Weapons agreed at their twenty-first Annual Conference in November that their mandate on improvised explosive devices for the following year would refer to the importance of having balanced involvement of men and women in its Group of Experts. Participants agreed that such balance would support the Group's efforts to address the threats posed by improvised explosive devices.[22]

At the fourth Review Conference of the States parties to the Anti-Personnel Mine Ban Convention in November, participants decided to amend the mandates of its implementation Committees to include matters related to gender and the diverse needs and experiences of people in affected communities in every aspect of its work. They further agreed that each Committee would appoint a focal point among its members to provide advice on addressing gender-related issues. Gender was also included in the Oslo Action Plan,[23] which determined the priority areas of work under the Convention for the upcoming five years.

Nuclear weapons

During the 2019 session of the Preparatory Committee for the 2020 Review Conference of the Parties to the Treaty on the Non-Proliferation of Nuclear Weapons (Nuclear Non-Proliferation Treaty), States parties demonstrated increased interest in promoting the inclusion of gender perspectives and women's equal participation. For the first time, two events on gender, held on the margins of the meeting, took place during the session: "When participation becomes meaningful: advancing the conversation on gender diversity in the [Nuclear Non-Proliferation Treaty]", organized by Australia, Canada, Ireland, Namibia, Netherlands, Sweden and the United Nations Institute for Disarmament Research; and "Gender and the [Nuclear Non-Proliferation Treaty]: Building Momentum to 2020 and Beyond", organized by Ireland. Meanwhile, separate collaborations between Member States and the United Nations Institute for Disarmament Research resulted in three working papers on gender: "Improving gender equality and diversity in the Non-Proliferation Treaty review process";[24] "Integrating gender perspectives in the implementation of the Treaty on the Non-Proliferation of Nuclear Weapons";[25] and "Gender in the Non-Proliferation

---

[22] For more information on Amended Protocol II, also known as the Protocol on Prohibitions or Restrictions on the Use of Mines, Booby-traps and Other Devices as amended on 3 May 1996, see chap. III.

[23] APLC/CONF/2019/5/Add.1, pp. 4–22.

[24] NPT/CONF.2020/PC.III/WP.25.

[25] NPT/CONF.2020/PC.III/WP.27.

Treaty: recommendations for the 2020 Review Conference".[26] At the conclusion of the session, the Chair issued a working paper[27] in which he (a) reaffirmed the importance of promoting the full, equal and effective participation and leadership of women in nuclear disarmament, non-proliferation and the peaceful use of nuclear energy and (b) encouraged States parties to actively support gender diversity in their delegations to meetings related to the Nuclear Non-Proliferation Treaty, in accordance with Security Council resolution 1325 (2000). In his recommendations, the Chair also recalled the need for States parties to recognize the disproportionate impact of ionizing radiation on women and girls.

During the First Committee, progress by the General Assembly was decidedly more mixed. While language on gender parity was included for the first time in the resolution on nuclear disarmament verification (74/50),[28] the resolution entitled "Joint Courses of Action and Future-oriented Dialogue towards a world without nuclear weapons" (74/63)[29] no longer recognized the importance of ensuring the equitable representation and participation of women and men in disarmament discussions to enable a truly comprehensive approach to nuclear non-proliferation and disarmament. Instead, the Assembly noted in the resolution that efforts to encompass different genders in disarmament and non-proliferation education underscore efforts and create momentum towards achieving a world without nuclear weapons.

Other weapons of mass destruction

Progress was also achieved in 2019 with regard to integrating gender perspectives and encouraging women's equal participation in forums related to chemical and biological weapons.

For the first time, the General Assembly encouraged the equitable participation of men and women in the framework of the Biological Weapons Convention with its resolution 74/79 of 12 December, entitled "Convention on the Prohibition of the Development, Production and Stockpiling of Bacteriological (Biological) and Toxin Weapons and on Their Destruction".

On the margins of the twenty-fourth Conference of States Parties to the Chemical Weapons Convention, the United Nations Institute for Disarmament Research launched *Missing Links*,[30] a research report analysing possible sex- and

---

[26] NPT/CONF.2020/PC.III/WP.48.

[27] NPT/CONF.2020/PC.III/WP.49.

[28] As noted in the separate section entitled "Equal participation" in this chapter, language in the resolution called for equitable representation of men and women in upcoming groups of governmental experts on nuclear disarmament verification.

[29] In previous years, the resolution was entitled "United action with renewed determination towards the total elimination of nuclear weapons".

[30] Renata Hessmann Dalaqua, James Revill, Alastair Hay and Nancy Connell, *Missing Links: Understanding Sex- and Gender-related Impacts of Chemical and Biological Weapons* (Geneva, United Nations Institute for Disarmament Research, 2019).

gender-specific effects of chemical and biological weapons and offering ideas to promote gender-responsive assistance within the Chemical Weapons Convention and Biological Weapons Convention regimes. At a dedicated launch event co-organized by the Institute and Norway, participants explored how gender was relevant in considering the effects of chemical weapons, why gender mattered when providing assistance under article X of the Chemical Weapons Convention, and how to improve the collection of gender-disaggregated data and support research on the gendered impacts of chemical weapons.

Women's perspectives and insights were also incorporated into the year's intersessional meetings of the Biological Weapons Convention. On the margins of the Meeting of Experts on Assistance, Response and Preparedness, the United Nations Institute for Disarmament Research and Norway organized another side event entitled "Gender-responsive [Biological Weapons Convention]? Understanding gender-related impacts of biological weapons and implications for assistance, response and preparedness". Meanwhile, the Convention's Implementation Support Unit continued encouraging women to pursue senior positions in its capacity-development activities, as well as in regional workshops and the Convention's Sponsorship Programme. Notably, the Office made particular efforts to attract a diverse and gender-balanced applicant pool for a workshop in August on fostering biosecurity networks in the Global South, including through a tailored call for applications and outreach to networks that promote women's participation. Of the 20 life scientists selected solely on the basis of merit, 13 were young women. The Office aimed to ensure that the young participants received capacity-development opportunities.

New weapons technologies

In 2019, awareness grew considerably of the differential impact of new weapons technologies on men, women, boys and girls. The equal and meaningful participation by women in forums related to issues of science and technology and international peace and security, such as meetings, workshops and symposiums, remained a priority for the Office for Disarmament Affairs.

During the meeting of the Group of Governmental Experts on Emerging Technologies in the Area of Lethal Autonomous Weapons Systems, held under the Convention on Certain Conventional Weapons, several High Contracting Parties referenced the need to take into account gender perspectives when discussing the issue of lethal autonomous weapon systems, given the potential impact of gender on emerging technologies.

During the first substantive session of the Open-ended Working Group on Developments in the Field of Information and Telecommunications in the Context of International Security,[31] which was held from 9 to 13 September, a number of delegations expressed concern about the gendered impacts of incidents involving information and communications technologies, as well as the global gender gap in access to and use of the Internet. Canada called for gender to be addressed throughout capacity-building efforts. In addition, it was suggested that the relationship between the security of information and communications technologies and the women, peace and security agenda should be further analysed.[32] Several delegations also underscored the importance of promoting women's equal and meaningful participation in intergovernmental processes on international security.

Another process in that area, led by the Group of Governmental Experts on Advancing Responsible State Behaviour in Cyberspace in the Context of International Security,[33] approached gender balance with a composition of 10 women and 15 men. During consultations that the Chair and members of the Group held with regional organizations throughout 2019,[34] Member States organized various events, held on the margins of the meetings, to promote women's participation in the field of security for information and communications technologies, further raising awareness around the topic. In addition, the Office for Disarmament Affairs ensured gender parity in the composition of expert panels during all of the Group's regional consultations. The United Nations Institute for Disarmament Research also produced in December a fact sheet entitled "Gender in Cyber Diplomacy", presenting numbers on gender balance, as well as ideas to promote gender considerations in cybersecurity discussions.

Separately, the Office for Disarmament Affairs made efforts to ensure that both women and men were represented in a workshop on the peace and security implications of artificial intelligence in August, as well as a joint table-top exercise with the United Nations Institute for Disarmament Research in September on the implications of hypersonic weapons for international stability and arms control.

Further to Action 12 of the Secretary-General's Agenda for Disarmament, the Office for Disarmament Affairs, in partnership with the Office for Outer Space Affairs and the Institute, sought to facilitate engagement by the private sector and non-governmental organizations in United Nations deliberations on outer-space security. That included an explicit focus on ensuring the full and

---

[31] The Open-ended Working Group on Developments in the Field of Information and Telecommunications in the Context of International Security was established pursuant to General Assembly resolution 73/27.

[32] Delegate of Canada, statement delivered during the general debate of the Open-ended Working Group, New York, 9 September 2019.

[33] The Group of Governmental Experts on Advancing Responsible State Behaviour in Cyberspace in the Context of International Security was established pursuant to General Assembly resolution 73/266.

[34] Pursuant to resolution 73/266, regional consultations were organized with the Organization for Security and Co-operation in Europe on 17 and 18 June, with the European Union on 19 and 20 June, with the Organization of American States on 15 and 16 August, with the Association of Southeast Asian Nations and Dialogue Partners on 2 October, and with the African Union on 11 October.

equal participation of women in activities carried out in 2019. In that connection, each of the three panels organized at the open-ended intersessional informal consultative meeting, convened on 31 January and 1 February by the Chair of the Group of Governmental Experts on Further Practical Measures for the Prevention of an Arms Race in Outer Space, included at least an equal number of women, representing national space agencies, commercial space actors and civil society. For a second consecutive iteration, the 2019 joint panel discussion of the First and Fourth Committees on possible challenges to space security and sustainability, organized by the Office for Outer Space Affairs and the Office for Disarmament Affairs in accordance with General Assembly resolutions 73/72 and 73/91, included an all-women panel, representing think-tanks, the Government and commercial sectors, and civil society. Notably, that panel took place in the context of an under-representation of women experts and leaders in intergovernmental discussions on that topic.

In accordance with Action 19 of the Secretary-General's Agenda for Disarmament, efforts continued in 2019 to explore common standards for the transfer, holdings and use of armed uncrewed aerial vehicles in order to ensure accountability, transparency and oversight for their use.[35] Further to the 2015 study prepared by the Office for Disarmament Affairs at the recommendation of the Advisory Board on Disarmament Matters, the Office maintained that measures for increasing transparency, oversight and accountability pertaining to the use of armed uncrewed aerial vehicles should include disclosure through appropriate channels of various information, including sex-disaggregated data, on the impact of targeted strikes, including civilian casualties, the identity of the target and criteria used in the selection of targets.

Regional disarmament and arms control

In 2019, the Vienna Office and three regional centres of the Office for Disarmament Affairs continued to engage in capacity-building and other initiatives to foster gender equality and empower women in disarmament, non-proliferation, security and related fields.

The United Nations Regional Centre for Peace, Disarmament and Development in Latin America and the Caribbean continued to pursue equal participation by women and men in its work, including by (a) requiring all its activities to have at least 25 per cent participation by both genders[36] and (b) highlighting gender dimensions in its trainings, workshops and seminars.

In March 2019, the Regional Centre held a course on firearms and ammunition evidence management in the Dominican Republic for a class of 28

---

[35] For more information, see the section on armed uncrewed aerial vehicles in this chapter.
[36] From January to December 2019, at least 35 per cent of participants in every activity at the Regional Centre were women.

representatives from the national security and justice sector,[37] 50 per cent of whom were women. The training applied a gender perspective to determine possible cases of violence against women, becoming the first of its kind in the country to both underline the gendered aspects of firearms and highlight the link between armed violence and violence against women. Meanwhile, the Centre convened two additional evidence-management courses during the year, engaging a total of 24 women and 58 men from the national-security and justice sectors in Costa Rica and in El Salvador.

The Regional Centre also continued collaborating with national and regional authorities to implement gender-sensitive approaches to armed-violence reduction measures through a Canadian-funded multi-year project. As part of that effort, the Centre undertook a series of extensive legal reviews in 2019, cross-referencing small arms laws with domestic violence provisions in 22 Latin American and Caribbean States. Through those studies, the Centre provided recommendations for restricting the ability of convicted domestic-violence perpetrators to acquire or renew firearms licenses. In addition, the studies provided a basis for future discussions on enhancing gender accountability in policies and laws to control small arms.

The Centre also organized two subregional seminars, targeted towards national authorities from Central American[38] and Caribbean States,[39] that addressed arms control as a fundamental pillar of the public-policy response to gender-based violence. Intended for personnel directly involved in controlling arms and preventing violence against women and girls, the courses provided opportunities for representatives of both Governments and non-governmental organizations to exchange ideas, discuss strategies and consider possibilities for joint initiatives to address armed violence against women.

Meanwhile, the United Nations Regional Centre for Peace and Disarmament in Asia and the Pacific continued to implement the region-wide project "Gun Violence and Illicit Small-Arms Trafficking from a Gender Perspective" in Asia and the Pacific. From 12 to 15 November, the Centre organized a workshop in Suva, Fiji, funded by the European Union, that brought together 15 representatives from civil society organizations and parliamentarians from seven States in the Pacific to discuss issues of armed violence and illicit small-arms trafficking

---

[37] National Police, Public Ministry, Ministry of Interior and Police, Ballistic Laboratory, Ministry of Defence and Customs.

[38] Colombia, Costa Rica, Dominican Republic, El Salvador, Guatemala, Honduras, Mexico, Nicaragua and Panama. Also participating were officials and experts from the United Nations Development Programme, the United Nations Office on Drugs and Crime, the United Nations Entity for Gender Equality and the Empowerment of Women (UN-Women), the Organization of American States, the Central American Integration System, and the Center of Excellence for Statistical Information on Government, Crime, Victimization and Justice.

[39] Antigua and Barbuda, Barbados, Belize, Dominica, Guyana, Jamaica, Saint Kitts and Nevis, Saint Vincent and the Grenadines, and Suriname. Three regional organizations and 12 civil society organizations also participated.

from a gender perspective. The workshop focused on increasing control of small arms and light weapons through the development of joint initiatives between non-governmental organizations and legislators. The broader project had led to interactive grass-roots initiatives, lobbying and campaigning activities, workshops, and meetings, while also enhancing collaboration between key actors.

In a separate effort to further strengthen gender-responsiveness as a cross-cutting theme in its projects and training activities, the Regional Centre provided government practitioners with support to effectively incorporate gender perspectives and other intersecting issues into national action plans to reduce illegal arms flows. Notably, it held a workshop on developing such plans based on the Modular Small-arms-control Implementation Compendium (MOSAIC) and the International Ammunition Technical Guidelines, providing six South-East Asian States with training that emphasized the importance of gender perspectives in the control of small arms and light weapons, as well as the need for any effective, long-term violence-reduction strategy to counter enduring associations between small arms, violence, power and masculinity.

In parallel, the United Nations Regional Centre for Peace and Disarmament in Africa continued to systematically encourage Member States to prioritize the nomination of women as delegates to its capacity-building and other events. Those events—organized or facilitated by the Centre throughout the year in its various mandated areas of small arms and light weapons, weapons of mass destruction, and peace and security—offered channels to promote gender equality in peace and disarmament with participating Member States and the media, including through use of social media.

Through its Vienna Office, the Office for Disarmament Affairs administered the Scholarship for Peace and Security for a second year in cooperation with the Organization for Security and Co-operation in Europe (OSCE). That initiative, which received the OSCE "Gender Champion Award" in March, provided to a group of young professionals—90 per cent of whom were women—online and in-person training on key conceptual and practical aspects of conflict prevention and resolution, arms control, non-proliferation of weapons of mass destruction, disarmament and development, peace and development–related technologies, and gender aspects. The Scholarship was aimed at further motivating recipients to deepen their activity and involvement in the disarmament and non-proliferation fields, while also connecting them with colleagues in similar fields.[40]

Peace operations

In 2019, the Office of Rule of Law and Security Institutions in the Department of Peace Operations, through its Disarmament, Demobilization and

---

[40] According to a follow-up assessment survey conducted by the Vienna Office on previous edition alumni.

Reintegration Section and Security Sector Reform Unit and in collaboration with the Department's Gender Unit, organized a consultation in Entebbe on the topic "Strengthening gender responsive [Disarmament, Demobilization and Reintegration] and [Security Sector Reform] in peacekeeping operations: Leveraging opportunities and lessons learned". That consultation brought together women leaders from ex-combatants' groups, civil society organizations and national security forces in the Central African Republic, Colombia and Mali, as well as representatives from the United Nations Headquarters and United Nations missions in the three countries. The participants agreed that, despite significant efforts at Headquarters and in the field to strengthen the delivery of gender-responsive disarmament, demobilization and reintegration and security sector reform, enhancing implementation would require tackling remaining challenges—namely, the limited availability of resources targeting women's specific priorities and concerns, a lack of country-specific data to promote evidence-based decision making at the mission level, and a need to strengthen accountability with national counterparts. During the discussions, participants identified good practices, exchanged lessons learned and formulated concrete recommendations to peace operations, Member States and the Security Council that were later endorsed by the Under-Secretary-General for Peace Operations.

During the year, the United Nations Office to the African Union also continued to support the Union's efforts to integrate gender in the African Peace and Security Architecture and African Governance Architecture, including through collaboration with the regional economic commissions and Member States. Additionally, the Office provided gender-sensitive advice to the African Union Commission on developing and implementing policies and guidance to help member States in updating their approaches to security sector reform; disarming, demobilizing and reintegrating their ex-combatants; managing their stockpiles; controlling the flux of small arms and light weapons; and dealing with mine action.

On 29 and 30 May, the United Nations Office to the African Union participated in an event entitled "Path to Peaceful Studies: Consultation on Harnessing Women's Leadership on Arms Control to Prevent Violence and Advance Development", held in Addis Ababa at the African Union Headquarters. That event brought together women from across Africa who were leading on issues of disarmament and violence prevention to (a) map out ongoing local practices in those areas and (b) set the course for future emerging research priorities, all in consultation with representatives of the African Union, the United Nations, government agencies and think tanks. During the two-day workshop, the group developed a range of relevant activities and priorities, including linkages to prevention under the women, peace and security agenda, as well as the necessity for the greater inclusion of civil-society actors at all levels of dialogue.

Disarmament, demobilization and reintegration

Gender-responsive disarmament, demobilization and reintegration continued to help protect women, ensure their access to benefits and increase their participation in society. Promoting it at all stages was considered crucial to the success and sustainability of interventions, making it a continued priority despite operational challenges and funding constraints. In that context, the Disarmament, Demobilization and Reintegration Section of the Office of Rule of Law and Security Institutions undertook a range of gender-related work in 2019.

While women had typically represented a small percentage of individuals targeted by disarmament, demobilization and reintegration programmes, their engagement increased with the implementation of community-violence-reduction projects. By providing formal education, vocational training and income-generating initiatives, those projects empowered women with opportunities to contribute to peace, including through work to mitigate local violence and prevent the recruitment of at-risk youth into armed groups.

In 2019, the Inter-Agency Working Group on Disarmament, Demobilization and Reintegration officially launched the revised United Nations Integrated Disarmament, Demobilization and Reintegration Standards, which provides the agreed policies and procedures of the United Nations for designing, planning and implementing processes in that area. One entity in the Inter-Agency Working Group, the United Nations Entity for Gender Equality and the Empowerment of Women (UN-Women), provided dedicated expertise for addressing gender issues throughout the revised Standards.

In Darfur, women represented 19 per cent of the combatants demobilized in 2019 with technical and logistical support provided by the African Union-United Nations Hybrid Operation in Darfur. In addition, 37 per cent of the direct beneficiaries of community stabilization projects implemented by the peacekeeping operation were women. To ensure women's meaningful participation, it also conducted targeted consultations to identify needs and gender-specific interventions.

In the Democratic Republic of the Congo, women represented 44 per cent of the direct beneficiaries of community-violence-reduction projects in 2019, a high participation rate supported by the requirement of the United Nations Organization Stabilization Mission in the Democratic Republic of the Congo for project proposals to substantively address gender. Furthermore, the Mission introduced the collection of gender disaggregated data in the monitoring of its projects. Women made up 2 per cent of the combatants demobilized with support from the Mission.

In Mali, women made up 38 per cent of the beneficiaries of community-violence-reduction projects during the year, and gender-responsive initiatives received 15 per cent of programmatic funding for disarmament, demobilization and reintegration. Notably, one woman combatant participated in the accelerated disarmament, demobilization and reintegration process, which included signatory armed groups. Women represented 5 per cent of the militia elements who participated in the first phase of the Government-led Community Rehabilitation Programme (central region).

In Haiti, women represented 49 per cent of direct beneficiaries targeted through community-violence-reduction projects in 2019, while 14 per cent of programmatic funds went to activities specifically targeting women. In that regard, the United Nations Mission for Justice Support in Haiti engaged with women associations, promoted gender-equality campaigns and raised awareness about gender-based violence. Moreover, the Haitian National Police launched a project in 2019 to strengthen its capacity to establish a gender-sensitive recruitment mechanism, with the support of UN-Women and the police component of the United Nations Mission for Justice Support in Haiti through its community-violence-reduction programme. A total of 60 women from the most violence-prone and impoverished areas of Port-au-Prince benefited from a workshop to prepare them for each stage of the national police-recruitment process.

In the Central African Republic, women represented 27 per cent of direct community-violence-reduction beneficiaries and 6 per cent of demobilized combatants.

Security sector reform

The Security Sector Reform Unit, located in the Office of Rule of Law and Security Institutions, led the United Nations throughout the year in efforts to foster the establishment of effective and accountable security institutions on the basis of non-discrimination, full respect for human rights and the rule of law. The Unit pursued its work in line with the 2012 Security Sector Reform Integrated Technical Guidance Note on Gender-Responsive Security Sector Reform,[41] which called for women to be included in the reform of security institutions, while also recognizing that increasing women's participation in the process of security sector reform would be critical both to effectively delivering security services to all segments of society and to establishing public trust in the State.

In March, the United Nations Groups of Friends of Security Sector Reform and for Gender Parity convened a high-level round-table discussion in New York to call on the United Nations and Member States to increase their political commitment to strengthening gender-responsive security sector reform. The discussion underlined that social stereotypes and conditions could deter women from joining the security sector, while women already working in the sector risk faced obstacles such as gender bias in the recruitment process, male-designed

---

[41] Security Sector Reform: Integrated Technical Guidance Notes (New York, pp. 9–10. https://peacekeeping.un.org/sites/default/files/un_integrated_technical_guidance_notes_on_ssr_1.pdf.

facilities, uniforms and equipment, assignment to non-combat functions, unfriendly policies on maternity leave and childcare, sexual harassment in the workplace, and limited access to promotion and career opportunities. In addition to identifying lessons from national and regional experiences, participants recommended targeted measures to overcome gender bias through advocacy, accountability, experience-sharing and adequate support. The event underscored the need for Member States and the United Nations to increase the proportion of women at all levels of security sector institutions, while also improving practical measures and consistent leadership to help prevent and respond to gender-based discrimination in the security sector workplace.

Security sector reform teams in peace operations supported national efforts to prevent and respond to sexual and gender-based violence in conflict, including by developing strategies and plans to enhance security sector capacities to protect women against any form of violence, in particular sexual violence. At the United Nations Multidimensional Integrated Stabilization Mission in Mali, for example, the security sector reform team helped create four integrated service centres for survivors of sexual abuse, further enhancing reporting and response efforts. Meanwhile, the Mission supported the establishment of vetting mechanisms to prevent perpetrators of sexual violence from joining the Army of Mali, while also advising the Permanent Secretariat to Counter the Proliferation of the Small Arms and Light Weapons to restrict access to guns by individuals associated with sexual violence.

In Libya, the Security Institutions Service of the United Nations Support Mission in Libya supported the ministers of interior and justice in organizing the "Consultative Forum for the Support and the Empowerment of Women in the Security Sector", held in Tripoli from 25 to 27 November. Funded by the Support Mission in Libya and the Policing and Security Joint Programme of the United Nations Development Programme, the forum was aimed at helping its 40 participants to develop a strategy for strengthening the role of women in the security sector. Meanwhile, to further advance the integration of women in the police service, the United Nations Support Mission in Libya assisted women police units in developing guidance on their responsibilities, along with detailed action plans that informed the strategic objectives of Libya's national security directorates. Additionally, the Support Mission's Security Institutions Service helped hold a second workshop in Tripoli from 3 to 5 December on "the institutional responsiveness to violence against women", with the aim of assisting and empowering rule of law institutions. Both workshops were organized in the context of the 16 Days of Activism against Gender-Based Violence, observed each year from 25 November to 10 December.

Separately, the security sector reform team of the Office of the Special Envoy of the Secretary-General for Yemen provided support to women of Yemen seeking to meaningfully participate in the security sector reform process. On 24 March, it organized a daylong training and coaching workshop to build the capacity of six women—representing police, the judiciary and civil society—to fully influence political negotiations and decisions on security sector reform. As part of the peace process, the security sector reform team also held a dedicated informal consultation on options for temporary security arrangements with 20 women, including a significant number of young women, from geographically diverse locations in Yemen. In addition, the Office of the Special Envoy teamed with the Geneva Centre for Security Sector Governance to assist the authorities in Yemen in ensuring that women would make up 30 per cent of the participants in a security sector reform dialogue held in Tripoli in November. That level of representation enabled women's issues and concerns to be reflected in the planning and design of associated security sector governance arrangements.

In Somalia, the landmark Somali Women's Charter received endorsement at a three-day Somali Women's Convention led by the Ministry of Women and Human Rights Development with the participation of the Federal Government, the federal member States' line ministries, and civil society organizations. In the Charter, the Convention's participants called for a 50 per cent representation quota at all levels of Government, including in the security sector. They also called for zero tolerance of gender-based violence and for women's rights to be enshrined in the revised Constitution, as well as in electoral, security and political legislative frameworks. To that end, the Ministry of Internal Security of Somalia—supported by the United Nations Assistance Mission in Somalia and the United Nations Development Programme through their joint mission, the Integrated Security Sector Reform Section—conducted a capacity-building session on the women, peace and security agenda and the National Gender Policy of Somalia for 73 Ministry of Internal Security officials, including 22 women and 51 men. As a result of the workshop, the Ministry established a Human Rights Directorate and appointed a focal point for women, peace and security.

In September, the Ministry of Women and Human Rights Development of Somalia and its Ministry of Ports and Marine Transport convened the "Consultative Conference on Women in the Maritime Sector". Organized with support from the United Nations Assistance Mission in Somalia and the United Nations Development Programme through their Integrated Security Sector Reform Section, as well as from the European Union Capacity Building Mission in Somalia, the event was intended to consider avenues for women to meaningfully participate in the maritime field, including in governance, policy and security delivery. The conference drew 60 attendees, including ministers of the Federal Government and federal member states, officials and experts, and representatives from academia and civil society. Participants agreed on actionable goals to enhance women's participation in the maritime sector through a Joint Statement of Intent. In October, the Federal Government of Somalia and the international partners endorsed the 2019-2020 Mutual Accountability Framework for Somalia, which includes a commitment by the Federal Government and the federal member states to develop a force generation plan for the formation of inclusive security services.

United Nations police

The United Nations Police Division is an integrated part of the Office of Rule of Law and Security Institutions responsible for doctrine development, planning, coordination, selection and recruitment for United Nations police components in peacekeeping operations and special political missions, which totalled over 10,000 uniformed personnel in the field in 2019. During the year, the Division significantly increased the training and deployment of women police officers in command, technical and operational roles, contributing to broader gender perspectives in all mandated activities, particularly those related to disarmament, demobilization and reintegration in the complex contexts of stabilization and peacebuilding.

An important role of the United Nations police involved their mandated contribution to security, advisory and oversight of transitional weapons and ammunition management activities conducted both by host States and by the disarmament, demobilization and reintegration components of United Nations missions, with particular attention to gender-related aspects. In that regard, the United Nations Multidimensional Integrated Stabilization Mission in Mali fulfilled that role by undertaking community-oriented policing programmes that engaged women in advanced disarmament, demobilization and reintegration activities.

In the Central African Republic, the United Nations police conducted continuous outreach to women and, in particular, leveraged the key role of women in supporting disarmament, demobilization and reintegration programmes and sustaining weapon-free zones following the adoption of a landmark peace agreement on 6 February.[42] The commitment of the United Nations police to gender-sensitive disarmament and preventing sexual and gender-based violence yielded especially notable impacts in South Sudan, Darfur and Abyei, specifically by enhancing women's involvement to more effectively respond to firearms illegally introduced into protection of civilian sites.

Mine action

In 2019, the United Nations Mine Action Service continued to prioritize diversity and gender-responsive programming, both by promoting gender-inclusive opportunities and by giving consideration to differing levels of individual exposure to and knowledge of risks from explosive ordnance. Both men and women retained essential responsibilities as deminers, trainers, mentors, risk educators, programme managers and survey-team members. In line with the Secretary-General's Initiative on Action for Peacekeeping, women in mine action continued to play an active role in reconstructing communities, as well as in rebuilding trust and sustainable peace.

---

[42] S/2019/145.

Throughout the year, the Mine Action Service undertook a range of gender-specific projects in support of integrating gender-related matters in mine action. Those efforts were in line with the United Nations Mine Action Strategy 2019-2023, in particular its cross-cutting Strategic Outcome dedicated to responding to the specific needs of women, men and youth from diverse groups and facilitating their empowerment and inclusion.

In November, the Mine Action Service published the third edition of the United Nations Gender Guidelines for Mine Action Programmes, developed through extensive inter-agency consultations to help field operations integrate gender and diversity considerations throughout programme life cycles. The Guidelines were expected to become available in other official languages of the United Nations, a step that would ensure their effective use in a variety of settings and further strengthen the quality of United Nations mine action activities.

Also during the year, the Mine Action Service trained eight women in explosive-ordnance disposal, helping to address a gender imbalance in that area both at its headquarters and on its teams in Colombia, Lebanon, the State of Palestine and the Syrian Arab Republic. The beneficiaries of that project broke barriers in a traditionally male-dominated field, while also serving as role models in affected communities and the United Nations system as a whole. For their work highlighting the importance of women's participation in peace operations, those women received the 2019 Secretary-General Award for Gender Parity.

The Mine Action Service also continued to incorporate gender considerations in recruitment processes, helping to increase the representation in mine action within peacekeeping missions from 28 per cent in 2018 to 32 per cent in 2019. For instance, in South Sudan, the Mine Action Service made specific efforts to increase the number of women working in male-dominated areas such as mine clearance and vehicle repair and maintenance. Those efforts also provided one response to the wage gaps and occupational blockages that women in South Sudan continued to face.

Meanwhile, the Mine Action Service launched a second mixed-gender demining project in Afghanistan in April, increasing the visibility of women in their communities and empowering them to act as agents of change.

In Iraq, the Mine Action Service worked with the Ministry of Interior to train 20 women police officers in explosive ordnance disposal. In addition to creating new opportunities for women in a country where the field of explosive ordnance clearance and management was often limited to individuals with military experience, that initiative helped close the gender parity gap in the mine-action sector. Additionally, the mixed-gender demining teams brought together individuals of different religions and ethnicities, supporting women's empowerment while building bonds between groups that could help sustain peace.

chapter

VII   Disarmament machinery

Tatiana Valovaya (left), Director-General of the United Nations Office at Geneva and Secretary-General of the Conference on Disarmament, speaks with Izumi Nakamitsu, High Representative for Disarmament Affairs, during the third part of the Conference on Disarmament in Geneva, 26 August 2019.

UN Photo/Jean Marc Ferré

CHAPTER VII

Disarmament machinery

If its members wish to reclaim the place for the Conference on Disarmament that was envisaged by its founders, they must return to seeking multilateral agreements.

ANTÓNIO GUTERRES, SECRETARY-GENERAL OF THE UNITED NATIONS[1]

Developments and trends, 2019

THE DETERIORATING INTERNATIONAL SECURITY ENVIRONMENT continued hindering the multilateral disarmament machinery throughout 2019. The unresolved matter of the issuance of visas affected disarmament organs at the United Nations Headquarters, resulting in the cancellation of the annual session of the United Nations Disarmament Commission and a delay of the substantive session of the First Committee of the General Assembly. The States members of the Conference on Disarmament in Geneva failed to overcome the deadlock that has lasted over two decades.

The work of the First Committee was overshadowed by growing tensions among major powers, particularly between the United States of America on one side and China and the Russian Federation on the other. Yet, despite the challenging global security environment and the considerable time devoted to addressing matters not necessarily related to its substantive work, the First Committee fulfilled its mandates for the year, approving 59 draft resolutions and decisions under various agenda items.

Separately, the States members of the Conference on Disarmament continued their efforts to begin substantive work, building on momentum created during the 2018 session. However, although proposals for a programme of work for 2019 were introduced by three presidencies of the Conference—Bolivarian Republic of Venezuela, Ukraine and Viet Nam—the Conference did not reach agreement on a proposal and, again, failed to start substantive work. With little prospect of adopting a programme of work, the United Kingdom of Great Britain and Northern Ireland, which assumed the second presidency in mid-February, sought to establish new subsidiary bodies and special coordinators with a view to structuring the current session to build on progress from the previous year. Yet, despite the efforts of the United Kingdom presidency, agreement on its proposal proved elusive.

---

[1] Remarks to the Conference on Disarmament, Geneva, 25 February 2019.

Nevertheless, consultations held under each of the six presidencies in 2019 enabled the Conference to discuss and examine various possibilities and potential language for a programme of work. In particular, during the presidency of Viet Nam, the Conference considered alternative approaches inspired by a suggestion put forward by the Netherlands to return to an earlier conceptualization of the programme of work. In a broader effort to commence substantive work, the Conference also held extensive thematic discussions on all core agenda items, while continuing to consider its working methods and the possible expansion of its membership. Despite more than two decades of paralysis in the Conference, a growing level of interest in its work was apparent from the requests of 50 States—a record number—to attend the 2019 session as observers.

Elsewhere, the United Nations Disarmament Commission was unable to hold its substantive session for the first time since 2005, dealing a blow to the effort to revitalize the multilateral disarmament machinery. Following its successful adoption in 2017 of recommendations on confidence-building measures in the field of conventional weapons, the Commission had started a new three-year cycle in 2018, addressing one fresh substantive agenda item, entitled "Transparency and confidence-building measures in outer space activities", alongside an existing item on nuclear disarmament and non-proliferation of nuclear weapons. The Commission was unable in 2019 to complete its organizational session and, therefore, could not hold its substantive session from 9 to 25 April, as mandated by the General Assembly in its resolution 73/82 of 5 December 2018.[2] Nevertheless, Member States held informal discussions on the two agenda items of its current three-year cycle in a bid to advance the deliberations on those issues.

Additionally, the Secretary-General's Advisory Board on Disarmament Matters held its seventy-first and seventy-second sessions, addressing two substantive agenda items. Regarding the first item, "Measures to mitigate civilian harm resulting from contemporary armed conflict", the Board, inter alia, recommended encouraging the General Assembly to further consider the issue of the use of explosive weapons in populated areas, potentially leading to mandates for the further development of criteria, indicators and methodologies to measure the reverberating civilian impacts of such use. In addition, the Board recommended developing a systematic approach and consistent methodologies to pool data on the effects of such use of explosive weapons, possibly including economic effects in order to underscore the multidimensional impact. On its second substantive agenda item, "The role of the disarmament, arms control and non-proliferation regime in managing strategic competition and building trust", the Board encouraged the Secretary-General to continue his high-level engagement with the five permanent members of the Security Council on the importance of cooperation aimed at reducing strategic competition and nuclear risks. The Advisory Board also highlighted the potential value of further engagement by

---

[2] The United Nations Disarmament Commission was unable to hold its organizational and substantive sessions in 2019 due to an unresolved matter concerning the non-issuance of visas.

the High Representative for Disarmament Affairs to identify options aimed at reversing current impediments to progress on disarmament. In that connection, its members called for a forthcoming study by the Office for Disarmament Affairs to include a review of the state of existing disarmament machinery.

First Committee of the General Assembly

Organization of work

The First Committee of the General Assembly held its seventy-fourth session from 3 October to 8 November under the chairmanship of Sacha Sergio Llorentty Soliz (Plurinational State of Bolivia).

The Committee delayed its substantive work due to the non-issuance of visas to some delegates. At the organizational meeting on 3 October, the Russian Federation maintained that the Committee should discuss that matter before approving its programme of work.[3] The body therefore continued to address organizational matters, especially with regard to visas, at the beginning of its substantive session on 7 and 8 October. It subsequently agreed to commence the general debate on 10 October and revisit organizational matters thereafter.[4]

The Committee resumed its consideration of organizational matters[5] on 21 October, adopting a revised programme of work and indicative timetables, while agreeing to defer its consideration of the remaining organizational matter (visas) under the agenda item "Revitalization of the work of the General Assembly". While deferring those matters enabled the Committee to first complete its thematic debates and take action on draft resolutions and draft decisions proposed under all of its substantive agenda items, the prolonged discussions on the organization of

---

[3] The Russian Federation proposed that the adoption of the First Committee's programme of work be postponed, noting that, because some of its experts were denied visas, the Russian delegation had again been put in a position that did not allow it to participate fully in the work of the First Committee. The United States reiterated that the organizational meeting of the Committee was not the proper forum in which to raise visa issues and that the appropriate forum was the Committee on Relations with the Host Country. (A/C.1/74/PV.1)

[4] Following three meetings to discuss organizational matters, the Chair noted that adopting the programme of work by a vote was not the right way to start the Committee's work and proposed that the body proceed with the adoption of the section concerning the general debate of its programme of work. He further proposed that, after the general debate, the Committee return to the various issues raised by several delegations and then decide on the rest of the programme of work. (A/C.1/74/PV.2)

[5] The Russian Federation emphasized that no progress had been made in improving or resolving the situation with regard to the United States' fulfilment of its obligations under the United Nations Headquarters Agreement of 1947 and that, unless the United States would end its discriminatory policy and issue visas to all the members of the delegations, the Russian Federation would be obliged to firmly insist on moving the work of both the First Committee and the United Nations Disarmament Commission to Vienna, Geneva or any other venues. The United States noted that the issue of visas was being actively dealt with by the Committee on Relations with the Host Country, and that the process had to play out. (A/C.1/74/PV.11)

work nonetheless had negative consequences for time management, resulting in shortened speaking times for the remainder of the session so that the Committee could complete its work within the period allotted for its seventy-fourth session.

During the main part of its session, the Committee considered its 20 allocated agenda items[6] in 27 meetings, with 8 devoted to the general debate and 10 to the thematic debates. The body took action on draft resolutions and decisions during the final segment of its work. Member States engaged in thematic debates on the following seven clusters: (a) nuclear weapons; (b) other weapons of mass destruction; (c) outer space (disarmament aspects); (d) conventional weapons; (e) other disarmament measures and international security; (f) regional disarmament and security; and (g) disarmament machinery. The Committee heard 132 statements during the general debate and 354 statements during the thematic debates, despite having devoted significant time to discussions not necessarily related to substantive work within its purview.[7]

Over the course of the thematic debate, the Committee held an exchange with the High Representative for Disarmament Affairs, Izumi Nakamitsu, and heard a briefing by García Moritán (Argentina),[8] representing the Agency for the Prohibition of Nuclear Weapons in Latin America and the Caribbean. Furthermore, the Committee heard briefings by, and held informal exchanges with, the chairs of the following bodies: (a) the Group of Governmental Experts to Consider the Role of Verification in Advancing Nuclear Disarmament;[9] (b) the Group of Governmental Experts on Further Practical Measures for the Prevention of an Arms Race in Outer Space;[10] (c) the Group of Governmental Experts on the United Nations Register of Conventional Arms;[11] (d) the Group of Governmental Experts on Advancing Responsible State Behaviour in Cyberspace in the Context of International Security; and (e) the Open-ended Working Group on Developments in the Field of Information and Telecommunications in the Context of International Security.[12] The Committee was also updated by the Office for Disarmament Affairs on the work of its three regional centres, in Kathmandu, Lima and Lomé,[13] and received briefings, via videoconference, from

---

[6] Agenda items 89 to 105, 121 and 136.

[7] The severe liquidity crisis at the United Nations forced the First Committee to cancel all the additional meetings that had been envisaged and to manage time very strictly. (A/74/PV.46)

[8] The Committee decided to ask regional groups to nominate their representatives to participate in the exchange with the High Representative for Disarmament Affairs. The Group of Latin American and Caribbean States nominated their representative. (A/C.1/74/PV.8 and A/C.1/74/PV.15)

[9] Owing to the extension of the general debate, the briefing by and informal exchange with the Chair of the Group of Governmental Experts to Consider the Role of Verification in Advancing Nuclear Disarmament were held after the end of the general debate. (A/C.1/74/PV.8 and A/C.1/74/PV.10)

[10] A/C.1/74/PV.18.

[11] A/C.1/74/PV.16.

[12] A/C.1/74/PV.17.

[13] A/C.1/74/PV.19.

the Chair of the Secretary-General's Advisory Board on Disarmament Matters and a representative of the United Nations Institute for Disarmament Research on the work of their respective organizations.[14] In addition, the current President of the Conference on Disarmament presented a report to the Committee on the work of the Conference and held an informal exchange with delegates.[15]

Following the general debate, the Committee heard statements[16] from members of civil society, with 16 non-governmental organizations delivering statements or joint statements on a range of issues in the field of disarmament, non-proliferation and arms control.

During its action phase, the First Committee approved 59 draft resolutions and decisions under various agenda items. One draft resolution was withdrawn[17] and one draft decision was not adopted after a vote.[18] Of the 59 drafts adopted, 40 were adopted as a whole by recorded vote, with separate votes requested for 58 drafts. Only 22 draft proposals (37 per cent) were adopted as a whole without a vote, reflecting what appeared to be a further hardening of divisions between Member States.[19] On 12 December, the General Assembly adopted the 59 drafts approved by the First Committee, as well as a procedural decision on the Committee's provisional agenda of work and timetable for 2020.[20]

Overview of key substantive discussions in the Committee

The seventy-fourth session of the First Committee was characterized by heightened tensions between the United States and the Russian Federation, particularly with regard to the issue of visas[21] and mutual allegations of non-compliance with treaty obligations. Divisions between the United States and China were also increasingly apparent. Furthermore, as in previous years, the session included sharp exchanges between States in the Middle East over the use of chemical weapons.

Many States expressed concern about the worsening international security environment and the continued erosion of the global disarmament, non-proliferation and arms control architecture. In particular, those States voiced regret about the demise of previous arms control agreements—especially the Treaty between the United States of America and the Union of Soviet Socialist Republics on the Elimination of Their Intermediate-Range and Shorter-Range

---

[14] A/C.1/74/PV.21.

[15] Ibid.

[16] Office for Disarmament Affairs, "Seventy-Fourth Session of the General Assembly, First Committee: Disarmament and International Security" (Civil Society and NGO Presentations).

[17] A/C.1/74/L.55/Rev.1.

[18] A/C.1/74/L.57/Rev.1.

[19] At the seventy-third session, the Committee adopted 68 drafts with 29 of them, 43 percent, without a vote. (A/73/PV.45)

[20] A/74/PV.46.

[21] Concerns about the non-issuance of visas were further addressed by the Committee on Relations with the Host Country during its seventy-fourth session. For more information, see A/74/26.

Missiles of 1987 (Intermediate-Range Nuclear Forces Treaty)—as well as concern about the uncertain future of the Treaty between the United States and the Russian Federation on Measures for the Further Reduction and Limitation of Strategic Offensive Arms (New START Treaty). In that context, such States called for the existing international norms and security architecture to be strengthened.

Commenting on the nature and root causes of the deteriorating security environment, the United States maintained that China and the Russian Federation were expanding their arsenals and deploying new destabilizing weapons while engaging in activities that impeded the ability to make progress on disarmament. Stressing the current insufficiency of the cold war approach, with its bilateral treaties that covered limited types of nuclear weapons or only certain ranges of adversary missiles, the United States called on Member States from every region to demand that China and the Russian Federation join the United States at the negotiating table in good faith in order to initiate a new era of arms control for the sake of international peace and security.[22]

The Russian Federation, for its part, accused the United States of pursuing a policy aimed at dismantling the entire system of international legal instruments on arms control, disarmament and non-proliferation, and it stressed the need to strengthen existing arrangements and elaborate new consensus-based treaty regimes.[23] In that regard, the Russian Federation introduced a new resolution on "Strengthening and developing the system of arms control, disarmament and non-proliferation agreements" (74/66),[24] which the Committee adopted by a vote of 174 to none, with 5 abstentions.[25]

China categorically rejected the aforementioned accusations levelled against it by the United States. It added that the United States, in an attempt to gain security supremacy over others, was continually lowering the threshold for the use of nuclear weapons and turning outer space and cyberspace into new

---

[22] A/C.1/74/PV.3.

[23] The Russian Federation added that the United States was undermining strategic stability by engaging in, inter alia, the unrestricted global deployment of missile defence capabilities, development of high-precision strategic offensive non-nuclear weapons, consideration of deploying strike weapons in outer space, and attempts to weaken the defence potential of other countries by using illegitimate methods of unilateral pressure bypassing the Security Council. Furthermore, the Russian Federation criticized the existence of non-strategic nuclear weapons in Europe, as well as the North Atlantic Treaty Organization's practice of "nuclear sharing", which it contended was a direct violation of the Treaty on the Non-Proliferation of Nuclear Weapons (Nuclear Non-Proliferation Treaty). (A/C.1/74/PV.4)

[24] In introducing the resolution, the Russian Federation said that its adoption would be an important contribution to the creation of conditions for the success of a number of important events in 2020 and 2021—the review conferences of the Nuclear Non-Proliferation Treaty, the Biological Weapons Convention and the Chemical Weapons Convention, as well as the extension of the New START Treaty. (A/C.1/74/PV.4)

[25] The United States voted in favour of the resolution but stressed that the Russian Federation's sponsorship of the draft resolution stood in sharp contrast to its history of violating those principles, in spirit and deed (A/C.1/74/PV.25). On 12 December, the General Assembly adopted it as resolution 74/66 by a vote of 179 to none, with 3 abstentions.

battlegrounds, severely undermining global strategic stability and increasing the risk of nuclear war.[26]

Meanwhile, more than 30 States and a number of regional organizations expressed support for the Secretary-General's Agenda for Disarmament and underscored its contribution to disarmament and international security.[27] In particular, the Association of Southeast Asian Nations, the European Union and the Group of Nordic Countries welcomed the Agenda's strong focus on chemical weapons and biological weapons.[28] Furthermore, a number of States expressed support for the Agenda's pillar on conventional weapons, "Disarmament that Saves Lives," welcoming its focuses on the interrelationship between disarmament and sustainable development, the use of explosive weapons in populated areas, the impact of arms control on conflict prevention and management, and the excessive accumulation of conventional arms and the illicit trade in such arms.

The Committee adopted five resolutions containing references to the Secretary-General's Agenda. Although separate votes were requested for all paragraphs referring to the Agenda, each was adopted with over two thirds of Member States voting in favour.[29]

Nuclear weapons

The First Committee's discussions on nuclear weapons were particularly contentious in 2019, reflecting deteriorating relations between the Russian Federation and the United States following the termination of the Intermediate-Range Nuclear Forces Treaty, as well as the real possibility of an expiration, in

---

[26] China added that, by breaching its commitments and exerting maximum pressure, the United States had continued to escalate the nuclear issue concerning the Islamic Republic of Iran and pushed tensions in the Middle East to the breaking point. (A/C.1/74/PV.4)

[27] New Zealand noted that one of the few factors for optimism lay, in fact, in the Secretary General's efforts to promote dialogue and more positive security outcomes via the launch of his Agenda for Disarmament in 2018 (A/C.1/74/PV.5). Referring to speech of the President of China, Xi Jinping, at the Palais des Nations in Geneva in January 2017, China noted that his initiative was highly compatible with the Agenda (A/C.1/74/PV.4). Meanwhile, Japan described the Secretary-General's Agenda for Disarmament as an excellent initiative for promoting dialogue and enhancing trust-building, and it expressed readiness to translate its implementation plan into concrete action (A/C.1/74/PV.5).

[28] A/C.1/74/PV.13.

[29] Approximately 30 States abstained in separate votes on paragraphs containing a reference to the Secretary-General's Agenda for Disarmament in draft resolutions on nuclear weapons— namely, the resolutions entitled "Towards a nuclear-weapon-free world: accelerating the implementation of nuclear disarmament commitments" (74/46) and "Follow-up to the advisory opinion of the International Court of Justice on the legality of the threat or use of nuclear weapons" (74/59), with the United States voting against them. Paragraphs referencing the Agenda's pillar on conventional weapons—namely, those on the Arms Trade Treaty and the Convention on Cluster Munitions—received more votes and no negative vote, with 15 or 16 abstentions. A separate vote was requested for a paragraph on the Agenda in a new resolution on "Youth, disarmament and non-proliferation" (74/64), which was adopted by 175 to none, with 2 abstentions. The resolution itself was adopted without a vote.

2021, of the New START Treaty. There was also widespread concern among States about the limited scope of the strategic dialogue between the nuclear-weapon States, particularly with respect to the absence of negotiations on further strategic nuclear arms reductions beyond the expiration of the New START Treaty in 2021. Only 4 of the 22 resolutions that the Committee adopted on nuclear weapons received consensus. (For more information on issues related to nuclear disarmament and non-proliferation, see chap. I).

Bilateral issues

The United States said the Russian Federation had serially violated its commitments on arms control and European security while pursuing a deliberate strategy to undermine the sovereignty of neighbouring States.[30] Highlighting a Russian material breach of the Intermediate-Range Nuclear Forces Treaty as a major negative development, the United States said that the Russian Federation bore sole responsibility for that Treaty's termination.[31] It further accused the Russian Federation of not only replacing ageing systems but also inventing new weapons of war, some of which would not be subject to the New START Treaty.[32] Furthermore, the United States criticized China for amassing a vast arsenal of intermediate-range, ground-launched missiles under no international restraints and for expanding its nuclear arsenal[33] while resisting meaningful bilateral dialogue with the United States on nuclear arms control and risk reduction.

The Russian Federation stated that, as long ago as the 1990s, the United States had decided to withdraw from the Anti-Ballistic Missile Treaty, "destroy" the Biological Weapons Convention and Chemical Weapons Convention, the Treaty on Conventional Armed Forces in Europe and the Intermediate-Range Nuclear Forces Treaty, adding that, if that destructive trend continued, the First Committee would

---

[30] The United States stated that the Russian Federation had failed to comply with its obligations under not only the Intermediate-Range Nuclear Forces Treaty but also the Open Skies Treaty, the Vienna Document 2011, the Chemical Weapons Convention and the moratorium on nuclear weapons testing. (A/C.1/74/PV.3)

[31] The United States stated that, while the Russian Federation was dangling the notion of a moratorium on the deployment of missiles covered by the Treaty, it had already fielded multiple battalions of 9M729 ground-launched cruise missiles throughout the Russian Federation, including in western Russian Federation within range of dozens of European capitals. (A/C.1/74/PV.12)

[32] The United States referred, as an example, to a nuclear-powered, nuclear-armed underwater drone designed to destroy cities and ports in radioactive tidal waves. In reference to a separate incident linked to Russian weapons development, the United States said that it had determined that an explosion on 8 August 2019 near Nenoksa, Russian Federation, was the result of a nuclear reaction that occurred during the recovery of a Russian nuclear-powered cruise missile from the White Sea following a failed test in early 2018. (A/C.1/74/PV.3)

[33] The United States noted that China looked set to double the size of its nuclear stockpile over the next decade, and that it threatened to target allies of the United States that hosted any of its missiles, even though China had already deployed thousands of intermediate-range missiles with the purpose of holding the United States and its allies and partners under threat. (A/C.1/74/PV.12)

have nothing to discuss, and there would be no Intermediate-Range Nuclear Forces Treaty, no New START Treaty, no Biological Weapons Convention or Chemical Weapons Convention.[34] The Russian Federation added that in seeking to prevent a new missile crisis, it had unilaterally declared and would implement a moratorium on ground-based, intermediate-range missiles, as long as no United States missiles of that type appeared in the relevant regions. The country called on the United States and its allies to reciprocate with similar steps.[35]

China voiced regret that the United States had withdrawn from the Intermediate-Range Nuclear Forces Treaty, and it expressed firm opposition to attempts by the United States to deploy intermediate-range missiles in the Asia-Pacific region, while also blaming the United States for the erosion of the international nuclear disarmament process. As the possessor of the largest and most advanced nuclear arsenal, the United States should work to meet its special and primary responsibility for nuclear disarmament by responding to the call of the Russian Federation to extend the New START Treaty, China stated. The country also called on the United States to substantially reduce its nuclear arsenal and create conditions conducive to enabling other nuclear-weapon States to join multilateral nuclear-disarmament negotiations.[36]

Treaty on the Non-Proliferation of Nuclear Weapons

Pessimism surrounding the prospects for a successful 2020 Review Conference of the Treaty on the Non-Proliferation of Nuclear Weapons (Nuclear Non-Proliferation Treaty) provided another backdrop for discussion on nuclear issues. Member States reaffirmed their commitment to the Treaty and expressed hope for a successful conclusion of the Review Conference.[37] However, many

---

[34] The Russian Federation contrasted its constructive approaches with actions by the United States, such as destroying the Nuclear Non-Proliferation Treaty; placing nuclear weapons on the territory of other States and training non-nuclear States in conducting nuclear strikes; repudiating the New START Treaty; expanding the placement of short- and intermediate-range ground-based missiles now that it had dismantled the Intermediate-Range Nuclear Forces Treaty; refusing to ratify the Comprehensive Nuclear-Test-Ban Treaty and preparing a test site to resume nuclear testing; blocking a dialogue on a zone in the Middle East free of weapons of mass destruction; blatantly violating obligations under the Joint Comprehensive Plan of Action on the nuclear programme of the Islamic Republic of Iran and punishing those who were implementing theirs; fuelling an arms race in outer space; and undermining the Biological Weapons Convention after refusing to submit to verification and installing its military biological facilities all over the world. (A/C.1/74/PV.4)

[35] The Russian Federation also noted with concern the continuing lack of clarity on the part of the United States with regard to the future of the New START Treaty, adding that, under the current circumstances, it would make sense to extend the agreement, which would prevent the strategic stability situation from completely deteriorating and would buy time to explore possible approaches to new emerging weapons and military technologies. (A/C.1/74/PV.13)

[36] China stated that, until the United States reduced its arsenal to the level of China's, any accusations it might make about China's military strength were as hypocritical and hollow as they were feeble and futile. (A/C.1/74/PV.4)

[37] On behalf of the member States of the Non-Proliferation and Disarmament Initiative—Canada, Chile, Germany, Japan, Mexico, the Netherlands, Nigeria, the Philippines, Poland, Turkey, the

States expressed deep concern that the prevailing security environment and the recent erosion of the nuclear-related arms control architecture might foreclose the possibility of progress in disarmament and arms control, in particular by preventing a successful outcome at the Review Conference.[38]

On behalf of the five nuclear-weapon States recognized by the Nuclear Non-Proliferation Treaty, the United Kingdom reported to the Committee on the state of play in their process dialogue, while also reaffirming their commitment to the Treaty in all its aspects. In particular, the United Kingdom stated their commitment to article VI, expressing their support for the goal of a world without nuclear weapons with undiminished security for all, as well as their commitment to working to ease international tension, which would be conducive to further progress on nuclear disarmament.[39]

While many Member States shared concerns about the prospects for a positive outcome at the 2020 Review Conference, a number of States endeavoured to inject momentum into the current review cycle and put forward proposals that might contribute towards a successful outcome. In that respect, various States welcomed the "Stepping Stones" initiative,[40] led by Sweden, and the "Creating an

---

United Arab Emirates and itself—Australia noted that the Initiative had reaffirmed the critical importance of dialogue and concerted action in achieving our shared goal of a world free of nuclear weapons and reiterated their deep commitment to their core mandate of strengthening the implementation of the Nuclear Non-Proliferation Treaty based on the 2010 Action Plan. (A/C.1/74/PV.11)

[38] In that context, the New Agenda Coalition, echoed by the Non-Aligned Movement, highlighted the vital importance of the nuclear-weapon States fulfilling their obligations under article VI of the Nuclear Non-Proliferation Treaty and their previous commitments agreed upon during its previous review cycles, noting that a presumption of the indefinite possession of nuclear weapons ran counter to the Treaty's object and purpose and threatened to erode its credibility and effectiveness. Egypt, speaking on behalf of the Coalition (Brazil, Ireland, Mexico, New Zealand, South Africa and itself), stressed that it was time for States to deliver on their commitment to the elimination of nuclear weapons in line with the Treaty's obligations, in order to safeguard future generations from the danger arising from the existence of nuclear weapons, adding that that was the only way to maintain the integrity and sustainability of the nuclear-disarmament and non-proliferation regime and that that aim must guide all future efforts. (A/C.1/74/PV.3)

[39] The United Kingdom also reported on progress on the five areas of work agreed upon at the last meeting of the five nuclear-weapon States: (a) nuclear doctrines and policies; (b) engagement with the Association of Southeast Asian Nations member States on the Protocol to the Treaty on the Southeast Asia Nuclear Weapon-Free Zone; (c) Glossary of Key Nuclear Terms (second phase); (d) co-operation on the peaceful use of nuclear energy, nuclear security and nuclear safety; and (e) a fissile material cut-off treaty. (A/C.1/74/PV.3)

[40] Sweden noted that the Stockholm initiative on nuclear disarmament, launched on 11 June, strived to mobilize momentum for an ambitious yet realistic outcome of the Nuclear Non-Proliferation Treaty Review Conference and beyond, through the "Stepping Stones" approach. In close dialogue with nuclear- and non-nuclear-weapon States, a group of 16 countries sought to identify actionable measures related to article VI. (A/C.1/74/P.12)

Environment for Nuclear Disarmament" initiative.[41] In addition, Japan introduced a new resolution, entitled "Joint course of action and future-oriented dialogue towards a world without nuclear weapons" (74/63), that focused on six practical and concrete actions to tangibly advance nuclear disarmament efforts in line with article VI of the Nuclear Non-Proliferation Treaty, while also stressing the importance both of future-oriented dialogue in promoting disarmament and of a set of initiatives focusing on strengthening the Treaty.[42]

Other matters

The thematic debate on nuclear weapons, as in previous years, reflected the wide gap in the views of nuclear-weapon States and of non-nuclear-weapon States.[43] While the former continued to emphasize their commitment to and achievements in nuclear disarmament, including through the initiatives explained above,[44] non-nuclear-weapon States expressed deep concern about the following issues: (a) the increasing threat posed by the continued existence of nuclear weapons and their humanitarian and environmental consequences; (b) backtracking by nuclear-weapon States on their disarmament commitments, particularly through efforts to modernize and expand their nuclear arsenals;[45] and (c) the possibility that the current deteriorating security environment and the erosion of the international security architecture would prompt a new arms race and undermine disarmament and non-proliferation efforts around the world.[46] Reiterating that achieving and maintaining a world without nuclear weapons remained its primary goal, the New Agenda Coalition introduced its

---

[41] The United States said that it remained committed to improving prospects for further progress towards nuclear disarmament and that, earlier that year, it had launched the "Creating the Environment for Nuclear Disarmament" initiative. (A/C.1/74/PV.12)

[42] At the thematic debates, Japan highlighted those six courses of actions: (a) transparency; (b) nuclear risk reduction; (c) the negotiation of a fissile material cut-off treaty; (d) the entry into force of the Comprehensive Nuclear-Test-Ban Treaty; (e) nuclear disarmament verification; and (f) disarmament and non-proliferation education (A/C.1/74/PV.12). The Committee adopted that resolution by a vote of 148 to 4, with 26 abstentions. China and the Russian Federation voted against it, while the United States abstained.

[43] For statements during the thematic debate on nuclear weapons, see verbatim records A/C.1/74/PV.11-13.

[44] Stressing that the current security environment was not conducive for progress in nuclear disarmament, nuclear-weapon States reiterated the view that nuclear disarmament could be achieved only through a gradual, step-by-step approach, which was echoed by their allies. See the statements delivered to the First Committee during the thematic debate on nuclear weapons by China (A/C.1/74/PV.4), France (A/C.1/74/PV.12), the Russian Federation (A/C.1/74/PV.13), the United Kingdom (A/C.1/74/PV.11) and the United States (A/C.1/74/PV.12).

[45] The Non-Aligned Movement expressed concern about the plans by nuclear-weapon States to modernize their nuclear arsenals, including with new delivery vehicles, as provided for in some of their military doctrines, including the latest United States Nuclear Posture Review, which set out rationales for the use of such weapons against non-nuclear-weapon States. (A/C.1/74/PV.3)

[46] The New Agenda Coalition expressed deep concern about the fact that new international security challenges continue to be cited as justifications for the slow progress in nuclear disarmament. The group stressed that the global security environment was not an excuse for

Participation in major disarmament treaties related to weapons of mass destruction

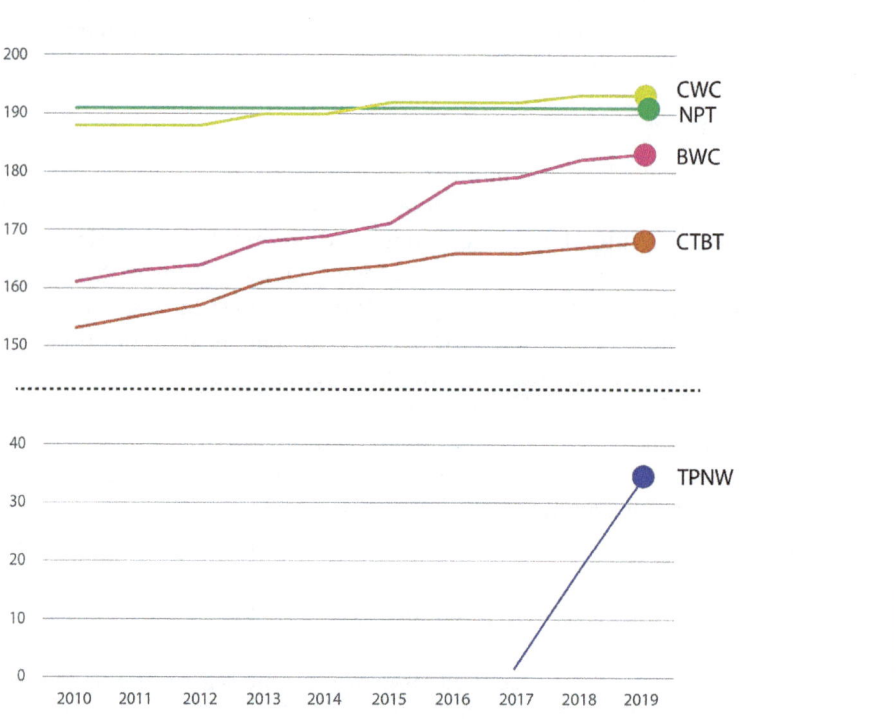

Over the past decade, membership in multilateral treaties related to disarmament and non-proliferation of weapons of mass destruction has continued to increase. In that time, the Chemical Weapons Convention (CWC) and the Nuclear Non-Proliferation Treaty (NPT) have achieved near-universal status, with the Biological Weapons Convention (BWC) and the Comprehensive Nuclear-Test-Ban Treaty (CTBT) both making significant strides towards that end. After its adoption in 2017, the Treaty on the Prohibition of Nuclear Weapons (TPNW) continues to make steady progress towards the threshold of 50 ratifications required for its entry-into-force. Taken together, these trends indicate that, even in the face of a difficult and deteriorating global security environment, States continue to value multilateral treaties related to the elimination of all weapons of mass destruction and the security benefits that they provide.

annual resolution entitled "Towards a nuclear-weapon-free world: accelerating the implementation of nuclear disarmament commitments" (74/46),[47] which the Committee adopted by a vote of 132 to 32, with 17 abstentions. All nuclear-armed States either voted against it or abstained.[48]

In that context, a large number of States welcomed the adoption of the Treaty on the Prohibition of Nuclear Weapons by the General Assembly in 2017 and the significant progress made towards its entry into force.[49] However, polarization over the Treaty persisted. While nuclear-weapon States and allied countries reiterated their opposition to the Treaty,[50] many other States highlighted its contribution to the existing nuclear disarmament and non-proliferation regime by addressing the gaps and imbalances therein, underlined its complementarity with the Nuclear Non-Proliferation Treaty, and called on all remaining countries to sign and ratify it.[51] The First Committee adopted the resolution entitled "Treaty

---

inaction but rather reinforced the need for urgency, pointing to the lack of political will, not favourable conditions. (A/C.1/74/PV.3)

[47] Egypt explained that the New Agenda Coalition's resolution highlighted an area of focus in the current Nuclear Non-Proliferation Treaty review cycle, namely calling on the nuclear-weapon States to fulfil their obligations flowing from article VI without further delay, and the importance of the Nuclear Non-Proliferation Treaty review process evaluating compliance with existing obligations and developing new measures, while putting forward specific recommendations to improve greater transparency, measurability and accountability for compliance. (A/C.1/74/PV.11)

[48] Subsequently, the New Agenda Coalition's resolution was adopted by the General Assembly by a vote of 137 to 33, with 16 abstentions.

[49] On behalf of the Caribbean Community, Jamaica stated that a special Caribbean Regional Forum on the Treaty was convened in June in Georgetown, Guyana, bringing representatives from all over the region to discuss ways of furthering support for it. It culminated in the adoption of the Georgetown Statement and a reaffirmation of the Caribbean Community's commitment to the Treaty (A/C.1/74/PV.11). The Non-Aligned Movement also expressed the hope that when the Treaty entered into force, it would contribute to furthering the global objective of the total elimination of nuclear weapons.

[50] On behalf of the United Kingdom, the United States and itself, France, in explaining their negative votes, noted that the Treaty on the Prohibition of Nuclear Weapons did not take into account the security considerations necessary for nuclear disarmament and delayed the implementation and strengthening of the Nuclear Non-Proliferation Treaty regime in all its aspects, by widening the gap between the States parties of the Nuclear Non-Proliferation Treaty (A/C.1/74/PV.22). The United Kingdom stated that it did not intend to support, sign or ratify the Treaty on the Prohibition of Nuclear Weapons, which risked undermining the Nuclear Non-Proliferation Treaty, ignored the security environment and did not address the technical and procedural challenges that must be overcome to achieve nuclear disarmament in a secure and responsible manner (A/C.1/74/PV.11). The United States noted that the Treaty on the Prohibition of Nuclear Weapons would not move the world any closer to eliminating nuclear weapons and had increased political divisions, making future disarmament efforts more difficult (A/C.1/74/PV.12).

[51] Austria said that the Treaty on the Prohibition of Nuclear Weapons was indispensable to fulfilling the ambition of the Nuclear Non-Proliferation Treaty to achieve a nuclear-weapon-free world, and that it was now an established part of the nuclear-disarmament architecture (A/C.1/74/PV.6). The Arab Group also emphasized that the Nuclear Non-Proliferation Treaty did not run counter to the Nuclear Non-Proliferation Treaty, but rather, complemented it in a manner conducive to the full implementation of its objectives (A/C.1/74/PV.11).

on the Prohibition of Nuclear Weapons (74/41) by a vote of 119 to 41, with 15 abstentions.[52]

In addition to that resolution, the members of the New Agenda Coalition led a large number of States on separate efforts to promote the humanitarian initiative on nuclear disarmament. Nuclear-weapon States and many of their allies voted against, or abstained from voting on, the resolutions entitled "Humanitarian consequences of nuclear weapons" (74/42) and "Ethical imperatives for a nuclear-weapon-free world" (74/47), even though each received support from a two-thirds majority of States.[53]

Meanwhile, the Non-Aligned Movement reaffirmed its long-standing position on nuclear disarmament, pressing nuclear-weapon States to comply urgently with their legal obligations and undertakings and to fully eliminate their nuclear weapons in a transparent, irreversible and internationally verifiable manner. The Movement also demanded that those States immediately cease any modernization or extension of their facilities related to nuclear weapons.[54] Furthermore, the Non-Aligned Movement reiterated its call for the convening of a United Nations high-level international conference on nuclear disarmament as a follow-up to the high-level meeting of the General Assembly on nuclear disarmament held in 24 September 2013.[55] The Committee also adopted the annual resolution sponsored by Myanmar, entitled "Nuclear disarmament" (74/45), which followed almost the same voting pattern as in 2018, by a vote of 117 to 40, with 22 abstentions.[56]

---

[52] On 12 December, the General Assembly formally adopted the resolution by a vote of 123 to 41, with 16 abstentions.

[53] The resolution entitled "Humanitarian consequences of nuclear weapons" (74/42h) was adopted by the First Committee by a vote of 136 to 14, with 27 abstentions and by the General Assembly by a vote of 144 to 13, with 28 abstentions. The resolution entitled "Ethical imperatives for a nuclear-weapon-free world" (74/47) was adopted by the First Committee by a vote of 129 to 37, with 12 abstentions and by the General Assembly by a vote of 135 to 37, with 13 abstentions.

[54] See the statement made by Indonesia on behalf of the Non-Aligned Movement (A/C.1/74/PV.3).

[55] As in previous years, the Committee adopted a resolution entitled "Follow-up to the 2013 high-level Meeting of the General Assembly on nuclear disarmament" (74/54), but about 40 States, particularly nuclear-weapon States and their allies, either voted against it or abstained. Nuclear-weapon States and their allies again criticized that resolution for ignoring their position on nuclear disarmament. (A/C.1/74/PV.22) By this resolution, which was adopted on 12 December by a vote of 142 to 34, with 10 abstentions, the Assembly reiterated its decision to convene a high-level United Nations conference on nuclear disarmament. However, it did not set specific dates for the conference, which the Assembly had decided in earlier resolutions to hold no later than 2018. (A/74/PV.46)

[56] The General Assembly adopted the resolution entitled "Nuclear disarmament" by a vote of 120 to 41, with 22 abstentions. As in previous years, the majority of non-nuclear-weapons States, particularly Non-Aligned Movement member States, supported the resolution, but France, the Russian Federation, the United Kingdom and the United States voted against it, along with their allies, particularly member States of the North Atlantic Treaty Organization. China was the only State with nuclear weapons that supported the resolution; the Democratic Republic of Korea, India and Pakistan abstained.

Separately, a large number of States expressed satisfaction with the convening in November of the first annual session of the Conference on the establishment of a Middle East zone free of nuclear weapons and all other weapons of mass destruction, pursuant to General Assembly decision 73/546 of 22 December 2018. However, Israel stressed that initiatives of the Arab Group, such as the Conference in November, went against the guidelines and principles of the nuclear-weapon-free zones agreed by consensus in the United Nations Disarmament Commission of 1999. Israel further declared that it would not participate in the Conference in November and, owing to that initiative, would also refrain from participating in future forums dealing with regional arms control topics.[57] As in the previous session, Israel and the United States voted against the resolution entitled "Establishment of a nuclear-weapon-free zone in the region of the Middle East" (74/30).[58]

A number of States, including nuclear-weapon States, underscored the importance of nuclear disarmament verification and expressed support for the work of the Group of Governmental Experts to Consider the Role of Verification in Advancing Nuclear Disarmament. As that Group had completed its work earlier in the year, Norway introduced a recurring resolution entitled "Nuclear disarmament verification" (74/50), whereby the General Assembly would establish another group of governmental experts to continue work in 2021 and 2022. The Committee adopted the resolution by a vote of 173 to 1, with 4 abstentions.[59]

The Committee also adopted a number of other resolutions regarding specific measures to promote nuclear disarmament and non-proliferation, including the resolutions entitled "Comprehensive Nuclear-Test-Ban Treaty" (74/78), "Conclusion of effective international arrangements to assure non-nuclear-weapon States against the use or threat of use of nuclear weapons" (74/31), "Reducing nuclear danger" (74/44) and "Convention on the Prohibition of the Use of Nuclear Weapons" (74/68),[60] as well as three resolutions and a decision on treaties that established nuclear-weapon-free zones.[61]

Many States continued to express their commitment to and support for the Joint Comprehensive Plan of Action, while expressing regret or concerns about the withdrawal of the United States and the phased reduction of commitments on

---

[57] A/C.1/74/PV.9.
[58] This resolution had been adopted by consensus annually until 2018, when the General Assembly decided to convene a conference on the establishment of a Middle East zone free of nuclear weapons and all other weapons of mass destruction.
[59] The text was subsequently adopted by the General Assembly by a vote of 150 to 1, with 26 abstentions. The Russian Federation cast the only negative vote.
[60] Those four resolutions and many others on nuclear weapons were adopted by the Committee on 1 November.
[61] Those are the resolutions entitled "African Nuclear-Weapon-Free Zone Treaty" (74/26), "Treaty for the Prohibition of Nuclear Weapons in Latin America and the Caribbean (Treaty of Tlatelolco)" (74/27) and "Nuclear-weapon-free southern hemisphere and adjacent areas" (74/48), as well as the decision entitled "Treaty on the South-East Asia Nuclear-Weapon-Free Zone (Bangkok Treaty) (74/510).

nuclear-related provisions by the Islamic Republic of Iran. A number of countries criticized the United States for obstructing the implementation of the Plan of Action and Security Council resolution 2231 (2015), urged the Islamic Republic of Iran to return to the full implementation of its commitments and called on all sides to work together to preserve the Plan.[62] Israel, however, said that it had always been unequivocal about the agreement's threats and its dangerous implications for the security and the stability of the Middle East. In that connection, Israel noted that the Islamic Republic of Iran had in recent months breached core nuclear obligations contained in Security Council resolution 2231 (2015). Meanwhile, responding to a statement by Saudi Arabia, the Islamic Republic of Iran said it was committed to nuclear non-proliferation and had no ambitions to possess nuclear weapons, noting its adoption of an additional protocol to its safeguards agreement with the International Atomic Energy Agency. It further quoted the Agency's Director General as saying that the Islamic Republic of Iran had the most comprehensive and robust verification regime of any country in the world.[63]

The denuclearization of the Korean Peninsula received less attention in the First Committee than in previous years, as the Democratic People's Republic of Korea and the United States undertook bilateral talks on the matter. The United States said that its goal remained to be the final, fully verified denuclearization of the Democratic People's Republic of Korea, and it underscored the importance of all Member States continuing to fully implement and enforce existing sanctions as mandated by Security Council resolutions.[64] However, the Democratic People's Republic of Korea stressed that its weapons tests in recent months were measures to bolster its self-defence capability and were part of its routine exercises, adding that its possession of nuclear forces was a defensive measure for coping with the

---

[62] Switzerland pointed out that the Joint Comprehensive Plan of Action established the strictest verification regime that had ever been applied to a civil nuclear programme and deplored the United States' withdrawal from the agreement and its reimposition of sanctions. It expressed concern about recent steps that the Islamic Republic of Iran had taken to advance its civilian nuclear capabilities and stressed the importance of full cooperation with the International Atomic Energy Agency, calling on all States to refrain from actions that would run counter to the objectives of the Joint Comprehensive Plan of Action. (A/C.1/74/PV.11)

[63] Saudi Arabia stressed the importance of concluding a comprehensive international agreement on the nuclear programme of the Islamic Republic of Iran that would prevent the country from possessing nuclear weapons (A/C.1/74/PV.12). In its response, the Islamic Republic of Iran suggested that the representative of Saudi Arabia refrain from proposing rehashed, uncreative ideas and proposals and asked him to study Security Council resolution 2231 (2015), which endorsed the Joint Comprehensive Plan of Action, a comprehensive international agreement intended to reassure and build confidence in countries such as Saudi Arabia that had misgivings about the peaceful nature of the nuclear programme of the Islamic Republic of Iran (A/C.1/74/PV.13).

[64] A/C.1/74/PV.12. In its right of reply, the United States further noted that President Donald Trump, had held out the prospect of a brighter future for the Democratic People's Republic of Korea if it made the strategic decision to denuclearize and therefore, again, called on the Democratic People's Republic of Korea to come back to the negotiating table in order to move forward on the commitment to denuclearization made at the 2018 Singapore summit. (A/C.1/74/PV.13)

hostile policy of the United States.[65] The Republic of Korea, meanwhile, pointed out that although recent working-level talks in Stockholm between the United States and the Democratic People's Republic of Korea had not produced tangible results, both sides were keeping the door open for dialogue, which was the only possible avenue towards peace.[66] In response, the Democratic People's Republic of Korea said that it had no intention of further talks until the United States took significant steps to completely and irreversibly cease its hostile policy towards it.[67]

Other weapons of mass destruction

As in previous years, the Committee's consideration of issues related to other weapons of mass destruction was dominated by tense exchanges over the use of chemical weapons in the Syrian Arab Republic. More broadly, the body's discussions on chemical weapons again demonstrated the deep international divisions over how to address the serious challenge to the international taboo and total ban on those weapons,[68] while further highlighting how ongoing regional conflicts in the Middle East had complicated discussions on disarmament and proliferation issues.[69] (For more information on issues related to other weapons of mass destruction, see chap. II.)

Member States reiterated strong support for the Chemical Weapons Convention and called for its universalization and full implementation. A large number of States—particularly some members of the Non-Aligned Movement, as well as China, the Russian Federation and the Syrian Arab Republic—urged the United States to make concrete efforts to complete the destruction of its chemical weapons.[70] Many States also expressed grave concern about the continued use of chemical weapons, in violation of international law and with impunity, sounding

---

[65] The Democratic People's Republic of Korea stated that resumed joint military exercises in the southern part of the Korean Peninsula and simulation tests for intercepting its intercontinental ballistic missiles conducted on the other side of the Pacific ran counter to the spirit of the joint statement of 12 June 2018 by the Democratic People's Republic of Korea and the United States, adding that peace and security on the Korean Peninsula would depend entirely on the future attitude of the United States. (A/C.1/74/PV.12)

[66] A/C.1/74/PV.12.

[67] Exercising its right of reply, the Democratic People's Republic of Korea reminded the United States that its Foreign Ministry, in a statement after the Stockholm working-level talks, had asked the United States to come up with a new way to solve the problem. (A/C.1/74/PV.13)

[68] In recent years, those weapons had been used not only in the Syrian Arab Republic but also other parts of the world, such as Iraq, Malaysia and the United Kingdom, highlighting a growing challenge to the authority of the Chemical Weapons Convention, which established a global legal prohibition on the entire category of those weapons of mass destruction.

[69] For statements during the thematic debate on other weapons of mass destruction, see verbatim records A/C.1/74/PV.13-14.

[70] Noting that the core objective and purpose of the Chemical Weapons Convention was chemical-weapon disarmament, China welcomed the successive completion by the Syrian Arab Republic, the Russian Federation, Libya and Iraq of the destruction of their chemical weapons and urged the United States, as the only remaining State party possessing chemical weapons, to make concrete efforts to fulfil its obligations and complete the destruction of its chemical weapons by the specified deadline. (A/C.1/74/PV.14)

the alarm about the erosion of the global norm against chemical weapons. On behalf of the States participating in the International Partnership against Impunity for the Use of Chemical Weapons, France stressed their determination to continue to combat the re-emergence of the use of chemical weapons and prevent impunity for those who resort to their use of such weapons or contribute to their development.[71]

Despite the widespread concern regarding the use of chemical weapons in the Syrian Arab Republic, the Committee's discussion on the question of accountability revealed a sharp divergence of views. While many States identified the Government of the Syrian Arab Republic as the responsible party, that Government and the Russian Federation, in particular, pointed to the ability of non-State actors such as Islamic State in Iraq and the Levant to launch such attacks. Recalling its earlier determination that the Government of the Syrian Arab Republic had used chlorine as a weapon on 19 May in an attack in the Syrian city of Latakia, the United States warned that such atrocities threatened to desensitize the world to the use and proliferation of chemical weapons and insisted that the Russian Federation must take concrete actions to prevent the Syrian Arab Republic from using chemical weapons.[72] Other States demanded that those responsible for that atrocity must be held accountable, while commending the Technical Secretariat of the Organisation for the Prohibition of Chemical Weapons (OPCW) for its impartial and objective work.[73]

In the meantime, the Syrian Arab Republic reiterated its opposition to any use of chemical weapons, stating that after acceding to the Chemical Weapons Convention and implementing all its commitments thereunder, the Government no longer possessed any of the chemical weapons or chemical substances banned by the Convention.[74] Many States, however, continued to express serious reservations about gaps and discrepancies in the chemical weapons declaration of the Syrian Arab Republic. The Group of Nordic Countries, for example, expressed deep concern about the continued possession by the Syrian Arab Republic of chemical

---

[71] France noted that the International Partnership against Impunity for the Use of Chemical weapons was founded on 23 January 2018 to strengthen cooperation and protect the Chemical Weapons Convention and that 40 States from all geographical regions and the European Union had joined it so far. (A/C.1/74/PV.13)

[72] Michael R. Pompeo, Secretary of State of the United States, press availability at the Palace Hotel, New York, 26 September 2019. (A/C.1/74/PV.3)

[73] The European Union and the Group of Nordic countries noted the conclusion of the report of the OPCW Fact-finding Mission concerning the incident in 2018 in Douma, Syrian Arab Republic, which confirmed an attack with chemical weapons. (A/C.1/74/PV.13)

[74] The Syrian Arab Republic stated that it had ended its chemical weapons programme and ensured the destruction of all its production facilities and chemical stocks, which was done outside Syrian territory on Western ships, first among them the United States vessel *MV Cape Ray*. Furthermore, the Government accused certain Western States of misleading the international community with lies and fabrications and of supporting and training terrorist organizations in the use of chemical weapons in Syrian territories by France, Israel, Turkey, the United Kingdom and the United States, and, together with various other States. (A/C.1/74/PV.14)

weapons, stressing that all such weapons in the country's possession should have been declared and destroyed.[75]

The question of accountability rendered the First Committee's discussions on chemical weapons highly contentious, mirroring sharp differences among the Security Council's permanent members over how to investigate and attribute responsibility for the use of such weapons. A number of States in the Committee welcomed the establishment of the Investigation and Identification Team pursuant to the decision adopted at the fourth special session of the Conference of the States Parties to Review the Operation of the Convention in 2018,[76] while also expressing strong support for the OPCW Technical Secretariat in its mission to establish arrangements for identifying the perpetrators of the use of chemical weapons in the Syrian Arab Republic. However, the Russian Federation stated that OPCW had become divided through the excessive politicization of the chemical-weapon issue concerning the Syrian Arab Republic; what the country said was a staged attempt in 2018 to assassinate Sergei Skripal, a former Russian military intelligence officer; and the "illegitimate attributive function" that a group of Western States had imposed on OPCW.[77] Meanwhile, the Non-Aligned Movement voiced deep regret over the failure to adopt the report of the fourth special session of the Conference of the States Parties to Review the Operation of the Chemical Weapons Convention, owing to a lack of consensus and the politicization of some issues.

The disagreement over the chemical-weapon issue of concerning the Syrian Arab Republic resulted in the adoption by a vote for a sixth consecutive year of the annual resolution on the chemical weapons convention entitled "Implementation of the Convention on the Prohibition of the Development, Production, Stockpiling and Use of Chemical Weapons and Their Destruction" (74/40), in which the General Assembly, inter alia, strongly condemned the use of chemical weapons in the Syrian Arab Republic attributed to the Syrian Arab Armed Forces and Islamic State in Iraq and the Levant, as well as the use of chemical weapons in Iraq, Malaysia and the United Kingdom.[78] The General Assembly adopted the resolution by a vote of 151 to 8, with 21 abstentions; China, the Russian Federation and the Syrian Arab Republic cast negative votes. In addition, separate

---

[75] Referring to the conclusion by the OPCW Declaration Assessment Team that the declarations provided by the authorities of the Syrian Arab Republic were insufficient and marred by errors, Norway, on behalf of the Nordic States (Denmark, Finland, Norway and Sweden), strongly urged the Syrian Arab Republic to immediately disclose all the relevant information and completely fulfil its declaration obligations. (A/C.1/74/PV.13)

[76] OPCW, document C-SS-4/DEC.3.

[77] In that regard, the Russian Federation contended that granting the OPCW Technical Secretariat the function of attributing responsibility for the use of chemical weapons went beyond the provisions of the Chemical Weapons Convention, changing the OPCW technical nature and encroaching on the exclusive authority of the Security Council. The Russian Federation added that it was quite certain that the mechanism would not result in objective investigations. (A/C.1/74/PV.14)

[78] A/C.1/74/PV.23.

votes were requested for five paragraphs of the resolution, which were all adopted by similarly divided votes.[79]

Separately, the United States referred to the 2018 chemical attack on Sergei Skripal in Salisbury, United Kingdom, in calling for the Novichok chemical families to be added to the Annex of Chemicals of the Convention Weapons Convention at the twenty-fourth session of Conference of the States Parties to the Convention in November, noting that those agents had no use other than to harm or kill.[80] However, the Russian Federation firmly rejected allegations by the United Kingdom that Russian citizens had been implicated in incidents involving toxic chemicals in Salisbury and Amesbury, adding that the United Kingdom refused to cooperate legally with the Russian Federation in the "Skripal case" and had yet to present any serious evidence.

With regard to biological weapons issues, many States reiterated support for the Biological Weapons Convention and called for universal adherence thereto and full implementation thereof.[81] Recognizing that the Convention's lack of a verification system continued to pose a challenge to its effectiveness, the Non-Aligned Movement members that were party to the Convention, in a call echoed by other States, sought the resumption of the multilateral negotiations to conclude a non-discriminatory, legally binding protocol dealing with all articles of the Convention, including through verification measures. The United States noted that a small number of States parties had repeatedly blocked practical steps to strengthen the Convention, insisting that the only way ahead was to return to negotiations on a Protocol to the Convention.[82] To strengthen the Convention's institutional framework, the Russian Federation encouraged States parties to support the initiatives to use mobile medical units and establish a Scientific

---

[79] Those five paragraphs are the following: the fifth preambular paragraph that re-emphasized the General Assembly's unequivocal support for the decision of the OPCW Director General to continue the mission to establish the facts surrounding the allegations of the use of chemical weapons; the second operative paragraph that condemned the use of chemical weapons in Iraq, Malaysia, the Syrian Arab Republic and the United Kingdom; the third operative paragraph that took note with great concern of the reports of the OPCW Fact-finding Mission regarding alleged incidents in Ltamenah, Saraqib and Douma in the Syrian Arab Republic; the fourth operative paragraph that recalled the adoption of decision (C-SS-4/DEC.3) of the fourth special session of the Conference of the States Parties, entitled "Addressing the threat from chemical weapons use", of 27 June 2018 and stressed the importance of its implementation; and the sixteenth operative paragraph that expressed that the OPCW Technical Secretariat could not fully verify the accuracy of the declaration of the Syrian Arab Republic. (A/74/PV.46)

[80] The United States noted that 24 nations, including the United States, had sponsored a draft decision that would make clear the understanding that the aerosolized use of central-nervous-system-acting chemicals, such as fentanyl, was inconsistent with law-enforcement purposes as a "purpose not prohibited", calling on Chemical Weapons Convention States parties to support the draft decision. (A/C.1/74/PV.13)

[81] The United Kingdom welcomed the accession of the United Republic of Tanzania, which deposited its instrument of ratification in London on 14 August 2019 and called on all States that have not yet done so to follow suit. (A/C.1/74/PV.13)

[82] A/C.1/74/PV.13.

Advisory Committee within the Convention, as well as to update its confidence-building measures.[83] China noted that it had actively promoted the development of a voluntary model code of conduct for biological scientists and proposed a regime for biological non-proliferation export controls and international cooperation within the Convention's framework.[84]

While welcoming an agreement by the Meeting of States Parties in December on measures to ease the Convention's financial crisis and provide stability to its Implementation Support Unit, a number of States still expressed concern about the financial situation. In that context, those States called on all States parties to pay their assessed contributions in full and on time.

As in previous years, the Committee adopted the resolution entitled "Convention on the Prohibition of the Development, Production and Stockpiling of Bacteriological (Biological) and Toxin Weapons and on Their Destruction" (74/79) without a vote.[85]

Conventional weapons

The conventional weapons issues considered by the First Committee included the illicit trade in small arms and light weapons, conventional ammunition, the Arms Trade Treaty, anti-personnel landmines, cluster weapons and the use of explosive weapons in populated areas.[86] (For more information on issues related to conventional weapons, see chap. III).

Member States continued to express strong support for the Programme of Action to Prevent, Combat and Eradicate the Illicit Trade in Small Arms and Light Weapons in All Its Aspects. Although some States regretted the lack of consensus on elements of the outcome document of the third Review Conference of the Programme of Action, held in June 2018, many expressed hope to achieve concrete progress in considering the Programme's national, regional and global implementation at the seventh Biennial Meeting of States, scheduled for 2020. The Committee adopted the annual omnibus resolution entitled "Small arms and light weapons in all its aspects" (74/60) without a vote; however, Israel and the United States voted against its seventh preambular paragraph and sixth operative paragraph, which welcomed the outcome document of the third Review Conference, because the two States opposed that document's language on the issue of ammunition controls.[87]

---

[83] The Russian Federation stated its opposition to the concept of "peer reviews" of dual-use microbiological facilities, as well as the initiative to create a certain "standing capacity" within the United Nations Secretariat to investigate alleged biological weapons incidents. (A/C.1/74/PV.14)

[84] A/C.1/74/PV.14.

[85] A/C.1/74/PV.23.

[86] For statements during the thematic debate on conventional weapons, see verbatim records A/C.1/74/PV.14-16.

[87] A/C.1/74/PV.24.

While States expressed divergent views in the First Committee as to whether ammunition should be addressed in the framework of the Programme of Action, Member States more widely supported the ongoing process mandated by the General Assembly to address the question of conventional ammunition. In that regard, a number of States, including the United States and the United Kingdom, welcomed the establishment in 2020 of a group of governmental experts on conventional ammunition.[88] States also continued to express support for the International Ammunition Technical Guidelines, including in the resolution entitled "Problems arising from the accumulation of conventional ammunition stockpiles in surplus" (74/65), which the Committee adopted without a vote.

Meanwhile, the Arms Trade Treaty gained further positive attention in the Committee as States continued to sign and ratify the agreement.[89] The Treaty garnered expressions of support from the majority of Member States, particularly members of the Caribbean Community, the European Union, the Group of Nordic Countries, Jamaica and the United Kingdom.[90] Yet, opposition to and reservations about the Treaty persisted, as indicated by the adoption by vote of its eponymous resolution (74/49),[91] as well as by the separate votes requested on all paragraphs containing reference to it. Egypt reiterated its call for States parties to the Treaty to ensure that its implementation was consistent with the Charter of the United Nations and in no way infringed on the right of States to meet their national security and self-defence needs.[92] Meanwhile, a number of States welcomed the steady progress by States parties in deliberations on a number of issues, particularly during the fifth Conference of States Parties to the Treaty. Those States also commended the presidency of Latvia during the Conference, especially for its effort to mainstream the gendered impact of armed violence in the context of the Treaty. (See chap. III for more information on the Arms Trade Treaty and chap. VI for more details on thematic gender and gender-based violence as the thematic priority of the fifth Conference of States Parties.)

---

[88] A/C.1/74/PV.14.

[89] In 2019, Lebanon and Palau ratified the Arms Trade Treaty, and Botswana, Canada and Maldives ratified it.

[90] China stated that its Foreign Minister informed the General Assembly that China had initiated the domestic legislative process for its accession to the Arms Trade Treaty. (A/C.1/74/PV.9 and A/C.1/74/PV.4) China further noted that it has consistently voted in favour of the annual resolution on the Arms Trade Treaty and that year had become a sponsor of the draft resolution (A/C.1/74/L.25) for the first time. (A/C.1/74/PV.16)

[91] The Committee adopted the resolution entitled "Arms Trade Treaty" by a vote of 150 to 1, with 26 abstentions. On 12 December, the General Assembly adopted it by a vote of 153 to 1, with 28 abstentions.

[92] Egypt reiterated that various shortcomings of the Arms Trade Treaty, especially its lack of clear definitions and criteria, largely undermined its possible effectiveness and made it possible to misuse it as a tool to manipulate and monopolize the legitimate trade in conventional weapons in a politicized manner, while ignoring the importance of preventing the intentional supply of weapons to unauthorized recipients such as terrorists and illegal armed groups. (A/C.1/74/PV.14)

Many States also underscored the contribution of the Anti-Personnel Mine Ban Convention and expressed hope for a successful fourth Review Conference of the States Parties, to be held in Ottawa in November. Norway, which held the presidency of the Review Conference, noted a need to step up progress on landmine clearance, address the use of improvised landmines under the Convention, strengthen mine-risk education and prevention measures for at-risk populations, and integrate a gender perspective into all aspects of mine action.[93]

A number of States also expressed support for the Convention on Cluster Munitions, along with the hope that more countries would sign and ratify the Convention ahead of its Review Conference in 2020, the tenth anniversary of its entry into force. The Committee adopted the resolution entitled "Implementation of the Convention on the Prohibition of the Use, Stockpiling, Production and Transfer of Anti-Personnel Mines and on Their Destruction" (74/61) by a vote of 161 to none, with 19 abstentions, and the resolution entitled "Implementation of the Convention on Cluster Munitions" (74/62) by a vote of 138 to 1, with 39 abstentions.

Furthermore, a number of States expressed support for ongoing discussions on the issue of lethal autonomous weapon systems within the framework of the Convention on Certain Conventional Weapons. In that regard, States welcomed progress made in the work of the Group of Governmental Experts on Emerging Technologies in the Area of Lethal Autonomous Weapons Systems, and they expressed hope for further progress at the annual Meeting of High Contracting Parties to the Convention, to be held in November. In addition, States including Japan and Ireland welcomed the adoption by consensus of 11 guiding principles by the Group of Governmental Experts, as well as its decision to continue discussions and work on recommendations towards the Convention's Review Conference in 2021.[94] States also reiterated their belief that such weapons must always remain under human control and that only human accountability could ensure full compliance with international humanitarian law.

A large number of States also voiced deep concern about the use of explosive weapons in populated areas. Austria, which hosted the Vienna Conference on Protecting Civilians in Urban Warfare in October, noted that it was heartened by the participation of 133 States from every region, along with many international organizations and representatives of civil society, reflecting broad interest in advancing the protection of civilians from the use of explosive weapons with wide-area effects in populated areas. Austria further encouraged all States to take part in drafting a political declaration, a process that would start in Geneva on 18 November.[95] Separately, on behalf of 69 States, Ireland delivered a joint

---

[93] A/C.1/74/PV.15.

[94] A/C.1/74/PV.15.

[95] Austria noted that the increasing urbanization of conflict was a major challenge to the protection of civilians, and that it was well documented that when explosive weapons with wide-area effects were used in populated areas, more than 90 per cent of the victims were

statement expressing serious concern over many violations of international humanitarian law that were taking place in current conflicts, including through the use of explosive weapons with wide-area effects in populated areas.[96] In that regard, those States welcomed the ongoing work of the International Committee of the Red Cross, civil society and the United Nations, while also urging further immediate action both for the protection of civilians and civilian objects and for compliance with international humanitarian law. They also welcomed the joint appeal made on that issue in September by the Secretary-General and the President of the International Committee of the Red Cross. (For more information, see chap. III.)

Other issues, including disarmament machinery

The growing tensions among major powers were notably reflected in the Committee's deliberations on other strategic issues, especially outer space and cybersecurity. (For more information on these issues, see chap. V).

Pursuant to resolutions 73/72 and 73/91, the First Committee and the Fourth Committee held a joint panel discussion on possible challenges to space security and sustainability.[97] Presided over jointly by their Chairs, the panel heard presentations by the Deputy to the Permanent Representative for Disarmament Affairs and the Director of the Office for Outer Space Affairs, as well as briefings by experts. The discussion demonstrated that there was convergence among States on the benefits of close coordination in that area between relevant bodies in Geneva, New York and Vienna.

In the meantime, the consideration of issues related to outer space in the First Committee revealed deepening differences of views over how to address threats to space security and sustainability.[98] China and the Russian Federation continued to strongly advocate a new treaty that would prohibit the placement of weapons in outer space, while the United States and its allies pursued further transparency and confidence-building measures. Reflecting entrenched divisions on the best way to address threats to space security, the Committee adopted all four resolutions on outer space by vote.

Many States welcomed the work of the Group of Governmental Experts on Further Practical Measures for the Prevention of an Arms Race in Outer

---

civilians (A/C.1/74/PV.15). The United States, which participated in the Vienna Conference on Protecting Civilians in Urban Warfare, stated that efforts to ban or stigmatize the use of explosive weapons were impractical and counterproductive, because they would hamper efforts to protect civilians from bad actors such as the Islamic State in Iraq and the Sham or encourage bad actors to use human shields and to hide in urban areas, adding that sharing and promoting good practices through non-political, military-to-military exchanges should be the common focus. (A/C.1/74/PV.14)

[96] A/C.1/74/PV.15.

[97] A/C.1/74/PV.20.

[98] For statements during the thematic debate on outer space (disarmament aspects), see verbatim records A/C.1/74/PV.17-18.

Space, while also expressing regret that the Group failed to adopt a final report by consensus. For the third time, the Committee adopted the resolution entitled "Further practical measures for the prevention of an arms race in outer space" (74/34), with 124 States in favour and 41—including the United States—against, with 10 abstentions.[99] Separately, the United States presented an alternative[100] to the annual resolution on transparency and confidence-building measures in outer space activities (74/67). Despite ultimately withdrawing that proposal, the United States still voted against the Russian text, which was adopted by a vote of 166 to 2, with 5 abstentions.[101]

The Committee also approved a resolution sponsored by the Russian Federation entitled "No first placement of weapons in outer space" (74/33) by a vote of 123 to 14, with 40 abstentions. In addition, it approved the annual resolution entitled "Prevention of an arms race in outer space" (74/32) by a vote of 175 to 2, with no abstentions. (For more information on outer space, see chap. V.)

Meanwhile, States expressed growing interest and engagement in issues related to cyber issues.[102] There remained general agreement among Member States on the conclusions contained in the 2013 and 2015 reports[103] of the groups of governmental experts on developments in the field of information and telecommunications in the context of international security, especially that international law, and the Charter of the United Nations in particular, is applicable and essential to the maintenance of peace and stability and the promotion of an open, secure, stable, accessible and peaceful information and communications technology environment. However, the Committee again adopted resolutions that had, in 2018, established separate processes for addressing cyber issues: an open-ended working group set up by the resolution sponsored by the Russian Federation (73/27) and a group of governmental experts mandated by the resolution sponsored by the United States (73/266). Member States broadly agreed

---

[99] That resolution was first introduced by the Russian Federation and China in 2017 and, over the objection of the United States, established a group of governmental experts to study the issue of further measures on the prevention of an arms race in outer space. Notably, its 2019 iteration contained an operative paragraph singling out one expert of the Group for the failure to reach consensus on its final report. A separate vote was requested for that paragraph and it was adopted by a five-vote margin (55 in favour, 50 against, 48 abstentions), but the reference was deleted from the revised resolution that was submitted to the General Assembly and adopted on 12 December.

[100] Entitled "Advancing transparency and confidence-building measures for outer space activities" (A/C.1/74/L.55/Rev.1).

[101] The United States had co-sponsored that resolution with the Russian Federation and China before 2018. In explaining its vote against the resolution entitled "Transparency and confidence-building measures in outer space activities", the United States stated that that did not mean that it had changed its long-standing support of voluntary transparency and confidence-building measures in outer space, but that United States support for such measures ended where they were linked to legally binding measures. (A/C.1/PV.24)

[102] For statements during the thematic debate on other disarmament issues and international security, including cyber issues, see verbatim records A/C.1/74/PV.16-17.

[103] A/68/98 and A/70/174.

that those groups were both of utility and could serve complementary functions, but, despite efforts to merge the resolutions, the First Committee adopted each by vote.[104]

As in previous years, the Committee adopted three annual resolutions sponsored by the Non-Aligned Movement: the resolution entitled "Observance of environmental norms in the drafting and implementation of agreements on disarmament and arms control" (74/52) without a vote; the resolution entitled "Promotion of multilateralism in the area of disarmament and non-proliferation" (74/55) by a vote of 124 to 4, with 52 abstentions; and the resolution entitled "Relationship between disarmament and development" (74/57) without a vote.

The Committee also adopted, without a vote, a new resolution entitled "Youth, disarmament and non-proliferation" (74/64), by which the General Assembly encouraged Member States, the United Nations, relevant specialized agencies and regional and subregional organizations to promote the meaningful and inclusive participation of young people in discussions in the field of disarmament and non-proliferation, including through dialogue. Referring in its preamble to the Secretary-General's Agenda for Disarmament, in which he described the young generation as the ultimate force for change and committed to actions promoting youth engagement, the Assembly requested the Secretary-General to seek specific measures to promote the meaningful and inclusive participation and empowerment of youth on disarmament and non-proliferation issues.

As in previous sessions of the First Committee, Member States expressed deep concern over the prolonged paralysis in the Conference on Disarmament and the United Nations Disarmament Commission and stressed the need to revitalize the work of the disarmament machinery.[105] In particular, States expressed concern about the cancellation of the Disarmament Commission's 2019 substantive session due to the non-issuance of a visa to the head of the Russian delegation. Although many States concurred with the Russian Federation on the importance of unimpeded access to the United Nations Headquarters and called for an early resolution of the issue of visas, they did not necessarily agree with the country's insistence that the issue should be discussed by the First Committee or that the Committee and the Disarmament Commission should be held in Geneva or Vienna. In that regard, States expressed the view that the Host Country Committee

---

[104] The resolution entitled "Developments in the field of information and telecommunications in the context of international security" (74/29) was adopted by the First Committee by a vote of 124 to 6 with 48 abstentions and the General Assembly by a vote of 129 to 6, with 45 abstentions. The resolution entitled "Advancing responsible State behaviour in cyberspace in the context of international security" (74/28) was adopted by the First Committee by a vote of 161 to 10, with 8 abstentions, and the General Assembly by a vote of 163 to 10, with 6 abstentions.

[105] For statements during the thematic debate on the disarmament machinery, see verbatim record A/C.1/74/PV.21.

and the Sixth Committee should deal with the issue while the First Committee and the Disarmament Commission should hold their sessions in New York.

In a bid to ensure that the Disarmament Commission would hold its substantive session in 2020, Australia and Hungary introduced a draft decision entitled "2020 session of the Disarmament Commission".[106] The Russian Federation then introduced an amendment[107] to a revised draft decision[108] in order to condition the convening of the session on the resolution of visa issues. The Russian Federation also introduced a draft decision entitled "Improving the effectiveness of work of the First Committee", requesting the Secretary-General to report on compliance with the Host Country Agreement and on his effort to ensure such compliance, as well as providing for the General Assembly to consider convening the Committee's 2020 session in Geneva or Vienna if the visa issue was not resolved.[109]

The Russian Federation did not succeed in securing enough votes for either proposal.[110] In early December, the Russian Federation again introduced the same draft decision[111] on the work of the First Committee and the same amendment[112] to the decision on the 2020 session of the Disarmament Commission for consideration by the General Assembly at its plenary meeting on 12 December, but the Assembly rejected both proposals.[113]

In 2019, there was little progress towards the convening of the fourth special session of the General Assembly devoted to disarmament. The Committee adopted the annual draft resolution entitled "Convening of the fourth special session of the General Assembly devoted to disarmament" (74/56), introduced by Indonesia on behalf of the Non-Aligned Movement, whereby the General Assembly encouraged Member States to continue consultations on the next steps for the convening of the fourth special session.[114]

---

[106] A/C.1/74/L.52.

[107] A/C.1/74/L.62.

[108] A/C.1/74/L.52/Rev.1.

[109] A/C.1/74/L.57/Rev.1.

[110] The Russian draft decision on the work of the First Committee was defeated by a vote of 69 to 18, with 72 abstentions. Its amendment to the draft decision on the 2020 session of the Disarmament Commission was also defeated by a vote of 66 to 21, with 59 abstentions. The Committee adopted this decision (74/511) without a vote, although the Russian Federation requested separate votes for two operative paragraphs and voted against them.

[111] A/74/L.28.

[112] A/74/L.29.

[113] The draft decision entitled "Improving the effectiveness of the work of the First Committee" was rejected by a vote of 66 to 17, with 63 abstentions. The draft amendment to the draft decision entitled "The 2020 session of the Disarmament Commission" was rejected by a vote of 65 to 18, with 63 abstentions.

[114] In 2017, the Open-ended Working Group on the fourth special session of the General Assembly devoted to disarmament adopted by consensus the recommendation on the objectives and the agenda of the fourth session. See the Working Group's report (A/AC.268/2017/2).

United Nations Disarmament Commission

The United Nations Disarmament Commission was unable to hold its substantive session in 2019. The Chair of the 2018 session of the Commission, Gillian Bird (Australia), opened the 2019 organizational session on 14 February, but immediately suspended it over unspecified technical issues. When she resumed the session on 2 April to deal with organizational matters, including the election of its Chair and officers for 2019, the Russian Federation objected to proceeding with the adoption of the organizational session's agenda.

It stated that the United States, in violation of its obligations under article 4 of the Agreement between the United Nations and the United States of America regarding the Headquarters of the United Nations of 1947 (United Nations Headquarters Agreement), was actively hindering the arrival of the head of the Russian delegation in New York to participate in the Commission's substantive session.[115] Invoking many years of consensus by the Commission on procedural and substantive decisions, the Russian Federation expressed opposition to adopting the agenda for the organizational session and requested to delay the session, so the Secretariat could prepare a specific proposal on options to address the concerns of the Russian Federation or so the substantive session could be moved to Geneva, Vienna or any country that could fulfil its obligations to the Organization. The Russian Federation further noted that if the situation regarding the head of the Russian delegation was not resolved, the delegation would have to oppose any procedural or substantive decisions of the Commission's organizational and substantive sessions.

Belarus and the Syrian Arab Republic supported the request of the Russian Federation to postpone the organizational meeting until the issue raised by the Russian Federation was resolved. The two countries concurred that the Commission should take decisions by consensus, in line with many years in which it had followed that practice in its work. In that connection, they reminded the Commission that consensus did not exist at that point.

The Chair then highlighted a paragraph of the final document of the first special session of the General Assembly devoted to disarmament, elaborating the Commission's working methods.[116] In that context, she pointed out that the draft

---

The Committee adopted the eponymous resolution (74/56) by a vote of 175 to none, with 3 abstentions.

[115] The Russian Federation noted that in response to its many attempts to address the issue bilaterally, the Russian Federation received one response: that the leading Russian expert in multilateral disarmament would not receive a visa to the United States under any circumstances and the Russian Federation needed to look for another representative. (A/CN.10/PV.375)

[116] The Chair read out paragraph 118 of the final document, which sets out: "The Disarmament Commission shall function under the rules of procedure relating to the committees of the General Assembly with such modifications as the Commission may deem necessary and shall make every effort to ensure that, in so far as possible, decisions on substantive issues be adopted by consensus."

agenda for the organizational session was a procedural matter and expressed hope that the Commission would agree to allow the organizational session to proceed.

However, the Russian Federation said that the question of facilitating the participation of the head of its delegation in the session's work was indeed a substantive issue. Stressing the need to undertake that work by consensus, it insisted on postponing the meeting to provide the Secretariat with time to find a solution. Responding both to assurances from the Chair that the concerns and issues of the Russian Federation would be reflected in the record and to an attempt she made to adopt the organizational meeting's agenda, the Russian Federation observed that the Chair was creating an unprecedented situation that broke with consensus, and it demanded a vote by all delegations on the question of whether consensus was the basis of the Commission's work.[117]

The United States acknowledged the concerns of the Russian Federation but framed them as a bilateral matter that should not slow down the Commission's work, particularly its adoption of an agenda for the organizational session that would enable the body to prepare for the start of substantive discussions the following week. The United States therefore recommended that the Russian Federation work bilaterally on the meeting's margins to seek a way forward on the visa matter, allowing the Commission to convene and take all the decisions necessary to prepare for the substantive session.[118]

Recalling the obligations of the United States as host country of the United Nations Headquarters, pursuant to the United Nations Headquarters Agreement,[119] the Russian Federation stressed that bilateral relations with the United States were not at issue and, rather, the United States had obligations it needed to fulfil. The only possible solution, the Russian Federation insisted, was to postpone the meeting to a later date so that the United States might duly grant a visa to the Russian representative, thereby enabling the Russian Federation to fully participate in the work of the session.

Referring to the Russian Federation's proposal to postpone the organizational meeting, the Chair stressed that a failure to adopt the draft agenda for the

---

[117] In addition to Belarus and the Syrian Arab Republic, Cuba and Nicaragua supported the Russian request, expressing the belief that it was important that all delegations be duly represented in the Disarmament Commission. Insisting that the host country abide by its obligations pursuant to the United Nations Headquarters Agreement and the 1961 Vienna Convention on Diplomatic Relations, Cuba noted that, as a State that had been affected by those issues, Cuba rejected the arbitrary and selective application of conditions by the host country in abiding by the United Nations Headquarters Agreement, in particular with regard to delaying or refusing to grant visas to representatives of Member States to participate in the work of the Commission. (A/CN.10/PV.375)

[118] The United States stressed that its permanent mission in New York had not been formally informed of the issue until that day, despite what might have occurred between the United States capital and its embassy in Moscow. (A/CN.10/PV.375)

[119] The Russian Federation stated that the provisions of Section 11 shall be applicable irrespective of the relations existing between the Governments of the persons referred to in that section and the Government of the United States." (A/CN.10/PV.375)

organizational session and take the actions set out therein would, in her view, put the substantive session at risk.[120] Nonetheless, the Commission decided to postpone the organizational session.

In the absence of the necessary organizational decisions, the United Nations Disarmament Commission was unable to begin its substantive session on 8 April as requested by the General Assembly in its resolution 73/82 of 5 December 2018. The Chair of the 2018 session of the Commission, together with the Chair-designate of its 2019 session, Katalin Bogyay (Hungary), continued to hold consultations on finding a way forward, with a view to commencing its substantive session. After holding informal consultations on organizational matters on 12 April, the outgoing Chair informed Member States that there did not appear to be sufficient support for convening the organizational meeting in coming days but added that she was encouraged by the support for proceeding with informal consultations on the substantive agenda items agreed upon for the current three-year cycle.[121]

Following consultations with the Chair-designate, the Chair informed Member States that under her responsibility as Chair, she had requested Diedre Mills (Jamaica), Chair of Working Group I, and Jeroen Cooreman (Belgium), Chair of Working Group II,[122] to facilitate informal discussions on the Commission's substantive agenda items: (a) agenda item 4, entitled "Recommendations for achieving the objective of nuclear disarmament and non-proliferation of nuclear weapons"; and (b) agenda item 5, entitled "Preparation of recommendations to promote the practical implementation of transparency and confidence-building measures in outer space activities with the goal of preventing an arms race in outer space, in accordance with the recommendations set out in the report of the Group of Governmental Experts on Transparency and Confidence-Building Measures in Outer Space Activities".[123] Thus, with the facilitation of the Chairs of the two working groups and pursuant to the schedule of meetings circulated by the Chair, Member States held a series of informal meetings aimed at advancing discussions on the two substantive agenda items.

---

[120] The Chair made the point that, if the Commission was unable to proceed with adopting its draft agenda for its organizational session that day, it would be unable to elect a Chair and other officers or to adopt the agenda for its substantive meetings, which were due to begin the following Monday.

[121] At its organizational session on 21 February 2018, the Disarmament Commission decided that the agenda for its substantive session in 2018 should serve for the period 2018–2020. (A/73/42)

[122] At its 369th meeting, on 2 April 2018, the Disarmament Commission elected Diedre Mills (Jamaica) as Chair of Working Group I, on agenda item 4, and Jeroen Cooreman (Belgium) as Chair of Working Group II, on agenda item 5. (A/73/42)

[123] In her communication with Member States, the Chair clarified that convening those informal discussions on substantive issues would allow the experts who were currently in New York to take advantage of the technical resources assigned to the current session of the Commission and make progress in preparing on an informal basis for the 2020 substantive session. She also reiterated that such discussions set no precedent for the Commission's future work.

Meanwhile, despite continued consultations by the Chair of the 2018 session, it became evident that the Commission would not be able to convene its substantive session. On 24 April, the Chair informed Member States that several attempts to convene organizational meetings had been inconclusive, and it had become clear that the Commission could not fulfil the mandate it had received from the General Assembly by resolution 73/82 of 5 December 2018. She added that her delegation (Australia), with the support of the Chair-designate (Hungary) and in consultation with all Member States, intended to submit to the First Committee at its seventy-fourth session a draft resolution or decision on the Disarmament Commission that would establish its mandate for 2020. (For more information, see the section on the First Committee in this chapter.)

Although the Commission held no substantive session in 2019, Member States submitted two working papers. On 25 April, Nigeria, on behalf of the African Group, circulated a working paper entitled "Recommendations to promote the practical implementation of transparency and confidence-building measures in outer space activities with the goal of preventing an arms race in outer space, in accordance with the recommendations set out in the report of the Group of Governmental Experts on Transparency and Confidence-Building Measures in Outer Space Activities".[124] The Group annexed to that working paper the text of a draft report of the Group of Governmental Experts on Further Practical Measures for the Prevention of an Arms Race in Outer Space,[125] prompting concerns among some States as the Group had not ultimately adopted it. On 30 April, the United States submitted a working paper entitled "Concerns of the United States of America regarding the publication of non-consensus reports of the Group of Governmental Experts on further practical measures for the prevention of an arms race in outer space", expressing regret that one State had decided to publish a working paper containing the non-consensus report.[126]

Conference on Disarmament

Recognized by the General Assembly[127] in 1978 and succeeding other Geneva-based disarmament forums, the Conference on Disarmament negotiated multilateral disarmament treaties including the Nuclear Non-Proliferation Treaty,

---

[124] A/CN.10/2019/WP.1.

[125] The Group of Governmental Experts on further practical measures for the prevention of an arms race in outer space was established by the General Assembly pursuant to its resolution 72/250 of 24 December 2017.

[126] In its working paper, the United States said that it could not support the submission or consideration of a working paper that included the non-consensus work of the Group of Governmental Experts. The United States further noted that the Group had not reached consensus owing to concerns that the report was not balanced and did not reflect the substantive discussions of the Group. (A/CN.10/2019/WP.2)

[127] The Conference was established in 1979 as the single multilateral disarmament negotiating forum of the international community, following the first special session of the General Assembly devoted to disarmament.

Multilateral treaties and conventions negotiated in and outside of the Conference on Disarmament

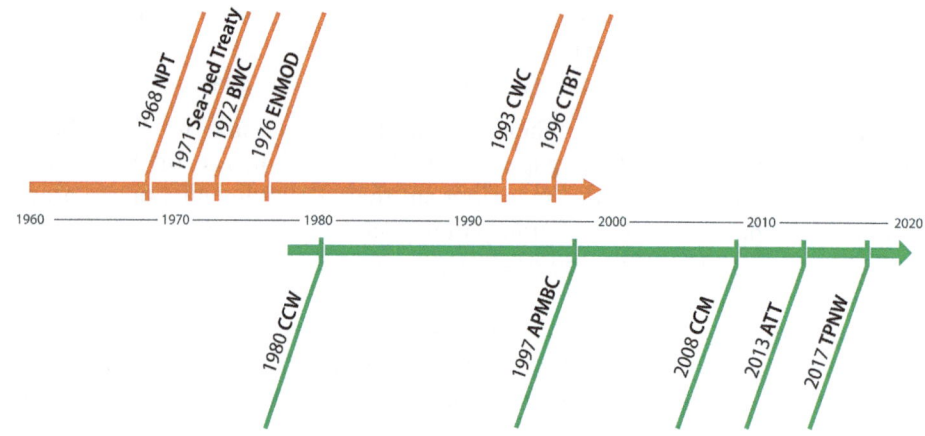

Negotiated in the Conference on Disarmament (or a predecessor)

1968 NPT
1971 Sea-bed Treaty
1972 BWC
1976 ENMOD
1993 CWC
1996 CTBT

1960 — 1970 — 1980 — 1990 — 2000 — 2010 — 2020

1980 CCW
1997 APMBC
2008 CCM
2013 ATT
2017 TPNW

Negotiated in other forums

ATT	Arms Trade Treaty	CTBT	Comprehensive Nuclear-Test-Ban Treaty
APMBC	Anti-Personnel Mine Ban Convention	CWC	Chemical Weapons Convention
BWC	Biological Weapons Convention	ENMOD	Convention on Environmental Modification Techniques
CCM	Convention on Cluster Munitions	NPT	Treaty on the Non-Proliferation of Nuclear Weapons
CCW	Convention on Certain Conventional Weapons	TPNW	Treaty on the Prohibition of Nuclear Weapons

Predecessor bodies: Ten-Nation Committee on Disarmament (1960), Eighteen-Nation Committee on Disarmament (1962–1969), Conference of the Committee on Disarmament (1969–1978), Committee on Disarmament (1979–1984)

The international community has maintained a single negotiating body since the 1960s for Governments to develop and agree on new multilateral disarmament treaties that are open to all States. Today's forum is called the Conference on Disarmament and offers a venue for its member States to regularly meet to pursue new disarmament measures by consensus.

The Conference on Disarmament in Geneva built on the legacy of its predecessor institutions well into the 1990s, most notably through the development of the Chemical Weapons Convention and the Comprehensive Nuclear-Test-Ban Treaty. Since 1996, the body has not negotiated new legal instruments.

Countries have initiated ad-hoc processes to negotiate a treaty regulating the conventional arms trade as well as separate bans on landmines, cluster munitions and nuclear weapons.

the Biological Weapons Convention, the Chemical Weapons Convention and the Comprehensive Nuclear-Test-Ban Treaty.

2019 session of the Conference on Disarmament

In a statement opening the session, Michael Møller, then Secretary-General of the Conference, said current realities made a compelling case for a renewed sense of urgency, as well as a collective commitment and determination, in pursuing disarmament. He pointed to the progress that the Conference had achieved the previous year, when it established five subsidiary bodies, and he expressed hope that the resulting momentum would continue in future sessions.[128]

The High Representative for Disarmament Affairs delivered a video message on 7 February, briefing the Conference on the progress of consultations and implementation of the Secretary-General's Agenda for Disarmament and calling on member States to exert "every effort to burnish the credibility of that forum for multilateral engagement at a time in which no discernible alternatives are in sight and disarmament efforts are so sorely needed".[129]

The Conference held its high-level segment from 25 to 27 February under the presidency of the United Kingdom. Thirty-six dignitaries spoke,[130] an increase of 39 per cent over 2018. The United Nations Secretary-General addressed the Conference on 25 February, stating that "key components of the international arms control architecture are collapsing" and urging member States "in the strongest possible terms to take decisive action to safeguard and preserve the existing system through dialogue that will help restore trust". He called on the member States to explore "a new vision for arms control in the complex international security environment of today".[131]

On 14 August, Tatiana Valovaya, the new Secretary-General of the Conference,[132] addressed the forum for the first time. Speaking at the 1517th plenary meeting, she said that the Conference must move forward to deliver on its mandate to negotiate and agree new instruments governing complex, sensitive and urgent issues of national and international security, issues impacting every living being on the planet. She also stressed the need for greater gender balance in the field of disarmament.[133]

---

[128] CD/PV.1475.

[129] CD/PV.1479.

[130] The dignitaries comprised 14 ministers; 18 deputy, vice or assistant ministers; and 4 ambassadors.

[131] Secretary-General's remarks to the Conference on Disarmament, Geneva, 25 February 2019.

[132] On 6 August, Tatiana Valovaya, the incoming Director-General of the United Nations Office at Geneva, was nominated by the United Nations Secretary-General and appointed by the member States of the Conference as the Secretary-General of the Conference on Disarmament, in accordance with rule 13 of the Rules of Procedure.

[133] CD/PV.1517.

Despite the efforts of three out of the six presidents of the 2019 session—Ukraine, the United Kingdom, the United States, the Bolivarian Republic of Venezuela, Viet Nam and Zimbabwe—to identify agreeable language for a programme of work that would allow the resumption of negotiations, the Conference could not achieve consensus on a text. Meanwhile, interest in the Conference increased: 50 non-member States requested to participate in 2019 as observers, the highest number in the past two decades.

During the first presidency from 21 January to 15 February, the Conference adopted the agenda[134] for its 2019 session. At the 1476th plenary meeting, the President, Yurii Klymenko (Ukraine), introduced a proposal[135] for a programme of work for the session. Following intensive consultations and plenary discussions, the President circulated a second revised version[136] of the proposal, suggesting negotiation mandates for agenda items 1 to 4[137] and the establishment of two coordinators, one on membership expansion and one on working methods. The members of the Conference could not reach agreement on that proposal.

During the second presidency from 18 February to 15 March, the President, Aidan Liddle (United Kingdom), presented a draft decision[138] subsequently circulated in two revised versions.[139] Noting that an absence of preparatory work meant the Conference had only a remote prospect of adopting a programme of work with meaningful negotiating mandates, the President proposed establishing new subsidiary bodies and special coordinators to structure its 2019 work to build on the previous year's activities, deepen the understanding of the technical and political issues crucial for negotiations, and seek common ground on a possible mandate and structure for negotiations. He proposed giving the subsidiary bodies clearer and more focused mandates than in 2018, with each built around one of the Conference's four core issues: nuclear disarmament, fissile material, preventing an arms race in outer space, and negative security assurances. One of two proposed special coordinators would examine the impact of emerging issues and new technologies on the Conference agenda, building on work by Subsidiary Body 5 in 2018, while the second special coordinator would examine the question of working methods and Conference membership. Despite the efforts of the President and intense discussions among the member States, the Conference could not agree on that proposal.

Robert Wood (United States), who held the third presidency from 18 March to 24 May, organized four panel discussions with participation by outside experts.

---

[134] CD/2153.

[135] CD/WP.618.

[136] CD/2172.

[137] Respectively, agenda items 1 to 4 are entitled "Cessation of the nuclear arms race and nuclear disarmament", "Prevention of nuclear war, including all related matters", "Prevention of an arms race in outer space" and "Effective international arrangements to assure non-nuclear-weapon States against the use or threat of use of nuclear weapons".

[138] CD/WP.619.

[139] See CD/2166 for the final revised draft.

Each of the four discussions was devoted to a substantive topic: substantive challenges facing arms control, non-proliferation and disarmament;[140] creating the environment for nuclear disarmament;[141] deterrence;[142] and transparency.[143]

Under the fourth presidency from 27 May to 21 June, Jorge Valero (Bolivarian Republic of Venezuela) held intensive consultations on a proposed programme of work,[144] in which he suggested negotiation mandates on agenda items 1 to 4, but he took no further action as consensus seemed out of reach. The President of the Bolivarian Republic of Venezuela also convened three plenary meetings respectively covering agenda items 1 and 2, item 3 and items 5, 6 and 7.[145]

Duong Chi Dung (Viet Nam), who held the fifth presidency from 24 June to 16 August, circulated a draft programme of work,[146] which, in recognition of the efforts of the previous year's subsidiary bodies, proposed the establishment of four working groups respectively dedicated to agenda items 1 to 4, as well as a fifth working group on agenda items 5 to 7. With the aim of preparing the ground for the adoption of a programme of work in 2020, the President also introduced the draft decision as a set of recommended elements for consideration for future programmes of work, without prejudice to any future decisions by the Conference.[147] That text included suggestions for future programmes of work to incorporate a schedule of activities, establish subsidiary bodies on the agenda items of the Conference and take into consideration possible mechanisms to discuss other issues, including the improved and effective functioning of the Conference.[148]

That second draft decision by the fifth President triggered a discussion on the framework and possible elements for a programme of work, during which the Netherlands submitted a working paper entitled "Back to basics".[149] By that working paper, the Netherlands posited that the Conference should return to the original conceptualization of the programme of work simply as a planning tool in which the allocation of time for each agenda item was set for the session ahead. At the end of his tenure, Mr. Duong summarized his observation of that discussion in a statement,[150] delivered in his capacity as the President of the Conference.

---

[140] CD/PV.1479.

[141] CD/PV.1499.

[142] CD/PV.1500.

[143] CD/PV.1501.

[144] CD/2162.

[145] Respectively, agenda items 5 to 7 are entitled "New types of weapons of mass destruction and new systems of such weapons; radiological weapons", "Comprehensive programme of disarmament" and "Transparency in armaments".

[146] CD/2173.

[147] CD/2174.

[148] Under the fifth Presidency, the Conference heard remarks from Lim Jock Hoi, Secretary-General of the Association of Southeast Asian Nations and Lassina Zerbo, Executive Secretary of the Preparatory Commission for the Comprehensive Nuclear-Test-Ban Treaty Organization.

[149] CD/2165.

[150] CD/2175.

Taonga Mushayavanhu (Zimbabwe), the sixth and final President of the 2019 session, successfully organized the negotiation of the final report of the Conference to the seventy-fourth session of the General Assembly.[151] At the 1522nd plenary meeting on 3 September, the member States of the Conference adopted the report by consensus.

Advisory Board on Disarmament Matters

The Advisory Board on Disarmament Matters held its seventy-first session in Geneva from 30 January to 1 February and its seventy-second session in New York from 26 to 28 June, dealing with two substantive agenda items: "Measures to mitigate civilian harm resulting from contemporary armed conflict"; and "The role of the disarmament, arms control and non-proliferation regime in managing strategic competition and building trust". In July, the Secretary-General submitted a report to the General Assembly summarizing the Board's deliberations and recommendations.[152]

In its discussions on measures to mitigate civilian harm resulting from contemporary armed conflict, the Board considered a myriad of factors, including the urbanization of conflict and its disproportionate impact on women, children and minority groups; the shift from State to non-State actors as the main combatants; the fact that small arms and light weapons from both licit and illicit sources were becoming a major driver of harm done to civilians; the increasing impact of new technologies; and the protraction of armed conflict. At its seventy-first session, the Board engaged with a panel of experts[153] on relevant trends. During the following session, the International Committee of the Red Cross gave a presentation in which it stressed, inter alia, the following points: (a) the difficult and delicate balance between military necessity and the principle of humanity and (b) the fundamentally pragmatic and reasonable nature of international humanitarian law.

The Board noted that the need to protect civilian populations from indiscriminate attacks featured prominently in the Secretary-General's Agenda for Disarmament and used seven categories to frame its review and recommendations.

With regard to the first category, on avoiding the use of explosive weapons in populated areas, the Board's suggestions included exploring a legislative basis for a report of the Secretary-General that would encourage further debate in the General Assembly, potentially resulting in relevant United Nations entities being tasked to further develop criteria, indicators and appropriate methodologies to measure the reverberating civilian impacts.

---

[151] CD/2179.

[152] A/74/247.

[153] The panel included representatives of the non-governmental organization Article 36, the International Committee of the Red Cross, the Office for the Coordination of Humanitarian Affairs and the United Nations Institute for Disarmament Research.

Looking at the second category, concerning sharing policy and practice to protect civilians, the Board noted that accurate reporting and collection of data were required to raise awareness and facilitate sharing. It recommended developing a systematic approach, including consistent methodologies, to pooling data on the effects of the use of explosive weapons in populated areas, and it expressed support for efforts to collect data on the economic impact in order to demonstrate the multi-dimensional impact on human lives. Furthermore, the Board's members suggested exploring ways to publish and actively communicate data, while also noting their belief that the impact of existing mitigation approaches should be examined.

Considering the third category, on strengthening inter-agency coordination on improvised explosive devices, the Board shared its view that accurate and comprehensive statistics were required to support the establishment of a whole-of-system approach.

On the fourth category, on developing common standards for armed uncrewed aerial vehicles, the Board recommended that, given the current lack of interest among Member States in exploring regulatory frameworks, consideration could be given to exploring the scope of existing arrangements for arms export control to incorporate information on the accountable transfer, holding and use of such weapon systems.

Reviewing the fifth category, concerning the establishment of the Saving Lives Entity, a dedicated trust fund on small arms, the Board supported the concept and underscored the importance of national capacity-building on weapons and ammunition management. The Board therefore recommended developing criteria and guidance for country-level proposals, as well as giving consideration to ensuring a sufficient United Nations pool of expertise that could support the development and implementation of projects.

Addressing the sixth category, on the gendered impact of arms, the Board recommended that disarmament issues be systematically integrated in the meetings of the women, peace and security agenda. It further recommended encouraging States parties to the Arms Trade Treaty to provide, in their national reports on implementation, detailed information responding to the Treaty's criteria on gender. The Board further recommended mainstreaming gender in disarmament issues in the agenda of the United Nations Entity for Gender Equality and the Empowerment of Women, as well as continuing to address gendered aspects of disarmament in the Secretary-General's report on the work of the Organization.

Looking at the seventh category, concerning building understanding on the impact of arms on conflict management", the Board considered field-level experiences and insights to be a requirement for better understanding the impact of arms that should be integrated into assessments, risk analyses and conflict prevention activities. Emphasizing the adverse impact of arms on development, it encouraged the Secretary-General to ensure that arms and arms control issues were mainstreamed across all United Nations entities.

Discussing its second substantive agenda item, "The role of the disarmament, arms control and non-proliferation regime in managing strategic competition and building trust", the Board noted its obligation to highlight the importance of preserving and bolstering the overall structure of arms control efforts, and it underlined that it was especially important for the Secretary-General to continue to promote and defend the essential principles of disarmament and arms control. Considering the urgent need for multilateral efforts to reduce the risk of use of nuclear weapons, the Board found that such efforts must be a priority for the Review Conference of the Nuclear Non-Proliferation Treaty. In addition, the Board found that the impact of new technologies, including cyberspace, outer space and artificial intelligence, should be fully taken into consideration.

The Board also reaffirmed the goals outlined in the Secretary-General's Agenda for Disarmament, expressed full support for the implementation plan crafted by the Office for Disarmament Affairs and urged the continuance of ongoing efforts to that end. Despite challenges posed by increasing competition among the major powers and the ongoing deterioration of existing disarmament, non-proliferation and arms control arrangements, the Board recognized four short-term opportunities for the Secretary-General to keep the implementation of part II of his agenda ("Disarmament to Save Humanity") moving forward— namely, the Nuclear Non-Proliferation Treaty Review Conference, the Conference on the Establishment of a Middle East Zone Free of Nuclear Weapons and All Other Weapons of Mass Destruction, the continued high-level diplomatic engagement with the Democratic People's Republic of Korea and groups of governmental experts providing an important means of facilitating discussion and helping to manage complex challenges.

The Board identified four recommendations to the Secretary-General: (a) continuing to engage with high-level officials of the five permanent members of the Security Council on the need for cooperation to, inter alia, reduce strategic competition and nuclear risks; (b) continuing to encourage support for and participation in the Conference on the Establishment of a Middle East Zone Free of Nuclear Weapons and All Other Weapons of Mass Destruction by all States in the region, the five permanent Security Council members and organizations; (c) initiating new expert-level engagement through the High Representative for Disarmament Affairs to identify actions; and (d) ensuring that action point 32 of the Agenda for Disarmament, which calls for a study of "ways to better coordinate and integrate the work and expertise among the various disarmament bodies", includes a review of the state of existing disarmament machinery.

As the Board of Trustees of the United Nations Institute for Disarmament Research, the Board welcomed the Institute's investment in communications and its leadership on several Agenda actions, including efforts to reduce the risk of use of nuclear weapons. The Board also endorsed the Institute's commitment to increased activities outside Geneva and New York. The Board's members positively reviewed a number of aspects of the Institute's work—particularly its focus on expanding partnerships to support outreach, diversity and impact—and suggested potential entry points for new partnerships, including with key relevant regional organizations. The Board also considered and approved the report of the Director on the activities of the Institute and the proposed programme of work and financial plan. Highlighting 2020 as the Institute's fortieth anniversary, the Board encouraged the Institute to support dialogue and new thinking on elements that might constitute effective arms control in the future.

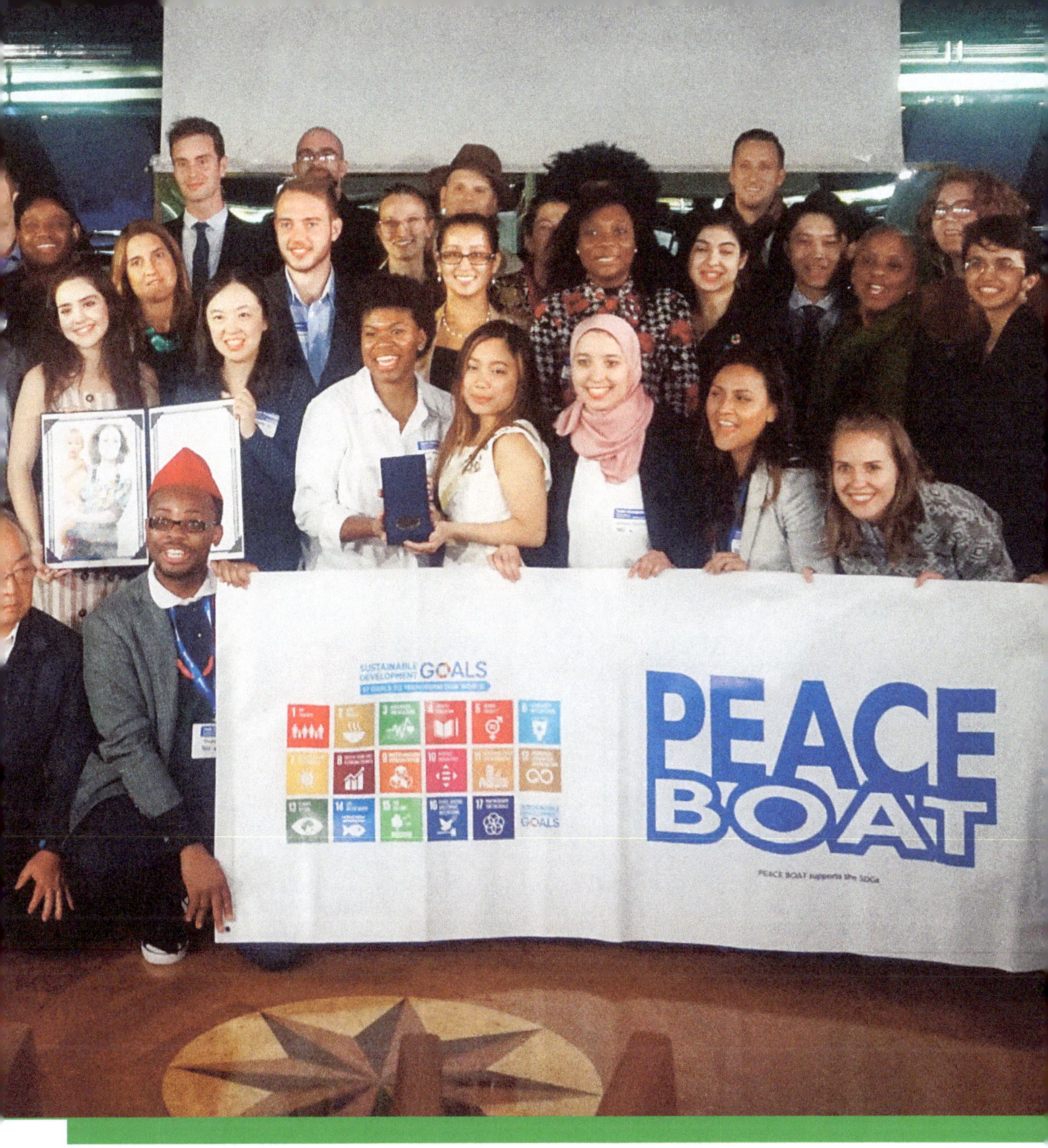

chapter

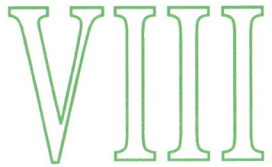

VIII Information and outreach

Participants of the event "Youth Champions for Securing our Common Future", organized by the United Nations Office for Disarmament Affairs and the non-governmental organization Peace Boat. The event, held in New York on 11 October 2019, was part of the Youth4Disarmament initiative and featured keynote speakers, educational panel discussions, workshops and musical performances. The participating "Youth Champions" had the opportunity to engage with United Nations officials, diplomats and civil society representatives working towards disarmament worldwide.

CHAPTER VIII

Information and outreach

In times of crisis, we achieve success only when we work together.

IZUMI NAKAMITSU, UNITED NATIONS HIGH REPRESENTATIVE FOR DISARMAMENT AFFAIRS[1]

Developments and trends, 2019

THROUGH ITS DISARMAMENT INFORMATION PROGRAMME, the United Nations Office for Disarmament Affairs continued to provide Member States, the diplomatic community, non-governmental organizations and the public at large with unbiased, up-to-date and relevant information on multilateral disarmament, non-proliferation and arms control activities. In support of that objective, the Office issued the forty-third annual edition of its flagship publication, the *United Nations Disarmament Yearbook*, as well as a wide range of other written materials.

The publications of the Office for Disarmament Affairs included two new Occasional Papers, issued in October and November. In the first paper, *United Nations Efforts to Reduce Military Expenditures: A Historical Overview*, the Office provided a historical survey of efforts within the United Nations to reduce military spending as a distinct objective within broader negotiations on general and complete disarmament. The second Occasional Paper, *Anti-Personnel Mine Ban Convention: 20 Years of Saving Lives and Preventing Indiscriminate Harm*, contained analyses of achievements and shortfalls under the Convention during its first 20 years. Published with the aim of presenting diverse perspectives, the paper was composed of separate chapters written by pioneers and luminaries of the movement that helped achieve the adoption of the Convention and have committed themselves towards realizing its full implementation.

The Office also issued several ad hoc publications throughout the year, including *Hypersonic Weapons: A Challenge and Opportunity for Strategic Arms Control*, a study that considered novel long-range strike options under development by several nuclear-armed States in the context of potential implications for security, arms control and disarmament. The study, which was prepared on the recommendation of the Secretary-General's Advisory Board on Disarmament Matters, also included a review of options for addressing the implications of such weapons in a multilateral context. Meanwhile, in support

---

[1] Briefing to the Conference on Disarmament in Geneva (by video conference), New York, 7 February 2019.

of the United Nations Saf*er*Guard Programme, the Office issued three practical support guides for applying the International Ammunition Technical Guidelines.

The Office for Disarmament Affairs also issued a new edition of the series *Programmes Financed from Voluntary Contributions* for the period 2018–2019. In that publication, the Office showcased concrete results of its partnerships with donors, while also highlighting the vital role of such support in attaining important disarmament goals.

The Office promoted the disarmament goals of the United Nations through a variety of media outreach and engagement activities undertaken throughout the year. Those included interviews of the United Nations High Representative for Disarmament Affairs, Izumi Nakamitsu, with international television and print outlets on issues related to disarmament, non-proliferation and arms control. Furthermore, the High Representative published two opinion articles in which she advocated for efforts aimed at protecting civilians in combat zones and for placing gender issues at the heart of arms policy.

The main website of the Office for Disarmament Affairs (www.un.org/ disarmament), which received over half a million unique visitors in 2019, continued to provide a vital means of communication with Member States, civil society, academia and staff members. Redesigned during the year with a more contemporary aesthetic, the website continued to provide a vital channel for disseminating new information, updates, speeches and remarks in the area of multilateral disarmament, non-proliferation and arms control.

The International Day against Nuclear Tests on 29 August was commemorated at the United Nations in Vienna and New York, as well as in Nur-Sultan. The Executive Secretary of the Preparatory Commission for the Comprehensive Nuclear-Test-Ban Treaty Organization, Lassina Zerbo, joined six prominent authors from France and Madagascar in authoring an op-ed for the ratification of the Comprehensive Nuclear-Test-Ban Treaty by the eight remaining Annex 2 States, whose ratification is needed for the Treaty to enter into force. On 9 September, the Secretary-General and the President of the seventy-third session of the General Assembly delivered remarks during a commemoration held at the United Nations Headquarters.

The Office for Disarmament Affairs continued to support the General Assembly's annual commemoration on 26 September of the International Day for the Total Elimination of Nuclear Weapons, which Member States established in 2013 to call for the urgent commencement of negotiations to prohibit the possession, development, production, acquisition and testing of nuclear weapons. A high-level plenary meeting took place at the United Nations Headquarters to mark the International Day, with statements delivered by the President of the General Assembly's seventy-fourth session, the Secretary-General, delegates of 55 Member States, two permanent observers and two representatives of civil society.

In 2019, 25 diplomats and other officials participated in the United Nations Programme of Fellowships on Disarmament, bringing to 1,033 the total number of officials who had participated in the programme since its inception in 1978.

Meanwhile, as part of its continued engagement with Vienna-based organizations and entities, the Office for Disarmament Affairs continued to partner with the Organization for Security and Co-operation in Europe to administer the Scholarship for Peace and Security, a capacity-building and training programme that provided early-career professionals with 100 scholarships, 90 of which were reserved for women.

Another highlight of 2019 was the achievement of a number of milestones in efforts to increase youth engagement in the field of disarmament. By its resolution 74/64, adopted on 12 December, entitled "Youth, Disarmament and Non-proliferation", the General Assembly reaffirmed the important and positive contribution that young people can make in sustaining peace and security. In addition, the Office for Disarmament Affairs launched a new youth outreach initiative, called "Youth4Disarmament", with the aim of connecting geographically diverse young people with experts to learn about current international security challenges, the work of the United Nations and how they can be active participants.

Disarmament Information Programme

Print and e-publications

The *United Nations Disarmament Yearbook* continued to serve as the flagship publication of the Office. Part I of the 2018 edition was distributed in 2019 to permanent missions at the plenary meeting of the United Nations Disarmament Commission, and the circulation of Part II to delegations was timed to coincide with the general debate of the General Assembly First Committee. The Office also issued the latest versions of the Yearbook in PDF and e-book formats and announced their publication on Twitter and in the "Spotlight" section of its website.

The Office for Disarmament Affairs published two titles under its Occasional Papers series during the year. In October, it issued *United Nations Efforts to Reduce Military Expenditures: A Historical Overview* (No. 33), providing a historical survey of efforts within the United Nations to reduce military spending. In the paper, the following were considered: how discussions on reducing military budgets had evolved in disarmament forums over the last decades, including through early efforts to pursue the reduction of military spending throughout the cold-war period as a distinct objective of general and complete disarmament; the emergence of efforts related to promoting transparency on military matters; and the various workstreams carried out under the banner of the relationship between disarmament and development.

In November 2019, the Office launched a second Occasional Paper, *The Anti-Personnel Mine Ban Convention: 20 Years of Saving Lives and Preventing Indiscriminate Harm* (No. 34), during the Convention's Fourth Review Conference. Designed to bring together diverse perspectives on that key instrument of humanitarian disarmament, the edition was written by pioneers and luminaries of the movement that helped achieve the Convention and that committed themselves towards realizing the its full implementation. With each chapter focused on a different element of the Convention, the publication was intended to give readers insight into its accomplishments to date and, of equal emphasis, challenges that the world must still overcome to finally end the appalling suffering caused by landmines.

The Office also produced the publication *Hypersonic Weapons: A Challenge and Opportunity for Strategic Arms Control,* a study prepared on the recommendation of the Secretary-General's Advisory Board on Disarmament Matters. Matters considered in the study included novel long-range strike options under development by several nuclear-armed States in the context of their potential implications for security, arms control and disarmament, as well as possible ways to address those implications in a multilateral context. The publication provided overviews of the current state of technology, possible implications for international peace and security and for existing and future arms control and disarmament efforts, and different approaches States may pursue to address those challenges.

Meanwhile, in support of the SaferGuard Programme, the Office issued three practical support guides for applying the International Ammunition Technical Guidelines. The first of those publications, entitled *Critical Path Guide to the International Ammunition Technical Guidelines*, provided clarification about how the measures within the Guidelines were to be interpreted and applied in practice while explaining technical concepts and processes in a simple, clear and concise manner. The second publication, *A Guide to Developing National Standards for Ammunition Management*, was designed to assist State authorities in the development of national standards for ammunition management based on the Guidelines and towards implementing those standards across State institutions. The third publication in the series, *Utilizing the International Ammunition Technical Guidelines in Conflict-Affected and Low-Capacity Environments*, was developed by the United Nations Institute for Disarmament Research (UNIDIR) to provide practical information and guidance on improving basic ammunition stockpile safety and security and reducing risks in ammunition storage and processing facilities in particularly challenging contexts (for more information about the SaferGuard Programme and the Guidelines, see chap. III).

In October, the Office issued the 2018–2019 edition of *Programmes Financed from Voluntary Contributions*, a report showcasing the concrete results of partnerships between the Office and its donors and the essential role of such support in attaining important disarmament goals.

The extrabudgetary activities explored in that publication included, among several, support for informal high-level discussions, funded by Germany, on how to take forward priority areas under the second pillar of the Secretary-General's Agenda for Disarmament, "Disarmament that Saves Lives". Those discussions, held between government and independent experts at New York's Greentree Estate in February, covered areas such as addressing concerns relating to the use of explosive weapons in populated areas; integrating United Nations efforts to address problems posed by small arms and light weapons at the country and regional levels; increasing transparency, accountability and oversight on armed uncrewed aerial vehicles; and dealing with excessive and poorly maintained ammunition stockpiles.

The publication also described a European Union–funded initiative to convene three thematic seminars and four regional meetings aimed at helping to facilitate a successful outcome at the next quinquennial Review Conference of the Treaty on the Non-Proliferation of Nuclear Weapons. The aim of those discussions was to gain a better understanding of the priorities of States parties for the Treaty's current review cycle, support dialogue on potential obstacles to a consensus outcome, identify areas of common ground and build trust between States parties.

Meanwhile, the Office continued throughout the year to produce the "UNODA Update", an online chronicle of events and activities of the Office and of various disarmament forums. In 2019, the Office published 65 articles for the Update that it collated in a quarterly mode.

Also in 2019, the Office for Disarmament Affairs updated and expanded its series of two-page fact sheets on various disarmament, non-proliferation, arms control and related issues, providing readers with relevant and up-to-date information about those topics in a clear, easy-to-read format. The Office continued its biannual updates of 38 fact sheets in areas such as weapons of mass destruction, conventional arms, the disarmament machinery and regional disarmament, and it introduced a new fact sheet entitled "Disarmament and Youth".

For more information on the Office's 2019 publications, including those of its regional centres, see annex I to this chapter.

Websites

The websites of the Office for Disarmament Affairs remained a key resource for engagement with delegates, civil society stakeholders and the general public. Throughout the year, those websites continued to act as the Office's main channels for disseminating information in support of the Disarmament Information Programme.

In 2019, the Office redesigned its main website (www.un.org/disarmament) to give it a more modern look and feel. Through a streamlined menu, a dynamic "hero" banner and other new features, the new design assigned greater prominence to key disarmament-related issues and events, simplified access to information and reduced visual clutter, all while retaining previously hosted information and remaining responsive to fit multiple screen sizes. The Office continued to maintain the website as a source of the latest information, updates, speeches, remarks and news in the area of multilateral disarmament, non-proliferation and arms control, including through an updated "Spotlight" section that regularly featured new links to substantial articles and event information.

The main website of the Office for Disarmament Affairs received over half a million unique visitors in 2019 and continued to serve as a connecting point for Member States, non-governmental organizations, research institutes and interested individuals, as well as staff members. The Office continued its efforts to provide as much content as possible in the six official languages of the United Nations.

The Office for Disarmament Affairs also undertook initiatives during the year to revamp other aspects of its web presence. Those included, most notably, the development of a new platform[4] to serve as a central repository for information about meetings and processes serviced by the Office. That new platform, called the "UNODA Meetings Place", was launched in December 2019 with the aim of making it easier for staff and external users to find information on meetings and conferences, as well as relevant documents. Additionally, the Office updated its web page on global military expenditures entitled "The World is Overarmed and Peace is Underfunded" to include more current figures.

Databases

In 2019, the Office maintained and updated the following public databases:

- General Assembly Resolutions and Decisions, which hosted information about every disarmament-related resolution the Assembly had adopted since its fifty-second session

- Disarmament Treaties,[2] which housed information on disarmament-related treaties, including a list of their States parties and signatories

- Documents Library database, a specialized archive of United Nations disarmament-related documents

- Military Expenditures Database, which catalogued the national reports received from Member States

- The Global Reported Arms Trade—the United Nations Register of Conventional Arms, which presented data provided by Member States in an interactive information platform.

---

[2] Since 1978, the United Nations has published the status of multilateral arms regulation and disarmament agreements, presenting data on signatories, parties of relevant agreements and the texts of the agreements themselves.

International days

International Day against Nuclear Tests

The International Day against Nuclear Tests[3] on 29 August was commemorated at the United Nations in Vienna and New York, as well as in Nur-Sultan. At the ceremony in Kazakhstan, Lassina Zerbo, the Executive Secretary of the Preparatory Commission for the Comprehensive Nuclear-Test-Ban Treaty Organization, and Beibut Atamkulov, Foreign Minister of Kazakhstan, adopted a joint statement.[4] A separate commemorative ceremony, held at the headquarters of the Preparatory Commission in Vienna, included a reading of the joint statement, a message[5] delivered on behalf of the Secretary-General and an exhibition of winning entries from a children's art campaign launched in 2018 by the Preparatory Commission and Paz y Cooperación, a Spanish non-governmental organization.

Also on the occasion of the International Day, the Preparatory Commission's Executive Secretary joined six prominent authors from France and Madagascar in writing an op-ed[6] for the ratification of the Comprehensive Nuclear-Test-Ban Treaty by the eight remaining Annex 2 States, whose ratification is needed for the Treaty to enter into force. The appeal was published by the French newspaper *Libération* in the context of an international campaign launched earlier in 2019 by the Parliamentary Assembly of the Francophonie.

At the United Nations Headquarters in New York, a high-level plenary meeting of the General Assembly took place on 9 September to commemorate and promote the International Day. The opening ceremony included remarks by the Secretary-General and the President of the seventy-third session of the General Assembly, María Fernanda Espinosa Garcés (Ecuador), as well as a speech by the Preparatory Commission's Executive Secretary.

---

[3] Through resolution 64/35 of 2 December 2009, introduced at the initiative of Kazakhstan, the General Assembly declared 29 August the International Day against Nuclear Tests to commemorate the closure of the Semipalatinsk nuclear test site on 29 August 1991, to raise awareness on the effects of nuclear-weapon test explosions and to strengthen the international norm against all nuclear tests as a valuable step towards achieving a world free of nuclear weapons.

[4] Preparatory Commission for the Comprehensive Nuclear-Test-Ban Treaty Organization, "Joint Statement by H.E. Mr. Beibut Atamkulov, Minister of Foreign Affairs of the Republic of Kazakhstan, and Dr. Lassina Zerbo, Executive Secretary of the Comprehensive Nuclear-Test-Ban Treaty Organization", Nur-Sultan, 29 August 2019.

[5] António Guterres, Secretary-General, message on the occasion of the International Day against Nuclear Tests, New York, 29 August 2019.

[6] Bruno Tertrais, Michel Fanget, Jacques Krabal, Richard Rakotonirina, Christine Razanamahasoa, Lova Rinel and Lassina Zerbo, "En finir avec les essais nucléaires", *Libération*, 28 August 2019.

In his opening remarks[7] to the plenary, the Secretary-General pointed out the terrible toll unleashed on pristine environments and local populations around the world as a result of more than 2,000 nuclear tests conducted over the previous seven decades. While acknowledging the significant progress to date in banning nuclear tests, he reaffirmed his call for all States to sign and ratify the Comprehensive Nuclear-Test-Ban Treaty without further delay and for the remaining Annex 2 States to do so with a sense of urgency. The President of the General Assembly noted the reverberating multigenerational effects of nuclear tests on lives and livelihoods, human health and the environment, with profound impacts on all aspects of sustainable development. She concluded that working together in pursuit of a world free of nuclear weapons was the best way to honour the victims of nuclear bombs and tests and to ensure that no more join their ranks in the future.[8]

In his statement[9] to the plenary meeting, the Executive Secretary said that the International Day was an opportunity to send a clear and unmistakable message that the business of ending nuclear tests for all time remained unfinished. He expressed hope that the commemoration would help inspire countries to take concrete measures to finally reach the objective of a world free from the dangers of nuclear testing, including through the universalization of the Comprehensive Nuclear-Test-Ban Treaty.

International Day for the Total Elimination of Nuclear Weapons

The 2019 International Day for the Total Elimination of Nuclear Weapons[10] was observed on 26 September at a high-level plenary meeting convened by the President of the seventy-fourth session of the General Assembly, Tijjani Muhammad Bande (Nigeria). In his opening remarks,[11] the President of the

---

[7] António Guterres, Secretary-General, remarks to the high-level plenary meeting to commemorate and promote the International Day against Nuclear Tests, New York, 9 September 2019.

[8] María Fernanda Espinosa Garcés, President of the General Assembly at its seventy-third session, statement at the high-level meeting to commemorate and promote the International Day against Nuclear Tests, New York, 9 September 2019.

[9] Lassina Zerbo, Executive Secretary of the Preparatory Commission for the Comprehensive Nuclear-Test-Ban Treaty Organization, statement at the high-level meeting to commemorate and promote the International Day against Nuclear Tests, New York, 9 September 2019.

[10] The International Day was established in 2013 through an initiative of the Non-Aligned Movement following the first high-level meeting of the General Assembly on nuclear disarmament. The initiative was advanced under General Assembly resolutions 68/32 of 5 December 2013, 69/58 of 2 December 2014, 70/34 of 7 December 2015, 71/71 of 5 December 2016, 72/251 of 24 December 2017, 73/40 of 5 December 2018 and 74/54 of 12 December 2019, through which the General Assembly called for immediately commencing negotiations in the Conference on Disarmament on a comprehensive convention on nuclear weapons, as well as for enhancing public awareness and education about the threat of nuclear weapons and the necessity of their total elimination.

[11] Tijjani Muhammad Bande, President of the General Assembly at its seventy-fourth session, statement at the high-level plenary meeting of the General Assembly to commemorate and

General Assembly welcomed ideas on, inter alia, how to further mobilize international efforts towards achieving the common goal of a nuclear-weapon-free world. The Secretary-General, in separate remarks,[12] said he feared that past progress in reducing the danger of nuclear weapons was going in reverse. He urged that steps be taken in good faith to eliminate nuclear weapons, and he reiterated his call for all States to fully implement their nuclear non-proliferation and disarmament commitments.

The commemorative event included remarks from 55 Member States,[13] as well as the Holy See and the League of Arab States. Representatives of Peace Boat[14] and the International Campaign to Abolish Nuclear Weapons[15] also provided statements.

Commemoration of Hiroshima and Nagasaki

On 6 August, the High Representative for Disarmament Affairs participated in the seventy-fourth Hiroshima Peace Memorial Ceremony and delivered a message[16] from the Secretary-General. In his message, the Secretary-General paid homage to those who perished in the initial blast of the atomic bombing in Hiroshima and to the many whose lives were devastated by its lingering long-term effects. Highlighting a worsening international security environment, especially rising tensions between the nuclear-armed States, he warned that the disarmament and arms control institutions that had made the world a more secure place for decades were being called into question. While expressing his sincere gratitude to the hibakusha and the people of Hiroshima and Nagasaki for their dedication to remind the world about the human cost of nuclear war, the Secretary-General

---

promote the International Day for the Total Elimination of Nuclear Weapons, New York, 26 September 2019.

[12] António Guterres, Secretary-General, remarks at the high-level plenary meeting of the General Assembly to commemorate and promote the International Day for the Total Elimination of Nuclear Weapons, New York, 26 September 2019.

[13] Argentina, Algeria, Austria, Bahrain (on behalf of the Group of Arab States), Bangladesh, Belarus, Brazil, Cambodia, China, Colombia, Costa Rica, Côte d'Ivoire, Cuba, Ecuador, Egypt, El Salvador, Equatorial Guinea, Fiji, Ghana, Guatemala, Guyana, Honduras, India, Indonesia, Iraq, Iran (Islamic Republic of), Ireland, Japan, Kenya, Kazakhstan, Kyrgyzstan, Lebanon, Liechtenstein, Malaysia, Maldives, Mexico, Mongolia, Morocco, Nepal, New Zealand, Nicaragua, Nigeria, Peru, Philippines, Saint Vincent and the Grenadines, Samoa, South Africa, Sweden, Thailand, Trinidad and Tobago, Uganda (on behalf of the Group of African States), Ukraine, United Republic of Tanzania, Uruguay and Venezuela (Bolivarian Republic of) (on behalf of the Non-Aligned Movement). For their statements, see United Nations (PaperSmart), "International Day for Total Elimination of Nuclear Weapons", 26 September 2019.

[14] Peace Boat, statement at the high-level plenary meeting of the General Assembly to commemorate and promote the International Day for the Total Elimination of Nuclear Weapons, New York, 26 September 2019.

[15] International Campaign to Abolish Nuclear Weapons, statement at the high-level plenary meeting of the General Assembly to commemorate and promote the International Day for the Total Elimination of Nuclear Weapons, New York, 26 September 2019.

[16] António Guterres, Secretary-General, message at the at the Hiroshima Peace Memorial Service, Hiroshima, 6 August 2019.

called upon world leaders to intensify efforts towards the goal of nuclear disarmament. He reiterated his firm commitment to working with the hibakusha and all peoples of the world to realize the common vision of a world free of nuclear weapons.

On 9 August, the High Representative for Disarmament Affairs attended the seventy-fourth Nagasaki Peace Memorial Ceremony and delivered a message[17] from the Secretary-General. In his remarks, he paid tribute to the victims of the atomic bombing of Nagasaki in 1945 and recalled his emotional visit to the city in 2018, particularly his participation in the peace ceremony and the testimony of the hibakusha. Recognizing the persisting nuclear danger, the Secretary-General called on the international community to work together to strengthen cooperation, trust and transparency and to safeguard the security benefits of the existing treaties. He also sent a message to young people, future peacemakers of the world, that they were the ultimate force for change to secure our common future.

Media

In 2019, the Office promoted the disarmament goals of the United Nations through a variety of media outreach and engagement activities, many of them undertaken by the High Representative for Disarmament Affairs.

To promote the Secretary-General's Agenda for Disarmament on its one-year anniversary, the High Representative participated in a television interview with GCTV to discuss the Agenda's impact in the area of nuclear weapons and emerging technologies. The High Representative and senior staff of the Office also spoke about disarmament, non-proliferation and arms control issues in numerous other interviews with international television and print outlets, including Fuji TV, Huffington Post Japan, Jiji Press, the *Journal of International Affairs*, *Kommersant*, Kyodo News, *Mainichi Shimbun*, NHK, RIA Novosti, *Tokyo Shimbun* and the *Yomiuri Shimbun*.

Furthermore, the High Representative published two opinion articles highlighting actions that Member States and the public could take to address related concerns in a manner consistent with United Nations disarmament goals. She used those articles to respectively advocate for, inter alia, protecting civilians in combat zones[18] and placing gender issues at the heart of arms policy.[19]

Meanwhile, the High Representative took part in interviews and wrote several articles to commemorate the passing of Sadako Ogata, the former United Nations High Commissioner for Refugees, and promote her legacy of global cooperation. Those appearances and articles were featured by the Fusae Ichikawa

---

[17] António Guterres, Secretary-General, message at the Nagasaki National Peace Memorial Ceremony, Nagasaki, 9 August 2019.

[18] Izumi Nakamitsu, "Protecting civilians in combat zones", *Express Tribune*, 19 May 2019.

[19] Izumi Nakamitsu, "Let's not forget: gender must be at the heart of arms policy", Friends of Europe, 8 March 2019.

Center for Women and Governance, Jiji Press, Kyodo News, *Mainichi Shimbun*, NewsPicks, NHK, *Lancet* and *Tokyo Shimbun*.

The High Representative also participated in two informal media briefings: in Tokyo on 31 October, held on the margins of the Daiwa Capital Markets Conference in Tokyo; and in the Hague, Netherlands, on 26 November, as part of the conference entitled "Urgent Appeal for a Nuclear Weapons Free World". Questions during the press encounters addressed recent developments concerning, inter alia, disarmament, arms control, non-proliferation and the international security environment.

Separately, other officials of the Office for Disarmament Affairs participated in a briefing about disarmament, non-proliferation and arms control issues for young international media representatives and journalists who participated in the Reham Al-Farra Memorial Journalism Fellowship. That engagement resulted in an article[20] in the *Philippine Star*.

The Office also conducted a social media campaign to publicize the launch of the "Joint Appeal by the Secretary-General and the President of the International Committee of the Red Cross on Use of Explosive Weapons in Cities".[21] The appeal, in which the authors advocated for an end to the use of explosive weapons in populated areas, was featured in a variety of newspapers and online media, including Al Arabiya, *Business Recorder*, China.org, *Jordan Times*, Just Security, *Libya Observer*, *Malaysia Sun*, Reliefweb, *Sierra Leone Times*, *European Sting*, *National (United Arab Emirates)*, *Siasat Daily*, United News of India and Xinhua News.

Exhibits

On 26 November, the United Nations welcomed the addition of a watch, ingot and bracelet made from destroyed, illicit firearms to its permanent disarmament exhibition in New York.

The display of products made from "Humanium Metal" became a part of the exhibit at the United Nations Headquarters in an inauguration ceremony attended by United Nations staff and representatives of Member States and civil society. The Office for Disarmament Affairs, El Salvador and Sweden co-organized the event with IM Swedish Development Partner, the non-governmental organization that pioneered a supply chain to produce commercial metal from illicit small arms.

---

[20] Janvic Mateo, "Philippines urges UN to ratify ban on nuke tests", *Philippine Star*, 29 September 2019.

[21] António Guterres and Peter Maurer, joint appeal on use of explosive weapons in cities (SG/2251), 18 September 2019.

Today's youth: the largest generation in history

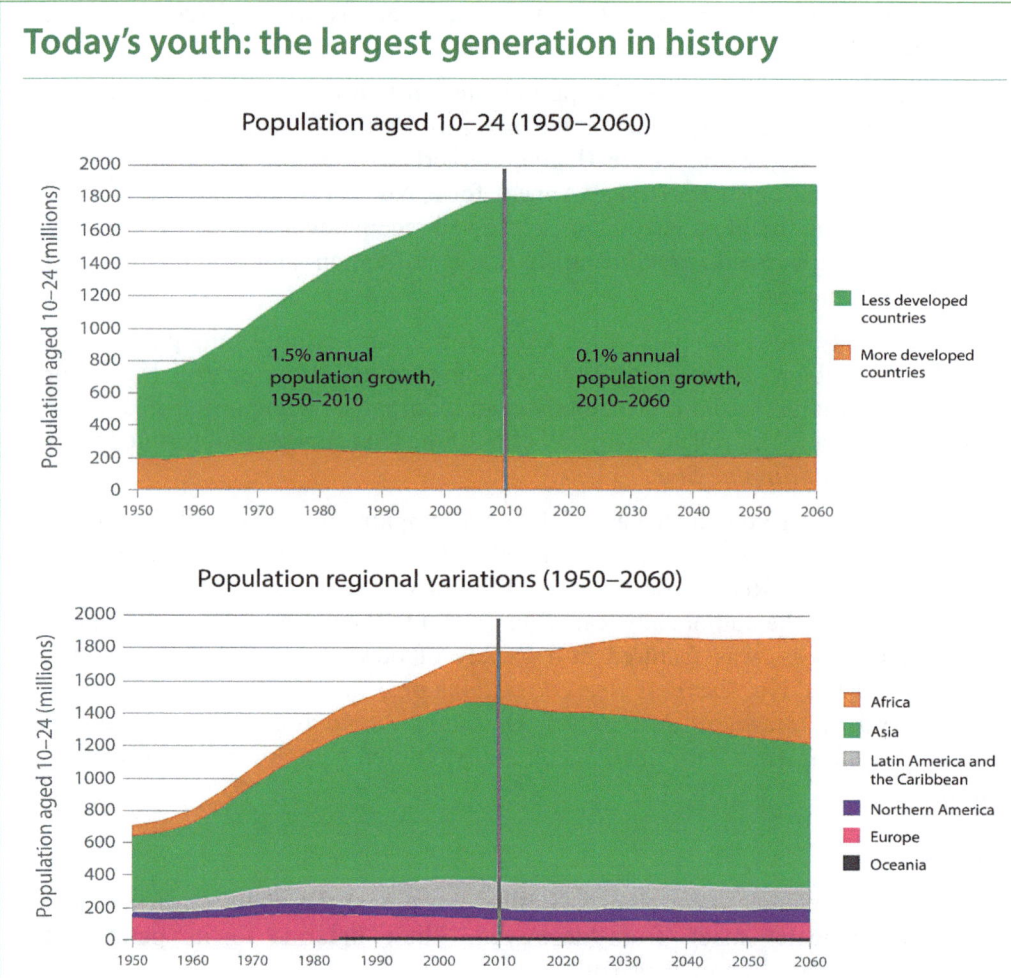

Population aged 10–24 (1950–2060)

1.5% annual population growth, 1950–2010

0.1% annual population growth, 2010–2060

Less developed countries

More developed countries

Population regional variations (1950–2060)

Africa

Asia

Latin America and the Caribbean

Northern America

Europe

Oceania

Figures courtesy of UNFPA.

There are 1.8 billion young people in the world today, more than 90 per cent of whom live in developing countries. Recognizing today's youth* as "the ultimate force for change", the Secretary-General committed in his Agenda for Disarmament to create a platform for the sustainable entry of young people from all parts of the world into the field of disarmament.

As a contribution towards this platform, the United Nations Office for Disarmament Affairs launched "#Youth4Disarmament", an outreach initiative focused on 3 "E"s of Engagement, Education and Empowerment. The ultimate goal is to increase youth participation and create space for young people to make meaningful substantive contributions to facilitating progress on disarmament. Imparting knowledge and skills to young people empowers them to make their contribution, as national and world citizens.

---

*While there is no universally accepted definition of "youth", the Security Council defined the term to include people from 18 to 29 years old in resolution 2250 (2015), "Youth, peace and security".

Disarmament and non-proliferation education

The Office for Disarmament Affairs continued throughout 2019 to build on its work promoting disarmament and non-proliferation education in line with the recommendations of the 2002 United Nations study[22] on disarmament and non-proliferation education.

On 11 June, the Office released its first e-learning module as part of a new initiative to provide accessible and comprehensive training on disarmament. Entitled "Introduction to Disarmament: Machinery, Processes and the Role of the United Nations", the 30-minute, self-paced course examined the operations and achievements of the three main disarmament organs—namely, the General Assembly First Committee, the Disarmament Commission and the Conference on Disarmament—as well as relevant entities such as the Security Council, the International Atomic Energy Agency, the Organisation for the Prohibition of Chemical Weapons and UNIDIR. Designed both for diplomats and the public, the module can be accessed by creating a free account on the Office's Disarmament Education Dashboard.

The Office also partnered with Hibakusha Stories, an initiative of the non-governmental organization Youth Arts New York, to host a workshop aimed at helping 38 New York City public high school teachers to encourage critical thinking by their students on nuclear-weapon issues. The "teach-the-teacher" workshop at the United Nations Headquarters included featured testimony from hibakusha advocates, a briefing on developments in the seventy-fourth session of the First Committee and a presentation on the destructive effect of a nuclear explosion in a populated urban area. The participants then joined a "meet the author" event at the United Nations Bookshop, where the Japanese-American author Kathleen Burkinshaw presented her book, *The Last Cherry Blossom*. Based on her mother's first-hand experience surviving the atomic bombing of Hiroshima, the book highlighted the living conditions of Japanese children during the war and the immense damage caused by the explosion of atomic bombs in Hiroshima and Nagasaki on 6 and 9 August 1945, respectively. The workshop on 5 November was the eighth of its kind that coincided with United States Election Day, when public school teachers in New York City receive time to participate in professional development activities.

Youth and disarmament

By its resolution 74/64 adopted on 12 December, entitled "Youth, disarmament and non-proliferation", the General Assembly reaffirmed the important and positive contribution that young people could make in sustaining peace and security.

---

[22] A/57/124.

Also in 2019, the Office for Disarmament Affairs launched a new youth outreach initiative, called "Youth4Disarmament", in conjunction with the Secretary-General's Agenda for Disarmament.[23] Recognizing the importance of young people in effecting change, the Office established the initiative with the aim of connecting geographically diverse young people with experts to learn about current international security challenges, the work of the United Nations and how they can be active participants.[24]

Three events took place under the Youth4Disarmament initiative during the year with support from the Office for Disarmament Affairs.

The first activity, held at the United Nations Headquarters on 16 August, brought together young people from across the New York area to join an expert-led discussion on the implications of artificial intelligence for international peace and security. A panel of experts from Scientists against Inhumane Weapons, the United Nations University and the Office for Disarmament Affairs discussed artificial intelligence in the context of its role in modern warfare, its strategic implications, and moral and ethical questions linked to its weaponization. Their interactive discussion was interspersed with questions and comments by young participants, including on possible modes of governance, the roles of non-military companies and how future generations could thrive in a technology-driven future.

The second event, entitled "Youth Champions for Securing our Common Future", was a full-day programme on 11 October co-organized by the Office for Disarmament Affairs and Peace Boat, an international non-governmental organization. The activity drew 75 young people between the ages of 18 and 30 to learn about the work of the United Nations, including by observing the First Committee during its general debate. The programme included a session with the theme "Building Empathy through Learning from Atomic Bomb Survivors", during which a hibakusha shared his memories of the atomic bombing of Hiroshima and a documentary film entitled *Pictures from a Hiroshima Schoolyard* was screened to underscore young people's ability to build bridges and confidence through people-to-people exchange. The second half of the programme took place on the Peace Boat, where youth participants could engage with representatives of States, civil society and the Office for Disarmament Affairs on the three pillars of the Secretary-General's Agenda for Disarmament. After a series of

---

[23] In his Agenda for Disarmament, issued in May 2018, the Secretary-General recognized young people as a tremendous force for change in the world who have "proved their power time and again in support of the cause of disarmament". In that connection, he committed the Office for Disarmament Affairs, in partnership with all interested entities, to further invest in disarmament education, including through the establishment of a platform for youth engagement.

[24] By placing youth engagement and empowerment at the core of its disarmament education efforts, the Office for Disarmament Affairs aimed to support the Secretary-General's recommendation to improve youth access to technical support and capacity-building while providing space for their participation. In the framework of its disarmament education programme, the Office aimed to impart knowledge and skills to young people and empower them to make their contribution to disarmament and sustaining peace, as national and world citizens.

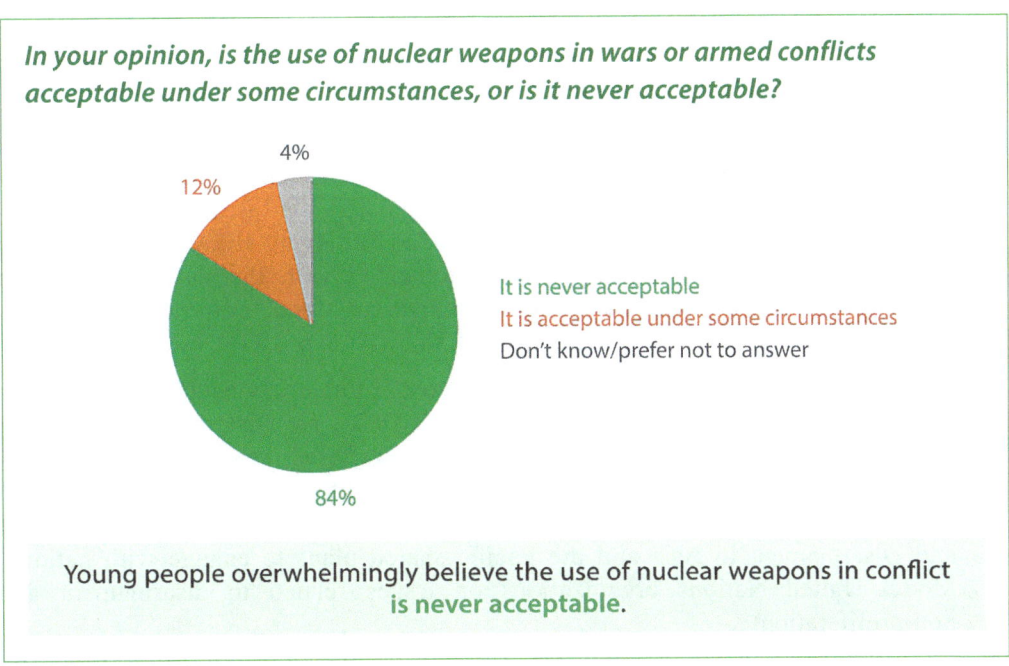

In your opinion, is the use of nuclear weapons in wars or armed conflicts acceptable under some circumstances, or is it never acceptable?

4%

12%

It is never acceptable
It is acceptable under some circumstances
Don't know/prefer not to answer

84%

Young people overwhelmingly believe the use of nuclear weapons in conflict **is never acceptable**.

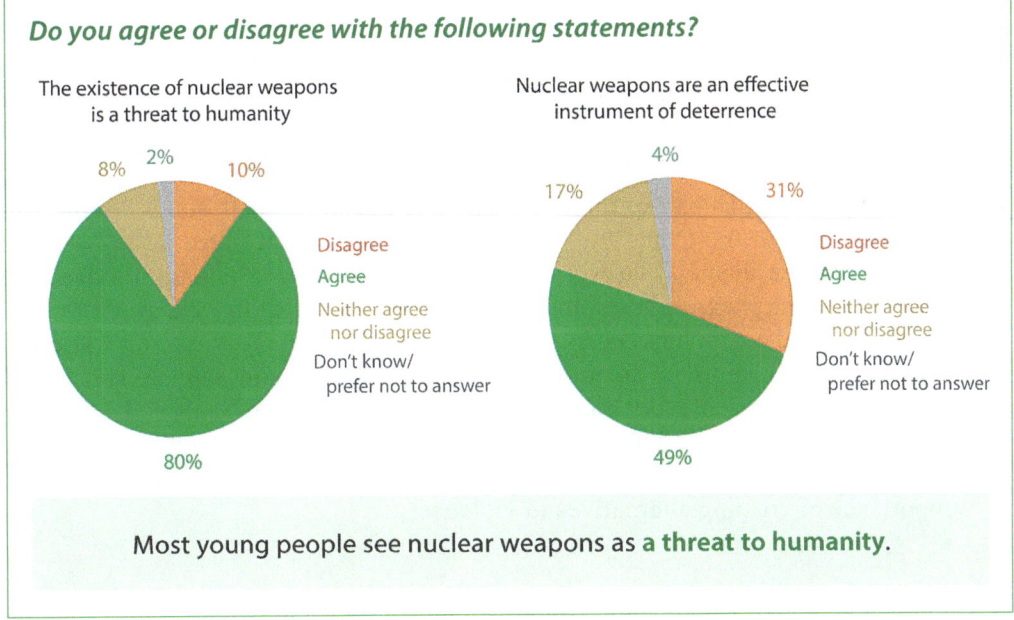

Do you agree or disagree with the following statements?

The existence of nuclear weapons is a threat to humanity

8%   2%   10%

Disagree
Agree
Neither agree nor disagree
Don't know/ prefer not to answer

80%

Nuclear weapons are an effective instrument of deterrence

4%
17%   31%

Disagree
Agree
Neither agree nor disagree
Don't know/ prefer not to answer

49%

Most young people see nuclear weapons as **a threat to humanity**.

Source: "Millennials on War", an ICRC survey of 16,288 respondents ages 20 to 35 in 16 countries* from 29 June to 1 October 2019. For more information, see **https://www.icrc.org/en/millennials-on-war**.

* Afghanistan, Colombia, France, Indonesia, Israel, Malaysia, Mexico, Nigeria, Russian Federation, South Africa, State of Palestine, Switzerland, Syrian Arab Republic, Ukraine, United Kingdom and United States.

expert presentations, the participants broke into groups to formulate proposals aimed at achieving new progress in the area of disarmament, arms control and non-proliferation.

On 26 November, the Office held the third Youth4Disarmament event in collaboration with IM Swedish Development Partner, another civil society organization, to raise awareness about the potential for disarmament and arms control to contribute towards saving lives and achieving the 2030 Agenda for Sustainable Development. The activity coincided with the inauguration of a permanent exhibit of items made from "Humanium Metal" at the United Nations Headquarters (for more information, see "Exhibits" on p. 287).

Events held earlier in the year included a video exchange on 4 April in which interns and young professionals of the Office for Disarmament Affairs in New York, Geneva, Lima, Lomé and Kathmandu shared ideas for future projects and discussed strategies for advancing disarmament and engaging youth in the years to come. For example, colleagues from the Regional Centre for Peace and Disarmament in Asia and the Pacific shared plans to engage with national Model United Nations organizations on issues related to disarmament and non-proliferation.

On 5 April, Peace Boat and the Office for Disarmament Affairs organized a luncheon event entitled "Youth Ambassadors Working towards a Nuclear-free Future". In the event's keynote remarks, a youth activist from the Marshall Islands described the suffering that her family and community continued to endure from the radiological legacy of cold war–era nuclear testing. She also discussed her experiences advocating for peace and disarmament as one of Peace Boat's "Ocean and Climate Youth Ambassadors".

Additionally, as part of the Economic and Social Council Youth Forum held on 8 and 9 April, the Office for Disarmament Affairs contributed an infographic display with the theme "The world is overarmed and peace is underfunded". To help put military expenditure into context for participating youth—including activists, digital media influencers and media representatives—the display stressed how resources committed to militaries, if redirected, could support substantial progress towards achieving the Sustainable Development Goals.[25] During the opening event of the exhibit, an intern of the Office talked with youth participants about trends in military spending, militarized perceptions of security and the importance of creating alternatives to violence.

---

[25] It was noted, for example, that the cost of a single fighter jet could send 200,000 children to school for one year or allow 15,000 children to attend school from kindergarten through high school (13 years).

Disarmament fellowships

Launched by the General Assembly in 1978 at its first special session devoted to disarmament,[26] the Programme of Fellowships on Disarmament is designed to train and build the capacity of officials from Member States to participate more effectively in international disarmament deliberating and negotiating forums.

As at the end of 2019, the Programme had trained 1,033 officials, many of whom went on to hold important disarmament-related positions within their Governments or in international organizations. In addition to preparing those participants to more effectively support regional and global disarmament efforts, the Programme had created an informal, world-spanning network among officials representing 170 States, enabling them to work cooperatively and constructively in pursuit of disarmament and non-proliferation goals.

In 2019, diplomats and other officials from 25 Member States[27] participated in the Programme, which was implemented by the Office for Disarmament Affairs. A total of 16 of the 25 Fellows for the year were women, contributing to the cadre of women with qualifications to hold multilateral disarmament-related posts within their Governments.

As per the established practice, the 2019 Fellowship Programme incorporated three segments comprising a variety of theoretical activities and practical exercises. Those activities included lectures and round-table debates on current disarmament topics with senior diplomats and representatives of international, regional, bilateral and civil society organizations and academia; an ambassadorial-level panel discussion on nuclear disarmament; a simulated session on a draft resolution on lethal autonomous weapon systems; and case studies on conventional weapons. The Fellows also undertook field visits to locations that included a destruction facility for conventional weapons, a former nuclear test site, a tokamak reactor, a nuclear fuel production plant and several laboratories engaging in disarmament-related work.

The initial segment of the Fellowship Programme, which began in Geneva on 19 August, exposed the Fellows to the work of the Conference on Disarmament and of various treaty regimes, in particular the Biological Weapons Convention

---

[26] Pursuant to paragraph 108 of the Final Document of the first special session on disarmament (resolution S-10/2), "In order to promote expertise in disarmament in more Member States, particularly in the developing countries, the General Assembly decides to establish a programme of fellowships on disarmament".

[27] Argentina, Armenia, Bahrain, Benin, Burundi, Cambodia, Cameroon, Dominican Republic, Egypt, France, Gabon, Germany, India, Iraq, Panama, Republic of Korea, Romania, Serbia, South Africa, Sri Lanka, State of Palestine, Switzerland, Timor-Leste, Trinidad and Tobago and United Republic of Tanzania.

(1972),[28] the Convention on Certain Conventional Weapons (1980),[29] the Anti-Personnel Mine Ban Convention (1997),[30] the Convention on Cluster Munitions (2008), the Arms Trade Treaty (2013) and the Treaty on the Prohibition of Nuclear Weapons (2017). The Fellows received background information on weapon systems, their effects and applicable law, in particular international humanitarian law; took part in case-study exercises on weapons law; and heard briefings on the impact of new technologies on the means and methods of warfare, relevant work by civil society and the activities of the Geneva Centres.[31]

During the second segment of the programme, the Fellows participated in study visits to several international organizations, structures or arrangements related to disarmament, arms control and non-proliferation. In Vienna, those included visits to the Preparatory Commission for the Comprehensive Nuclear-Test-Ban Treaty Organization, the International Atomic Energy Agency, the Organization of Security and Co-operation in Europe and export control regimes such as the Wassenaar Arrangement. In The Hague, Netherlands, the Fellows visited the Organisation for the Prohibition of Chemical Weapons, the International Court of Justice and the International Criminal Court. The Fellows also participated in country-specific study visits at the invitation of Brazil, China, Germany, Japan, Kazakhstan, the Republic of Korea and Switzerland, as well as a visit to European Union institutions in Brussels, organized by the European Union Non-Proliferation and Disarmament Consortium pursuant to Council decision 2018/299.[32]

The third segment of the Programme took place in October at the United Nations Headquarters in New York, where the Fellows followed the work of the General Assembly First Committee and developments on key issues related to disarmament, non-proliferation and arms control. In parallel, the fellows prepared and discussed research work on various disarmament and arms control topics.

After completing the Programme at the United Nations Headquarters on 25 October, the 2019 Fellows were awarded certificates of participation by the High Representative for Disarmament Affairs and the Chair of the First Committee.

---

[28] Convention on the Prohibition of the Development, Production and Stockpiling of Bacteriological (Biological) and Toxin Weapons and on Their Destruction.

[29] Convention on Prohibitions or Restrictions on the Use of Certain Conventional Weapons Which May Be Deemed to be Excessively Injurious or to Have Indiscriminate Effects.

[30] Convention on the Prohibition of the Use, Stockpiling, Production and Transfer of Anti-Personnel Mines and on Their Destruction.

[31] Geneva International Centre for Humanitarian Demining, Geneva Centre for Security Policy and Geneva Centre for the Democratic Control of Armed Forces.

[32] Council Decision (CFSP) 2018/299 of 26 February 2018 promoting the European network of independent non-proliferation and disarmament think tanks in support of the implementation of the EU Strategy against proliferation of weapons of mass destruction, *Official Journal of the European Union*, L 56, 28 February 2018, p. 46–59.

Vienna Office of the United Nations Office for Disarmament Affairs

In 2019, the Vienna Office continued to expand its awareness-raising and education activities by organizing a range of outreach activities and capacity-building programmes for young professionals with a particular focus on women. The Office also added new self-paced courses to its Disarmament Education Dashboard, an online learning platform for disarmament- and non-proliferation-related issues, and further improved the system's substance and functionality.[33]

The Vienna Office collaborated with relevant staff across the Office for Disarmament Affairs to develop two in-depth, self-paced courses—on Security Council resolution 1540 (2004) and cyber diplomacy—for access by expert-level practitioners. Meanwhile, the Vienna Office continued to expand the Dashboard's offering of short introductory courses on key disarmament and non-proliferation issues, while also overseeing thematic and methodological improvements to the Dashboard's existing education modules by the Office for Disarmament Affairs. The platform received approximately 3,500 new registrations during the year, a significant increase in its user base, reflecting its increasingly essential role for course participants in related professional fields and the general public, as well as for partners and donors.

As part of its continued engagement with Vienna-based organizations and entities, the Office continued to partner with the Organization for Security and Co-operation in Europe (OSCE) to implement the Scholarship for Peace and Security, a capacity-building and training programme for young professionals in the OSCE region. In 2019, the Scholarship provided early-career professionals with 100 scholarships, 90 of which were reserved for women. The programme consisted of two components: (a) eight weeks of online coursework and one week of in-person training for young professional women; and (b) a separate eight-week online training open to female and male participants. The training courses not only increased the substantive knowledge and skills of participants, but also contributed to the creation of a network of young professionals from the wider OSCE area, particularly women, who were active in various relevant fields. The Scholarship for Peace and Security 2019 was the second round of training courses organized by the Vienna Office in close partnership with the OSCE, which jointly decided to build on the programme's success in 2018 and 2019 by relaunching in 2020.

The Vienna Office also conducted outreach aimed at increasing awareness in the diplomatic community and the general public about disarmament- and non-proliferation-related issues, including the Office's own work in those

---

[33] Intended to expand the number and quality of training opportunities in the field of disarmament and non-proliferation, the Dashboard offers training materials and resources, developed in cooperation with relevant entities, in the field of arms control, disarmament and non-proliferation, as well as cross-cutting issues, including gender and development. It allowed new training courses to be tailor-made in accordance with audience demand.

areas. It organized two events under its "Conversations Series": (a) "Emerging Technologies: A Blessing or a Curse?", a talk show-style discussion held on 9 May between relevant experts and audience members participating in person and via Facebook; and (b) "Disarmament and Non-Proliferation Education: The Way Forward", a panel event held on 14 November. The success of that discussion series prompted plans for additional events that would focus on cross-cutting issues to attract wider audiences.

Meanwhile, the Vienna Office continued to initiate and participate in outreach activities in cooperation with other Vienna-based organizations and entities. On 26 September, the Office participated in a commemorative event for the International Day for the Total Elimination of Nuclear Weapons, helping to raise awareness about the grave risks to humanity posed by the continued existence of nuclear weapons.

United Nations Institute for Disarmament Research

One of the few policy institutes in the world focused on disarmament, UNIDIR carried out activities throughout 2019 to generate knowledge and promote dialogue and action on disarmament and security. Its work in those areas included producing policy-relevant research and analysis, building capacity on traditional and emerging issues and delivering tools to assist Member States in implementing their disarmament commitments. Acting in its capacity as an autonomous institute within the United Nations, UNIDIR offered research and policy support to Member States, United Nations bodies, international and regional organizations and other stakeholders. Under its strategic research agenda,[34] UNIDIR focused on four multi-year programmes: conventional arms; gender and disarmament; security and technology; and weapons of mass destruction and other strategic weapons. It aimed to proactively identify new issues in those areas in a manner responsive to diverse security concerns, integrated with relevant peace, security and development priorities and accessible to a global audience.

UNIDIR accomplished the following in 2019:

- Carried out research on topics such as nuclear risk reduction and verification, space security, urbanization of violence, weapons and ammunition management, conflict prevention, cyber stability, artificial intelligence, the weaponization of autonomous technologies, and gender and disarmament.

- Engaged in over 50 countries and facilitated dialogue between and among disarmament stakeholders through more than 30 conferences, workshops and events, ranging from events on gender and disarmament held on the margins of the Conference of States Parties to the Chemical Weapons Convention to a table-top exercise exploring the implications of the use of hypersonic

---

[34] The UNIDIR programme of work and financial plan for 2018 and 2019 received approval from its Board of Trustees in 2018. See A/73/259.

weapon systems. In addition to its annual Cyber Security Conference and Space Security Conference, UNIDIR convened a new flagship event, the Innovations Dialogue, to discuss the international security implications of new technologies.

- Offered advisory services to intergovernmental processes and forums, including by serving as consultant to the groups of governmental experts on further practical measures for the prevention of an arms race in outer space, the role of verification in advancing nuclear disarmament, and advancing responsible state behaviour in cyberspace in the context of international security.

- Issued 42 publications (and seven translations) on subjects as varied as the changing role of conventional arms control in preventing and managing violent conflicts, nuclear disarmament verification, electronic and cyberwarfare in outer space and gender issues related to cyber diplomacy (for a list of UNIDIR publications, see annex II).

- Launched a revamped website that increased the average monthly web traffic by 36 per cent, produced over 50 videos and built a significantly stronger presence on social media, garnering 2.5 million impressions on Twitter over the year.

The following subsections identify 2019 highlights from UNIDIR research programmes, all four of which supported the implementation of the Secretary-General's Agenda for Disarmament.[35]

Weapons of mass destruction and other strategic weapons

UNIDIR work in the programme on weapons of mass destruction and other strategic weapons fell into five main areas: reducing the risk of nuclear-weapon use; nuclear verification and transparency approaches; space security; enhancing compliance and enforcement of weapons of mass destruction-relevant international treaties (especially the nuclear, chemical and biological regimes); and work on addressing new challenges to curbing such weapons. In all those areas, UNIDIR published new studies while also carrying out meetings and other activities with the disarmament community. For example, building on a study on hypersonic weapons published in February in collaboration with the Office for Disarmament Affairs, UNIDIR undertook a table-top exercise with the Office on 19 September to examine the arms control implications of those systems. Separately, UNIDIR hosted its annual outer space conference on 28 and 29 May, drawing record interest and attendance. In addition, UNIDIR continued to provide technical input and support to two groups of governmental experts—on the role of

---

[35] UNIDIR provided a full account of its activities, as well as its proposed programme of work and financial plan for 2019, in the annual report of its Director to the General Assembly (A/74/180). Detailed information about specific projects, as well as the entirety of the research programme and activities, is available on its website (www.unidir.org).

verification in advancing nuclear disarmament verification and on prevention of an arms race in outer space—as well as to subsidiary bodies of the Conference on Disarmament on several matters, the United Nations Disarmament Commission on space security, and regional consultations for the 2020 Review Conference of the Parties to the Treaty on the Non-Proliferation of Nuclear Weapons in support of the Office for Disarmament Affairs and the Chair-designate.

Conventional arms

UNIDIR conducted research through its conventional arms programme on three priority areas: supporting national and regional policy and practice for weapon and ammunition management; conventional arms control in prevention and peacemaking; and adapting arms control to address urbanization of violence. Those activities supported the active engagement of States in various multilateral instruments, including the United Nations Programme of Action on Small Arms and Light Weapons and the Arms Trade Treaty.

In 2019, UNIDIR promoted knowledge among States and regional organizations on strengthening national and regional policy and practice for weapon and ammunition management. Its key achievements included helping States assess baselines and develop national weapon and ammunition management road maps in West Africa in cooperation with the Economic Community of West African States Commission, facilitating dialogue and generating ideas on key issues and processes pertinent to conventional ammunition management on which progress could be made at the national, regional and multilateral levels prior to the commencement of the group of governmental experts in 2020, and providing advisory support to the Secretary-General in assessing the implementation of the arms embargo in Somalia.

Meanwhile, in integrating conventional arms control into prevention and peacemaking, UNIDIR convened the "Building the Bridges" initiative, intended to promote knowledge and dialogue among peace, security and development actors on ways to apply arms control to reduce violence, prevent conflict and advance sustainable development.

Continuing its research on adapting arms control to address the urbanization of violence, UNIDIR generated ideas on opportunities to improve policy and practice to reduce civilian harm from conventional weapons in urban environments. In particular, UNIDIR facilitated dialogue among States and their militaries on ways to reduce risk to civilians from explosive weapons in urban warfare. Additionally, UNIDIR initiated the development of a practical tool to help States self-assess their preventative and preparedness measures to counter the threat of improvised explosive devices. The tool was scheduled for launch in 2020.

Security and technology

Through its security and technology programme, UNIDIR aimed to help practitioners and multilateral disarmament processes respond effectively to the security challenges raised by technological innovation. Its objectives were to support norm development and implementation, increase understanding of digital destabilization and help modernize the "arms control toolbox".

The programme was focused on three priority areas of technological innovation: cyber stability; artificial intelligence and the weaponization of increasingly autonomous technologies; and the security dimensions of innovations in science and technology. Within each area, UNIDIR aimed to build knowledge and awareness on the international security implications and risks of specific technological innovations and convene stakeholders to explore ideas and develop new thinking on ways to address them.

In 2019, the programme continued to support the advancement of the international cyber debate by, inter alia: (a) continuously maintaining and further developing the UNIDIR Cyber Policy Portal;[36] (b) providing advice and support to the United Nations Secretariat and Member States on the establishment both of the Open-ended Working Group on Developments in the Field of Information and Telecommunications in the Context of International Security and the Group of Governmental Experts on Advancing Responsible State Behaviour in Cyberspace in the Context of International Security;[37] and (c) convening the UNIDIR annual Cyber Stability Conference in June. Notably, the Conference was convened in New York on an exceptional basis in order to build the capacity of New York–based delegations to actively participate in the historic open-ended working group process. The event also was live-streamed for the first time to further amplify its reach.

In addition to its work on cyber issues under the security and technology programme, UNIDIR held the inaugural edition of a new flagship event, the Innovations Dialogue. The event on 19 August focused on the implications of digital technologies—such as Internet of things, distributed ledger technologies and quantum—on international security and disarmament. The dialogue drew high participation, with 180 registrations and an average of 130 participants in the room throughout the day.

Through the programme, UNIDIR also advanced its portfolio of work on artificial intelligence and autonomy in 2019, including through the publication of research papers on the role of data in algorithmic decision-making and on swarming technologies.

Gender and disarmament

In 2019, the UNIDIR programme on gender and disarmament continued to assist the diplomatic community in bridging gender and disarmament frameworks. In order to provide Member States and disarmament stakeholders with a

---

[36] The Cyber Policy Portal was launched in January 2019 and showcased at the Paris Peace Forum, held from 11 to 13 November.

[37] In 2019, UNIDIR served as expert consultant to both Groups of Governmental Experts.

baseline analysis on women's participation and gender balance in arms control and disarmament, UNIDIR conducted an extensive quantitative and qualitative analysis that it published in the report *Still Behind the Curve*.[38]

The study found that women diplomats were still significantly under-represented in multilateral forums dealing with weapons, making up only a third of diplomats accredited to arms control and disarmament conferences. In smaller, more specialized forums, the average proportion of women dropped to 20 per cent. Furthermore, drawing on views gathered from diplomats and others, UNIDIR analysed obstacles to the full and equal participation of women in the field of disarmament and international security. The analysis highlighted a need for concerted action to promote gender equality in disarmament diplomacy, in line with Actions 36 and 37 of the Secretary-General's Agenda for Disarmament, as well as Goal 5 of the 2030 Agenda for Sustainable Development.

Furthermore, to promote gender mainstreaming in multilateral arms control and disarmament deliberations, UNIDIR organized events held on the margins of the third session of the Preparatory Committee for the 2020 Review Conference of the Parties to the Nuclear Non-Proliferation Treaty, the fifth Conference of States Parties to the Arms Trade Treaty, the fourth Meeting of Experts to the Biological Weapons Convention, and the twenty-fourth session of the Conference of the States Parties to the Chemical Weapons Convention.

While meetings of States parties of the Arms Trade Treaty and the Nuclear Non-Proliferation Treaty had previously featured gender-related discussions, multilateral debates on chemical and biological weapons had systematically considered neither the relevance of sex- and age-disaggregated data on the effects of those weapons nor knowledge of gender dynamics in the implementation of the Biological Weapons Convention and the Chemical Weapons Convention. As an initial step towards overcoming that gap, UNIDIR published *Missing Links*,[39] a research report analysing possible sex- and gender-specific effects of those weapons. The authors of the report offered an overview of existing literature relevant to understanding the linkages between gender and biological and chemical weapons, as well as a proposal for gender-responsive assistance aimed at helping States and their populations to become more resilient to and recover more rapidly from chemical or biological incidents.

In collaboration with Member States and civil society organizations, UNIDIR also produced working papers and fact sheets tailored to delegates attending arms control and disarmament meetings. Those included a fact sheet entitled "Gender in the Arms Trade Treaty", as well as two working papers for the Nuclear Non-Proliferation Treaty Preparatory Committee: "Improving gender equality

---

[38] Renata Hessmann Dalaqua, Kjølv Egeland and Torbjørn Graff Hugo, *Still Behind the Curve*, (Geneva, UNIDIR, 2019).

[39] Renata Hessmann Dalaqua, James Revill, Alastair Hay and Nancy Connell, *Missing Links: Understanding Sex- and Gender-Related Impacts of Chemical and Biological Weapons* (Geneva, UNIDIR, 2019).

and diversity in the Non-Proliferation Treaty review process"[40] and "Integrating gender perspectives in the implementation of the Treaty on the Non-Proliferation of Nuclear Weapons".[41]

As part of a collaboration with the International Gender Champions Disarmament Impact Group,[42] UNIDIR published in January 2019 the *Gender and Disarmament Resource Pack for Multilateral Practitioners*, containing information on the relevance of gender perspectives to arms control, non-proliferation and disarmament, as well as practical ideas that can support diplomats in applying a gender lens to their work. UNIDIR distributed the *Resource Pack* to chairs and presidents of various multilateral arms control, non-proliferation and disarmament meetings in 2019.

UNIDIR also produced a short animated video, "How does gender relate to arms control and disarmament?", as well as an online hub on gender and disarmament. The video was translated into all official United Nations languages, as well as Japanese, and widely shared on social media. The online hub also attracted attention from the disarmament community, providing easy access to a compilation of gender-related resources.

---

[40] NPT/CONF.2020/PC.III/WP.25.

[41] NPT/CONF.2020/PC.III/WP.27.

[42] Co-chaired by the Director of UNIDIR and the Ambassadors of Canada, Ireland, Namibia and the Philippines, the International Gender Champions Disarmament Impact Group seeks to promote dialogue, shared knowledge and the pursuit of concrete opportunities to advance gender-responsive action within disarmament processes.

Annex I

United Nations Office for Disarmament Affairs publications and other information materials in 2018

- *United Nations Disarmament Yearbook*, vol. 43 (Parts I and II): 2018 (Sales Nos. E.19.IX.3 and E.19.IX.4) (also available in e-book format)
- *United Nations Efforts to Reduce Military Expenditures: A Historical Overview*, United Nations Office for Disarmament Affairs Occasional Papers, No. 33, October 2019 (Sales No. E.20.IX.1)
- *The Anti-Personnel Mine Ban Convention: Twenty Years of Saving Lives and Preventing Indiscriminate Harm*, United Nations Office for Disarmament Affairs Occasional Papers, No. 34, November 2019 (Sales No. E.20.IX.2)
- *Programmes Financed from Voluntary Contributions: 2018–2019*
- *Hypersonic Weapons: A Challenge and Opportunity for Strategic Arms Control—A Study Prepared on the Recommendation of the Secretary-General's Advisory Board on Disarmament Matters*
- *A Guide to Developing National Standards for Ammunition Management*
- *Critical Path Guide to the International Ammunition Technical Guidelines*
- *Utilizing the International Ammunition Technical Guidelines in Conflict-Affected and Low-Capacity Environments*
- UNODA Update (online news updates): First Quarter, Second Quarter, Third Quarter and Fourth Quarter
- Fact sheets on disarmament issues

Regional Centre for Peace and Disarmament in Africa

- UNREC Focus (newsletter): No. 34 (February 2019) and No. 35 (June 2019)
- Fact sheet, July 2019

Regional Centre for Peace, Disarmament and Development in Latin America and the Caribbean

- Fact sheet, July 2019

Regional Centre for Peace and Disarmament in Asia and the Pacific

- Newsletter: No. 16 (2019)

Annex II

United Nations Institute for Disarmament Research publications in 2019[43]

Weapons of mass destruction and other strategic weapons

- Shared risks: An examination of universal space security challenges — Briefing paper for the United Nations Disarmament Commission
- Hypersonic Weapons: A Challenge and Opportunity for Strategic Arms Control (with Office for Disarmament Affairs)
- Reversing the Slide: Intensified Great Power Competition and the Breakdown of the Arms Control Endeavour
- Mandate and Working Methods in the Conference on Disarmament
- Nuclear Risk Reduction: The State of Ideas
- Electronic and Cyber Warfare in Outer Space
- Nuclear Risk Reduction: A Framework for Analysis
- UNIDIR Space Security Conference 2019
- Watch Them Go: Simplifying the Elimination of Fissile Materials and Nuclear Weapons
- Eyes on the Sky: Rethinking Verification in Space
- The Implications of Hypersonic Weapons for International Stability and Arms Control: Report on a UNIDIR-UNODA Turn-based Exercise
- Compliance and Enforcement in WMD-related Treaties
- IAEA Mechanisms to Ensure Compliance with NPT Safeguards
- Compliance Management under the Chemical Weapons Convention
- Compliance and Enforcement in the Biological Weapons Regime
- Monitoring, Verification, And Compliance Resolution In U.S.-Russian Arms Control
- Compliance and Enforcement: Lessons from across WMD-related regimes

Conventional arms

- Building the Bridge: A Commentary on Arms Control to Reduce Violence, Prevent Conflict and Advance Sustainable Development
- Conventional Ammunition Management: A Gap Analysis

---

[43] To access the publications listed in this annex, see United Nations Institute for Disarmament Research, "Publications".

- Key Issues and Processes Pertinent to the Management of Conventional Ammunition: Report of the First Seminar (Also available in French and Spanish)
- Key Issues and Processes Pertinent to the Management of Conventional Ammunition: Report of the Second Seminar (Also available in French and Spanish)
- Key Issues and Processes Pertinent to the Management of Conventional Ammunition: Report of the Third Seminar (Also available in French and Spanish)
- Opportunities to Improve Military Policy and Practice to Reduce Civilian Harm from Explosive Weapons in Urban Conflicts: An Options Paper
- Opportunities to Strengthen Military Policies and Practices to Reduce Civilian Harm From Explosive Weapons: A Food for Thought Paper
- Preventing Diversion in Conventional Arms Transfers: Exploring Contributions of Industry and Private Sector Actors
- Enhancing the Understanding of Roles and Responsibilities of Industry and States to Prevent Diversion: An Issue Brief
- A Menu of Options to Enhance the Common Understanding of End Use/r Control Systems to Strengthen their Role in Preventing Diversion
- The Role of Weapon and Ammunition Management in Preventing Conflict and Supporting Security Transitions
- Utilizing the International Ammunition Technical Guidelines in Conflict-Affected and Low-Capacity Environments

Security and technology

- The Role of Regional Organizations in Strengthening Cybersecurity and Stability
- Electronic and Cyber Warfare in Outer Space
- Stemming the Exploitation of ICT Threats and Vulnerabilities (Also available in French)
- Cyber Stability Conference 2019: Strengthening Global Engagement
- The Role of Data in Algorithmic Decision-Making
- Innovations Dialogue Report

Gender

- Still Behind the Curve
- Fact Sheet on Gender in the ATT
- Gender and Disarmament Resource Pack

- Missing Links: Understanding Sex- and Gender-Related Impacts of Chemical and Biological Weapons
- Gender in Cyber Diplomacy Fact Sheet

Annex III

Events held on the margins of the 2019 session of the First Committee

10 October	Launch of the Middle East Weapons of Mass Destruction Free Zone Project (Organized by UNIDIR)
14 October	Launch of the Online Training Course on United Nations Security Council Resolution 1540 (2004) (Organized by the Permanent Missions of Japan, the Republic of Korea and the United States with the Office for Disarmament Affairs)
16 October	Scientific and Technological Capacity for Disarmament and Non-proliferation (Organized by the Office for Disarmament Affairs and the Verification Research, Training and Information Centre)
17 October	Nuclear Risk Reduction: Pathways Forward (Organized by the Permanent Missions of Australia, Finland, Sweden and Switzerland with UNIDIR)
22 October	Hypersonic Weapons: A Challenge and Opportunity for Strategic Arms Control (Organized by the Permanent Missions of Poland and Switzerland with the Office for Disarmament Affairs)
	Containing the Oxygen of Conflict: Issues and Priorities for Ammunition Life Cycle Management (Organized by the Permanent Mission of Germany with UNIDIR)
23 October	Digital Technologies and Conventional Arms Trade: Opportunities and Challenges (Organized by UNIDIR)
	Rethinking Unconstrained Military Spending (Organized by the Office for Disarmament Affairs)

24 October   Disarmament that Saves Lives: Supporting Country-Level Small Arms Control and Violence Reduction for Sustainable Development
(Organized by the Office for Disarmament Affairs)

25 October   Gender-Responsive Small Arms Control
(Organized by Small Arms Survey and the Office for Disarmament Affairs)

25 October   Enhancing Arms Control Policy in United Nations Peace Operations Practice
(Organized by the Department of Peacekeeping Operations and the Office for Disarmament Affairs)

25 October   Transparency Commitments on Arms Transfers and Military Budgets: Tools for Conflict Prevention
(Organized by the Office for Disarmament Affairs)

28 October   Navigating Space: Charting a Course for a Sustainable Space Environment
(Organized by UNIDIR)

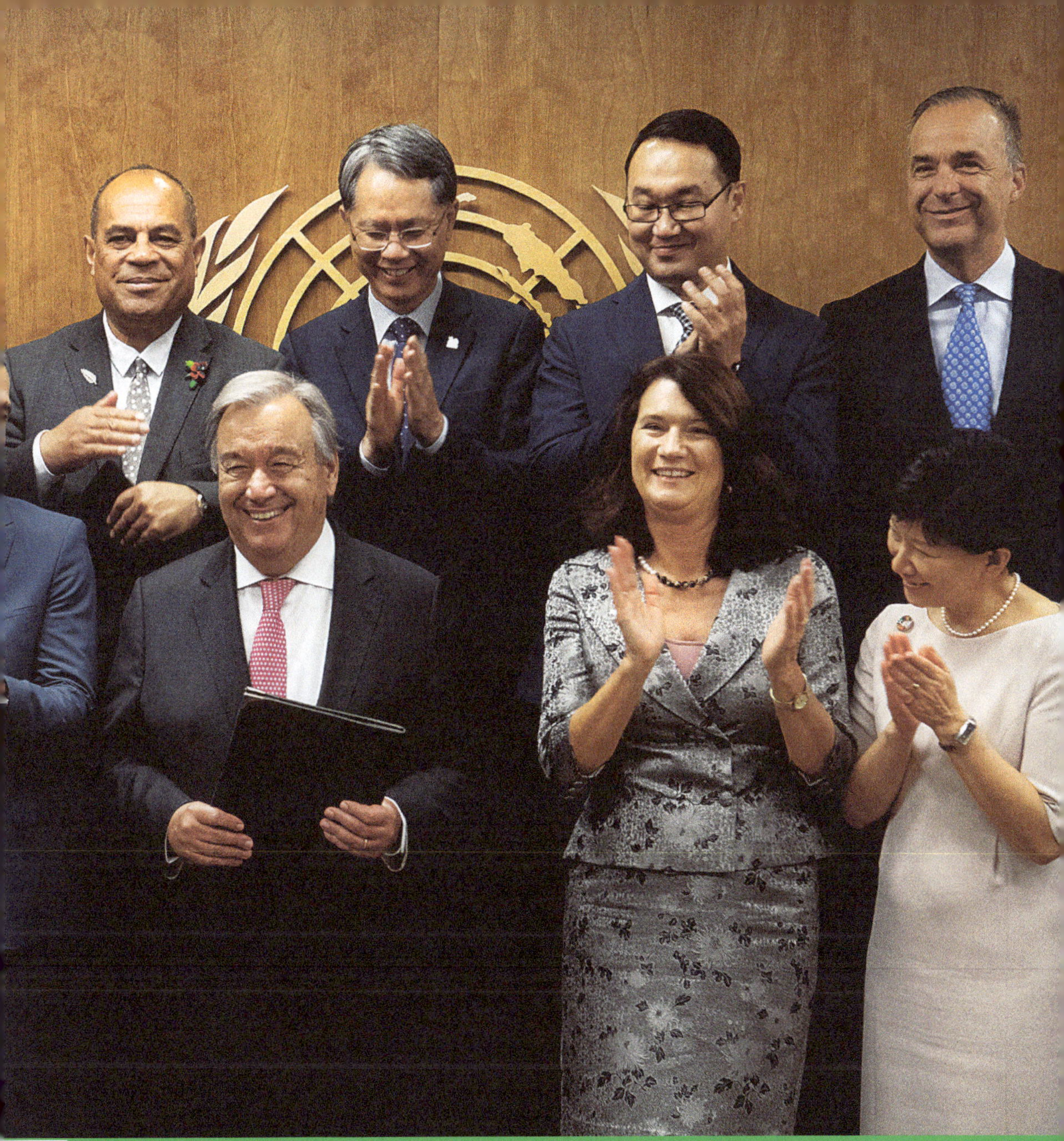

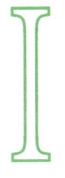

appendix

I Status of multilateral arms regulation and disarmament agreements

Secretary-General António Guterres is handed the joint ministerial declaration from the Stockholm Ministerial Meeting on Nuclear Disarmament and the Non-Proliferation Treaty, Stockholm, 26 September 2019.

The declaration was adopted on 11 June 2019 at the Ministerial Meeting in Stockholm to gather momentum in support of the Nuclear Non-Proliferation Treaty ahead of the Treaty's Review Conference the following year.

Status of multilateral arms regulation and disarmament agreements

The most up-to-date information on disarmament treaties, including their status of adherence, are available at the website of the United Nations Office for Disarmament Affairs:

http://disarmament.un.org/treaties/

The data contained in this appendix has been provided by the depositaries of the treaties or agreements. Inclusion of information concerning the treaties and agreements of which the United Nations Secretary-General is not the depositary is as reported by the respective depositaries and implies no position on the part of the United Nations with respect to the data reported.

The treaties are presented below by depositary.

Secretary-General of the United Nations

Agreement Governing the Activities of States on the Moon and Other Celestial Bodies

Arms Trade Treaty

Central African Convention for the Control of Small Arms and Light Weapons, Their Ammunition and All Parts and Components That Can Be Used for Their Manufacture, Repair and Assembly (Kinshasa Convention)

Comprehensive Nuclear-Test-Ban Treaty

Convention on Cluster Munitions

Convention on Prohibitions or Restrictions on the Use of Certain Conventional Weapons Which May Be Deemed to Be Excessively Injurious or to Have Indiscriminate Effects

Convention on the Prohibition of Military or Any Other Hostile Use of Environmental Modification Techniques

Convention on the Prohibition of the Development, Production, Stockpiling and Use of Chemical Weapons and on Their Destruction

Convention on the Prohibition of the Use, Stockpiling, Production and Transfer of Anti-Personnel Mines and on Their Destruction (Anti-Personnel Mine Ban Convention)

International Convention for the Suppression of Acts of Nuclear Terrorism

Treaty on the Prohibition of Nuclear Weapons

African Union

African Nuclear-Weapon-Free Zone Treaty (Pelindaba Treaty)

Canada and Hungary

Treaty on Open Skies

France

Protocol for the Prohibition of the Use in War of Asphyxiating, Poisonous or Other Gases, and of Bacteriological Methods of Warfare (1925 Geneva Protocol)

Kyrgyzstan

Treaty on a Nuclear-Weapon-Free Zone in Central Asia

Mexico

Treaty for the Prohibition of Nuclear Weapons in Latin America and the Caribbean (Treaty of Tlatelolco)

Netherlands

Treaty on Conventional Armed Forces in Europe

Organization of American States

Inter-American Convention Against the Illicit Manufacturing of and Trafficking in Firearms, Ammunition, Explosives and Other Related Materials

Inter-American Convention on Transparency in Conventional Weapons Acquisitions

Pacific Islands Forum

South Pacific Nuclear Free Zone Treaty (Rarotonga Treaty)

Russian Federation, United Kingdom and United States

Convention on the Prohibition of the Development, Production and Stockpiling of Bacteriological (Biological) and Toxin Weapons and on Their Destruction

Treaty Banning Nuclear Weapon Tests in the Atmosphere, in Outer Space and Under Water (Partial Test Ban Treaty)

Treaty on Principles Governing the Activities of States in the Exploration and Use of Outer Space, including the Moon and Other Celestial Bodies (Outer Space Treaty)

Treaty on the Non-Proliferation of Nuclear Weapons

Treaty on the Prohibition of the Emplacement of Nuclear Weapons and Other Weapons of Mass Destruction on the Sea-Bed and the Ocean Floor and in the Subsoil Thereof (Sea-bed Treaty)

Thailand

Treaty on the Southeast Asia Nuclear Weapon–Free Zone (Bangkok Treaty)

United States

Antarctic Treaty

Actions reported for the period 1 January to 31 December 2019

The following list shows actions, if any, during the period from 1 January to 31 December 2019 with regard to multilateral arms regulation and disarmament agreements, as reported by the depositaries. The order in which the agreements are listed is according to the date of signature or opening for signature.

A new State party is listed below based on the date of deposit with the respective depositary of a State's instrument of ratification, acceptance, approval or accession. However, please refer to the footnotes to ascertain whether that State actually becomes a State party at a later date, as some treaties only enter into force for a State after a specified period of time from the date of deposit. If a State expressed its consent to be bound by a means other than ratification, the date of deposit is further noted as follows: (a) = accession, (A) = acceptance, (AA) = approval, (P) = consent to be bound and (s) = succession.[a]

In the case of multi-depositary clauses, depositary action may be completed with one or more of the several depositaries. The following notation indicates where the reported action was completed: (M) = Moscow, (L) = London and (W) = Washington.

Certain treaties that establish nuclear-weapon-free zones (Bangkok Treaty, Pelindaba Treaty, Rarotonga Treaty, Treaty of Tlatelolco and Treaty on a Nuclear-Weapon-Free Zone in Central Asia) have associated protocols concerning security guarantees from the nuclear-weapon States and some also have protocols for States outside the zone of application, but which have some territory within the zone. They are at different stages with regard to signature, ratification and entry into force. For the status of adherence of these protocols, see the table in chapter 4 on p. 136.

Protocol for the Prohibition of the Use in War of Asphyxiating, Poisonous or Other Gases, and of Bacteriological Methods of Warfare (1925 Geneva Protocol)

SIGNED AT GENEVA: 17 June 1925
ENTERED INTO FORCE: 8 February 1928
DEPOSITARY: France
    NEW PARTIES: Tajikistan   —15 November (a)
    TOTAL NUMBER OF PARTIES: 143

Antarctic Treaty

SIGNED AT WASHINGTON: 1 December 1959
ENTERED INTO FORCE: 23 June 1961
DEPOSITARY: United States
    NEW PARTIES: Slovenia   — 22 April (a)
    TOTAL NUMBER OF PARTIES: 54

---

[a] A glossary of terms relating to treaty actions is available from http://treaties.un.org/Pages/Overview.aspx?path=overview/glossary/page1_en.xml (accessed 20 June 2018).

Treaty Banning Nuclear Weapon Tests in the Atmosphere, in Outer Space and Under Water (Partial Test Ban Treaty)

SIGNED BY THE ORIGINAL PARTIES[b] IN MOSCOW: 5 August 1963
OPENED FOR SIGNATURE AT LONDON, MOSCOW AND WASHINGTON: 8 August 1963
ENTERED INTO FORCE: 10 October 1963
DEPOSITARY: Russian Federation (M), United Kingdom (L) and United States (W)
    NEW PARTIES: None
    TOTAL NUMBER OF PARTIES: 125

Treaty on Principles Governing the Activities of States in the Exploration and Use of Outer Space, including the Moon and Other Celestial Bodies (Outer Space Treaty)

OPENED FOR SIGNATURE AT LONDON, MOSCOW AND WASHINGTON: 27 January 1967
ENTERED INTO FORCE: 10 October 1967
DEPOSITARY: Russian Federation (M), United Kingdom (L) and United States (W)
    NEW PARTIES: Bahrain   —7 August (a) (M)
                         Slovenia   — 8 February (a) (L)
    TOTAL NUMBER OF PARTIES: 110

Treaty for the Prohibition of Nuclear Weapons in Latin America and the Caribbean (Treaty of Tlatelolco)

OPENED FOR SIGNATURE AT MEXICO CITY: 14 February 1967
ENTERED INTO FORCE: for each Government individually
DEPOSITARY: Mexico
    NEW PARTIES: None
    TOTAL NUMBER OF PARTIES: 33

    Amendment to article 7[c]
    NEW PARTIES: None
    TOTAL NUMBER OF PARTIES: 24

    Amendment to article 25[d]
    NEW PARTIES: None
    TOTAL NUMBER OF PARTIES: 24

    Amendment to articles 14, 15, 16, 19 and 20[e]
    NEW PARTIES: None
    TOTAL NUMBER OF PARTIES: 28

---

[b] The original parties are the Russian Federation, the United Kingdom and the United States.
[c] Amendment adopted by the General Conference of OPANAL, pursuant to resolution 267 (E-V) of 3 July 1990.
[d] Amendment adopted by the General Conference of OPANAL, pursuant to resolution 268 (XII) of 10 May 1991.
[e] Amendment adopted by the General Conference of OPANAL, pursuant to resolution 290 (VII) of 26 August 1992.

Treaty on the Non-Proliferation of Nuclear Weapons

OPENED FOR SIGNATURE AT LONDON, MOSCOW AND WASHINGTON: 1 July 1968
ENTERED INTO FORCE: 5 March 1970
DEPOSITARY: Russian Federation (M), United Kingdom (L) and United States (W)
    NEW PARTIES: None
    TOTAL NUMBER OF PARTIES: 191

Treaty on the Prohibition of the Emplacement of Nuclear Weapons and Other Weapons of Mass Destruction on the Sea-Bed and the Ocean Floor and in the Subsoil Thereof (Sea-bed Treaty)

OPENED FOR SIGNATURE AT LONDON, MOSCOW AND WASHINGTON: 11 February 1971
ENTERED INTO FORCE: 18 May 1972
DEPOSITARY: Russian Federation (M), United Kingdom (L) and United States (W)
    NEW PARTIES: None
    TOTAL NUMBER OF PARTIES: 94

Convention on the Prohibition of the Development, Production and Stockpiling of Bacteriological (Biological) and Toxin Weapons and on Their Destruction

OPENED FOR SIGNATURE AT LONDON, MOSCOW AND WASHINGTON: 10 April 1972
ENTERED INTO FORCE: 26 March 1975
DEPOSITARY: Russian Federation (M), United Kingdom (L) and United States (W)
    NEW PARTIES: United Republic of Tanzania —14 August (L)
    TOTAL NUMBER OF PARTIES: 183

Convention on the Prohibition of Military or Any Other Hostile Use of Environmental Modification Techniques

OPENED FOR SIGNATURE AT GENEVA: 18 May 1977
ENTERED INTO FORCE: 5 October 1978
DEPOSITARY: Secretary-General of the United Nations
    NEW PARTIES: None
    TOTAL NUMBER OF PARTIES: 78

Agreement Governing the Activities of States on the Moon and Other Celestial Bodies

OPENED FOR SIGNATURE AT NEW YORK: 18 December 1979
ENTERED INTO FORCE: 11 July 1984
DEPOSITARY: Secretary-General of the United Nations
    NEW PARTIES:[f]   Armenia   —19 January (a)
    TOTAL NUMBER OF PARTIES: 18

---

[f] Article 19, paragraph 4, states:
    "For each State depositing its instrument of ratification or accession after the entry

Convention on Prohibitions or Restrictions on the Use of Certain Conventional Weapons Which May Be Deemed to Be Excessively Injurious or to Have Indiscriminate Effects

OPENED FOR SIGNATURE AT NEW YORK: 10 April 1981
ENTERED INTO FORCE: 2 December 1983
DEPOSITARY: Secretary-General of the United Nations
    NEW PARTIES:[g]   None
    TOTAL NUMBER OF PARTIES: 125

Amendment to Article 1 of the Convention on Certain Conventional Weapons (entered into force on 18 May 2004)
NEW PARTIES: None
TOTAL NUMBER OF PARTIES: 86

Amended Protocol II (entered into force on 3 December 1998)
NEW PARTIES: Benin   —27 September (P)
TOTAL NUMBER OF PARTIES: 106

Protocol IV (entered into force on 30 July 1998)
NEW PARTIES: Benin   —27 September (P)
TOTAL NUMBER OF PARTIES: 109

Protocol V (entered into force on 12 November 2006)
NEW PARTIES: Benin   —27 September (P)
TOTAL NUMBER OF PARTIES: 96

South Pacific Nuclear Free Zone Treaty (Rarotonga Treaty)

OPENED FOR SIGNATURE AT RAROTONGA: 6 August 1985
ENTERED INTO FORCE: 11 December 1986
DEPOSITARY: Secretary-General of the Pacific Islands Forum
    NEW PARTIES: None
    TOTAL NUMBER OF PARTIES: 13

---

into force of this Agreement, it shall enter into force on the thirtieth day following the date of deposit of any such instrument."

[g] Article 5, paragraphs 2 and 3, of the Convention state:
"2. For any State which deposits its instrument of ratification, acceptance, approval or accession after the date of the deposit of the twentieth instrument of ratification, acceptance, approval or accession, this Convention shall enter into force six months after the date on which that State has deposited its instrument of ratification, acceptance, approval or accession.
"3. Each of the Protocols annexed to this Convention shall enter into force six months after the date by which twenty States have notified their consent to be bound by it in accordance with paragraph 3 or 4 of Article 4 of this Convention."

Treaty on Conventional Armed Forces in Europe

SIGNED AT PARIS: 19 November 1990
ENTERED INTO FORCE: 9 November 1992
DEPOSITARY: Netherlands
    NEW PARTIES: None
    TOTAL NUMBER OF PARTIES: 30

Agreement on Adaptation

ADOPTED AND SIGNED AT ISTANBUL: 19 November 1999
NOT YET IN FORCE[h]
NEW SIGNATORIES: None
TOTAL NUMBER OF SIGNATORIES: 30

NEW PARTIES: None
TOTAL NUMBER OF PARTIES: 3

Treaty on Open Skies

SIGNED AT HELSINKI: 24 March 1992
ENTERED INTO FORCE: 1 January 2002
DEPOSITARY: Canada and Hungary
    NEW PARTIES: None
    TOTAL NUMBER OF PARTIES: 34

Convention on the Prohibition of the Development, Production, Stockpiling and Use of Chemical Weapons and on Their Destruction

SIGNED AT PARIS: 13 January 1993
ENTERED INTO FORCE: 29 April 1997
DEPOSITARY: Secretary-General of the United Nations
    NEW PARTIES:[i]   None
    TOTAL NUMBER OF PARTIES: 193

---

[h] Article 31, paragraph 3, states:
"This Agreement on Adaptation shall enter into force 10 days after instruments of ratification have been deposited by all States Parties listed in the Preamble, after which time the Treaty shall exist only in its amended form."

[i] Article XXI, paragraph 2, states:
"For States whose instruments of ratification or accession are deposited subsequent to the entry into force of this Convention, it shall enter into force on the 30th day following the date of deposit of their instrument of ratification or accession."

Treaty on the Southeast Asia Nuclear Weapon–Free Zone (Bangkok Treaty)

Signed at Bangkok: 15 December 1995
Entered into force: 27 March 1997
Depositary: Thailand
    New parties: None
    Total number of parties: 10

African Nuclear-Weapon-Free Zone Treaty (Pelindaba Treaty)

Signed at Cairo: 11 April 1996
Entered into force: 15 July 2009
Depositary: Secretary-General of the African Union
    New parties: None
    Total number of parties: 40

Comprehensive Nuclear-Test-Ban Treaty

Opened for signature at New York: 24 September 1996
Not yet in force[j]
Depositary: Secretary-General of the United Nations
    New signatories: None
    Total number of signatories: 184

    New parties: Zimbabwe   —13 February
    Total number of parties: 168

Convention on the Prohibition of the Use, Stockpiling, Production and Transfer of Anti-Personnel Mines and on Their Destruction (Anti-Personnel Mine Ban Convention)

Opened for signature at Ottawa: 3 December 1997
Entered into force: 1 March 1999
Depositary: Secretary-General of the United Nations
    New parties:[k]   None
    Total number of parties: 164

---

[j] Article XIV, paragraph 1, states:
"This Treaty shall enter into force 180 days after the date of deposit of the instruments of ratification by all States listed in Annex II to this Treaty, but in no case earlier than two years after its opening for signature."

[k] Article 17, paragraph 2, states:
"For any State which deposits its instrument of ratification, acceptance, approval or accession after the date of the deposit of the 40th instrument of ratification, acceptance, approval or accession, this Convention shall enter into force on the first day of the sixth month after the date on which that State has deposited its instrument of ratification, acceptance, approval or accession."

Inter-American Convention Against the Illicit Manufacturing of and Trafficking in Firearms, Ammunition, Explosives, and Other Related Materials

OPENED FOR SIGNATURE AT WASHINGTON, DC: 14 November 1997
ENTERED INTO FORCE: 1 July 1998
DEPOSITARY: Organization of American States
    NEW PARTIES:[1]   None
    TOTAL NUMBER OF PARTIES: 31

Inter-American Convention on Transparency in Conventional Weapons Acquisitions

OPENED FOR SIGNATURE AT GUATEMALA CITY: 7 June 1999
ENTERED INTO FORCE: 21 November 2002
DEPOSITARY: Organization of American States
    NEW PARTIES: None
    TOTAL NUMBER OF PARTIES: 17

International Convention for the Suppression of Acts of Nuclear Terrorism

OPENED FOR SIGNATURE AT NEW YORK: 14 September 2005
ENTERED INTO FORCE: 7 July 2007
DEPOSITARY: Secretary General of the United Nations

NEW PARTIES:[m]		
	Montenegro	—13 February
	Thailand	—2 May

    TOTAL NUMBER OF PARTIES: 116

Treaty on a Nuclear-Weapon-Free Zone in Central Asia

OPENED FOR SIGNATURE AT SEMIPALATINSK: 8 September 2006
ENTERED INTO FORCE: 21 March 2009
DEPOSITARY: Kyrgyzstan
    NEW PARTIES: None
    TOTAL NUMBER OF PARTIES: 5

---

[1] Article XXV states:
    "This Convention shall enter into force on the 30th day following the date of deposit of the second instrument of ratification. For each State ratifying the Convention after the deposit of the second instrument of ratification, the Convention shall enter into force on the 30th day following deposit by such State of its instrument of ratification."
[m] Article 25, paragraph 2 states:
    "For each State ratifying, accepting, approving or acceding to the Convention after the deposit of the twenty-second instrument of ratification, acceptance, approval or accession, the Convention shall enter into force on the thirtieth day after deposit by such State of its instrument of ratification, acceptance, approval or accession."

Convention on Cluster Munitions

OPENED FOR SIGNATURE AT OSLO: 3 December 2008
ENTERED INTO FORCE: 1 August 2010
DEPOSITARY: Secretary-General of the United Nations
    NEW PARTIES:[n]   —Maldives   —27 September
                      —Philippines   —3 January
    TOTAL NUMBER OF PARTIES: 107

Central African Convention for the Control of Small Arms and Light Weapons, Their Ammunition and All Parts and Components That Can Be Used for Their Manufacture, Repair and Assembly (Kinshasa Convention)

OPENED FOR SIGNATURE AT BRAZZAVILLE: 19 November 2010
ENTERED INTO FORCE: 8 March 2017
DEPOSITARY: Secretary-General of the United Nations
    NEW PARTIES:[o]   Equatorial Guinea   — 24 December
    TOTAL NUMBER OF PARTIES: 8

Arms Trade Treaty

OPENED FOR SIGNATURE AT NEW YORK: 3 June 2013
ENTERED INTO FORCE: 24 December 2014
DEPOSITARY: Secretary-General of the United Nations
    NEW PARTIES:[p]   Canada   —19 June (a)
                      Lebanon   —9 May
                      Maldives   —27 September (a)
                      Botswana   —7 June (a)
                      Palau   —8 April
    TOTAL NUMBER OF PARTIES: 105

---

[n] Article 17, paragraph 2, states:

"For any State that deposits its instrument of ratification, acceptance, approval or accession after the date of the deposit of the thirtieth instrument of ratification, acceptance, approval or accession, this Convention shall enter into force on the first day of the sixth month after the date on which that State has deposited its instrument of ratification, acceptance, approval or accession."

[o] Article 36, paragraph 2, states:

"For each State that deposits its instrument of ratification, acceptance, approval or accession after the date of deposit of the sixth instrument of ratification, acceptance, approval or accession, the Convention shall enter into force 30 days after the date of deposit of that instrument."

[p] Article 22, paragraph 2, states:

"For any State that deposits its instrument of ratification, acceptance, approval or accession subsequent to the entry into force of this Treaty, this Treaty shall enter into force for that State ninety days following the date of deposit of its instrument of ratification, acceptance, approval or accession."

Treaty on the Prohibition of Nuclear Weapons

OPENED FOR SIGNATURE AT NEW YORK: 7 July 2017
NOT YET IN FORCE[q]
DEPOSITARY: Secretary-General of the United Nations

NEW SIGNATORIES:		
	Botswana	—26 September
	Cambodia	—9 January
	Dominica	—26 September
	Grenada	—26 September
	Lesotho	—26 September
	Maldives	—26 September
	Nauru	—22 November
	Saint Kitts and Nevis	—26 September
	Trinidad and Tobago	—26 September
	United Republic of Tanzania	—26 September
	Zambia	—26 September

TOTAL NUMBER OF SIGNATORIES: 80

NEW PARTIES:		
	Antigua and Barbuda	—25 November
	Bangladesh	—26 September
	Bolivia (Plurinational State of)	—6 August
	Dominica	—18 October
	Ecuador	—25 September
	El Salvador	—30 January
	Kazakhstan	—29 August
	Kiribati	—26 September
	Lao People's Democratic Republic	—26 September
	Maldives	—26 September
	Panama	—11 April
	Saint Lucia	—23 January
	Saint Vincent and the Grenadines	—31 July 2019
	South Africa	—25 February
	Trinidad and Tobago	—26 September

TOTAL NUMBER OF PARTIES: 34

---

[q] Article 15, paragraph 1, states:

"This Treaty shall enter into force 90 days after the fiftieth instrument of ratification, acceptance, approval or accession has been deposited."

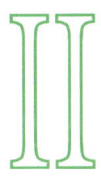

appendix

II Disarmament resolutions and decisions listed by chapter

A view of the gavel that was handed over from María Fernanda Espinosa Garcés, President of the seventy-third session of the General Assembly, to Tijjani Muhammad-Bande, President of the seventy-fourth session of the General Assembly, after the closing plenary meeting of the seventy-third session of the General Assembly, 16 September 2019.

Disarmament resolutions and decisions listed by chapter

At its seventy-fourth session, the General Assembly adopted 56 resolutions and three decisions related to disarmament. In this appendix, highlights of those texts and explanations of vote by Member States during the First Committee session are presented, with the information organized by chapter topic.[a] The accompanying boxes contain key data and cross references to Part I of the *Yearbook*, which can be consulted for the complete texts, the full lists of sponsors and the votes of States.[b]

Chapter I. Nuclear disarmament and non-proliferation

74/31. Conclusion of effective international arrangements to assure non-nuclear-weapon States against the use or threat of use of nuclear weapons

The General Assembly recommended that further intensive efforts be devoted to the search for a common approach or common formula and that the various alternative approaches, particularly those considered in the Conference on Disarmament, be further explored. It also recommended that the

> **Submitted by**: Pakistan (5 Oct.)
>
> **GA vote**: 122-0-64 (12 Dec.)
>
> **1st Cttee vote**: 118-0-63 (1 Nov.)
>
> See also *Yearbook, Part I*, pp. 27–31.

Conference actively continue intensive negotiations to reach agreement and conclude effective international agreements on security assurances, taking into account the widespread support for the conclusion of an international convention and giving consideration to any other proposals designed to secure the same objective.

First Committee. After the voting in favour, Belarus took the floor and called for full compliance with assurances for non-nuclear-weapon States against the use or threat of use of nuclear weapons.

---

[a] See A/C.1/74/PV.22–26 for the full text of the statements.
[b] The following are abbreviations used in the boxes:
o.p. = operative paragraph; p.p. = preambular paragraph. The order of the numbers for the voting statistics indicates votes in favour, votes against and abstentions, respectively.

74/36. Follow-up to nuclear disarmament obligations agreed to at the 1995, 2000 and 2010 Review Conferences of the Parties to the Treaty on the Non-Proliferation of Nuclear Weapons

The General Assembly recalled that the 2010 Review Conference of the Parties to the Treaty on the Non-Proliferation of Nuclear Weapons (Nuclear Non-Proliferation Treaty) reaffirmed the continued validity of the practical steps agreed to in the Final Document of the 2000 Review Conference of the Treaty. The Assembly also noted that the 2000 and 2010 Review Conferences had agreed that legally binding security assurances by the five nuclear-weapon States to the non-nuclear-weapon States parties to the Treaty strengthened the nuclear non-proliferation regime.

> **Submitted by**: Iran (Islamic Republic of) (30 Sep.)
>
> **GA vote**: 118-43-19; 119-4-46, p.p. 6 (12 Dec.)
>
> **1st Cttee vote**: 110-43-20; 109-5-50, p.p. 6 (1 Nov.)
>
> See also *Yearbook, Part I*, pp. 49–53.

74/41. Treaty on the Prohibition of Nuclear Weapons

The General Assembly welcomed the adoption of the Treaty on the Prohibition of Nuclear Weapons on 7 July 2017 and welcomed that already 79 States had signed the Treaty and 33 States had ratified or acceded to it as at 1 November 2019. It called upon all States that had not yet done so to sign, ratify, accept, approve or accede to the Treaty at the earliest possible date.

> **Submitted by**: Austria (10 Oct.)
>
> **GA vote**: 123-41-16; 115-40-12, o.p. 5; 118-26-22, o.p. 6 (12 Dec.)
>
> **1st Cttee vote**: 119-41-15; 108-40-13, o.p. 5; 109-26-23, o.p. 6 (1 Nov.)
>
> See also *Yearbook, Part I*, pp. 76–79.

First Committee. Before voting in favour, the **Islamic Republic of Iran** noted that the adoption of that Treaty was a step in the right direction.

Before voting against the draft resolution, the following States delivered statements:

- **Israel** expressed concern, inter alia, about arms control and disarmament processes that failed to give due regard to the security and stability context when drafting disarmament measures. With respect to procedural aspects, Israel firmly believed that such negotiations should be undertaken in the appropriate forums, under the appropriate rules of procedure, which would not undermine national security considerations.

- **Pakistan** said that at each stage of the disarmament process, the objective should be undiminished security at the lowest level of armaments and military forces. It believed that the cardinal objective could be achieved only as a cooperative and universally agreed undertaking through a consensus-based process involving all the relevant stakeholders. It asserted that the Treaty on the Prohibition of Nuclear Weapons did not fulfil those essential conditions.

After voting against the draft resolution, the following States explained their votes:

- The **United Kingdom**, speaking also on behalf of China, France, the Russian Federation and the United States, argued that the Treaty on the Prohibition of Nuclear Weapons failed to address the key issues that must be overcome to achieve lasting global nuclear disarmament, contradicted and risked undermining the Nuclear Non-Proliferation Treaty, ignored the international security context and regional challenges, and did nothing to increase trust and transparency among States.

- **Japan** was of the view that all States should focus on concrete and practical measures for advancing the common goal of nuclear disarmament, regardless of divergent views.

- **India** maintained that it would not become a party to the Treaty and should not be bound by any of the obligations that might arise from it. It reiterated its commitment to the goal of a nuclear-weapon-free world and believed that that goal could be achieved through a step-by-step process, underwritten by a universal commitment and an agreed global and non-discriminatory multilateral framework, as outlined in its working paper (CD/1816) entitled "Nuclear Disarmament", submitted to the General Assembly in 2006.

After they abstained from voting, the following States spoke:

- **Sweden** conveyed that, after careful consideration and extensive consultations, it announced in July that Sweden would refrain from signing or seeking the ratification of the Treaty on the Prohibition of Nuclear Weapons in its current form, largely because of its shortcomings, which Sweden addressed during the negotiations in 2017.

- **Argentina** believed that the Treaty on the Prohibition of Nuclear Weapons, and any future instrument, should strengthen the Nuclear Non-Proliferation Treaty, while avoiding duplication or generating parallel regimes on provisions that were well established and enjoyed strong acceptance within the framework of the Nuclear Non-Proliferation Treaty.

- **Switzerland** said that, while it supported the overall objective of the Treaty on the Prohibition of Nuclear Weapons, it continued to question some of the Treaty's provisions, including their impact on the existing nuclear disarmament and non-proliferation regime based on the Nuclear Non-Proliferation Treaty. It stated that it would reassess its position on the Treaty before the end of 2020.

- **Singapore** reiterated its view that the Treaty on the Prohibition of Nuclear Weapons should not in any way affect the rights and obligations of States parties to other treaties and agreements.

74/42. Humanitarian consequences of nuclear weapons

The General Assembly stressed that it was in the interest of the very survival of humanity that nuclear weapons never be used again, under any circumstances, and that the only way to guarantee that nuclear weapons are never used again would be their total elimination. Furthermore, the Assembly stressed that the catastrophic effects of a nuclear weapon detonation could not be adequately addressed and that awareness of those consequences must underpin all approaches and efforts towards nuclear disarmament. The Assembly called upon all States to prevent the use of nuclear weapons, to prevent their vertical and horizontal proliferation and to exert all efforts to totally eliminate the threat of those weapons.

> **Submitted by**: Austria (10 Oct.)
>
> **GA vote**: 144-13-28 (12 Dec.)
>
> **1st Cttee vote**: 136-14-27 (1 Nov.)
>
> See also *Yearbook, Part I*, pp. 80–83.

First Committee. Before voting in favour of the draft resolution, **North Macedonia** said that it had decided to withdraw its sponsorship after thorough consideration of the draft resolution.

Before voting against the draft resolution, **France** took the floor, speaking also on behalf of the United Kingdom and United States. It stated that some, including those who continued to promote the narrative on humanitarian consequences, maintained that the goal of nuclear disarmament called for a ban on the possession and use of nuclear weapons with immediate effect, even though States that possessed nuclear weapons that do not join the ban would not be bound by it. They believed that approach was deeply misguided.

After voting in favour, the following delivered statements:

- **Japan** emphasized that, as the only country to have suffered wartime atomic bombings, it shared the goal of the total elimination of nuclear weapons and recognized the humanitarian consequences of the use of nuclear weapons, based on its first-hand experience.

- **India** said that it shared concerns about the serious threat to the survival of humankind that could be posed by the use of nuclear weapons.

After they abstained from voting, the following States explained their votes:

- **China** pointed out that overemphasizing humanitarian issues while neglecting other important elements that were more closely related to nuclear disarmament would not be conducive to achieving results in the process of nuclear disarmament. Instead, China believed that it would interfere with and undermine the consensus-based conclusions already reached.

- **Pakistan** believed that the discourse on nuclear weapons could not be reduced solely to its humanitarian and ethical dimensions by trivializing and ignoring the fundamental security concerns of States that relied on them for their security.

74/44. Reducing nuclear danger

The General Assembly called for a review of nuclear doctrines and for immediate and urgent steps to reduce the risks of unintentional and accidental use of nuclear weapons. The Assembly requested the

> **Submitted by**: India (11 Oct.)
>
> **GA vote**: 123-49-15 (12 Dec.)
>
> **1st Cttee vote**: 117-49-14 (1 Nov.)
>
> See also *Yearbook, Part I*, pp. 87–89.

Secretary-General to intensify efforts and support initiatives that would contribute to the full implementation of the recommendations of the Secretary-General's Advisory Board on Disarmament Matters that would significantly reduce the risk of nuclear war, and to continue encouraging Member States to consider the convening of an international conference to identify ways of eliminating nuclear dangers.

First Committee. Before it abstained from voting, **Pakistan** stated that the sponsor of the draft resolution relied on the continuous expansion and modernization of its conventional and nuclear arsenals and increasing the readiness of its nuclear forces by taking steps—such as the canisterization of missiles, the induction of destabilizing weapon systems, and forced postures and security doctrines—that had an offensive, rather than defensive, intent.

74/45. Nuclear disarmament

The General Assembly urged the Conference on Disarmament to commence as early as possible its substantive work during its 2020 session, on the basis of a comprehensive and balanced programme of work that took into consideration all the real and existing priorities in the field of disarmament and arms control, including the immediate commencement of negotiations on a comprehensive nuclear weapons convention. It also called for the early entry into force, universalization and strict observance of the Comprehensive Nuclear-Test-Ban Treaty as a contribution to nuclear disarmament, while welcoming the latest signatory to the Treaty, Tuvalu, and its latest ratification, by Zimbabwe.

> **Submitted by**: Myanmar (11 Oct.)
>
> **GA vote**: 120-41-22; 113-37-15, p.p. 2; 148-4-14, o.p. 12; 163-1-10, o.p. 16 (12 Dec.)
>
> **1st Cttee vote**: 117-40-22; 108-38-14, p.p. 2; 144-4-17, o.p. 12; 157-1-10, o.p. 16 (1 Nov.)
>
> See also *Yearbook, Part I*, pp. 90–101.

First Committee. After they abstained from voting on the draft resolution, the following took the floor:

- The **Democratic People's Republic of Korea** maintained that the total elimination of nuclear weapons was the only solution to the threats posed by nuclear weapons. In that regard, it was of the view that the nuclear-weapon States with the biggest nuclear arsenals should take the lead in the nuclear disarmament process. However, it expressed reservations regarding the continued calls for adherence to the Nuclear Non-Proliferation Treaty and the Comprehensive Nuclear-Test-Ban Treaty.

- As a non-party to the Nuclear Non-Proliferation Treaty, **Pakistan** said that it could not subscribe to the implementation of the action plans and decisions of the Treaty's Review Conferences. Regarding paragraph 16 of the draft resolution, it considered ironic the continued promotion, in a draft resolution on nuclear disarmament, of a non-proliferation-centric treaty on fissile material; therefore it had decided to vote against the paragraph.

- **Switzerland** wished to put on record that it abstained in the voting on the draft resolution and on several votes on separate paragraphs of different draft resolutions with reference to the Treaty on the Prohibition of Nuclear Weapons.

- **India** explained that it had to abstain in the voting on the draft resolution because of certain references to the Nuclear Non-Proliferation Treaty and the Treaty on the Prohibition of Nuclear Weapons, on which its position was well known. However, it supported other provisions of the draft resolution, which it believed were consistent with India's position on nuclear disarmament and non-proliferation.

74/46. Towards a nuclear-weapon-free world: accelerating the implementation of nuclear disarmament commitments

The General Assembly acknowledged its decision 73/546 of 22 December 2018, in which it had decided to entrust to the Secretary-General the convening of a conference aimed at elaborating a treaty on the establishment of a Middle East zone free of nuclear weapons and all other weapons of mass destruction, on the basis of arrangements freely arrived at by the States of the region. The Assembly emphasized the importance of holding a constructive meeting that resulted in a substantive outcome at the 2020 Nuclear Non-Proliferation Treaty Review Conference, urging all Member States to step up their efforts in that regard. It also emphasized the vital importance of ensuring that the Review Conference (a) contributed to the strengthening of the Nuclear Non-Proliferation Treaty and making progress towards achieving its full implementation and universality, and (b) monitored the implementation of commitments made and actions agreed upon at the 1995, 2000 and 2010 Review Conferences.

> **Submitted by**: Egypt (13 Oct.)
>
> **GA vote**: 137-33-16; 141-1-29, p.p. 4; 115-37-14, p.p. 12; 160-4-8, p.p. 8; 159-4-9, o.p. 15; 114-38-17, o.p. 24 (12 Dec.)
>
> **1st Cttee vote**: 132-32-17; 133-1-29, p.p. 4; 110-37-12, p.p. 12; 153-3-7, p.p. 8; 153-4-7, o.p. 15; 111-36-12, o.p. 24 (1 Nov.)
>
> See also *Yearbook, Part I*, pp. 102–115.

First Committee. In a general statement, **Egypt** welcomed the draft resolution, which it believed represented a genuine call for concrete progress on nuclear disarmament and working towards achieving and maintaining a world without nuclear weapons through a set of realistic and practical measures. It urged all member States to support the relevant proposals and honour their previous obligations and unequivocal commitments.

Before voting against the draft resolution, **France**, speaking also on behalf of the United Kingdom and the United States, referred to the inclusion in the text of language welcoming of the adoption of the Treaty on the Prohibition of Nuclear Weapons, which it strongly opposed.

After voting in favour, **Switzerland** said that it continued to question some of the provisions of the Treaty on the Prohibition of Nuclear Weapons, including the impact on the existing nuclear disarmament and non-proliferation regime based on the Nuclear Non-Proliferation Treaty. It stated that it would reassess its position on the Treaty before the end of 2020. It voted in favour of its fourth preambular paragraph, regarding the Secretary-General's disarmament agenda, but believed changes made to other paragraphs of the draft resolution gave rise to several questions, in particular the twenty-sixth preambular paragraph and paragraph 22.

After the vote, **India** said that it voted against the draft resolution, as well as its operative paragraph 15, since it could not accept the call to accede to the Nuclear Non-Proliferation Treaty as a non-nuclear-weapon State.

After they abstained from voting, the following States took the floor:

- The **Democratic People's Republic of Korea** said that it considered the draft resolution biased and unbalanced because of the unilateral call upon it to denuclearize without any mention of eliminating the root cause of the problem.

- **Pakistan** conveyed its dismay towards the ritualistic and unrealistic call upon it in paragraph 15 to accede to the Nuclear Non-Proliferation Treaty as a non-nuclear-weapon State.

74/47. Ethical imperatives for a nuclear-weapon-free world

The General Assembly called upon all States to acknowledge the catastrophic humanitarian consequences and risks posed by a nuclear-weapon detonation, whether by accident, miscalculation or design, and it acknowledged the ethical imperatives for nuclear disarmament and the urgency of achieving and maintaining a nuclear-weapon-free world, which was a "global public good of the highest order", serving both national and collective security interests. The Assembly stressed that all States, with the support of all relevant stakeholders, shared an ethical responsibility to act with urgency and determination to take the effective measures, including legally binding measures, necessary to eliminate and prohibit all nuclear weapons, given their catastrophic humanitarian consequences and associated risks.

> **Submitted by**: South Africa (14 Oct.)
>
> **GA vote**: 135-37-13; 119-33-17, p.p. 11 (12 Dec.)
>
> **1st Cttee vote**: 129-37-12; 111-32-16, p.p. 11 (1 Nov.)
>
> See also *Yearbook, Part I*, pp. 116–121.

First Committee. Before voting against the draft resolution, **France** took the floor, speaking also on behalf of the United Kingdom and the United States. France said that some, including those who continued to promote the narrative on humanitarian consequences, maintained that the goal of nuclear disarmament called for a ban on the possession and use of nuclear weapons with immediate effect, even though States that possessed nuclear weapons that did not join the ban would not be bound by it. They believed that that approach was deeply misguided.

After voting against the draft resolution, **India** stated that questions relating to the immorality of nuclear weapons had to be examined in the framework of the sovereign responsibility of States to protect their security in a nuclearized global order assembled on the pillars of nuclear deterrence.

After they abstained from voting on the draft resolution, the following States spoke:

- **China** expressed the view that achieving the goal of nuclear disarmament could not be the only goal and that overemphasizing humanitarian issues while neglecting other important elements that were more closely related to nuclear disarmament would not be conducive to achieving results in the process of nuclear disarmament. Instead, China believed that that would interfere with and undermine the consensus-based conclusions already reached.

- **Pakistan** said that the discourse on nuclear weapons could not be reduced solely to the humanitarian and ethical dimensions by trivializing and ignoring the fundamental security concerns of States that relied on them for their security.

74/50. Nuclear disarmament verification

The General Assembly welcomed the adoption by consensus of the report of the Group of Governmental Experts on Nuclear Disarmament Verification, mandated in resolution 71/67. The Assembly requested the Secretary-General to seek the substantive views of Member States on the report of the Group. It also requested the Secretary-General to establish a group of governmental experts of up to 25 participants, which would meet in Geneva for four sessions of one week each in 2021 and 2022, to further consider nuclear disarmament verification issues. The Assembly requested the Chair of the group to organize, in New York, two informal intersessional consultative meetings so that all Member States could share their views, which the Chair should convey to the group of governmental experts for its consideration.

> **Submitted by**: Norway (29 Oct.)
> **GA vote**: 178-1-5 (12 Dec.)
> **1st Cttee vote**: 173-1-4 (7 Nov.)
> See also *Yearbook, Part I*, pp. 136–139.

First Committee. After voting in favour of the draft resolution, the following States took the floor:

- **Egypt** stated that it had multiple reservations about the report of the Group of Governmental Experts and its possible unintended negative implications on the objective of achieving nuclear disarmament and on the relevant agreed obligations.

- **Cuba** pointed out that the draft resolution contained significant changes that undermined the balance of the text, noting the elimination of various provisions of resolution 71/67.

After voting against the draft resolution, the **Russian Federation** said that verification activities, separate from any specific agreement in the area of arms control and reduction, had no practical value. In addition, it believed that focusing attention on verification issues distracted the attention of the international community from the primordial issues of international security, which had a direct impact on the prospects of nuclear disarmament. It was of the view that changing the mandate of the Group of Governmental Experts from consideration of the role of verification in advancing nuclear disarmament was premature.

74/54. Follow-up to the 2013 high-level meeting of the General Assembly on nuclear disarmament

The General Assembly expressed its concern that improvements in existing nuclear weapons and the development of new types of nuclear weapons (a) violated the legal obligations on nuclear disarmament of States party to the Nuclear Non-Proliferation Treaty, as well as the commitments of those States to diminish the role of nuclear weapons in their military and security

> **Submitted by**: Indonesia (4 Nov.)
> **GA vote**: 1142-34-10; 114-36-16, p.p. 14 (12 Dec.)
> **1st Cttee vote**: 137-33-10; 115-35-18, p.p. 14 (7 Nov.)
> See also *Yearbook, Part I*, pp. 153–158.

policies, and (b) contravened the negative security assurances provided by the nuclear-weapon States. The Assembly requested the Secretary-General to undertake all the arrangements to commemorate and promote the International Day for the Total Elimination of Nuclear Weapons, including a one-day high-level plenary meeting of the Assembly, and to continue to update the platform for the promotion of those activities.

First Committee. Before voting in favour of the draft resolution, **Cuba** expressed support for the concern about improvements in existing nuclear weapons and the development of new types of nuclear weapons.

After voting against the draft resolution, the following States took the floor:

- The **Netherlands** expressed regret that the proposals it put forward during the 2013 high-level meeting were not acknowledged in the draft resolution. It therefore did not believe that the United Nations high-level international conference on nuclear disarmament, to be convened at a date to be decided later, set the right mandate for such negotiations. It asserted that the central role of the Nuclear Non-Proliferation Treaty and its review cycle was not acknowledged in the draft resolution.

- **France**, speaking also on behalf of the United States and the United Kingdom, expressed the view that nuclear proliferation and the non-compliance of some States with their non-proliferation obligations, as well as nuclear terrorism and the deterioration of the international security environment, constituted serious threats to international peace and security that were not taken into account in the text. They also considered its inclusion of only one reference to the Nuclear Non-Proliferation Treaty—to article VI—to be insufficient, incidental and unbalanced. In addition, they did not support the language in the text noting the adoption of the text of the Treaty on the Prohibition of Nuclear Weapons.

After it abstained from voting, **Switzerland** expressed the belief that the negotiation of a comprehensive nuclear-weapons convention was not the only possible option and was perhaps not the most promising. It noted that it had several questions concerning the new fourteenth preambular paragraph.

74/58. Prohibition of the dumping of radioactive wastes

The General Assembly requested the Conference on Disarmament to continue to consider a convention on the prohibition of radiological weapons, one that took into account radioactive wastes, and to include in its report to the Assembly at its seventy-fifth session the progress recorded in the negotiations on the subject.

> **Submitted by**: Nigeria (16 Oct.)
>
> **GA vote**: w/o vote (12 Dec.)
>
> **1st Cttee vote**: w/o vote (1 Nov.)
>
> See also *Yearbook, Part I*, pp.169–171.

74/59. Follow-up to the advisory opinion of the International Court of Justice on the legality of the threat or use of nuclear weapons

The General Assembly underlined once again the unanimous conclusion of the International Court of Justice that there existed an obligation to pursue in good faith and bring to a conclusion negotiations leading to nuclear disarmament in all its aspects under strict and effective international control. It called once again upon all States to immediately engage in multilateral negotiations leading to nuclear disarmament in all its aspects under strict and effective international control, including under the Treaty on the Prohibition of Nuclear Weapons.

> **Submitted by**: Malaysia (16 Oct.)
>
> **GA vote**: 138-33-15; 143-1-29, p.p. 9; 118-36-15, p.p. 17; 120-36-13, o.p. 2 (12 Dec.)
>
> **1st Cttee vote**: 132-32-17; 135-1-30, p.p. 9; 116-36-14, p.p. 17; 114-36-15, o.p. 2 (7 Nov.)
>
> See also *Yearbook, Part I*, pp. 172–178.

74/63. Joint courses of action and future-oriented dialogue towards a world without nuclear weapons

The General Assembly reaffirmed that all States parties to the Nuclear Non-Proliferation Treaty were committed to the ultimate goal of eliminating nuclear weapons and called upon all States parties to the Treaty to identify concrete measures to put the commitments into practice towards the 2020 Review Conference. It encouraged all States, in particular the nuclear-weapon States, to take concrete measures to enhance transparency and mutual confidence, to take actions to reduce the risks of nuclear detonation occurring either by miscalculation or by misunderstanding, and to make every effort—including declaring and maintaining moratoriums on the production of fissile material for use in nuclear weapons or other nuclear explosive devices, as well as deepening substantive discussions in the Conference on Disarmament—to start negotiations on a treaty banning the production of fissile material

> **Submitted by**: Japan (31 Oct.)
>
> **GA vote**: 160-4-21; 157-2-18, p.p. 2; 166-2-7, p.p. 4; 168-2-6, p.p. 8; 162-3-8, p.p. 16; 161-0-15, p.p. 18; 165-2-6, p.p. 19; 148-7-20, o.p. 1; 157-3-13, o.p. 3; 146-5-19, o.p. 3; 153-2-18, o.p. 3; 162-2-8, o.p. 3; 159-3-11, o.p. 5 (12 Dec.)
>
> **1st Cttee vote**: 148-4-26; 149-2-16, p.p. 2; 158-2-7, p.p. 4; 155-2-8, p.p. 8; 150-3-9, p.p. 16; 147-0-18, p.p. 18; 155-2-5, p.p. 19; 133-7-20, o.p. 1; 145-3-15, o.p. 3; 132-5-21, o.p. 3; 139-2-20, o.p. 3; 151-2-8, o.p. 3; 149-3-10, o.p. 5 (1 Nov.)
>
> See also *Yearbook, Part I*, pp. 199–216.

for use in nuclear weapons or other nuclear explosive devices. The Assembly also encouraged all States to immediately sign and ratify the Comprehensive Nuclear-Test-Ban Treaty, among other actions.

First Committee. Before voting against the draft resolution, the **Democratic People's Republic of Korea** categorically rejected the draft resolution, asserting that the text did not indicate willingness or intention to engage in dialogue towards a world free of nuclear weapons. It expressed its rejection of the central resolutions of the Security Council mentioned in the draft resolution.

Before it abstained from voting on the draft resolution, **Algeria** drew attention to the draft resolution's operative paragraphs, which it believed introduced different language and removed relevant references to the Nuclear Non-Proliferation Treaty that were reflected in previous versions. It was in favour of the eighteenth preambular paragraph and operative paragraph 1, despite concerns regarding the language of the draft resolution. With regard to the eighteenth preambular paragraph, it said that the text did not faithfully reflect the agreed language of the 2010 Nuclear Non-Proliferation Treaty Review Conference, which emphasized the deep concerns about the humanitarian consequences of any use of nuclear weapons, and similarly, operative paragraph 1 did not cover the implementation of obligations under the Nuclear Non-Proliferation Treaty and the agreed steps and actions from previous Review Conferences of the Treaty.

After voting in favour, the following States explained their votes:

- **Belarus** welcomed the fact that the draft resolution called for the establishment of new nuclear-weapon-free zones on the basis of agreements among States in the relevant regions and that the draft reflected the importance of further efforts to achieve the immediate signing and ratification of the Comprehensive Nuclear-Test-Ban Treaty.

- **France**, which abstained from voting on the eighteenth preambular paragraph and paragraph 3 (c), explained that it rejected any link established between the catastrophic humanitarian consequences of the use of nuclear weapons and nuclear disarmament. It pointed out that there was no consensus that such an approach underpinned efforts towards nuclear disarmament. On paragraph 3 (c), it recalled that any negotiations on a fissile material cut-off treaty should be based on document CD/1299 and the mandate therein, and the failure to mention that document in the operative part of the draft resolution was the reason for its abstention in the voting on the paragraph.

After voting against the draft resolution, **China** explained its votes against the sixteenth and nineteenth preambular paragraphs and operative paragraphs 3 (c), 3 (e), 3 (f) and 5. With regard to the fissile material cut-off treaty, it (a) maintained that reaching a comprehensive and balanced programme of work in the Conference on Disarmament and negotiating the treaty under the Shannon Mandate was the only viable way forward, and (b) objected to the moratorium, as it did not have a clear definition or scope and could not be verified. Noting that certain paragraphs contained reference to concrete exercises on nuclear disarmament verification, China expressed the view that either the Group of Governmental Experts, under the United Nations framework, or the Conference on Disarmament must decide whether or not to take that approach. It also could not support the operative paragraph on the Democratic People's Republic of Korea, its main concern being the inclusion of content that went above and beyond the provisions of Security Council resolutions.

After they abstained from voting, the following States spoke:

- **Mexico** explained that the language in several paragraphs reinterpreted prior agreements made by the parties to the Nuclear Non-Proliferation Treaty, in particular the obligations and provisions listed in article VI of the Treaty. It stated that the draft resolution included notions of conditionalities for compliance with obligations for nuclear disarmament and did not acknowledge differentiated responsibilities of nuclear and non-nuclear States. It was also concerned that the draft resolution included references to the Comprehensive Nuclear-Test-Ban Treaty that did not match the language agreed in other resolutions and documents.

- **Liechtenstein** considered the formulation in operative paragraph 1 unacceptable, as it introduced a qualification to the clear obligations of the nuclear-weapon States under article VI of the Nuclear Non-Proliferation Treaty and undermined the unequivocal undertaking by the nuclear-weapon States to accomplish the total elimination of their nuclear arsenals, as previously agreed. It also expressed dissatisfaction with the approach of the draft resolution towards the urgent entry into force of the Comprehensive Nuclear-Test-Ban Treaty, as it believed that the text suggested that a moratorium on testing could be an acceptable effort by the nuclear-weapon States to comply with past commitments.

- **Brazil** pointed out that some elements of the draft text seemed to reinterpret or limit the obligations and commitments derived from the Nuclear Non-Proliferation Treaty and its review process. With regard to the second preambular paragraph, it would have preferred the use of the term "cornerstone" to refer to the relevance of the Treaty to the nuclear disarmament and non-proliferation regime, in line with long-standing practice. With regard to operative paragraph 1, it believed that the language contained therein suggested that the achievement of a world free of nuclear weapons, which was a legally binding obligation derived from article VI of the Treaty, was contingent upon the easing of international tensions and the strengthening of trust among States. It was also very concerned about the most recent revision of the draft, which it believed suggested that the goal of eliminating nuclear weapons was dependent upon the strengthening of the international non-proliferation regime. It also explained that the moratoriums on nuclear tests elevated in paragraph 3 (d), while important interim measures, were by no means a substitute for the entry into force of the Comprehensive Nuclear-Test-Ban Treaty.

- **Ireland** said that certain elements reinterpreted important outcomes and undertakings related to the Nuclear Non-Proliferation Treaty, and it could not accept any implication that conditionality applied to disarmament obligations. It reiterated that entry into force of the Comprehensive Nuclear-Test-Ban Treaty and its universalization were key priorities for Ireland, and the language on that point was insufficient. It said that it abstained in the voting on preambular paragraph 18, which it believed insufficiently captured the devastating consequences that would result from the use of nuclear weapons and the urgency of the issue. It also regretted the lack of a comprehensive gender perspective in the draft resolution.

- The **Republic of Korea** strongly believed that the term used to refer to the atomic bomb survivors should have been phrased in a more appropriate manner, in order to fully represent all survivors, regardless of their nationalities. It was also disappointed to see that some language used in operative paragraphs moved away from previously agreed language and did not reflect a well-crafted balance.

- **Egypt** was of the view the draft resolution implicitly linked the implementation of nuclear disarmament obligations to an ambiguous set of preconditions and aimed to lower the level of expectation regarding the pace of implementing the relevant agreed commitments. In subparagraph 3 (b), it noted that the term "States possessing nuclear weapons" did not observe the established categorization within the context of the Nuclear Non-Proliferation Treaty, which recognized only nuclear-weapon States and non-nuclear-weapon States, and it strongly cautioned against the unintended consequences of using such terms. It also deeply regretted that the new version of the draft resolution omitted the previous reference to the agreed objective of the establishment of a nuclear-weapon-free zone in the Middle East.

- **Pakistan** said that it could not support the universalization of the Nuclear Non-Proliferation Treaty, as it was a highly unrealistic and impractical objective. It also expressed concern that the draft resolution sought only to address the non-proliferation aspects of fissile materials.

- The **United States** stated that, while it could not support a number of elements in the draft resolution, it thanked Japan for streamlining the text and refocusing it on the future. It also noted with satisfaction that the draft resolution encouraged States to conduct a candid dialogue on the relationship between nuclear disarmament and security and said that it stood ready to engage in such a refreshing and realistic endeavour.

- **New Zealand** expressed regret that paragraph 1 of the draft resolution distorted the fundamental commitments laid out in article VI of the Nuclear Non-Proliferation Treaty and drew attention to paragraph 3 (d), which, in its view, considerably devalued the importance of the entry into force of the Comprehensive Nuclear-Test-Ban Treaty. Similarly, with respect to paragraph 3 (e), it said that it was not opposed to any efforts to advance nuclear disarmament verification, but it did not think that that should be done through the framework of only one process.

- **Austria** was very concerned about the potential negative impact of the changed language on the integrity of the Nuclear Non-Proliferation Treaty and the ongoing review process of the Treaty. Although it voted in favour of the eighteenth preambular paragraph, it expressed regret that the paragraph departed from consensus language on the catastrophic humanitarian consequences of nuclear weapons found in the final document of the 2010 Nuclear Non-Proliferation Treaty Review Conference (NPT/CONF.2010/50 (Vol. I), para. 80). On paragraph 3 (d), it noted with regret the strongly diluted language on the Comprehensive Nuclear-Test-Ban Treaty. Furthermore, it regretted that the draft resolution followed the narrative that the total elimination of nuclear weapons would occur only after rebuilding confidence and trust.

- **India** was of the view that the text had fallen short on the objective of nuclear disarmament. It abstained in the voting on operative paragraph 3 (c), as it supported the commencement of negotiations on a fissile material cut-off treaty in the Conference on Disarmament on the basis of document CD/1299 and the mandate contained therein.

- The **Islamic Republic of Iran** considered the language used in the fifth preambular paragraph and in operative paragraph 5 as contrary to the unequivocal undertaking of the nuclear-weapon States to accomplish the total elimination of their nuclear arsenals. It also believed that the draft resolution failed to strike an acceptable balance between nuclear disarmament and non-proliferation, and it pointed out that the eighteenth preambular paragraph failed to use the agreed language of the final document of the 2010 Nuclear Non-Proliferation Treaty Review Conference. It believed that negotiations at the Conference on Disarmament of a treaty banning the production of fissile material for use in nuclear weapons should commence within the context of an agreed comprehensive and balanced programme of work that also included the commencement of negotiations on a comprehensive convention on nuclear disarmament, which it believed was not reflected in the draft resolution. It voted in favour of the second, fourth and nineteenth preambular paragraphs and of operative paragraph 3 (f).

• **Ecuador** was of the view that the absence of a reference to the Treaty on the Prohibition of Nuclear Weapons rendered the draft resolution an unambitious tool. Ecuador supported the denuclearization of the Korean Peninsula but considered the draft resolution insufficient, as it left out other cases that were equally indispensable to achieving a world free of nuclear weapons. It also stated that the draft resolution undermined efforts towards the early entry into force of the Comprehensive Nuclear-Test-Ban Treaty. It believed that the text did not give the issue of humanitarian consequences the consideration it deserved, as it merely recognized the catastrophic nature of such consequences as fact and did not express the General Assembly's deep concern in that regard. For all of those reasons, it abstained in the voting on the draft resolution and its second, eighth, sixteenth and eighteenth preambular paragraphs, as well as on operative paragraphs 1, 3 (c), 3 (d) 3 (e) and 5.

74/68. Convention on the Prohibition of the Use of Nuclear Weapons

The General Assembly reiterated its request to the Conference on Disarmament to commence negotiations in order to reach agreement on an international convention prohibiting the use or threat of use of nuclear weapons under any circumstances, and it requested the Conference to report to the General Assembly on the results of those negotiations.

> **Submitted by**: India (11 Oct.)
>
> **GA vote**: 118-50-15 (12 Dec.)
>
> **1st Cttee vote**: 115-50-15 (1 Nov.)
>
> See also *Yearbook, Part I*, pp. 234–236.

First Committee. After the vote, **Ecuador** explained that it voted in favour of the draft resolution because of the recognition in the seventh preambular paragraph that a legally binding prohibition of the use of nuclear weapons was not contrary, but in fact contributed, to international efforts for the achievement and maintenance of a world free of nuclear weapons. However, it pointed out that the true path for achieving that goal was through the universalization of the existing Treaty on the Prohibition of Nuclear Weapons.

After it abstained from voting on the draft resolution, **Pakistan** argued that the lead sponsor had pursued the continuous expansion and modernization of conventional and nuclear arsenals while increasing the readiness of its nuclear forces by taking steps that included honing its missiles and introducing destabilizing weapon systems and force postures and security doctrines that had an offensive, rather than defensive, intent. It said that, given the gaping hole between the practices and declared policies of the lead sponsor of the draft resolution, it was difficult to vote in its favour.

74/78. Comprehensive Nuclear-Test-Ban Treaty

The General Assembly reiterated its condemnation of the six nuclear tests conducted by the Democratic People's Republic of Korea in violation of relevant Security Council resolutions and urged full compliance with the obligations under those resolutions, which included that the Democratic People's Republic of Korea abandon its nuclear weapons programme and not conduct any further nuclear tests. The Assembly noted with encouragement the statement of the Democratic People's Republic of Korea concerning a moratorium on nuclear tests and efforts towards the dismantlement of the Punggye-ri nuclear test site, reaffirmed its support for the complete, verifiable and irreversible denuclearization of the Korean Peninsula in a peaceful manner, welcomed all efforts and dialogue to that end, and encouraged all parties to continue such efforts and dialogue.

> **Submitted by**: New Zealand (14 Oct.)
>
> **GA vote**: 182-1-4; 165-0-10, p.p. 4; 171-0-5, p.p. 7 (12 Dec.)
>
> **1st Cttee vote**: 177-1-4; 160-0-10, p.p. 4; 168-0-5, p.p. 7 (1 Nov.)
>
> See also *Yearbook, Part I*, pp. 282–288.

First Committee. Before voting in favour of the draft resolution, **Israel** drew attention to the seventh preambular paragraph, which contained references to the Review Conferences of the Nuclear Non-Proliferation Treaty. It objected that decisions and resolutions adopted in the context of one forum could not be inserted into the work of another without the latter's explicit consent.

Before voting against, the **Democratic People's Republic of Korea** argued that the essence of the nuclear issue on the Korean Peninsula was distorted in the draft resolution. It was of the view that the text unilaterally denounced the Democratic People's Republic of Korea and ignored the principle of objectivity and impartiality.

After voting in favour, the following States delivered statements:

- **Brazil** said that it voted in favour of the draft resolution in light of its continued support for the integrity and entry into force of the Treaty as an important nuclear disarmament and non-proliferation measure. However, it regretted the continued reference made in the draft resolution to Security Council resolution 2310 (2016), which it believed was counterproductive in efforts towards the Treaty's entry into force and unduly encroached upon the responsibilities of the Preparatory Commission for the Comprehensive Nuclear-Test-Ban Treaty Organization. For that reason, it abstained in the voting on that paragraph.

- **Egypt** expressed its concern regarding its fourth preambular paragraph, which referred to Security Council resolution 2310 (2016).

- **Pakistan** recalled that it participated constructively in the Treaty negotiations in the Conference on Disarmament and voted in favour of its adoption by the General Assembly in 1996 and, since then, it had voted in favour of the annual draft resolution. Regarding the reference in the fourth preambular paragraph to Security Council resolution 2310 (2016), it stated that it was wary of the Security Council defining legislative requirements for Member States and entering into areas that were not necessarily under its jurisdiction.

It emphasized that it was not bound by any provisions that emanated from the Nuclear Non-Proliferation Treaty or its Review Conferences, including, as stated in the seventh preambular paragraph, any other instrument to which it was not a party. It had therefore abstained in the voting on the seventh preambular paragraph.

- The **Islamic Republic of Iran** noted that almost all nuclear-weapon States, in particular the United States, were modernizing and qualitatively upgrading their nuclear-weapon systems by using new technologies, including subcritical testing and simulations. It expressed regret that the nuclear-weapon States were not called upon in the draft resolution to refrain from such measures. It had abstained in separate votes on the fourth preambular paragraph and dissociated itself from its references to Security Council resolution 2310 (2016).

- **Ecuador** expressed full support for the prompt entry into force of the Comprehensive Nuclear-Test-Ban Treaty and believed that the draft resolution as a whole should be adopted by consensus. However, it regretted that the fourth preambular paragraph included a reference to Security Council resolution 2310 (2016).

After it abstained from voting, the **Syrian Arab Republic** argued that the Comprehensive Nuclear-Test-Ban Treaty offered no guarantees vis-à-vis the use or threat of use of nuclear weapons against non-nuclear-weapon States. It said that the text made no explicit reference to the illegitimacy of using or threatening to use nuclear weapons and recalled that the Treaty also did not explicitly call for the universalization of the Nuclear Non-Proliferation Treaty.

74/509. Treaty banning the production of fissile material for nuclear weapons or other nuclear explosive devices (decision)

The General Assembly decided to include in the provisional agenda of its seventy-fifth session, under the item entitled "General and complete disarmament", the sub-item entitled "Treaty banning the production of fissile material for nuclear weapons or other nuclear explosive devices".

> **Submitted by**: Canada (10 Oct.)
>
> **GA vote**: 181-1-4 (12 Dec.)
>
> **1st Cttee vote**: 177-1-4 (1 Nov.)
>
> See also *Yearbook, Part I*, pp. 295–296.

First Committee. Before voting against the draft resolution, **Pakistan** underscored that a treaty banning the future production of fissile material would simply freeze the status quo to the strategic advantage of a select few.

Before they abstained from voting on the draft resolution, the following States took the floor:

- **Israel** recalled its long-standing position that the notion of a fissile material cut-off treaty should be part of a new consensus-based regional security architecture. It maintained that that was an essential prerequisite, which was far from being fulfilled.

- The **Islamic Republic of Iran** strongly believed that any instrument that sought to ban the production of and provide for the total elimination of fissile material for nuclear weapons and other nuclear-explosive devices must cover the past, present and future production of fissile material for nuclear weapons and other nuclear-explosive devices and provide for the verifiable declaration and total elimination of all stocks of such materials worldwide, at a fixed date.

Chapter II. Biological and chemical weapons

74/40. Implementation of the Convention on the Prohibition of the Development, Production, Stockpiling and Use of Chemical Weapons and on Their Destruction

The General Assembly noted with appreciation the ongoing work of the Organisation for the Prohibition of Chemical Weapons (OPCW). It also welcomed the cooperation between the United Nations and OPCW within the framework of their relationship agreement.

First Committee. In a general statement, **Poland** underscored that as the integrity of the Chemical Weapons Convention and the credibility of OPCW was at stake, the draft resolution could not be silent on the continued use of chemical weapons. It explained that, accordingly, the text referred to decision C-SS-4/DEC.3, which comprehensively addressed the threat posed by the use of chemical weapons. Noting that building a common understanding on those issues had proved to be extremely challenging, Poland affirmed that it had done its utmost to address the situation in a balanced and adequate manner while taking into account the ongoing work of OPCW.

> **Submitted by**: Poland (8 Oct.)
>
> **GA vote**: 151-8-21; 131-7-25, p.p. 5; 119-11-30, o.p. 2; 120-11-26, o.p. 3; 116-16-29, o.p. 4; 112-12-36, o.p. 16 (12 Dec.)
>
> **1st Cttee vote**: 147-7-24; 125-7-31, p.p. 5; 116-13-36, o.p. 2; 117-12-35, o.p. 3; 111-18-38, o.p. 4; 106-13-46, o.p. 16 (4 Nov.)
>
> See also *Yearbook, Part I*, pp. 64–75.

Before voting in favour, **France** said that it would have liked the text to recognize and welcome the establishment of the Fact-finding Mission in the Syrian Arab Republic by OPCW, in accordance with the voting of States parties to the Chemical Weapons Convention in June 2017. It conveyed that the draft resolution reflected its serious concerns and stressed the need to re-establish robust deterrence mechanisms, and that is why it voted in favour. It wished to put on record that the chemical non-proliferation regime must not be held hostage and it was unacceptable for it to be the subject of politicization.

Before voting against the draft resolution, the following took the floor:

- **Russian Federation** objected that the document failed to call on the United States to complete the elimination of its chemical arsenal as soon as possible. It cited decision C-SS-4/DEC.3 and argued that it ran counter to the provisions of the Chemical Weapons Convention and infringed upon the mandate of the Security Council. It was of the view that the attributive mechanism established through illegitimate means, in accordance with the Convention, would not engage in any objective investigations; rather, its goal would be to serve the ambitions of those who created it. Against that backdrop, it considered the draft resolution weak with regard to counter-terrorism, as it did not take into account the consequences of any initiatives to stop weapons of mass destruction from falling into the hands of terrorists.

- The **Syrian Arab Republic** objected that despite its full cooperation in various fields with the OPCW-United Nations Joint Investigative Mechanism (JIM), the Mechanism had been exploited by some Western States, foremost among which were the United States, Britain and France, to make unfounded accusations against the Syrian Arab Republic, contained in unprofessional and non-scientific reports lacking any physical evidence. It drew attention to those accusations as also noted in draft resolution A/C.1/74/L.10.

- The **Islamic Republic of Iran** explained it would vote against the draft resolution, as a number of its paragraphs were highly politicized. It hoped that the politicization of the draft resolution and of OPCW's work would end, thereby enabling the Committee in the future to adopt a consensus-based draft resolution on the Convention's implementation.

Before it abstained from voting on the draft resolution, **Cuba** took the floor. It said that, with regard to paragraphs 2 and 3, it believed that it was unacceptable to accuse a State party to the Chemical Weapons Convention of using such weapons without an independent, impartial, comprehensive and conclusive investigation conducted by OPCW. It recalled that decision C-SS-4/DEC.3 was not supported by all States party to the Convention. It reiterated its rejection of that decision, as it believed that it was beyond the privileges accorded to the OPCW Technical Secretariat by the Chemical Weapons Convention and was aimed at modifying the organization's mandate. It was of the view that the draft resolution disregarded the cooperation of the Government of the Syrian Arab Republic in the destruction of its chemical weapons and weapons-production facilities, despite the country's complex security situation.

74/79. Convention on the Prohibition of the Development, Production and Stockpiling of Bacteriological (Biological) and Toxin Weapons and on Their Destruction

The General Assembly appreciated that the meeting of States parties in Geneva in December 2018 adopted a set of financial measures to be reviewed at the Ninth Review Conference, and resolved to continue to monitor the financial situation of the Convention. It noted that the meeting of States parties in 2018 agreed that the financial difficulties of the Convention stemmed from three principal sources, namely the non-payment of contributions by some States parties, delays in the receipt of contributions from other States parties and the financial requirements of the United Nations with respect to activities not funded from its regular budget, and called upon States parties to consider ways of addressing those serious issues as a matter of urgency. The Assembly encouraged the meeting of States parties in 2019 to consider and to agree upon practical arrangements for the Ninth Review Conference.

Submitted by: Hungary (17 Oct.)

GA vote: w/o vote (12 Dec.)

1st Cttee vote: w/o vote (4 Nov.)

See also *Yearbook, Part I*, pp. 289–294.

Chapter III. Conventional weapons

74/24. Objective information on military matters, including transparency of military expenditures

The Assembly requested the Secretary-General to promote international and regional or subregional symposiums and training seminars and to support the development of an online training course by the Secretariat, with the financial and technical support of interested States, with a view to explaining the purpose of the standardized reporting system and facilitating the secure online filing of the reports.

> **Submitted by**: Germany, Romania (17 Oct.)
>
> **GA vote**: 176-0-2 (12 Dec.)
>
> **1st Cttee vote**: 176-0-2 (6 Nov.)
>
> See also *Yearbook, Part I*, pp. 1–6.

74/38. Conventional arms control at the regional and subregional levels

The General Assembly recognized the importance of equitable representation of women in arms control discussions and negotiations. It requested the Conference on Disarmament to consider the formulation of principles to serve as a framework for regional agreements on conventional arms control, and looked forward to the subsequent report on the subject. It asked the Secretary-General, in the meantime, to seek the views of Member States on the subject and to submit a report to the General Assembly at its seventy-fifth session.

> **Submitted by**: Pakistan (5 Oct.)
>
> **GA vote**: 185-1-2; 174-2-0, p.p. 7; 125-1-47, o.p. 2 (12 Dec.)
>
> **1st Cttee vote**: 168-1-2; 149-2-3, p.p. 7; 107-1-46, o.p. 2 (7 Nov.)
>
> See also *Yearbook, Part I*, pp. 56–60.

First Committee. After the vote, **India** said that it voted against the draft resolution and its operative paragraph 2, which requested the Conference on Disarmament to consider the formulation of principles that could serve as a framework for regional agreements on conventional arms control. Recalling that the United Nations Disarmament Commission in 1993 adopted by consensus guidelines and recommendations on regional disarmament, it said there was therefore no need for the Conference on Disarmament to engage in formulating principles on the same subject. Furthermore, it believed that the security concerns of States extended beyond narrowly defined regions and, consequently, the notion of the preservation of balance in defence capabilities in the regional or subregional context was both unrealistic and unacceptable.

74/49. The Arms Trade Treaty

The General Assembly called upon all States parties to submit, in a timely manner, and to update their initial reports, thereby enhancing confidence, transparency, trust and accountability. The Assembly encouraged further steps to enable States to increasingly prevent and tackle the diversion of conventional arms and ammunition to unauthorized end uses and end users, and recognized that enhancing reporting rates, transparency and information-sharing was fundamental to achieving

> **Submitted by**: Argentina (14 Oct.)
>
> **GA vote**: 153-1-28; 160-0-16, p.p. 9; 142-1-31, o.p. 4; 137-2-32, o.p. 9 (12 Dec.)
>
> **1st Cttee vote**: 150-1-26; 155-0-15, p.p. 9; 137-1-31, o.p. 4; 136-2-31, o.p. 9 (5 Nov.)
>
> See also *Yearbook, Part I*, pp. 128–135.

that goal. It welcomed the adoption of action-oriented decisions on gender and gender-based violence and the fact that States parties agreed to review progress on those two aspects on an ongoing basis, and encouraged States parties and signatory States to ensure the full and equal participation of women and men in pursuing the object and purpose of the Treaty.

First Committee. Before they abstained from voting on the draft resolution, the following States spoke:

- **Cuba** expressed the view that the Arms Trade Treaty was adopted prematurely, noting that negotiations on it had not been concluded and no consensus had been reached. It cited considerable ambiguities, inconsistencies, a lack of clear definitions and legal gaps, which it believed all undermined its effectiveness and efficiency. It rejected the acknowledgement of artificial synergies among legal instruments, membership, scope and category of arms, which it saw as totally different elements. In addition, it underscored the fact that, because of the profound differences among Member States, no consensus had been reached on the synergies between the Programme of Action to Prevent, Combat and Eradicate the Illicit Trade in Small Arms and Light Weapons in All Its Aspects and the Arms Trade Treaty in the final document of the third Review Conference on the Programme of Action. It said that it disassociated itself from all paragraphs related to the Arms Trade Treaty contained in various draft resolutions on which the First Committee would take action.

- **Armenia** reiterated its concerns with regard to the preamble and principal section of the Arms Trade Treaty. It reaffirmed its position that the Treaty, in its current shape, may be interpreted as limiting the exercise of the sovereign right to self-defence, as well as hindering legitimate access to relevant technologies.

- **Egypt** was of the view that motivations related to the desire of some States to manipulate and politicize the legitimate arms trade had led to several shortcomings and loopholes in the Treaty, which made the implementation of the Treaty selective and subjective and allowed exporting States to abuse its provisions. It also argued that the Treaty completely ignored the prohibition of the intentional State-sponsored supply of weapons to unauthorized recipients, including terrorists and illegal armed groups, which represented the main real threat in that domain. Therefore, it noted, it would continue to abstain in the voting on the draft resolution, as well as on paragraphs that referred to the Treaty.

After voting in favour, **Brazil** abstained in the voting on operative paragraph 9, owing to the reference made therein to synergies between the Arms Trade Treaty and the Programme of Action.

After voting against the draft resolution, the following States took the floor:

- **Israel** stated that it did not consider the Programme of Action to be the right venue for addressing the issue of ammunition as another venue had been chosen for that task—the Group of Governmental Experts in 2020.

- The **United States** said that it opposed the inclusion of ammunition language in the final outcome document of the third Review Conference. As such, it explained that it could not accept language in the draft resolution that characterized the outcome of the Review Conference as a success, when consensus on two paragraphs with regard to a highly controversial issue clearly was not achieved.

After they abstained from voting on the draft resolution, the following took the floor:

- The **Islamic Republic of Iran** noted that the Arms Trade Treaty failed to prohibit arms transfers to countries that committed acts of aggression, including foreign occupation. Noting that the draft resolution called upon non-parties to accede to the Treaty, it said such a call for universalization was unacceptable because the Treaty was not adopted by consensus. It furthermore maintained that some States parties perpetrated major violations of the provisions of the Treaty, exporting billions of dollars in arms. It explained that its position on the Treaty applied to all paragraphs in the draft resolutions and draft decisions to be adopted by the Committee that year, and it therefore disassociated itself from all such references.

- **India** explained that it continued to keep the Treaty under review from the perspective of its defence, security and foreign policy interests and therefore abstained in the voting on the draft resolution.

- **Ecuador** expressed regret that the text of the Treaty submitted for consideration by the General Assembly in 2013 included shortcomings, such as the imbalance between the rights and responsibilities of exporting and importing countries; the importance of the fundamental principles of international law and its standing in treaties; the lack of an explicit ban on the transfer to non-authorized non-State actors; the lack of specific references to the crime of aggression and the fact that certain articles could be used in a subjective manner and based on double standards. Ecuador was currently examining the Arms Trade Treaty and observing how it was being implemented, as well as the conclusions reached at its conferences of States parties, in order to identify whether or not the problems in its text persisted during implementation.

74/51. Assistance to States for curbing the illicit traffic in small arms and light weapons and collecting them

The General Assembly recalled the report of the third Review Conference of the Programme of Action on Small Arms and Light Weapons. It encouraged the international community to support the implementation of the Economic Community of West African States Convention on Small Arms and Light Weapons, Their Ammunition and Other Related Materials. The Assembly also encouraged countries in the Sahelo-Saharan subregion to facilitate the effective functioning of national commissions to combat the illicit proliferation of small arms and light weapons and, in that regard, invited the international community to lend its support wherever possible.

> **Submitted by**: Mali (15 Oct.)
>
> **GA vote**: w/o vote; 151-1-21, p.p. 16 (12 Dec.)
>
> **1st Cttee vote**: w/o vote; 149-1-20, p.p. 16 (5 Nov.)
>
> See also *Yearbook, Part I*, pp. 140–144.

74/53. Transparency in armaments

The General Assembly emphasized that it was important for Member States to provide information on exports and imports of small arms and light weapons. The Assembly requested that the Secretary-General prepare a report on the continuing operation and relevance of the Register. The report would be written with the assistance of a group of governmental experts to be convened for a week each at the end of 2021 and at the beginning and in the middle of 2022 and would explore the relationship between the participation in, scope of and use of the Register, and its further development.

> **Submitted by**: Netherlands (15 Oct.)
>
> **GA vote**: 157-0-23; 135-1-32, p.p. 6 (12 Dec.)
>
> **1st Cttee vote**: 154-0-23; 138-1-26, p.p. 7 (5 Nov.)
>
> See also *Yearbook, Part I*, pp. 147–152.

First Committee. Before voting in favour, **Pakistan** stated that, for transparency measures to gain broader traction and acceptance, the recognition of different political and security conditions in various regions was essential. It reiterated that those measures also needed to be pursued in tandem with others, including on confidence-building and conflict resolution. It acknowledged the recognized value of voluntary measures outlined in the draft resolution.

Before it abstained from voting on the draft resolution, **Cuba** said that the draft resolution lacked balance as a result of its unwarranted focus on small arms and light weapons. It explained that it did not support partial analyses that disregarded serious problems related to the production, modernization, use and trade of highly sophisticated conventional weapons. It did not support the fact that the draft resolution mentioned the entry into force of the Arms Trade Treaty or that it endorsed the 2019 report of the Group of Governmental Experts, to which it had important objections. It did not support expanding the scope of the United Nations Register of Conventional Arms beyond the seven categories of weapons to include small arms and light weapons. It stressed that any attempt to expand the Register must begin with the inclusion of weapons of mass destruction, including nuclear weapons. It did not support the convening of a new group of experts in 2021 and 2022, as proposed in the draft resolution.

After voting in favour of the draft resolution as a whole, **Ecuador** said that it had abstained from voting on paragraphs of draft resolutions with reference to the Arms Trade Treaty. It stated that it was currently examining the Treaty and observing how it was being implemented, as well as the conclusions reached at its conferences of States parties, in order to identify whether or not the problems in its text persisted when the instrument was implemented.

After they abstained from voting on the draft resolution, the following States took the floor:

- The **Islamic Republic of Iran** underlined that the existing United Nations mechanism for transparency in conventional arms, without transparency in weapons of mass destruction, was not balanced nor comprehensive, in particular given the situation in the volatile region of the Middle East.

- The **Syrian Arab Republic** said that it considered the United Nations Register of Conventional Arms not comprehensive and noted that it did not include developments in conventional weapons. The Register also did not take into consideration the special situation in the Middle East, where the Arab-Israeli conflict was still ongoing. The delegation emphasized its reservation about all paragraphs referring to the Arms Trade Treaty in current or future draft resolutions and decisions consensually adopted by the First Committee.

74/60. The illicit trade in small arms and light weapons in all its aspects

The Assembly welcomed the establishment of the Saving Lives Entity fund and encouraged States in a position to do so to make voluntary financial contributions to the fund. It reaffirmed the importance of States undertaking to identify groups and individuals engaged in the illegal manufacture, trade, stockpiling, transfer and possession, as well as financing for acquisition, of illicit small arms and light weapons, and take action under appropriate national law against such groups and individuals.

> **Submitted by**: Colombia (16 Oct.)
>
> **GA vote**: w/o vote; 170-2-1, p.p. 7; 155-1-15, p.p. 2; 172-2-1, o.p. 6 (12 Dec.)
>
> **1st Cttee vote**: w/o vote; 170-2-0, p.p. 7; 151-1-16, p.p. 2; 169-2-0, o.p. 6 (5 Nov.)
>
> See also *Yearbook, Part I*, pp. 179–188.

The Assembly requested the Secretary-General to seek the views of Member States on best practices, lessons learned and new recommendations on preventing and combating the diversion and illicit international transfer of small arms and light weapons to unauthorized recipients.

First Committee. Before it abstained from voting, **Egypt** expressed the view that motivations related to the desire of some States to manipulate and politicize the legitimate arms trade led to several shortcomings and loopholes in the Treaty, in particular its deliberate lack of several necessary definitions and clear criteria, which made the implementation of the Treaty selective and subjective and allowed exporting States to abuse its provisions. It also argued that the Treaty completely ignored the prohibition of the intentional State-sponsored supply of weapons to unauthorized recipients, including terrorists and illegal armed groups, which represented the main real threat in that domain. Therefore, it noted, it would continue to abstain in the voting on paragraphs with references to the Arms Trade Treaty in various draft resolutions.

After voting in favour of the draft resolution, the **Syrian Arab Republic** said that it had voted in favour of the paragraphs that were adopted by a vote at the third Review Conference on the Programme of Action. Its vote in favour of those paragraphs was based on its conviction about the importance of the topic and on its consideration for its brothers and sisters in Africa and the Caribbean, despite its reservations about some of the new topics that were included in the document.

After voting against the draft resolution, the following States took the floor:

- **Israel** stated that it did not consider the Programme of Action to be the right venue for addressing the issue of ammunition since another venue already had been chosen for it—the Group of Governmental Experts in 2020.

- The **United States** recalled that it opposed the inclusion of ammunition language in the final outcome document of the third Review Conference. As such, it maintained that it could not accept language in the draft resolution that characterized the outcome of the Review Conference as a success, when consensus on two paragraphs with regard to a highly controversial issue clearly was not achieved.

After it abstained from voting on the draft resolution as a whole and also on paragraphs of other draft resolutions containing reference to the Arms Trade Treaty, **Ecuador** clarified that it was currently examining the Treaty and observing how it was being implemented, as well as the conclusions reached at its conferences of States parties in order to identify whether or not the problems in its text persisted when the instrument was implemented.

74/61. Implementation of the Convention on the Prohibition of the Use, Stockpiling, Production and Transfer of Anti-Personnel Mines and on Their Destruction

The General Assembly stressed the importance of the full and effective implementation of and compliance with the Convention, including through the continued implementation of the action plans under the Convention.

> **Submitted by**: Norway, Afghanistan, Sudan (17 Oct.)
>
> **GA vote**: 169-0-18 (12 Dec.)
>
> **1st Cttee vote**: 161-0-19 (5 Nov.)
>
> See also *Yearbook, Part I*, pp. 189–192.

First Committee. Before abstaining from voting on the draft resolution, the following States took the floor:

- **Cuba** stressed that, for six decades, the United States had subjected it to an ongoing policy of hostility and aggression, and therefore it had been unable to renounce the use of mines in an effort to preserve its sovereignty and territorial integrity, in line with the legitimate right of self-defence, stipulated in Article 51 of the Charter of the United Nations.

- **Egypt** believed that the Convention lacked balance between humanitarian concerns and those related to anti-personnel landmines and their possible legitimate military uses, especially in countries with long borders, facing extraordinary security challenges. Furthermore, it pointed out that the Convention did not establish any legal obligation on States to remove the anti-personnel mines they had placed in the territory of other States, making it almost impossible for many States to meet the demining requirements on their own.

After voting in favour, **Singapore** conveyed that, as a small State, it nonetheless firmly believed that the legitimate security concerns and the right to self-defence of any State could not be disregarded, and it was therefore of the view that a blanket ban on all types of cluster munitions and anti-personnel landmines might be counterproductive. It expressed support for international efforts to resolve the humanitarian concerns about anti-personnel landmines and cluster munitions.

After they abstained from voting on the draft resolution, the following States spoke:

- The **Islamic Republic of Iran** believed that the Convention focused mainly on humanitarian concerns and did not adequately take into account the legitimate military requirements of many countries, in particular those with long land borders, for the responsible unlimited use of mines to defend their territories.

- **Myanmar** stressed that capacity constraints were a major challenge, to some extent, preventing its ability to join the Convention. Nevertheless, it stated, relevant stakeholders in Myanmar were currently studying the instrument for a better understanding of it, with the aim of eventually joining the Convention.

- The **Republic of Korea** supported the objectives and purposes of the Ottawa Convention and of the draft resolution. However, it said that, owing to the security situation on the Korean Peninsula, it was currently not a party to the Convention and therefore had abstained from voting on the draft resolution. It clarified that that did not mean that it was any less concerned about the problems associated with anti-personnel mines.

- **India** reiterated that it supported the vision of a world free of anti-personnel landmines and was committed to their eventual elimination. It said that goal would be facilitated considerably by the availability of effective military and alternative technologies that were cost-effective and could perform the legitimate defensive role of anti-personnel landmines.

- **Pakistan** explained that, given its security considerations and the need to guard long borders, which were not protected by any natural obstacle, reliance on landmines was an integral part of Pakistan's defence.

74/62. Implementation of the Convention on Cluster Munitions

The General Assembly requested the Secretary-General to convene the second Review Conference of States Parties to the Convention on Cluster Munitions and to continue to render the necessary assistance and to provide such services as may be necessary to fulfil the tasks entrusted to him under the Convention and in the relevant decisions of the Meetings of States Parties and the first Review Conference.

> **Submitted by**: Switzerland (17 Oct.)
>
> **GA vote**: 144-1-38; 153-0-17, p.p. 14 (12 Dec.)
>
> **1st Cttee vote**: 138-1-39; 147-0-16, p.p. 14 (5 Nov.)
>
> See also *Yearbook, Part I*, pp. 193–198.

First Committee. Before it abstained from voting on the draft resolution, **Egypt** reiterated concerns about the selective and imbalanced nature of the Convention, which was developed and concluded outside the framework of the United Nations and lacked an equitable and clear definition of cluster munitions in a manner deliberately designed to fit the specific production requirements of some States.

After they abstained from voting, the following States took the floor:

- The **Islamic Republic of Iran** explained that it had abstained because it did not participate in the negotiations of the Convention and was neither a signatory nor a party thereto. It stressed it could not support an instrument negotiated outside the United Nations, in disregard for the concerns and the interests of many States.

- **Myanmar** underlined that capacity constraints were a major challenge, to some extent, preventing Myanmar's ability to join the Convention. Nevertheless, it stated, relevant stakeholders in Myanmar were currently studying the instrument for a better understanding of it, with the aim of eventually joining the Convention.

74/65. Problems arising from the accumulation of conventional ammunition stockpiles in surplus

The General Assembly reiterated its request to the Secretary-General to convene a group of governmental experts in 2020 on problems arising from the accumulation of conventional ammunition stockpiles in surplus, taking into account the exchanges in the open, informal consultations. It requested the Secretary-General to report to the General Assembly on the work of the group upon its completion.

> **Submitted by**: Germany, France (6 Nov.)
>
> **GA vote**: w/o vote (12 Dec.)
>
> **1st Cttee vote**: w/o vote (7 Nov.)
>
> See also *Yearbook, Part I*, pp. 220–224.

First Committee. After it joined the consensus in favour of the draft resolution, **Pakistan** highlighted three points: (a) the largest stockpiles of conventional armaments and ammunition were maintained by the major military powers, which therefore should take the lead in assessing surplus stockpiles and their safe disposal; (b) such efforts could be supplemented by actions at the regional and subregional levels to prevent excessive accumulation, as well as imbalances in conventional armaments and military forces; and (c) while it might not be possible to have a universal definition of surplus stockpiles of armaments or their ammunition, some general guidelines could be developed on the basis of previous work done under the auspices of the United Nations.

74/76. Convention on Prohibitions or Restrictions on the Use of Certain Conventional Weapons Which May Be Deemed to Be Excessively Injurious or to Have Indiscriminate Effects

The General Assembly recalled the decisions by the Meeting of the High Contracting Parties to the Convention in 2018 to clarify certain aspects of the financial measures adopted at the Meeting of the High Contracting Parties in 2017 and to continue to monitor the financial situation of the Convention, and to request the Chair-elect to continue consultations aimed at improving the stability of the Secretariat's support to the Convention. The Assembly welcomed the work of the Group of Governmental Experts related to emerging technologies in the area of lethal autonomous weapons systems, including its 2018 report, which had provided a basis for further work.

> **Submitted by**: Latvia (17 Oct.)
>
> **GA vote**: w/o vote (12 Dec.)
>
> **1st Cttee vote**: w/o vote (5 Nov.)
>
> See also *Yearbook, Part I*, pp. 270–274.

First Committee. Before joining the consensus in favour of the draft resolution, **Cuba** said it would do so with the understanding that the issue of mines that were different from anti-personnel mines was not on the agenda of the Meeting of the High Contracting Parties to the Convention on Certain Conventional Weapons, as decided at the meeting held in 2018.

Chapter IV. Regional disarmament

74/25. Implementation of the Declaration of the Indian Ocean as a Zone of Peace

The General Assembly requested the Chairman of the Ad Hoc Committee on the Indian Ocean to continue his informal consultations with Committee members and to report through the Committee to the General Assembly at its seventy-sixth session.

> **Submitted by:** Indonesia (15 Oct.)
>
> **GA vote:** 134-45-3 (12 Dec.)
>
> **1st Cttee vote:** 130-44-3 (7 Nov.)
>
> See also *Yearbook, Part I*, pp. 7–9.

74/26. African Nuclear-Weapon-Free Zone Treaty

The General Assembly called upon African States parties to the Nuclear Non-Proliferation Treaty that had not done so to conclude comprehensive safeguards agreements with the International Atomic Energy Agency as required by the Treaty of Pelindaba and to conclude additional protocols to their safeguards agreements on the basis of the model protocol approved by the Board of Governors of the Agency on 15 May 1997.

> **Submitted by:** Nigeria (16 Oct.)
>
> **GA vote:** w/o vote (12 Dec.)
>
> **1st Cttee vote:** w/o vote (1 Nov.)
>
> See also *Yearbook, Part I*, pp. 10–11.

First Committee. Before the draft resolution was adopted, **India** conveyed its assurance that it would respect the status of the African nuclear-weapon-free zone.

After the draft resolution was adopted, **Spain** noted that after very carefully considering the invitation extended to Spain to sign Protocol III of the Treaty of Pelindaba, its Government decided not to sign the Protocol. It recalled that the entire territory of Spain had been militarily denuclearized since 1976 and, consequently, it had already taken all of the necessary measures to ensure that the provisions of the Treaty of Pelindaba were implemented across its national territory. It noted it had joined the consensus on the draft resolution since it was introduced in 1997; however, it did not support the mentioned consensus on the fifth preambular paragraph and, for that reason, it had worked with other delegations to find more balanced wording that was acceptable to all parties.

74/27. Treaty for the Prohibition of Nuclear Weapons in Latin America and the Caribbean (Treaty of Tlatelolco)

The General Assembly noted with satisfaction that the year 2019 marked the fiftieth anniversary of the entry into force, on 25 April 1969, of the Treaty of Tlatelolco and of the establishment of the Agency for the Prohibition of Nuclear Weapons in Latin America and the Caribbean. It also encouraged the States members of the Agency for the Prohibition of Nuclear Weapons in Latin America and the Caribbean to continue the activities and efforts that they conducted jointly with the Agency.

> **Submitted by:** Mexico (10 Oct.)
>
> **GA vote:** w/o vote (12 Dec.)
>
> **1st Cttee vote:** w/o vote (1 Nov.)
>
> See also *Yearbook, Part I*, pp. 12–15.

74/30. Establishment of a nuclear-weapon-free zone in the region of the Middle East

The General Assembly called upon all countries of the region that had not yet done so, pending the establishment of the zone, to agree to place all their nuclear activities under International Atomic Energy Agency safeguards. It also requested the Secretary-General to continue to pursue consultations with the States of the region and other concerned States and to seek their views on the measures outlined in chapters III and IV of the study annexed to the report of the Secretary-General of 10 October 1990 (A/45/435) or other relevant measures in order to move towards the establishment of a nuclear-weapon-free zone in the region of the Middle East.

> **Submitted by**: Egypt (30 Sep.)
> **GA vote**: 175-2-3 (12 Dec.)
> **1st Cttee vote**: 172-2-2 (1 Nov.)
> See also *Yearbook, Part I*, pp. 23–26.

First Committee. Before voting in favour of the draft resolution, the **Islamic Republic of Iran** expressed the view that the situation had changed, as some had chosen to break the three-decade-long consensus on the draft, and it therefore believed that there was no longer any justification for refraining from updating the substance of the draft resolution.

Before voting against the draft resolution, the following States took the floor:

- The **United States** regretted that it could not support the draft resolution, as it believed that the divisive efforts by its sponsors, in cooperation with other States of the region, to advance separate initiatives ran contrary to the cooperative consensus-based principles that the draft resolution claimed to endorse in favour of approaches that did not have consensus support among the States of the region.

- **Israel** believed that it was very unfortunate that long-standing practice was broken by the Group of Arab States by imposing a new unilateral and destructive draft resolution in 2018, entitled "Convening a conference on the establishment of a Middle East zone free of nuclear weapons and other weapons of mass destruction". It argued that the Arab Group altered the status quo.

After voting in favour, the following States spoke:

- **Belarus** said that it saw the implementation of the decisions and requirements of the draft resolution as crucial factors for ensuring stability and security in the region.

- The **Syrian Arab Republic** argued that there was global consensus that the only real danger in the Middle East lay in the fact that Israel possessed nuclear weapons and had the means to deliver them far beyond its region. It noted that Israel also possessed a frightening chemical and biological arsenal.

74/37. Regional disarmament

The General Assembly called upon States to conclude, wherever possible, agreements for nuclear non-proliferation, disarmament and confidence-building measures at the regional and subregional levels. The Assembly welcomed the initiatives towards disarmament, nuclear non-proliferation and

> **Submitted by**: Pakistan (5 Oct.)
>
> **GA vote**: w/o vote (12 Dec.)
>
> **1st Cttee vote**: w/o vote (7 Nov.)
>
> See also *Yearbook, Part I*, pp. 54–55.

security undertaken at those levels, and it supported and encouraged efforts aimed at promoting confidence-building measures to ease regional tensions and further disarmament and nuclear non-proliferation at the regional and subregional levels.

74/39. Confidence-building measures in the regional and subregional context

The General Assembly called upon Member States to refrain from the use or threat of use of force in accordance with the purposes and principles of the Charter of the United Nations. It also called upon Member States to pursue confidence- and security-building measures through sustained consultations

> **Submitted by**: Pakistan (5 Oct.)
>
> **GA vote**: w/o vote (12 Dec.)
>
> **1st Cttee vote**: w/o vote (7 Nov.)
>
> See also *Yearbook, Part I*, pp. 61–63.

and dialogue and urged States to strictly comply with all bilateral, regional and international agreements, including arms control and disarmament agreements to which they were party. In addition, the Assembly encouraged the promotion of bilateral and regional confidence-building measures.

74/48. Nuclear-weapon-free southern hemisphere and adjacent areas

The General Assembly welcomed the steps taken to conclude further nuclear-weapon-free zone treaties on the basis of arrangements freely arrived at among the States of the region concerned, which included the steps taken towards the establishment of a nuclear-weapon-free zone in the Middle East.

> **Submitted by**: New Zealand (14 Oct.)
>
> **GA vote**: 148-5-30; 115-37-13, p.p. 6; 139-2-28, o.p. 6 (12 Dec.)
>
> **1st Cttee vote**: 142-5-30; 108-36-14, p.p. 6; 135-2-30, o.p. 6 (1 Nov.)
>
> See also *Yearbook, Part I*, pp. 122–127.

First Committee. Before voting against the draft resolution, **France** took the floor, speaking also on behalf of the United Kingdom and the United States. It stated that they considered proposing the establishment of a nuclear-weapon-free zone in an area made up mostly of the high seas, contradictory to stating that such a zone would be in full compliance with the applicable principles and rules of international law, including those of the United Nations Convention on the Law of the Sea that pertained to the freedom of the high seas and the right of passage through maritime space. They were of the view that the real objective of the draft resolution was to establish a nuclear-weapon-free zone on the high seas and did not believe that that ambiguity had been sufficiently clarified. Lastly, France noted that the draft resolution welcomed the adoption of the Treaty on the Prohibition of Nuclear Weapons, which they opposed.

74/69. United Nations Regional Centre for Peace and Disarmament in Asia and the Pacific

The General Assembly took note of the report of the Secretary-General and expressed its appreciation to the Regional Centre for its important work in promoting confidence-building measures through the organization of meetings, conferences and workshops in the region, including national

> **Submitted by:** Nepal (14 Oct.)
>
> **GA vote:** w/o vote (12 Dec.)
>
> **1st Cttee vote:** w/o vote (7 Nov.)
>
> See also *Yearbook, Part I*, pp. 237–239.

and subregional workshops on the control of small arms and light weapons; the seventeenth United Nations-Republic of Korea Joint Conference on Disarmament and Non-Proliferation Issues, held on Jeju Island, Republic of Korea, on 5 and 6 December 2018; subregional training courses for States of South and South-East Asia and Mongolia on conventional ammunition stockpile management in line with the International Ammunition Technical Guidelines and the SaferGuard programme; a project to build capacity towards ratification of the Arms Trade Treaty for States of Central Asia and Mongolia; and a capacity-building project for States of South and South-East Asia on gun violence and illicit small arms trafficking from a gender perspective.

74/70. United Nations regional centres for peace and disarmament

The General Assembly commended the three regional centres for peace and disarmament for their sustained support provided to Member States for over 30 years in implementing disarmament, arms control and non-proliferation activities through seminars and conferences, capacity-building and

> **Submitted by:** Indonesia (15 Oct.)
>
> **GA vote:** w/o vote (12 Dec.)
>
> **1st Cttee vote:** w/o vote (7 Nov.)
>
> See also *Yearbook, Part I*, pp. 240–242.

training, policy and technical expertise, and information and advocacy at the global, regional and national levels.

First Committee. In a general statement, **Armenia** explained its position on the draft resolutions with references to the eighteenth Midterm Ministerial Meeting of the Non-Aligned Movement, held in Baku from 3 to 6 April 2018. It regretted to mention that paragraph 577 of the final document of the Meeting ran counter to the long-established approach of the international community and contained biased and one-sided formulations that distorted the essence of the Nagorno Karabakh conflict and the principles of its peaceful settlement. It wished to put on record its reservations about all paragraphs of First Committee draft resolutions containing a reference to the said Midterm Ministerial Meeting. Accordingly, it disassociated itself from those paragraphs

74/71. United Nations Regional Centre for Peace and Disarmament in Africa

The General Assembly noted with appreciation the tangible achievements of the Regional Centre and the impact of the assistance that it provided to African States to control small arms and light weapons through capacity-building for national

> **Submitted by:** Nigeria (16 Oct.)
>
> **GA vote:** w/o vote (12 Dec.)
>
> **1st Cttee vote:** w/o vote (7 Nov.)
>
> See also *Yearbook, Part I*, pp. 243–246.

commissions on small arms and light weapons, defence and security forces, and United Nations peacekeeping mission personnel, as well as the support that the Centre had provided to States in preventing the diversion of such weapons, in particular to non-State armed groups and terrorist groups.

74/72. United Nations Regional Centre for Peace, Disarmament and Development in Latin America and the Caribbean

The Assembly recognized that the Regional Centre had an important role in the promotion and development of regional and subregional initiatives agreed upon by the countries of Latin America and the Caribbean in the field of weapons of mass destruction, in particular nuclear weapons, and conventional arms, including small arms and light

> **Submitted by:** Peru (16 Oct.)
> **GA vote:** w/o vote (12 Dec.)
> **1st Cttee vote:** w/o vote (7 Nov.)
> See also *Yearbook, Part I*, pp. 247–250.

weapons, in the relationship between disarmament and development, including the implementation of the Sustainable Development Goals, in the promotion of the participation of women in this field and in strengthening voluntary confidence-building measures among the countries of the region.

First Committee. In a general statement, **Peru** wished to highlight the important role played by the Regional Centre, as it helped the States of the region to conduct a series of initiatives and activities aimed at implementing peace and disarmament measures, as well as at their economic and social development, through the appropriate use of available resources.

74/73. Regional confidence-building measures: activities of the United Nations Standing Advisory Committee on Security Questions in Central Africa

The Assembly encouraged the development of mechanisms for Community regulation, and called for the holding of a high-level conference to discuss issues relating to pastoralism and cross-border transhumance, with a view to ensuring joint and integrated management thereof. It emphasized the importance of the ongoing reform process of the

> **Submitted by:** Democratic Republic of the Congo (17 Oct.)
> **GA vote:** w/o vote (12 Dec.)
> **1st Cttee vote:** w/o vote (7 Nov.)
> See also *Yearbook, Part I*, pp. 251–259.

Economic Community of Central African States and encouraged the States members of the Standing Advisory Committee and the international community to support that reform.

First Committee. In a general statement, the **Democratic Republic of the Congo** spoke on behalf of the Group of Central African States, noting that they would continue supporting the draft resolution. They called on all other delegations to do the same by adopting it by consensus in order to allow the Standing Advisory Committee, as an instrument of preventive diplomacy in the subregional peace and security architecture, to continue its work to promote peace and strengthen confidence-building measures.

74/75. The risk of nuclear proliferation in the Middle East

The General Assembly stressed that the resolution on the Middle East adopted by the 1995 Review and Extension Conference on the Nuclear Non-Proliferation Treaty was an essential element of the outcome of the 1995 Conference and of the basis on which the Treaty had been indefinitely extended without a vote in 1995. It reiterated that the resolution would remain valid until its goals

> **Submitted by:** Egypt (30 Sep.)
>
> **GA vote:** 152-6-24; 163-3-6, p.p. 5; 164-3-6, p.p. 6 (12 Dec.)
>
> **1st Cttee vote:** 151-6-22; 159-3-5, p.p. 5; 163-3-4, p.p. 6 (1 Nov.)
>
> See also *Yearbook, Part I*, pp. 263–269.

and objectives had been achieved and called for immediate steps towards the full implementation of the 1995 resolution on the Middle East.

First Committee. Before voting in favour of the draft resolution, the following States took the floor:

- The **Islamic Republic of Iran** explained that the draft resolution reflected the concern of the solid majority of States that the regime of Israel, as the only non-party to the Nuclear Non-Proliferation Treaty in the Middle East, was the source of nuclear proliferation in that region.

- The **Democratic People's Republic of Korea** expressed its strong support for the establishment of a nuclear-weapon-free zone in the Middle East. It underlined the importance of building confidence-building measures to enhance peace and security in the region. It said that it disassociated itself from the reference to a general call for universal adherence to the Nuclear Non-Proliferation Treaty.

Before voting against the draft resolution, **Israel** said that it considered unfortunate the attempt to divert the First Committee's attention away from the real proliferation challenges facing the Middle East. It pointed out that the authors of the draft resolution neglected to mention that Iraq, the Islamic Republic of Iran, Libya and the Syrian Arab Republic violated their obligations under the Treaty on the Non-Proliferation of Nuclear Weapons and promoted clandestine military nuclear programmes, in contravention of their international obligations.

74/77. Strengthening of security and cooperation in the Mediterranean region

The General Assembly reaffirmed that security in the Mediterranean was closely linked to that of Europe, as well as to international peace and security. It called upon all States of the Mediterranean region that had not yet done so to adhere to all the multilaterally negotiated legal instruments in force related to the field of disarmament and non-proliferation. The Assembly encouraged

> **Submitted by:** Angola (4 Oct.)
>
> **GA vote:** 179-0-2; 170-2-1, o.p. 2; 170-2-1, o.p. 5 (12 Dec.)
>
> **1st Cttee vote:** 172-0-2; 169-2-0, o.p. 2; 167-2-1, o.p. 5 (7 Nov.)
>
> See also *Yearbook, Part I*, pp. 275–281.

all States of the region to strengthen confidence-building measures by promoting openness and transparency on all military matters by participating, inter alia, in the United Nations Report on Military Expenditures and by providing accurate data and information to the United Nations Register of Conventional Arms.

First Committee. The following delivered general statements:

- The **European Union** took the floor, speaking also on behalf of the candidate countries Albania, Montenegro, the Republic of North Macedonia, Serbia and Turkey; the country of the Stabilization and Association Process and potential candidate Bosnia and Herzegovina; as well as, Georgia, the Republic of Moldova and Ukraine. The European Union noted that paragraph 5 had again been included in order to maintain consensus on the draft resolution, in which the General Assembly called upon all States of the Mediterranean region that had not yet done so to adhere to all the multilaterally negotiated legal instruments in force related to the field of disarmament and non-proliferation, thereby creating the conditions necessary for strengthening peace and cooperation in the region. It underlined that the proposed reference to legal instruments in force did not imply a change to its long-standing position in support of the Comprehensive Nuclear-Test-Ban Treaty, which it regretted had not yet entered into force.

- **Algeria** said that it had tried through exchange and dialogue to explain that, ultimately, the draft resolution called on the countries of the region to be willing to engage in collective efforts related to disarmament and, more broadly, peace.

After voting in favour of the draft resolution, the **Syrian Arab Republic** said it hoped that, in the future, the sponsors of the text would take into account the need to make clear a reference to Israel's violation of all instruments.

After it abstained from voting on the draft resolution, **Israel** explained that it voted against operative paragraphs 2 and 5 as they did not truly reflect the reality in the Middle East. With regard to operative paragraph 2, it affirmed that peace in the Mediterranean region was the ultimate goal of the State of Israel but believed that the one-sided paragraph was misleading. It argued that the draft resolution legitimized the atrocities that were perpetuated in its region, as well as dangerous proliferation. With regard to operative paragraph 5, it believed that joining arms control treaties was not an aim or goal in and of itself, because such treaties were useless if countries did not obey them or if they did not solve regional issues. It believed that the most important element was for the right conditions to be established, thereby creating trust and confidence, security and mutual recognition.

The **Islamic Republic of Iran**, which did not participate in the vote on the draft resolution as a whole, said that it voted in favour of operative paragraph 2 because of the call to ensure the withdrawal of foreign forces of occupation, respect the sovereignty, independence and territorial integrity of all countries of the region and the rights of peoples to self-determination, as well as for full adherence to the principle of the non-use or threat of use of force and the inadmissibility of the acquisition of territory by force. It also voted in favour of operative paragraph 5 because it called for adherence to all the multilaterally negotiated legal instruments on disarmament and non-proliferation, in line with repeated calls by successive Review Conferences of the Parties to the Nuclear Non-Proliferation Treaty for Israel to accede without any delay or precondition as a non-nuclear-weapon party to the Treaty. However, it did not participate in action on the draft resolution as a whole, as it was of the view the draft did not factually reflect the realities in the region and the situation in the occupied territories, including the continued killing of innocent Palestinian civilians in the occupied territories of the State of Palestine and the imposition by the Israeli regime of the most severe blockade on the Gaza Strip.

74/510. Treaty on the South-East Asia Nuclear-Weapon-Free Zone (Bangkok Treaty) (decision)

The General Assembly decided to include in the provisional agenda of its seventy-sixth session, under the item entitled "General and complete disarmament", the sub-item entitled "Treaty on the South-East Asia Nuclear-Weapon-Free Zone (Bangkok Treaty)".

> **Submitted by:** Thailand (16 Oct.)
>
> **GA vote:** w/o vote (12 Dec.)
>
> **1st Cttee vote:** w/o vote (1 Nov.)
>
> See also *Yearbook, Part I*, p. 297.

First Committee. Before it joined the consensus on the draft decision, the **United Kingdom** took the floor, speaking also on behalf of China, France, the Russian Federation and the United States. They reaffirmed their commitment to the aims and objectives of the South-East Asia Nuclear-Weapon-Free Zone.

Chapter V. Emerging, cross-cutting and other issues

74/28. Advancing responsible State behaviour in cyberspace in the context of international security

The General Assembly welcomed the commencement of the work of the Group of Governmental Experts on Advancing Responsible State Behaviour in Cyberspace in the Context of International Security and also welcomed the commencement of the work of the Open-ended

> **Submitted by:** United States (31 Oct.)
>
> **GA vote:** 163-10-6 (12 Dec.)
>
> **1st Cttee vote:** 161-10-8 (6 Nov.)
>
> See also *Yearbook, Part I*, pp. 16–19.

Working Group on Developments in the Field of Information and Telecommunications in the Context of International Security.

First Committee. Before voting in favour of the draft resolution, the **United States** said that it was dedicated to working constructively in both the Group of Governmental Experts and the Open-ended Working Group, as it had on cyber issues in the First Committee for the past two decades. While it believed it was necessary to have two draft resolutions to reflect that two processes had started, each with its own mandate and timeline, it saw no legitimate reason for the international community not to pursue complementary consensus cyber draft resolutions in the First Committee.

Before voting against the draft resolution, the **Russian Federation** said adopting a single draft resolution acceptable to all was the only logical way to turn the discussion on international information security towards consensus. The United States had refused that option, instead putting forward a separate document based on a completely different line of logic—that of dividing the international community into two tracks, with a specific expiration date. The Russian Federation called on Member States interested in restoring a genuine consensus to support the Russian draft resolution and to adopt a fair and balanced decision with respect to the draft text submitted by the United States.

After voting in favour, the following States explained their votes:

- **Malaysia** said it believed that both draft resolutions on information security carried value in moving forward the global discourse on developments in the field of information and telecommunications in the context of international security.

- The **United Kingdom** pointed out that the draft resolution contained only text that had been previously agreed upon and, for that reason, it co-sponsored and voted in favour of it.

- **Brazil** deeply regretted that the First Committee again had to vote on two competing draft resolutions. It said that it was committed to both dialogue processes—namely, the Group of Governmental Experts on Developments in the Field of Information and Telecommunications in the Context of International Security and the Open-ended Working Group.

- **Chile** was of the view that the two processes complemented each other and strengthened the multilateral cybersecurity structure and for that reason, it voted in favour of both draft resolutions.

- **Switzerland** voted in favour of the draft resolution, as it mirrored previous texts and relied essentially on long-standing consensus language.

After voting against the draft resolution, the following States took the floor:

- **China** called on the relevant country to join it and the vast majority of countries in jointly promoting complementarity and mutual reinforcement between the two processes, so as to ensure progress on both fronts.

- **Cuba** believed that the Working Group was the appropriate forum and the one best suited to address the issue in a transparent, inclusive, multilateral, democratic and open-ended way, with the full and equal participation of all Member States. It reiterated that the Groups of Experts working on the issue had exhausted discussions on the applicability of international law in the use of new information and telecommunications technology without reaching a consensus on the urgent measures needed to prevent covert or illegal use by individuals, organizations and States of information systems of other nations to attack third countries.

74/29. Developments in the field of information and telecommunications in the context of international security

The General Assembly welcomed the launch of the negotiation process in the format of the United Nations Open-ended Working Group on Developments in the Field of Information and Telecommunications in the Context of International Security, and also welcomed the Group of Governmental Experts on Developments in the Field of Information and Telecommunications in the Context of International Security. The Assembly underlined that the Open-ended Working Group and the Group of Governmental Experts were important independent mechanisms under United Nations auspices that should conduct their work in accordance with their mandates in a

> **Submitted by**: Russian Federation (30 Oct.)
>
> **GA vote**: 129-6-45 (12 Dec.)
>
> **1st Cttee vote**: 124-6-48 (6 Nov.)
>
> See also *Yearbook, Part I*, pp. 20–22.

constructive and pragmatic manner, adding to each other's efforts, and that their results should contribute to the implementation of the tasks of maintaining international peace and security in the use of information and communication technologies.

First Committee. Before it abstained from voting on the draft resolution, **Australia** noted that it had conducted outreach and made representations in Canberra, Moscow and New York to request simple changes to the fourth, tenth and twelfth preambular paragraphs and operative paragraph 1 with the intention of bringing the draft resolution back into line with agreed language. It expressed disappointment that those consensus-based changes that would have increased the likelihood of wider support were rejected.

After voting in favour, the following States spoke:

- **Malaysia** voted in favour of both draft resolutions on information security, as it believed that they carried value in moving forward the global discourse on developments in the field of information and telecommunications in the context of international security.

- **Brazil** deeply regretted that the First Committee had again had to vote on two competing draft resolutions on the issue. It said that it was committed to both dialogue processes.

- **Chile** understood that the two processes complemented each other and strengthened the multilateral cybersecurity structure and, for that reason, it voted in favour of both draft resolutions.

- **Switzerland** believed that the draft resolution could have benefited from greater support, even if it had not been adopted by consensus, had it relied more closely on agreed language and faithfully reflected the consensus outcomes of past Groups of Governmental Experts. It regretted that that was not possible and that corresponding changes were not made, notably with regard to the tenth and twelfth preambular paragraphs.

After voting against the draft resolution, the following States delivered statements:

- **Israel** believed that the discussions of the Open-ended Working Group should support, and not duplicate or impair, other efforts, including those undertaken within the United Nations and, in particular, by the Group of Governmental Experts on Developments in the Field of Information and Telecommunications in the Context of International Security. It also believed it essential to maintain agreed-upon language and to refrain from adding new non-agreed elements, such as referring to the process as negotiations, which was done in several paragraphs of the draft resolution.

- The **United Kingdom**, speaking also on behalf of Canada, noted the introduction of language that went beyond the mandate for the Open-ended Working Group prejudiced discussions.

After they abstained from voting on the draft resolution, the following States spoke:

- The **United States** explained that it generally supported the sentiment of the draft resolution, but was concerned that some of the language went beyond that of the Open-ended Working Group or was otherwise controversial or undefined.

- **Finland**, speaking on behalf of the European Union, stated that it engaged constructively on the draft resolution with the sponsor, proposing minor amendments in line with consensus language that would have enabled them to support it. It expressed disappointment that none of those minor amendments were incorporated into the final draft.

- **New Zealand** explained that the draft resolution retained language of concern to it. It was of the view that the text did not focus on the common ground shared by the Assembly.

- **Japan** expressed regret that the revisions and amendments proposed by several States to change non-consensus language to consensus language had not been incorporated in the draft resolution.

74/32. Prevention of an arms race in outer space

The Assembly recognized the growing convergence of views on the elaboration of measures designed to strengthen transparency, confidence and security in the peaceful uses of outer space, without prejudice to efforts towards the conclusion of an effective and verifiable multilateral agreement or agreements on the prevention of an arms race in outer space.

> **Submitted by**: Egypt, Sri Lanka (5 Oct.)
>
> **GA vote**: 183-2-0 (12 Dec.)
>
> **1st Cttee vote**: 175-2-0 (5 Nov.)
>
> See also *Yearbook, Part I*, pp. 32–36.

First Committee. The following States delivered general statements:

- **Egypt** said that it was regrettable to see that all five proposals under the cluster were being put to the vote, including a genuine, balanced attempt sponsored by 40 States, as contained in the draft resolution, to bridge the gaps and address the threats that were fully recognized by all States.

- **Cuba** supported the adoption of a legally binding treaty for the prevention and prohibition of the placement of arms in outer space and deplored the fact that one State had blocked consensus in adopting the final report of the Group of Governmental Experts on the Prevention of an Arms Race in Outer Space, established by the General Assembly to make recommendations on the substantive elements of a legally binding instrument for the prevention and prohibition of an arms race in outer space.

Before voting in favour of the draft resolution, **Venezuela** said that the text provided balanced and constructive support in the quest for achieving the overall objective of preventing an arms race in outer space, while seeking to take concrete steps and practical measures to prevent an arms race, offering viable and necessary options and reflecting on the existing concerns of the majority of the international community on the subject, with a view to ensuring a peaceful outer space worthy of the coexistence and shared development of humankind.

Before voting against the draft resolution, the **United States** clarified that its vote in no way detracted from its long-standing support for voluntary transparency and confidence-building measures for outer space activities. It considered unacceptable the linkage between proposals for voluntary, pragmatic transparency and confidence-building measures and the commencement of futile negotiations on fundamentally flawed arms control proposals. In particular, it noted the draft resolution's references to the draft treaty on the prevention of the placement of weapons in outer space and of the threat or use of force against outer space objects, put forward by the Russian Federation and China in 2014 at the Conference on Disarmament, which it opposed. It drew attention to its recent critique (CD/2129) of said draft treaty. It deeply regretted that the Committee must spend time debating paragraph 3 of the draft resolution, and it was of the view that the Assembly would not solve the challenges facing the outer space environment by singling out one expert's professional position in the Group of Governmental Experts.

74/33. No first placement of weapons in outer space

The General Assembly reiterated that the Conference on Disarmament had the primary role in the negotiation of a multilateral agreement or agreements on the prevention of an arms race in outer space in all its aspects. It urged an early start of substantive work based on the updated draft treaty, introduced by China and the Russian Federation at the Conference on Disarmament, on the prevention of the placement of weapons in outer space and of

> **Submitted by**: Russian Federation (17 Oct.)
>
> **GA vote**: 128-14-38; 117-42-13, p.p. 5 (12 Dec.)
>
> **1st Cttee vote**: 123-14-40; 114-42-10, p.p. 5 (5 Nov.)
>
> See also *Yearbook, Part I*, pp.37–40.

the threat or use of force against outer space objects. The Assembly stressed that, while such an agreement had not yet been concluded, other measures could contribute to ensuring that weapons were not placed in outer space.

First Committee. In a general statement, **China** recalled that some countries proposed, for the very first time, that separate votes be taken on specific paragraphs. It considered such proposals a move designed to undermine the voting on the draft resolution as a whole, with a view to creating international divisions. It called upon all countries that supported the draft resolution to continue to support the text as a whole, as well as to vote in favour of the fifth preambular paragraph.

Before voting in favour of the draft resolution, the following States took the floor:

- The **Bolivarian Republic of Venezuela** said that the draft resolution provided balanced and constructive support in the quest for achieving the overall objective of preventing an arms race in outer space, while seeking to take concrete steps and practical measures to prevent an arms race, offering viable and necessary options and reflecting on the existing concerns of the majority of the international community on the subject with a view to ensuring a peaceful outer space worthy of the coexistence and shared development of humankind.

- **Pakistan** said that it would vote in favour of the fifth preambular paragraph of the draft resolution, which contained references to the objective of shaping a community of shared future for humankind. It believed that, in the domain of outer space, such a noble goal assumed added relevance because the 1967 Outer Space Treaty already recognized that the exploration and use of outer space, including the moon and other celestial bodies, should be carried out for the benefit and in the interest of all countries.

Before voting against the draft resolution, the following spoke:

- The **European Union** argued that the no-first-placement initiative did not address the difficult issue of defining what a weapon in outer space was, which could lead a State to mistakenly assess that another State had placed weapons in outer space. It remained concerned about the continued development of all anti-satellite weapons and capabilities, including terrestrially based weapons, and underlined the importance of addressing such developments promptly and as part of international efforts to prevent an arms race in outer space. Rather than introducing a no-first-placement pledge, the European Union and its member States believed that it would be more useful to address the issue of behaviour in, and use of, outer space in order to advance meaningful discussions and initiatives on how to prevent space from becoming an arena for conflict and to ensure the long-term sustainability of the space environment.

- **France** was of the view that the no-first-placement initiative did not provide an adequate definition of what constituted a weapon in outer space. Secondly, it believed that there were limits to verifying objects launched into space, and the provisions of the no-first-placement initiative did not allow for the effective confirmation of a State's political commitment to not being the first to place weapons in outer space. Thirdly, it clarified that it could not support the reference made in the fourth preambular paragraph to the idea of a "common effort towards a community of shared future for humankind". It argued that that phrase had been inserted by China to promote its own vision of multilateralism and global geopolitics in the international system and that none should support the inclusion of language in multilateral documents that supported specific national interests. Lastly, it was of the view the draft resolution did not take into account the short-term threat posed by other anti-satellite weapons, such as lasers or systems that were launched from Earth.

After voting in favour, the following States delivered statements:

- **Mexico** clarified that its support should in no way be understood as tacit endorsement or acceptance of a putative right to place weapons in outer space or launch them from Earth if another State did so first or in response to an attack.

- **India** supported the substantive consideration in the Conference on Disarmament of the subject of preventing an arms race in outer space. It noted that, while not a substitute for legally binding instruments, transparency and confidence-building measures could play a useful and complementary role to legally binding instruments. It decided to vote against the fifth preambular paragraph of the draft resolution due to the inclusion of the phrase "a community of shared future for humankind".

After they abstained from voting on the draft resolution, the following States explained their positions:

- **Japan** was of the view that the draft resolution did not adequately deal with the question of what constituted a weapon in outer space. Secondly, with regard to verification, it did not believe that the initiative of no first placement of weapons in outer space would be effective or verifiable. Thirdly, it believed that the draft resolution focused solely on space-based weapons and therefore did not address the entire list of outer space activities, including ground-based activities. It explained that it abstained from voting on the fifth preambular paragraph because it contained language that did not enjoy consensus in the General Assembly.

- **Germany** was of the opinion that the draft resolution did not adequately respond to the short-term objective of strengthening trust and confidence among States.

- **Switzerland** reiterated that the draft resolution did not clearly define what constituted a weapon in outer space and did not address the development of ground-based systems that could attack or damage satellites, including the testing of such systems, although those capacities were a source of immediate concern. It also noted that the draft resolution did not address the potential second placement of weapons in outer space and, in that regard, believed that the draft resolution did not appear to be complete. Lastly, it stated that it continued to have questions with regard to the concept of the will to shape a community of shared future for humankind, referenced in the fifth preambular paragraph of the draft resolution, and therefore abstained from voting on the paragraph.

74/34. Further practical measures for the prevention of an arms race in outer space

The General Assembly emphasized that the work of the Group of Governmental Experts on Further Practical Measures for the Prevention of an Arms Race in Outer Space constituted an important contribution to international efforts to conclude the above-mentioned international legally binding instrument. It recommended that the work of the Group be taken into account in the search for further practical measures for the prevention of an arms race in outer space, in particular in the course of future

> **Submitted by**: Russian Federation (30 Oct.)
>
> **GA vote**: 131-6-45; 115-42-11, p.p. 4; w/o vote, o.p. 3 (12 Dec.)
>
> **1st Cttee vote**: 124-41-10; 111-40-12, p.p. 4; 55-50-48, o.p. 3 (5 Nov.)
>
> See also *Yearbook, Part I*, pp. 41–45.

negotiations at the Conference on Disarmament on the international legally binding instrument in that regard. It urged the international community to continue its efforts aimed at preventing an arms race, including the placement of weapons, in outer space, with a view to maintaining international peace and strengthen global security.

First Committee. In a general statement, **China** recalled that some countries proposed, for the very first time, that separate votes be taken on specific paragraphs. It considered such proposals a move designed to undermine the voting on the draft resolution as a whole, with a view to creating international divisions. It called upon all countries that supported the draft resolution to continue to support it as a whole, as well as to vote in favour of the fourth preambular paragraph.

Before voting in favour of the draft resolution, the following States took the floor:

- The **Bolivarian Republic of Venezuela** said that the draft resolution provided balanced and constructive support in the quest for achieving the overall objective of preventing an arms race in outer space, while seeking to take concrete steps and practical measures to prevent an arms race, offering viable and necessary options and reflecting on the existing concerns of the majority of the international community on the subject, with a view to ensuring a peaceful outer space worthy of the coexistence and shared development of humankind.

- **Pakistan** stated that it would vote in favour of the fourth preambular paragraph of the draft resolution, which contained references to the objective of shaping a community of shared future for humankind. It believed that, in the domain of outer space, such a noble goal assumed added relevance because the 1967 Outer Space Treaty already recognized that the exploration and use of outer space, including the moon and other celestial bodies, should be carried out for the benefit and in the interest of all countries.

Before voting against the draft resolution, the **United States** highlighted that it held extensive consultations on the text to try to find a mutually acceptable compromise on a unified resolution on transparency and confidence-building measures. It stated that, despite its best efforts, its calls for compromise were rebuffed by the primary sponsor of the draft resolution.

After voting in favour, **India** stated that it had always voted in favour of the draft resolution because it shared the goal of taking practical steps to prevent an arms race in outer space. However, it decided to vote against the fourth preambular paragraph of the draft resolution due to the inclusion of a new phrase—"a community of shared future for humankind".

After voting against the draft resolution, **Germany** pointed out that it changed its voting pattern because the main sponsors of the draft resolution chose, in operative paragraph 3,[c] to single out an expert who was working in full accordance with the rules of procedure of the Group of Governmental Experts on the Prevention of an Arms Race in Outer Space.

After they abstained from voting on the draft resolution, the following States took the floor:

- **Japan** explained that it abstained in the voting on the fourth preambular paragraph because that paragraph did not contain language that enjoyed consensus in the General Assembly. It also voted against operative paragraph 3 because it was the Group of Governmental Experts as a whole that did not reach consensus, and singling out an expert who broke the consensus was therefore not appropriate.

- **Switzerland** believed that it was essential for efforts to be monitored and, in that regard, it strongly deplored some elements of the draft resolution, in particular operative paragraph 3, which, in its view, not only broke with the practice established in the Committee but could also complicate the future work of the Group of Governmental Experts Lastly, it underscored that it continued to have questions with regard to the concept of the will to shape a community of shared future for humankind, referenced in the

---

[c] Operative paragraph 3 of the draft resolution (A/C.1/74/L.58/Rev.1) was deleted from the final text of resolution 74/34.

fourth preambular paragraph, and therefore abstained in the voting on that paragraph.

74/35. Role of science and technology in the context of international security and disarmament

The Assembly encouraged Member States to organize events such as conferences, seminars, workshops and exhibitions, at the national, regional and international levels, on the role of science and technology in the context of international security and disarmament on current developments in science and technology and their potential impact on international security and disarmament efforts.

> **Submitted by:** India (11 Oct.)
>
> **GA vote:** w/o vote (12 Dec.)
>
> **1st Cttee vote:** w/o vote (6 Nov.)
>
> See also *Yearbook, Part I*, pp. 46–48.

First Committee. Before voting in favour of the draft resolution, **France** took the floor, speaking also on behalf of the United States and United Kingdom. France underscored that the rights referenced in the fifth preambular paragraph of the draft resolution were those noted in specific provisions of a small number of treaties, such as the Chemical Weapons Convention, the Biological Weapons Convention and the Nuclear Non-Proliferation Treaty. It drew attention to the fifth preambular paragraph, which clearly stated that States must exercise those rights in accordance with their international obligations, including their obligations under those three treaties.

After voting in favour, the following spoke:

- **Pakistan** highlighted that it was important that the right of access to technologies for socioeconomic development be ensured on a non-discriminatory basis.

- **Brazil** said that the formulation of the fifth preambular paragraph of the resolution adopted in 2017 (resolution 72/28), although not ideal, contributed to a more balanced approach to the issues covered by the resolution. In that respect, it recalled that the right of States to develop, produce, transfer and use technologies for peaceful purposes was explicitly and unequivocally recognized in the Biological Weapons Convention, the Chemical Weapons Convention, the Treaty on the Non-Proliferation of Nuclear Weapons and the Treaty on the Prohibition of Nuclear Weapons. With regard to the fourth preambular paragraph of the draft resolution, it noted that the reference to the need to regulate the transfer of technologies for peaceful purposes to address the risk of proliferation by States or non-State actors referred to the specific provisions of relevant international obligations to which each State was bound.

74/43. Measures to prevent terrorists from acquiring weapons of mass destruction

The General Assembly called upon Member States to support international efforts to prevent terrorists from acquiring weapons of mass destruction and their means of delivery. It appealed to all Member States to consider early accession to and ratification of the International Convention for

> **Submitted by:** India (11 Oct.)
>
> **GA vote:** w/o vote (12 Dec.)
>
> **1st Cttee vote:** w/o vote (4 Nov.)
>
> See also *Yearbook, Part I*, pp. 184–86.

the Suppression of Acts of Nuclear Terrorism and encouraged States parties to the Convention to review its implementation.

74/52. Observance of environmental norms in the drafting and implementation of agreements on disarmament and arms control

The General Assembly called upon States to adopt unilateral, bilateral, regional and multilateral measures to contribute to ensuring the application of scientific and technological progress within the framework of international security, disarmament and other related spheres without detriment to the

> **Submitted by:** Indonesia (15 Oct.)
>
> **GA vote:** w/o vote (12 Dec.)
>
> **1st Cttee vote:** w/o vote (6 Nov.)
>
> See also *Yearbook, Part I*, pp. 145–146.

environment or to its effective contribution to attaining sustainable development. It invited all Member States to communicate to the Secretary-General the measures they had adopted and requested the Secretary-General to submit a report containing that information to the Assembly's seventy-fifth session.

First Committee. Before voting in favour of the draft resolution, the **United Kingdom**, speaking also on behalf of France, stated that it saw no direct connection, as stated in the draft resolution, between general environmental standards and multilateral arms control.

74/55. Promotion of multilateralism in the area of disarmament and non-proliferation

The General Assembly underlined the importance of preserving the existing agreements on arms regulation and disarmament and the multilateral disarmament forums, which constituted an expression of the results of international cooperation and multilateral negotiations in response to the challenges facing humankind.

> **Submitted by:** Indonesia (15 Oct.)
>
> **GA vote:** 127-5-51 (12 Dec.)
>
> **1st Cttee vote:** 124-4-52 (6 Nov.)
>
> See also *Yearbook, Part I*, pp. 159–162.

First Committee. After it abstained from voting on the draft resolution, **Armenia** explained its position on the draft resolutions with references to the eighteenth Midterm Ministerial Meeting of the Non-Aligned Movement, held in Baku from 3 to 6 April 2018. It regretted to mention that paragraph 577 of the final document of the Meeting ran counter to the long-established approach of the international community and contained biased and one-sided formulations that distorted the essence of the Nagorno Karabakh conflict and the principles of its peaceful settlement. It wished to register its reservations about all paragraphs of First Committee draft resolutions containing a reference to the said Midterm Ministerial Meeting. Accordingly, Armenia disassociated itself from those paragraphs.

74/57. Relationship between disarmament and development

The General Assembly reiterated its invitation to Member States to provide the Secretary-General with information regarding measures and efforts to devote part of the resources made available by the implementation of disarmament and arms

> **Submitted by:** Indonesia (15 Oct.)
>
> **GA vote:** w/o vote (12 Dec.)
>
> **1st Cttee vote:** w/o vote (6 Nov.)
>
> See also *Yearbook, Part I*, pp. 166–168.

limitation agreements to economic and social development, with a view to reducing the ever-widening gap between developed and developing countries.

First Committee. Before voting in favour of the draft resolution, the **United Kingdom** took the floor, speaking also on behalf of France. The United Kingdom said that they considered the notion of a symbiotic relationship between disarmament and development questionable, as the conditions conducive to effective arms control and disarmament were not necessarily dependent on development only, as seen with the growing military expenditure of some developing countries.

74/66. Strengthening and developing the system of arms control, disarmament and non-proliferation treaties and agreements

The General Assembly urged all States parties to arms control, disarmament and non-proliferation treaties and agreements to implement all provisions of such treaties and agreements in their entirety and called for continued efforts to strengthen the system of arms control, disarmament and non-proliferation treaties and agreements. The Assembly also called

> **Submitted by**: Russian Federation (30 Oct.)
>
> **GA vote**: 179-0-3 (12 Dec.)
>
> **1st Cttee vote**: 174-0-5 (6 Nov.)
>
> See also *Yearbook, Part I*, pp. 225–228.

upon all Member States to give serious consideration to the negative implications of undermining arms control, disarmament and non-proliferation treaties and agreements and their regimes for international security and stability, as well as for progress in the field of disarmament. It urged all Member States to support efforts aimed at the resolution of implementation issues by means consistent with arms control, disarmament and non-proliferation treaties and agreements and international law.

First Committee. Before voting in favour, **Finland** took the floor, speaking also on behalf of the member States of the European Union, Albania, Bosnia and Herzegovina, Canada, Iceland, Liechtenstein, Montenegro, North Macedonia, Norway and the Republic of Moldova. Finland underlined that the international community must ensure accountability, end impunity for violations and uphold global norms. It stressed that that was why the European Union had strongly supported the establishment of an international attribution mechanism to identify and hold accountable the perpetrators of the use of chemical weapons, and that also was why autonomous European Union sanctions had been adopted against the use of chemical weapons, as well as against nuclear proliferation and other violations of international law, notably the use of force against the territorial integrity or sovereignty of other States. It regretted that those aspects of compliance had not been included in the text by the main sponsor of the draft resolution. They also regretted that the main sponsor of the draft resolution did not accept amendments reflecting relevant gender considerations.

After voting in favour, the **United States** delivered a statement, speaking also on behalf of the United Kingdom. It stated that they had voted in favour because of their deep commitment to the principles contained in the draft resolution. It added, however, that the Russian Federation's sponsorship of the draft resolution stood in sharp contrast to its history of violating those principles, in spirit and deed.

74/67. Transparency and confidence-building measures in outer space activities

The General Assembly emphasized the importance of undertaking further work at the Disarmament Commission on preparing recommendations relating to the practical implementation of transparency and confidence-building measures in outer space activities with the goal of preventing an arms race in outer space. It also welcomed the convening of a joint half-day panel discussion of the First and Fourth Committees to address possible challenges to space security and sustainability during the seventy-fourth session of the General Assembly.

> **Submitted by**: Russian Federation (17 Oct.)
>
> **GA vote**: 173-2-6 (12 Dec.)
>
> **1st Cttee vote**: 166-2-5 (5 Nov.)
>
> See also *Yearbook, Part I*, pp. 229–233.

First Committee. Before voting in favour of the draft resolution, the following took the floor:

- The **Islamic Republic of Iran** noted that the draft resolution affirmed the importance of preventing an arms race in outer space and put the transparency and confidence-building measures in the right context—namely, as a means of reinforcing the objective of preventing an arms race in outer space. It recalled that the draft resolution had served for many years as a point of convergence for the international community on the application of transparency and confidence-building measures in outer space, while also helping to harmonize views and contributing towards an international consensus on such measures.

- The **Bolivarian Republic of Venezuela** said that the draft resolution provided balanced and constructive support in the quest for achieving the overall objective of preventing an arms race in outer space, while seeking to take concrete steps and practical measures to prevent an arms race, offering viable and necessary options and reflecting on the existing concerns of the majority of the international community on the subject, with a view to ensuring a peaceful outer space worthy of the coexistence and shared development of humankind.

Before voting against the draft resolution, the **United States** clarified that its vote in no way detracted from its long-standing support for voluntary transparency and confidence-building measures for outer space activities. It considered unacceptable the linkage between proposals for voluntary, pragmatic transparency and confidence-building measures and the commencement of futile negotiations on fundamentally flawed arms control proposals. In particular, it noted the draft resolution's references to the draft treaty on the prevention of the placement of weapons in outer space and of the threat or use of force against outer space objects, put forward by the Russian Federation and China in 2014 at the Conference on Disarmament, which it opposed. It drew attention to its recent critique (CD/2129) of the said draft treaty.

After voting in favour, the following States took the floor:

- **Japan** expressed concern about the ninth preambular paragraph, stating that it was not constructive or appropriate to include references to the most recent session of the United Nations Disarmament Commission in the draft resolution.

Chapter VII. Disarmament machinery

74/56. Convening of the fourth special session of the General Assembly devoted to disarmament

The General Assembly recalled the adoption by consensus of the recommendations on the objectives and agenda of the fourth special session of the General Assembly devoted to disarmament by the Open-ended Working Group on the fourth special session of the General Assembly devoted to disarmament, which had met in 2016 and 2017.

> **Submitted by:** Indonesia (15 Oct.)
>
> **GA vote:** 179-0-4 (12 Dec.)
>
> **1st Cttee vote:** 175-0-3 (7 Nov.)
>
> See also *Yearbook, Part I*, pp. 166–168.

The Assembly also recalled the Group's report and the substantive recommendations contained therein (A/AC.268/2017/2) and reiterated its appreciation to the participants of the Open-ended Working Group for their constructive contribution to its work.

74/74. Report of the Conference on Disarmament

The General Assembly requested the current President and successive Presidents of the Conference on Disarmament to cooperate with the States members of the Conference in the effort to guide the Conference to the early commencement of its substantive work, including negotiations, at its 2020 session.

> **Submitted by:** Zimbabwe (16 Oct.)
>
> **GA vote:** w/o vote (12 Dec.)
>
> **1st Cttee vote:** w/o vote (7 Nov.)
>
> See also *Yearbook, Part I*, pp. 260–262.

74/511. 2020 session of the Disarmament Commission (decision)

The General Assembly decided that the Disarmament Commission would continue consideration of the following items at its substantive session of 2020: recommendations for achieving the objective of nuclear disarmament and non-proliferation of nuclear weapons; preparation of recommendations to promote the practical implementation of transparency and confidence-building measures in outer space activities

> **Submitted by:** Australia, Hungary (3 Nov.)
>
> **GA vote:** w/o vote; 149-1-12, o.p. (a); 152-1-10, o.p. (b) (12 Dec.)
>
> **1st Cttee vote:** w/o vote; 133-1-14, o.p. (a); 133-1-15, o.p. (b) (7 Nov.)
>
> See also *Yearbook, Part I*, pp. 298–302.

with the goal of preventing an arms race in outer space, in accordance with the recommendations contained in the report of the Group of Governmental Experts on Transparency and Confidence-building Measures in Outer Space Activities. The Assembly also decided that the Disarmament Commission would continue its work in accordance with its mandate and to that end make every effort to achieve specific recommendations on the items on its agenda.

Chapter VIII. Information and outreach

74/64. Youth, disarmament and non-proliferation

The General Assembly encouraged Member States, the United Nations, relevant specialized agencies and regional and subregional organizations to promote the meaningful and inclusive participation of young people in discussions in the field of disarmament and non-proliferation, and called upon them to consider developing and implementing policies and programmes for young people to increase and facilitate their constructive engagement in the field of disarmament and non-proliferation. The Assembly encouraged Member States to continue efforts to raise awareness and strengthen coordination within the United Nations system and beyond on ongoing efforts to promote the role of youth. It stressed the importance of realizing the full potential of young people through education and capacity-building, bearing in mind the ongoing efforts and the need to promote the sustainable entry of young people into the field of disarmament and non-proliferation.

Submitted by: Republic of Korea (17 Oct.)

GA vote: w/o vote; 177-0-2, p.p. 8 (12 Dec.)

1st Cttee vote: w/o vote; 175-0-2, p.p. 8 (6 Nov.)

See also *Yearbook, Part I*, pp. 217–219.